'I can't think of a more brilliant Christmas book to give to one's significant other if they have even a passing interest in medieval Europe or the rich and extraordinary sex life of its inhabitants.' – *Erotic Review*

'An expansive, accessible and highly engaging account of what we do – and don't – know about western European sexual culture in the Middle Ages.' – BBC *History Magazine*

'This lively, engaging study combines a scholarly rigour with a sharp eye for telling detail, told in a fluid style that keeps the pages turning. A culture in which clerics commissioned sheelagh-na-gigs – graphic carvings of women displaying their genitals – to adorn their holy buildings perplex us. Harvey takes great care to explain this complicated culture.' – *Irish Times*

'[An] irresistibly eccentric cultural history ... Impeccably re   ched and impossibly entertaining, *The Fires of Lust* is a w transcends its scholarl

'A lively and readable accoun the scholarly literature on sexu   urope. Harvey's specialism in the histor   provides particular depth, and is integrated with legal and cultural material to create a sparkling and convincing whole.'
– RUTH MAZO KARRAS, author of *Sexuality in Medieval Europe*

'Learned, fun and full of surprises – a fascinating, wide-ranging guide to medieval sexual attitudes and experiences.'
– FARA DABHOIWALA, author of *The Origins of Sex*

'With unabashed directness, a delicate touch of wit, and constant humanity, Katherine Harvey surveys the world of medieval sex and sexuality ... Here, in its messy complexity, is medieval life – life laid bare, but always with respect and care. A triumph.'
– JOHN H. ARNOLD, author of *Belief and Unbelief in Medieval Europe*

THE FIRES OF LUST

SEX

IN THE

MIDDLE AGES

KATHERINE HARVEY

REAKTION BOOKS

Published by
REAKTION BOOKS LTD
Unit 32, Waterside
44–48 Wharf Road
London N1 7UX, UK

www.reaktionbooks.co.uk

First published 2021
First published in paperback 2022
Copyright © Katherine Harvey 2021

Printed and bound in Great Britain
by TJ Books Ltd, Padstow, Cornwall

A catalogue record for this book is available from the British Library

ISBN 978 1 78914 656 1

Contents

Introduction

On 2 December 2015, in his speech opening a parliamentary debate on military action against the so-called Islamic State in Syria, the British Prime Minister David Cameron described the organization's members as 'woman-raping, Muslim-murdering, medieval monsters'. This was not the first time he had identified Islamic State's use of sexual violence as something that belonged to a specific era in the distant past: a year earlier, he had told the United Nations that 'the cruelty being meted out – beheadings, eyes being gouged out, rape – is horrific. It is literally medieval in character.'[1]

Cameron's identification of repugnant sexual behaviour as somehow medieval was far from an original sentiment; rather, it sits within a long tradition of associating the Middle Ages with all the vices (also including superstition, torture and poor personal hygiene) that we like to think we have subsequently become too good for. His comments encapsulate the popular perception that medieval life was backwards and unthinkingly violent – and that sex, rather than offering some respite from this unremitting bleakness, was usually violent, deviant or both. All of these stereotypes have been oft-represented and reinforced by the entertainment industry, and this prime-ministerial version of our medieval past has much in common with the world depicted in the HBO television series *Game of Thrones*.

While this immensely popular programme is technically a fantasy set in a fictional world, its creators have made much of its medieval inspiration and historical authenticity. When asked by *The Atlantic* about the sexual violence depicted in the series, George R. R. Martin (author of the novels on which it is based) responded, 'Well, I'm not writing about contemporary sex – it's medieval.' Such assertions have been used to justify the inclusion of countless sexual encounters and scenes involving numerous naked prostitutes, most of which add little or nothing to the plot or character development. This is a world in which sexual violence (including rape) is endemic, incest is unremarkable and homosexuality is unnatural.

Virtually every female character is sexually assaulted, some of them repeatedly, while the main gay character, Loras Tyrell, is an effeminate and promiscuous man who is eventually executed for 'buggery'.[2]

Stereotypical representations of medieval sex are also characteristic of the romance genre, as demonstrated by Mills & Boon's Medieval Lords and Ladies Collection of historical novels. In comparison to *Game of Thrones*, these are rather gentle stories, but they are equally insistent that this was a violent world (most of the heroes are warriors of some kind), in which women faced constant physical danger. While Mills & Boon has generally moved away from sexual violence in recent years, many of the encounters described in its medieval volumes are still very dependent on ideas of dominance and submission. Heroines are often reluctant to recognize their attraction to the hero, and only realize their true feelings when they helplessly succumb to a combination of persistent harassment and rough sex. Such behaviour is rendered palatable by the formulaic nature of the books – the reader knows that there will be a happy ending, and that the heroine does love the hero really – but also by the distancing effect of several centuries.[3] Like *Game of Thrones*, these novels use the Middle Ages as a device that allows the modern cultural consumer to observe behaviours which would feel uncomfortable if presented in a contemporary scenario, but which can be unchallenging, enjoyable or even sexually gratifying if justified by the comfort blanket of history.

Popular belief in the strange and violent nature of medieval sexuality is further reinforced by the persistent myth that medieval lords were entitled (through a custom known as the *droit du seigneur*) to take the virginity of a bride on her wedding night.[4] Although there is no evidence that this ever happened in reality, it has been depicted in works as diverse as Wolfgang Amadeus Mozart's opera *The Marriage of Figaro* (1786) and the Hollywood blockbuster *Braveheart* (1995). In the latter, Scottish animosity towards the English is partly driven by Edward I's decision to reimpose this custom north of the border. This new right is enthusiastically embraced by the English commanders in Scotland, and leads indirectly to the death of William Wallace's beloved wife, and thus to his campaign against the English. It also serves to highlight the fundamental difference between the noble Scots and their English enemies, whose sexual deviance is represented not only by their enthusiasm for this brutal custom, but by Edward I's incestuous desire for his daughter-in-law Isabella, and by the homosexuality of his son Prince Edward (whose portrayal draws so heavily on contemporary stereotypes of gay men as weak, ineffectual and bitchy that it provoked protests at the time of the film's release, with one reviewer describing it as 'gay-baiting').[5]

Alongside the conviction that all medieval sex was deeply deviant and/ or violently misogynistic, there exists another strongly entrenched belief: that everyone in the Middle Ages was sexually repressed (thanks to the influence of the Church), but also sex mad. This idea is even included (in a very tame way) in the popular children's television series *Horrible Histories*, in which the title characters in the 'Funky Monks' Song' declare that for a monk to stick true to his vows he must live a life of no fun. As soon as the bishop's back is turned, they eat, drink and smuggle in a nun. More overtly, this idea is used as a source of humour in a number of films that employ another persistent medieval myth: the chastity belt. This device was supposedly used by jealous husbands to prevent their wives having adulterous relations while they were away from home, although there is little evidence that this was either a widespread problem, or a real solution.[6] Nevertheless, it has featured prominently in films such as *Up the Chastity Belt!* (1971), in which Frankie Howerd played Lurkalot, a seller of marital aids. The film is essentially a series of comic set pieces, including one in which Lurkalot sells a chastity belt to a husband who is about to go on Crusade, only to turn around and sell keys to a whole crowd of men. In another scene, he makes chastity belts for Saladin's harem, so that they can go on a sex strike and end the Crusades, which are presented largely as a getaway for bored husbands who want some sexual freedom.[7]

Representations of this sort ridicule medieval attitudes and highlight the differences between the past and the present, but are underpinned by a belief that medieval people were just like us, because ultimately sex is a universal human impulse. Yet while there are some obvious continuities – not least because the human body and its physical capabilities have changed very little over the past millennium – there have been significant changes in how sex has been regarded, and therefore in how it is understood and experienced. For one thing, the medieval mind tended to see sex as something that one person did to another, rather than an activity in which both partners were equally engaged. There was a strong tendency to emphasize active (implicitly male) and passive (female) roles, and to assume that one of each was involved in each act of intercourse. While this did not necessarily mean that medieval women were expected to simply lie back and think of England, it was considered significant that men did the penetrating, and women were penetrated. This way of thinking held true even in discussions of same-sex acts, so that one man would be considered passive and the other active. Female-female acts were only really considered as sex if one woman used an object to penetrate the other.[8]

If this view tended to prioritize penile-vaginal intercourse as the most significant – perhaps the only real – form of sex, the picture was further complicated by the existence of different categorizations of sexuality and sexual behaviour. We should not automatically assume that what seems sexual to us seemed sexual to them, or vice versa. In contemporary Britain, for example, kissing someone on the lips is almost inherently sexual, to the extent that some people object even to a parent kissing their young child on the mouth. But while medieval kisses certainly could be erotic, they could also be an expression of affection, or respect, or political bonds. Heterosexuality and homosexuality are both essentially nineteenth-century inventions; to apply either term to the pre-modern world is anachronistic, and arguably distorts our understanding of the past. Consequently, some historians have argued, we may need different categorizations – perhaps natural vs unnatural, licit vs illicit, or virginity vs everything else – to think about medieval sex.[9]

Besides the ideological differences between medieval and modern views of sex, it is worth considering the differences in how people learn about sex. Today, by the time we reach the age of consent, most of us will have acquired considerable knowledge from formal sex education, but also via exposure to our sex-saturated mass media – from, for example, news stories, advertising, sex scenes in films and on television, and perhaps even pornography. In contrast, most medieval people encountered only what could be gleaned from their local community, whether in the form of instruction from a parish priest, conversation with family and friends, or occasional glimpses of people or animals caught in the act.

Of course, there is a vast array of sexual attitudes and experience in the modern world, so that your perspective and mine might be very different, and the same was true in medieval Europe. This book focuses on western Europe, a sizeable area encompassing a range of peoples, cultures and attitudes, over a period of roughly four centuries, from circa 1100 to around 1500. Given such a geographical and chronological range, as well as the influence of individual circumstances, experiences and personalities, there would have been considerable variation in what people thought about sex and sexuality, and we should be cautious about trying to identify one single medieval view on any of the topics covered. Nevertheless, there were some extremely influential and widely shared ideas and attitudes in circulation, many of them rooted in two belief systems that were dominant throughout medieval Europe: Roman Catholic Christianity and Galenic medicine. It is with the influence of these complex ideologies on medieval sex and sexuality that we shall begin.

ONE

Guiding Principles

Although sexual intercourse is, in essence, a bodily function, individual attitudes and experiences are always shaped by the world in which one lives – by legal constraints, by medical ideas and (in many societies, including medieval Europe) by religious beliefs.

Religious Beliefs

In the tiny parish church of St Botolph's, Hardham, West Sussex, is a quartet of twelfth-century wall paintings that tell the story of Adam and Eve. In the best preserved, the first man and woman are unashamedly naked. Then Eve succumbs to the Temptation, represented by a strange winged serpent. The other images depict the couple after the Fall, performing agricultural tasks, immersing themselves in water to quell their newly emerged lust, and finally cowering in shame, hiding their nakedness with their arms.[1]

This familiar Bible story was at the heart of medieval understandings of sex. Before the Fall, Adam and Eve represented human nature as it was meant to be: they were immortal and free from suffering, and their sinless bodies functioned perfectly. After the Fall, everything changed.[2] As the early thirteenth-century English treatise *Holy Maidenhood* put it: 'If you ask why God created such a thing [as sex], this is my answer: God never created it to be like this, but Adam and Eve perverted it through their sin and corrupted our nature.'[3] Such was the importance of this process that the nature of sex in the Garden of Eden was the subject of considerable theological debate. Some authorities argued that prelapsarian people would have reproduced asexually, like angels, but this was very much a minority view.[4] Most theologians thought that God designed sexual intercourse as a means of perpetuating the human and animal races, and that He created sexual pleasure as an added incentive to the fulfilment of this goal.[5] It was, however, generally agreed that Adam and Eve did not have sex in Paradise, either because there was insufficient time before the Fall, or because God did not order them to do so.[6]

Nevertheless, medieval people were fascinated by the possibility of prelapsarian sex, and debated what it would have been like. Some argued that it would have been completely free of both sin and pleasure, with the genitals functioning like any other body part; having an erection would have felt no different to moving an arm or leg. Others thought that sex would have been more pleasurable before the Fall, when bodies were both healthier and more sensitive. However, because these perfect people were untroubled by lust, they would have had sex only in order to reproduce, with every act of intercourse producing healthy offspring.[7] Related physiological puzzles were also much discussed; it was, for example, deemed unlikely that Eve would have menstruated or that Adam would have experienced wet dreams, since their bodies were perfectly calibrated. Some even suggested that semen would not have existed in Paradise; Hildegard of Bingen (1098–1179) thought that men would instead have produced some sort of 'pureness'. Others disagreed, reasoning that Adam and Eve could not have obeyed God's command to 'be fruitful and multiply' without it.[8]

If many aspects of sex before and after the Fall were unknowable, the increased role played by shame was unquestionable. In a postlapsarian world, sex was irrevocably altered: the events that took place in Eden transformed a simple bodily function into something disruptive and uncontrollable. People were embarrassed by their over-sensitive genitals, which were no longer obedient to reason.[9] More troublingly, sex became the means by which Original Sin was transmitted: because sex was impossible without lust, children who were conceived through intercourse inevitably received this taint.[10]

These facts coloured all medieval discussions about sex. St Augustine (354–430), whose writings were widely read throughout the Middle Ages, thought that all sex was sinful, because it inverted the proper hierarchy of mind and body and caused, through orgasm, 'an almost total extinction of mental alertness'. It thus served as a reminder of, perhaps even a partial re-enactment of, the Original Sin which led to the Fall.[11] Such sentiments informed many of the texts that seem to suggest that the medieval Church disapproved, wholeheartedly and without nuance, of any form of sexual activity. For example, according to the *Quinque Verba* (a fourteenth-century manual for the instruction of priests):

> Lust is the seventh deadly sin, and lust means the desire for illicit pleasures in many forms such as fornication, whoring, adultery, debauchery, incest, sacrilege, unnatural vices, and other horrendous

Adam and Eve are tempted by the serpent, in a 12th-century wall painting
from St Botolph's Church, Hardham. The serpent, though now less visible from wear,
is depicted giving the apple to Eve.

sins. Still, it is not a good thing to dwell on these things or speak
of them at too great a length, but, rather, to grieve over and
fear them.[12]

The reason for such fear was explained by a twelfth-century English
sermon which proclaimed that 'Bodily pleasure is but for a moment; but
the fire which follows thereon will endure forever.'[13] The surest way to
avoid hellfire was to remain a virgin.

According to *Holy Maidenhood*, which was written to persuade holy women of the benefits of virginity, the best sexual deterrent was meditation on 'that sinful act through which your mother conceived you – that indecent heat of the flesh, that burning itch of physical desire, that animal union, that shameless coupling, that stinking and wanton deed, full of filthiness'.[14] Marriage was, the author claimed, the least meritorious of the three states in which a Christian might honestly live, 'for marriage brings forth her fruit thirtyfold in heaven, widowhood sixtyfold; maidenhood with a hundredfold outdoes both.'[15] Being a virgin placed a woman (or, indeed, a man) on the level of the angels, or perhaps even above them, since it was harder to remain pure on Earth than it was in Heaven.[16] Indeed, given that being a true virgin meant avoiding not just sex with a partner, but masturbation and even impure thoughts, it is surprising that any mere mortal achieved it. The scale of the challenge is illustrated by the case of an unfortunate young monk who was persecuted by a demon. Whenever he began to pray, the evil spirit rubbed his genitals until he was polluted by an emission of semen. Although the man was otherwise of good behaviour, Bishop Hildegard of Le Mans (1096–1125) ruled that he was no longer a virgin, since he had participated (however unwillingly) in a 'shameful act of fornication'.[17]

Yet despite the clarity of this verdict, and despite *Holy Maidenhood*'s assertion that virginity was 'a treasure that, if it be once lost, will never again be found', many authorities suggested that virginity could be regained. St Augustine believed that the will was central in such cases: if a woman had not experienced desire, then her spiritual virginity was intact, even if her body was not. According to Peter Damian (*c.* 1007–1072), those who questioned God's ability to restore virginity (either physical or spiritual) were guilty of questioning His power. If, Damian fumed, God could be born of a virgin, then of course He could achieve the much lesser feat of repairing lost virginity. For pious women who longed for the religious life, but were obliged to marry, such arguments offered the possibility of salvation.[18] The Norfolk mystic Margery Kempe (*c.* 1373– *c.* 1438), a married mother of fourteen who was tormented by her lost virginity, received the ultimate proof that sex did not have to signal the end of a woman's spiritual life when she tearfully bewailed her fallen state to Christ (with whom she regularly conversed). He reassured her that because she was 'a maiden in [her] soul', she would dance alongside the holy virgins in Heaven.[19]

Thanks to Adam and Eve, the idea that sex was sinful influenced all medieval lives. Nevertheless, most people opted for marriage over virginity – and unlike Margery Kempe, most do not seem to have felt like failures. Nor should we assume that those who took wedding vows were automatically seen as inferior to those who took vows of celibacy.

Marital sex (if performed correctly) was not seen as a barrier to salvation, and by the later Middle Ages the Church was increasingly willing to acknowledge that it could even be a good thing: it saved the souls of those who were incapable of lifelong abstinence and produced Christian offspring.[20] Moreover, as the English friar John Baconthorpe (*c.* 1290–1347) observed, marriage had wider benefits, for 'man does not just aim at generating offspring, for the multiplication of the species, like a beast; he aims at living a good and peaceful life with his wife.'[21]

How far the ordinary Christian absorbed and was influenced by these ideas is largely unknowable, but *Fasciculus Morum* (an early fourteenth-century English handbook for preachers) reveals the moral messages delivered from the pulpit. Churchgoers were, for example, taught that lechery was offensive to God, and pleasing to the Devil.[22] They were also reminded that great care must be taken over even seemingly harmless physical contact and conversations, since lust was like a fire and could be ignited by a spark.[23] Such general teachings were supplemented by warnings about specific forms of sexual sin, including fornication – which was a grave sin because it could never be justified (unlike, say, theft in time of need), because it suggested that humans were worse than animals (some of which mated for life), and because it caused social disorder, for 'if everybody could freely sleep with anyone, frequent struggles would arise, strife, hatred, homicide, and many more evils.'[24] The married faithful were also warned against infidelity, and reminded that husbands must not 'become adulterers with their own wives, using sex not for procreation but for their lustful pleasures alone'.[25] Finally, parishioners were taught about incest and sodomy, even though the latter was so repulsive that the author could not bring himself to discuss it, simply writing that 'I pass it over in horror and leave it to others to describe it.'[26]

The moral instruction of the medieval Christian also covered chastity, which in this context meant sexual restraint within or without marriage, rather than complete abstinence; it was achieved through a combination of self-control and self-mortification (such as fasting or flagellation). The message was reinforced with purportedly true tales of continence, including one about a man who suffered from bad breath. When he asked his wife why she had not told him, she replied that she 'thought that all men's mouths smell that way'. This proved that she was a truly chaste wife, who had never kissed another man.[27] Preachers also praised virginity as the ideal state, warning that it could be lost 'through unchaste touching and hugging' and reminding their flock that 'as a sign of his love and reverence of virginity, Christ chose to be a virgin, to be born of a virgin, and to be baptised by a virgin.' Those who imitated His life of exemplary sexual purity would 'follow Christ to the Kingdom of Heaven'.[28]

Such exhortations to emulate Christ were common in medieval Christianity; He, along with the saints, was constantly held up as an example of pious living to be imitated by the faithful. It was in this spirit that Bishop Herbert of Norwich (1090–1119) wrote to Thurstan the monk:

> My son, see to it that you maintain your chastity, without which it is impossible to please God. A virgin was Christ, a virgin was Mary the mother of Christ, a virgin was John the herald of Christ, a virgin was John the beloved of Christ; attend, and you shall find that everywhere in the mystery of our redemption virginity has had the utmost efficacy . . . Truly it is a blessed fellowship to dwell with Christ, and to sing the song which none but virgins sing.[29]

Such an exhortation was particularly appropriate in this context, since both men had taken monastic vows, but interest in such models of sexual conduct was not limited to the cloister. From the twelfth century onwards, there was both growing interest in the humanity of Jesus and the saints, and an increasing tendency for the devout to try to emulate them.

Since virginity has always been particularly valued as a feminine virtue, it is unsurprising that it was particularly associated with female saints, to the extent that some historians have argued that it was almost impossible for a non-virginal woman to be considered truly holy.[30] The most obvious embodiment of this ideal was the Virgin Mary, to whom many medieval Christians of both sexes were passionately devoted. It was widely believed that she remained a virgin after the conception and birth of Christ, and indeed for her entire life; some even suggested that she had been impregnated by a ray of pure light, possibly through the ear.[31] There was a strong desire to separate the Virgin from not only the indignities of sexual intercourse, but the related contaminations of the female body, so that it was widely believed that the birth of Christ was free from pain and from the polluting effects of afterbirth. Some authorities suggested that, thanks to her Immaculate Conception, Mary would not have menstruated.[32]

Although Mary was pre-eminent among the medieval virgin-saints, she had numerous popular counterparts, notably the Virgin Martyrs. These Roman girls were the heroines of highly formulaic tales in which they converted to Christianity against the wishes of their pagan families and died in defence of their faith and their virginity, often after undergoing extreme physical and mental trials. One of the best known was St Agnes, a thirteen-year-old girl who faced torments including imprisonment in a brothel and a miraculously unsuccessful burning before she was eventually stabbed to death.[33] Moreover, such powerfully disturbing stories were not confined to the history books. When Oda of Hainault's (*d.* 1158) parents arranged a marriage for her, she insisted that she intended to preserve her virginity for her heavenly spouse, and cut off her nose with a sword. Although Oda lived as a nun for many years after this incident, her hagiographer presented her as a martyr for virginity.[34]

The medieval Church also placed considerable value on male virginity, a virtue embodied by Christ. *The Golden Legend* notes that John the Baptist was also a lifelong virgin, while St George was 'like sand ... dry of the lusts of the flesh', and John the Evangelist abandoned his wedding feast at Cana to follow Jesus and live a life of perpetual virginity. Again, such figures were not restricted to the distant past. In the eleventh century, the virgin king emerged as a significant figure; Edward the Confessor, the English king whose death without issue in 1066 led to the Norman Conquest, is probably the best known.[35] Many bishops were similarly celebrated for their sexual purity: St Wulfstan of Worcester (1062–95), for example, was 'so exceptionally chaste that when his life was ended, he displayed in heaven the sign of his virginity which was still intact'.[36]

Despite its high ideals and strong rhetoric, medieval Christianity was ultimately a religion that offered hope and the possibility of forgiveness. The Virgin Mary seemed to have a particular weakness for sexual sinners, and collections of her miracles often include stories of fornicators who were saved by her intervention; the Castilian priest Gonzalo de Berceo (*c.* 1197–*c.* 1264) included three examples in his *Miracles of Our Lady*. The first concerned a sexton who left his abbey at night, in search of sexual adventures. As he returned, he fell into a river and drowned. Devils tried to carry off his soul, but the Queen of Heaven came to his rescue and the monk was restored to life. Henceforth, he was a changed man – although he remained devoted to Mary.[37] She also saved a Cluniac monk who had sex with his mistress before going on pilgrimage, and an abbess who found herself pregnant after a single lapse. This woman's sin was nearly uncovered, but Mary intervened by spiriting her baby away to be raised by a hermit, and eradicating all physical signs of her ordeal.[38]

What all of these individuals had in common, besides their sexual transgressions, was a genuine contrition for their sins. Perhaps the ultimate embodiment of such penitence was Mary Magdalene, whose cult exploded in popularity around 1200. The medieval Magdalene was a composite of several biblical Marys, and bore little resemblance to the woman depicted in the Gospels. According to *The Golden Legend*, she was 'a woman who

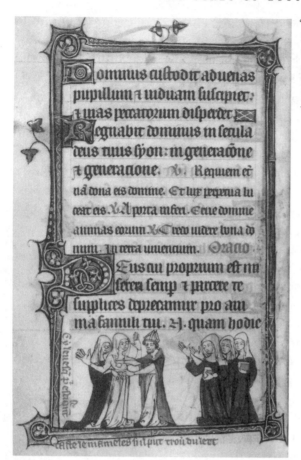

'The Abbess Delivered': a bishop investigates rumours that an abbess has recently given birth by examining her breasts, from a 14th-century Book of Hours (British Library Yates Thompson MS 13, f. 157v).

gave her body to pleasure', until she met Jesus. He forgave her sins and she became one of His most devoted followers. She received many 'marks of love' from Christ, who resurrected her brother and allowed her to do the housekeeping on His travels.[39] If Mary Magdalene's sexual sins did not bar her from Christ's inner circle, they also offered medieval Christians hope that they too might be redeemed. Consequently, they celebrated her enthusiastically: her feast was one of the most important in the Christian calendar, professions and institutions adopted her as their patron saint, and everything from Oxbridge colleges to daughters were named after her. As Humbert of Romans, the head of the Dominican order, preached in the mid-thirteenth century: 'no other woman in the world was shown greater reverence, or believed to have greater glory in Heaven.'[40]

Medical Theories

While religious belief underpinned most medieval ideas about sexuality, both attitudes and behaviour were also shaped by medical ideas about the human body. Although medieval medicine was very different to its twenty-first-century equivalent, it was based on an extremely sophisticated set of theories. At its heart was the humoral system, according to which health was based on the equilibrium of four humours (blood, phlegm, black bile and yellow bile), and illness the product of imbalance. The humours were balanced, and good health maintained, through the expulsion of various bodily fluids, including semen. Closely linked to this was the idea of complexion – that is, the balance of the qualities of hot and cold, wet and dry, in the human body. Each individual had their own unique complexion, but broadly speaking women were cold and wet, whereas men were hot and dry.

This meant that the genitals of a male foetus developed outside the body, but in a female they were largely internal: the ovaries were roughly equivalent to the testicles, and the womb was like an inverted penis.[41] Some authorities (adherents of the so-called one-sex model) went so far as to present the woman as a defective male; according to Albertus Magnus (d. 1280) 'the male penis is a sort of perfected and complete thing which moves to the exterior, whereas the womb, along with the parts associated with it, is a sort of incomplete and imperfect thing that is retained internally.' It was therefore theoretically possible for a woman to turn into a man if she overheated, forcing her internal organs out of her body.[42] But this interpretation was not universally accepted. As one English text of about 1400 pointed out:

> There are five differences between man and woman. The first difference is above their forehead, for there are some men who are bald, but women are not. The second difference is that some men are thick-haired on their beards, but women are smooth. The third difference is on the breasts, for men have only little warts but women have long paps. The fourth difference is between their legs, for men have a penis with other appendages, but women have an opening which is called a 'bel chos' or else a weket [gate] of the womb. The fifth difference is inside the body of the woman between her navel and her vagina, for there she has a vessel that no man has, which is called the matrix.[43]

Another crucial difference was that women menstruated, which they needed to do because they lacked the bodily heat to 'dry up the bad and

superfluous humours in them'.[44] Although medical sources rarely presented menstruation as a sin, it was a source of considerable repugnance.
Bartholomeus Anglicus (*fl.* 1230) described how menstrual blood flowed
into the uterus 'as filthe into a goter', and claimed that it could rust metal
and kill living things. After the menopause the evil humours built up
inside the body, so that sex with an old woman was potentially extremely
harmful. On the other hand, it was recognized that menstrual blood was
a useful thing: it nourished the embryo during pregnancy, and was also
the source of breast milk.[45]

If the female body was only partially understood, the same was true
of male anatomy. Erections were thought to result from a windy spirit
within the body, so a man who struggled to have sex might be advised
to eat wind-producing foods, such as chickpeas.[46] According to William
of Saliceto, the penis contained two distinct passages, one linked to the
neck of the bladder, from which urine was expelled, the other linked to
the sperm ducts, which produced semen. He dismissed the suggestion
that there was also a third passage, solely for the purpose of nocturnal
emissions during sleep.[47] There was also considerable debate about the
production of semen. It was widely agreed that it was derived from excess
food, which was turned into blood and then 'fermented and whitened by
the power of the testicles'.[48] But was it produced from the whole body,
or in the brain? Arguments in favour of the whole-body theory included
the fact that emitting semen produced pleasure throughout the body, but
it was clearly undermined by observation, which suggested that a man
who lost a body part was still able to reproduce. Supporters of the brain
theory pointed out that semen was white, soft and moist, like the brain; in
humoral terms the two substances were thought to be similar. There was
much circumstantial evidence of the link: the eyes unmistakeably looked
different during sex, and bathing the genitals of a drunk man brought
him to his senses.[49] Moreover, it was widely believed that cutting the
veins located to the side of a man's ears would make him infertile, which
seemed to prove the point.[50]

According to humoral theory, sex was a form of excretion; it was
therefore beneficial to the body, but only in moderation. Medical writings
included frequent warnings about the impact of overindulgence, with the
essential problem being that men were thought to lose both heat and
moisture during intercourse.[51] Too much sex could dry out the body, causing symptoms including hair loss, heart and lung problems, and kidney
failure. The eyes and brain were thought to be particularly vulnerable to
such drying, because of the 'strong link' between those organs and semen;
as a result, Albertus Magnus claimed, 'the eyes of those who copulate a

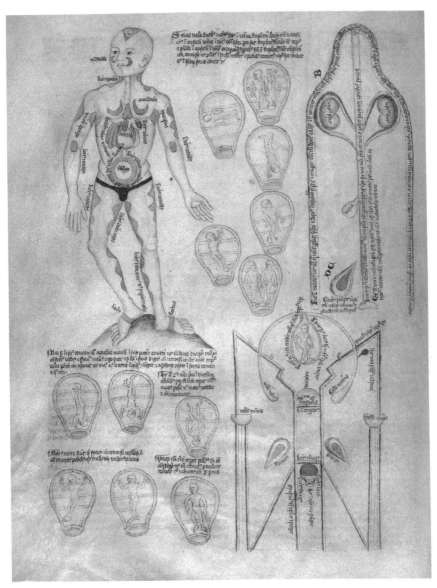

Reproductive organs depicted in a German miscellany, *c.* 1420 (Wellcome Collection, MS 49, f. 37v).

great deal are sunken and shrunk in size, and vision is weakened from frequent copulation.'[52] He also recounted the story of a monk who, 'half-starved', died after having 'desired' a beautiful woman seventy times before matins. A post-mortem found that his brain had shrunk to the size of a pomegranate, and his eyes had been destroyed.[53] Those who were merely weakened by too much sex were advised to abstain for a time; there were also remedies to replenish their strength, although some of these were sufficiently repulsive as to make death seem appealing. Arnau de Vilanova, for example, advised: 'let him sit naked in a clean tub in which 30 or 40 eggs have been broken, and draw all these eggs in through the anus.'[54]

But too little sex was also a health risk; as the eleventh-century monk-physician Constantine the African put it, 'no one who abstains from intercourse will be healthy. Intercourse is without doubt beneficial and an aid to health.'[55] Sex was one of the ways by which the superfluities of digestion were expelled from the body, which was necessary for good health, and long-term celibacy meant the retention of excess semen. Maino de Maineri (d. 1368), an Italian physician whose patients included Robert the Bruce, noted that 'occasionally corruption arises from the retention of sperm, corrupting not only the sperm ducts but also the whole body . . . in the manner of a poison.'[56] This would affect the heart, leading to anxiety and depression; other symptoms might include headaches and weight loss. Long-term abstinence could even lead to death.[57]

Sex was also important for female health, although in different ways. As *The Secrets of Women* explained, sex was beneficial for women, 'because through it they lose their superfluous cold and receive heat, and this tempers their frigid natures . . . Thus women who have much sexual intercourse do not have their lives shortened as men do.' Indeed, frequent sex could actually make women stronger and healthier.[58] A sensible individual would, however, consider her reproductive capacities; it was commonly believed that prostitutes rarely conceived because frequent intercourse made their wombs too smooth to retain semen.[59] And of course, sex often led to childbirth, with obvious risks.

Since women were also thought to release seed during intercourse, they too were at risk if they didn't have enough sex; indeed, some medical writers thought that celibacy was more dangerous for women than for men.[60] The most serious consequence of female abstinence was a disease known as suffocation of the womb, to which teenage girls and widows were especially prone. The symptoms included fainting, stomach upsets and loss of appetite, and the best treatment was marriage, so that the sufferer could have regular sex.[61] This was what a physician urged when the young Margaret of Ypres (1216–1237) fell ill.[62] If, like the deeply pious Margaret, the woman was unwilling or unable to take a husband, then lifestyle changes might help: the English physician John of Gaddesden (d. 1361) suggested foreign travel and frequent exercise.[63] But in many cases, medical intervention would be needed. Potential remedies included cupping of the inguinal and pubic area, various special drinks, and pessaries made from powdered fox penis.[64] Another oft-suggested treatment aimed to drive the womb back into the correct position by simultaneously using a feather to put a bad smell under the woman's nose, and fumigating her nether regions.[65]

In the most serious cases, doctors sometimes suggested treatments that were seemingly intended to bring the woman to orgasm, so that she would release the excess seed which was causing her illness. John of Gaddesden recommended that, if a sufferer had a fainting fit and needed urgent treatment, 'the midwife should insert a finger covered with oil of lily, laurel or spikenard into her womb, and move it vigorously about.'[66] Arnau of Vilanova's method was slightly less hands-on, involving the insertion of silk soaked in 'ground sage and natron with vinegar or salt water' into the vagina, but the intended consequences were similar: this, he said, would cause gripping, followed by the emission of excess seed. He also acknowledged that some women (especially, he claimed, the wives of Florentine merchants) masturbated, although he rejected this as a cure since it was clearly a sin.[67]

Despite agreeing on the importance of intercourse, most medical texts are infuriatingly vague about exactly how much sex was enough: it varied from person to person, and over the course of an individual's life. According to the thirteenth-century *Liber Minor de Coitu*, those who were particularly vulnerable to the effects of excess included those with sciatica and arthritis, men with fat, pale, humid bodies, and phlegmatics. These people were naturally cold; losing heat through the emission of seed made them colder. On the other hand, fleshy men with a hot, moist constitution needed to have sex in order to lose heat.[68] Female sexuality could also be explained in relation to complexion. For example, choleric women who lacked husbands would 'suffer physically and be debilitated', whereas melancholic women were 'healthier, stronger, and happier' if man-free.[69] Age was another important factor, especially for men: the diminution of natural heat and radical moisture was supposed to lessen desire, but regimens and other medical texts included frequent warnings that old men (that is, those over sixty) should have less sex, while the over-seventies should avoid it altogether.[70]

That a person could die of too much or too little sex was not merely a theory found in specialist medical writings, but a widespread phenomenon that was thought to pose a real danger to real people. Among those who supposedly died of excess was Ralph, count of Vermandois. In 1152, when he was probably in his seventies, he married for the third time, to a much younger woman. Shortly afterwards, he became seriously ill, and his doctor 'warned him, as he valued his life, to abstain from intercourse with his wife'. When the physician examined Ralph's urine, he quickly realized that his advice had been ignored, and predicted – correctly – that the patient would be dead within three days.[71] Even if sex did not kill a man, it could leave him more vulnerable to other diseases. During the plague epidemics that swept Europe in the fourteenth and fifteenth centuries, physicians warned that too much sex opened the pores, making men more vulnerable to contagion; to stay healthy, it was necessary to eschew 'fleshly lust'.[72] The plague tract that a Yorkshire gentleman copied into his commonplace book towards the end of the Middle Ages similarly included a solemn warning against intercourse, because it weakened the vital spirits just as they were needed to fight the disease.[73]

Abstinence was also a genuine health issue, especially for the clergy, who were required by their vocation to remain celibate. Soldiers were similarly vulnerable, since their campaigns took them away from their wives for long periods of time. According to the twelfth-century Norman poet Ambroise, thousands of Crusaders perished 'because from women they abstained'.[74] But even a layman who stayed peacefully at home could be at risk. In 1394, in the small Provençal town of Manosque, a young bride named Margarida de Portu was accused of poisoning her husband. During the course of her trial, it emerged that the couple had never had sex, due to her seizures: Margarida testified that 'whenever he lay beside me in bed, I trembled so badly that nothing could happen.'[75] The Jewish physician Vivas Josep, who examined the corpse, believed that Johan Damponcii had died because of his unconsummated marriage. Referring to the writings of Avicenna and Galen to support his theory, he suggested that frustrated lust had led to melancholy, which has in turn caused syncope and unbalanced humours. Thus Johan's heart was constricted and damaged, leading to his sudden death.[76]

Although medieval ideas about sexual health centred around the idea of balance, there is some evidence that, long before syphilis erupted onto the scene in the late fifteenth century, people recognized the possibility of sexually transmitted diseases, even if they did not understand them in terms of bacteria and viruses. The complexity of medieval attitudes and experiences is reflected in Arnaud de Verniolles' recollections of his student exploits:

> At the time they were burning the lepers, I was living in Toulouse; one day I did it with a prostitute. And after I had perpetrated this sin my face began to swell. I was terrified and thought I had caught leprosy; I thereupon swore that in future I would never sleep with a woman again.[77]

This was not an unusual story: there are many tales of medieval men who found themselves with undesirable symptoms after a brothel visit, and attributed their plight to their bad behaviour.[78] But too much has been made of the medieval tendency to interpret disease as a product of sexual sin, and such interpretations were not solely based on moral judgements.

Indeed, concerns about the sexual transmission of disease via prostitutes were often addressed in an entirely rational manner. Sometimes local authorities took preventative action: a set of regulations from late medieval Southwark banished women with a 'burning sickness' (probably gonorrhoea) from the local stews, and in 1497 the 'light women' of Aberdeen were ordered to cease trading, due to 'the infirmity come out of France and foreign parts' (that is, syphilis).[79] Although such measures surely had a moral element, they were firmly rooted in medical theory. The *Prose Salernitan Questions* (*c.* 1200) explained how a woman might seem unharmed after having intercourse with a leper, but the coldness of the female complexion meant that the leper's semen remained in her uterus, where it would turn to putrid vapour. When the penis of a healthy man came into contact with this vapour, the heat of his body would ensure that it was absorbed through his open pores. Sores would soon appear on his genitals, before spreading around his body.[80] Thus the fears of men like Arnaud de Verniolles made perfect sense within the context of contemporary medical ideas.

Fortunately, treatments were available; medical treatises and recipe collections contain numerous remedies for swollen, pustulent and itchy genitals, including various poultices and herbal washes. John of Gaddesden suggested that, if a man had sexual relations with a woman he believed to be leprous, he should immediately cleanse his penis, either with his own urine or with vinegar and water. Then he must undergo intensive phlebotomy, followed by a three-month course of purgation, ointments and medication.[81] Such treatments were undoubtedly unpleasant, but the

Diseases of the genitals, from an early 14th-century medical anthology (British Library Sloane MS 1977, f. 7v).

surgical remedies recommended by the English surgeon John of Arderne (*fl.* 1308–1377) were downright brutal. In one of his cases, 'the man's yard began to swell after coitus, due to the falling of his own sperm, whereof he suffered great grievousness of burning and aching as men do when they are so hurt.' He treated this unfortunate individual by cutting away the dead flesh, then applying quicklime – a process that must have been excruciatingly painful, but which apparently produced a cure.[82]

To us, it seems clear that these are remedies for venereal diseases acquired as a result of unsafe sex, but it is less than certain that medieval people would have understood them in this way. The man with the swollen yard, for example, may well have been viewed by his contemporaries as a victim not of infection, but of overindulgence. Nevertheless, cases such as his helped to reinforce the idea that sex was a powerful force with potentially dangerous consequences – and thus it needed to be controlled.

Mechanisms of Control

In one of his most powerful sermons, St Vincent Ferrer (1350–1419) preached about the necessity of controlling sexual behaviour within a city in order to avoid God's wrath. The sins of an individual, he warned, hurt not just them, but the whole community, for if

> there is a woman, concubine or [sexual] friend of someone in the town, the entire town is corrupted . . . and one such person can corrupt more than all the others can cure . . . If you have 1,000 apples in a bin, and one is rotten, all the others will rot . . . thus one bad person corrupts the good ones.[83]

Consequently, it was for the common good that medieval authorities policed individual sexual conduct, and punished those who acted in ways that were deemed unacceptable.

At the heart of the Church's moral efforts was the parish priest, who had a duty to teach his flock about sin and penance, and to hear their confessions.[84] Religious writers often drew parallels between confessing to a priest and seeking treatment from a doctor, with both consultations offering a form of healing. Being a confessor was thus a highly skilled job: he must be both authoritative and kindly, able to offer consolation as well as penance, persuasive enough to make even the reluctant confess, and restrained enough not to show any reaction to the confession, including disapproval.[85]

Because it was a private procedure, it is impossible to know exactly what medieval confession was like. The questions were supposed to reflect the identity of the penitent, considering the individual's age, gender and occupation. Merchants, for example, might be asked whether they had committed adultery or bigamy during their frequent travels, while married women should be challenged on their fidelity to their husbands.[86] Texts such as Roger of Flamborough's *Liber poenitentialis*, a guide for inexperienced confessors that included models for confession, give us a flavour of the process:

> Priest: Have you ever been corrupted by lust?
> Penitent: A good deal.
> Priest: Have you ever committed lust against nature?
> Penitent: A good deal.
> Priest: Even with a man?
> Penitent: A good deal.
> Priest: With a cleric or a layman?
> Penitent: Both.
> Priest: With married or unmarried laymen?
> Penitent: Both.
> Priest: How many of them were married?
> Penitent: I don't know.
> Priest: You therefore don't know their status?
> Penitent: Correct.
> Priest: Let us therefore get as much information as we can. How long did you sin with them?
> Penitent: Seven years.

Roger also explained that he never asked detailed questions about specific acts; rather, he spoke vaguely about commonly recognized sins, only probing as far as strictly necessary.[87] This reflected widespread fears that overly detailed questions gave people ideas – and that the answers might teach a simple priest about practices of which he was hitherto innocent.[88]

Once the priest had obtained a complete and sincere confession, he would usually provide a suitable penance.[89] (The gravest sins, including incest, were passed to a more senior cleric, usually a bishop, at this point.[90]) The penalties imposed could be arduous: prescriptive texts suggested that serious offences such as adultery or sex with a nun might require several years of fasting, genuflexions, beatings, prayers and/or sexual abstinence.[91] These rules may not, however, have been applied literally. In the early thirteenth century Thomas of Chobham noted that the rigour of canon law on such matters was not always observed; the human body could not sustain such harshness, and so prudent priests gave more bearable penances.[92] Pope Honorius III (1216–27) concurred: too light a penance would cause arrogance, but an overharsh penalty would deprive the penitent of hope.[93] Individual circumstances could also lead to relative clemency. It was, for example, recognized that the innate bodily heat of the young made them especially vulnerable to lust, while the delicate bodies of the high-born could not tolerate prolonged fasting.[94] Priests were also warned not to give penances that would alert a husband to his wife's sins, so an adulteress might have to eat less rather than fasting completely, or be told to say extra prayers or to give alms – an approach that suggests a surprising sensitivity on the part of the Church to the dangers posed by some husbands.[95]

Although the confession process was intended to be both straightforward and reassuring, in practice it was fraught with potential complications. Confessions were supposed to be confidential, but the fifteenth-century chaplain of Wokingham charged with revealing his parishioners' secrets was not unique in breaking the seal of the confessional. A more widespread problem was privacy: the confessional was not widely used until the sixteenth century, so it was quite likely that these conversations would be overheard. The fifteenth-century story of a lecherous man who failed to confess his sexual sins before taking the Easter communion and was consequently struck dead by lightning was probably fictitious, but it reflected a common concern: the man was supposedly motivated by fears that his neighbours would overhear his confession.[96] There was also some concern that penitents would identify their partner-in-crime, since it was considered inappropriate to confess to other people's sins on their behalf.[97] If a confession would unavoidably implicate someone else (for example, if a man confessed to incest with his sister), he should try to find a confessor who did not know the relevant party.[98]

From an ecclesiastical perspective, women were the biggest problem, both as sinners and as a cause of male sin. In a particularly memorable image, Odo of Cheriton (d. 1247) compared kissing a woman to biting into fruit: if a man realizes there is a worm in his apple, he will spit it out, and he should similarly eject his sins through confession.[99] Sermons depicted the concealment of sexual sins as a particularly feminine trait, and often included stories of women who failed to confess incest or adultery and were consequently damned.[100] There were also concerns about wives who confessed marital secrets, along with tales of husbands who eavesdropped on (or even dressed up as priests to hear) their wives' confessions.[101]

Women also endangered the clergy, and there was considerable disquiet about the dangers of discussing sexual matters with female parishioners.

According to the French theologian Jean Gerson (1363–1429), if a woman believed her confession would arouse her usual confessor (and especially if it was about him) she should go elsewhere.[102] Numerous authorities insisted that women must confess in full public view (to avoid both suspected and actual sin), and advised the priest to sit by her side so that he could not see her face, especially if she were young and attractive.[103] Despite these precautions, there were relatively frequent complaints that priests exploited their position to seduce female parishioners. In an early fourteenth-century case, a French matron knelt down for confession, but the priest embraced her, crying out that 'there was no woman in the world that he loved as much as me.' The woman was so upset that she left without confessing.[104] A London curate named Sir Geoffrey was allegedly in the habit of assailing young women after their Easter confession: he would kiss them, 'put his handis under their clothis', and ask if 'they might mete to do syne'. He ended up before the ecclesiastical courts – another important venue in the Church's war against sexual sin.[105]

Local Church courts such as the one in which Sir Geoffrey appeared spent most of their time dealing with similar offenders: in the early fourteenth century, roughly 90 per cent of the cases heard by both a rural dean's court in the diocese of Worcester and its equivalent in Cerisy, Normandy, concerned sex and marriage.[106] These institutions investigated public accusations supported by credible witnesses (until about 1200 these were the only acceptable kind), but also anonymous denunciations made directly to the court, or via parish priests; their judges were also able to take the initiative in investigating rumours.[107] Yet more immoral behaviour was uncovered by visitations, in which an authority figure (such as a bishop) conducted inspections of parishes and ecclesiastical institutions. When Bishop Trefnant of Hereford visited the village of Burghill in the spring of 1397, the parishioners

> reported that John Watys, a carpenter, committed adultery with Sybil Weston. Harry Daundevyl, a tiler, refuses to live with his wife, fails to love her as a husband ought, and has an adulterous relationship with Matilda, whom he keeps in a house at Pyon. Walter Herring commits fornication with Agnes, recent mistress of William Leper ... It is rumoured that Davy Matis is fornicating with Isabella Prestone.[108]

Once an individual was accused of a sexual offence, they could potentially clear themselves by compurgation – that is, by producing several witnesses willing to swear on oath that they believed him or her to be innocent. The credentials of these witnesses seem to have been subject to scrutiny, to ensure that they offered genuine testimony, and had not simply been paid for their services. After a successful purgation, the judge formally readmitted the accused into a state of good fame; the accusation was not to be spoken of again. A substantial number of cases ended with conviction, often following a confession. In 1499, in the Sudbury and Suffolk region, about two-thirds of those accused confessed, while the rest attempted compurgation – not all of them successfully. Cases could in theory be dismissed from court without penance or compurgation, especially if the individual concerned had already been suspended from church for some time, and had thus been sufficiently humiliated. Even these lucky individuals were probably given a good telling off by the judge.[109]

Most offenders were fined, required to pay court costs, and subjected to rituals that were intended to embarrass them before their friends and neighbours, and to deter others from similar offences.[110] The standard court-imposed penance required the offender to walk before the cross in the parish procession on a Sunday or major religious festival, carrying a candle, and then to stand or kneel in church for part of the service, before making an offering of the candle. This was usually repeated several times, typically in a state of semi-undress (that is, barefoot, barelegged or in a shirt/smock); women were obliged to leave their hair unbound. In some cases offenders were also whipped, although it is unclear whether this was meant as a serious physical punishment, or as further humiliation.[111] Gradually, however, solely financial punishments became the norm. Thus in the fourteenth century the episcopal courts at Tournai and Cambrai imposed mainly spiritual punishments, but later favoured fines, the amount of which was determined by the social status of the sinner.[112]

Individual sexual conduct was not just a religious concern; secular authorities also intervened in such matters, and could impose more serious penalties, including death. In late medieval Venice, for example, sexual offenders were investigated by the Avogadori, who were communal attorneys, and tried before the Council of Forty.[113] Like the ecclesiastical authorities, these bodies both responded to allegations and pursued potential cases, sometimes very proactively. In 1386 a London beadle accused of trespass said that it was the city's custom for law enforcement officials to enter a house if he heard that a sexual offence, such as adultery, was taking place there.[114] In rural areas, manorial courts dealt with men such as John Kenward of Hepworth, who was summoned to explain why he was living with a single woman named Alice, having driven his wife from the house. He was punished with a heavy fine.[115]

The relationship between secular and ecclesiastical justice was always complex, often fraught, and subject to considerable variation by region and over time. In theory, if an offender confessed and did penance, he could not be punished further.[116] But secular authorities exercised increasing control over lay morality towards the end of the Middle Ages – to the extent that, by the end of the fifteenth century, adultery had effectively been brought under secular jurisdiction in most countries.[117] This was partly driven by financial considerations; as one late fifteenth-century Exeter text put it, sexual offenders increasingly 'payed for their redemption with moneys'.[118] However, there were also important ideological changes, with urban government taking on a more religious tone. By the 1450s, cities including Nuremberg and Strasbourg had laws targeting immoral behaviour including fornication, blasphemy and drunkenness. Marriage was increasingly emphasized as the only acceptable context for sex, and there was growing hostility to prostitution.[119]

Within this context, the regulation of sexual behaviour was about both morality and civic order; rather than simply trying to shape individual conduct, the authorities were making a point about the sort of society they hoped to construct.[120] Public discipline punished the guilty, but also showed the wider community that such behaviour was innately reprehensible, unfitting in a good citizen, and offensive to God.[121] While we might assume that there was a clear distinction between clerical and lay attitudes, and that the authorities were imposing their vision of order on a reluctant populace, the evidence strongly suggests that many ordinary people had absorbed the prevailing religious and medical ideas about sex, and bought into the notion that the regulation of individual sexual behaviour was necessary for the greater good.[122] In the following chapters, we shall explore how these guiding principles – both imposed by the authorities and internalized by the masses – influenced the lives of real medieval people.

TWO

Getting Together

In order to have sex, it was first necessary to find a suitable partner, and in the Middle Ages (as today) this could be a challenging process, shaped by personal preference but also by various social constraints.

Criteria for Compatibility

What were the qualities a medieval person looked for in a sexual partner? At the most basic level, according to Andreas Capellanus (author of the twelfth-century treatise *On Love*), lovers must be of opposite sexes, since 'two persons of the same sex are in no way fitted to reciprocate each other's love or to practise its natural acts.'[1] It was also extremely important to ensure that your potential partner was not a relative, something which could be much harder than it sounds, since medieval definitions of incest were extremely broad. According to the rules set out by the Fourth Lateran Council (1215), anyone who shared a great-great-grandparent (that is, siblings, but also first, second and third cousins) was considered too closely related for marriage. Affinity (that is, a relationship created by sexual intercourse) also counted, so that once a man and woman had sex, they were barred from marrying each other's relatives. In addition, Christians were forbidden to marry spiritual relations (that is, people to whom they were connected through baptism), so that it was not possible to marry a godparent, a godchild, or any of their close kin.[2]

Age was also important, and canon law required that a girl must be at least twelve, and a boy at least fourteen, to marry. Marriage with an underage spouse was considered to be imperfect and was discouraged by the Church, although it could, in certain circumstances, be permitted by papal dispensation. Marriage with an infant below the age of reason (that is, under seven) could not, and while child marriages did happen, they were very unusual. Although adolescents were known to be prone to lust, sex was widely viewed as detrimental to their health, for which reason many

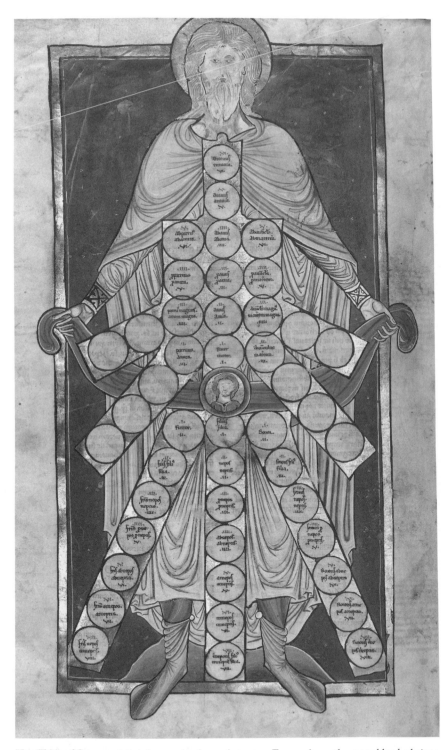

This 'Table of Consanguinity', drawn up in late 12th-century France, shows the many blood relations a medieval Christian was not permitted to marry (Getty Museum, MS Ludwig XIV 2, f. 227v).

authorities argued that it was best to postpone marriage until at least the late teens. According to Abbess Hildegard of Bingen, females were not ready for sex (in the sense that they would be capable of producing healthy offspring) until about twenty, while a boy's sexual maturity was best judged by his beard: once he had one, he was old enough to father offspring.[3] According to Giles of Rome (c. 1243–1316), early intercourse was bad for both sexes – because tastes formed at this stage would last a lifetime, but also because young girls were particularly likely to die in childbirth, and because young parents produced offspring who were feeble and lacking in reason. Consequently he thought that girls should be at least eighteen, and boys over twenty, before having sex.[4] Those who disregarded this guidance might come to regret their actions: in one of Thomas Becket's miracles, a knight expresses remorse over his wife's suffering in childbirth, for 'she was not yet of the age that she ought to become a mother.'[5]

As a result the average age at marriage seems to have been surprisingly high: across Europe urban girls typically married in their mid-twenties, and their rural counterparts in their early twenties. In the North, men were typically only slightly older than their wives (the English average seems to have been two or three years), but in Southern Europe (especially in Italy) it was not unusual for husbands to be at least a decade older.[6] Very large age gaps were possible, but were frowned upon and (as in the case of the union between January and May in Chaucer's 'The Merchant's Tale') ridiculed. This was partly because of attitudes to older people having sex. According to Andreas Capellanus, the elderly were ill-suited for love, 'because after a man's sixtieth year and a woman's fiftieth, one can admittedly have sexual intercourse but one's sensual pleasure cannot lead to love', because of the decline of natural heat.[7] Hildegard of Bingen was slightly more optimistic: she thought that, in those with a strong and youthful disposition, 'the heat of sexual pleasure' would wane at around seventy.[8]

Elite marriages were usually arranged by families or lords, and could involve very young people. In such circumstances, consummation would normally be postponed, and most child brides remained at home for several years after their marriage.[9] Even if a young child moved in with their future spouse, they were not supposed to share a bed. Jean de Joinville (c. 1225–1317), future biographer of Louis IX, was betrothed to Alix de Grandpré when they were both toddlers, and she went to live with his family when she was only two or three. Her mother received assurances from the Joinvilles that the child would be protected, and the couple were not married until they were both in their early teens. Even after this, the marriage was probably not consummated for some time, since their first child was born in 1247.[10] Similarly, Elizabeth Clifford was betrothed to Robert Plumpton in 1447, as a six-year-old. Her fiancé died three years later, so in 1453 Elizabeth (now twelve) was married to the second Plumpton son, William. Legally, she was old enough to consummate the marriage, but her father-in-law promised her father that this should not be done until she was sixteen. She had her first child at eighteen.[11]

Even outside the ranks of the nobility and gentry, family approval was an extremely important consideration when contracting a marriage, which effectively meant that your family got to decide who you could have (socially acceptable) sex with. The early fifteenth-century English verse 'How the Goodwife Taught Her Daughter' reminded girls:

> If any man pays court to you, and would marry you,
> Look that you scorn him not, whoever he is,
> But show it to your family and hide you it not.[12]

As late fifteenth-century Londoner Margery Sheppard put it: 'I will do as my father will have me; I will never have none against my father's will.'[13] In theory, peasants also needed their lord's permission to marry, although Pope Adrian IV ruled that the moral need to prevent fornication must trump a landowner's right to his serf's labour.

Families were especially likely to object to marriages that involved an obvious social mismatch, although there was some scope for women to marry up. When Margery Paston secretly married the family bailiff, her family was horrified: her mother Margaret considered this a 'lewd' union, and described her daughter as a 'brethel' (wretch).[14] In a case discussed by Angelo Gambiglioni (d. 1461), Philomena married a man of low birth without her father's permission. She thus forfeited her right to a dowry (the assets she brought to her husband on marriage), and when she tried to claim a share of her wealthy father's estate after his death, she was denied it due to her 'vile marriage' to 'a low person' of illegitimate birth, which had brought 'shame and ignominy' on the whole family.[15] Unions involving people of different religions were also frowned upon, and there was effectively no such thing as mixed marriage, since one partner would be required to convert. Such a conversion was likely to lead to shunning by one's community of origin, and a lack of resources to bring into marriage.[16]

Despite the many social and familial pressures involved in the making of a match, love and attraction undoubtedly could be a factor in medieval marriages. Andreas Capellanus warned that good character was the most important quality in a lover; although appearance was important, it could not form the basis of a lasting relationship.[17] Nevertheless, medieval

Europe had clear ideas about female beauty. Among the desirable features were golden hair, gleaming white skin, rosy cheeks, a delicate nose, white teeth, a small red mouth, long slender arms and fingers, small high breasts, a tiny waist, a rounded belly and dainty feet.[18] There were only a few small regional variations on this ideal: some popular literature from southern Italy presented tanned brunettes in a positive light, linking their appearance to sunlight and their healthy working conditions, and one Spanish text suggested that moist armpits were a desirable feminine feature.[19] Beauty was also strongly linked to social status, with literary texts often contrasting the good looks of the well-born with the darker skin and coarse, ill-proportioned features of the peasantry.[20] Men were warned to beware women who 'painted too heavily with the colours of the rainbow' – that is, they wore too much make-up.[21]

Although it has often been suggested that the medieval breast was solely a maternal or even (in the case of the Virgin Mary) a religious object, there is actually ample evidence that breasts were seen in sexual terms. Small, firm breasts were the medieval aesthetic ideal, and feature prominently in medieval literature: Chaucer's Troilus is enamoured by Criseyde's 'breasts round and little', and depictions of Bathsheba (late medieval Europe's ideal woman, at least in a physical sense) showed her with pert little breasts. One heroine was described as having 'firm breasts that lifted up her gown as if they were two round nuts'. Both poets and priests were well aware of the effect that breasts could have on men. The French poet Eustache Deschamps (c. 1346–c. 1406) favoured tight dresses with wide necklines 'through which the breasts and the throat could be more visible', while the mother in the German verse 'Stepmother and Daughter' advises her daughter that she can seduce a man by leaving her bodice unlaced, thus 'causing his courage to rise'. Late medieval clerics railed against cleavage-baring fashions, and sumptuary laws often prohibited revealing necklines.[22]

Large and loose breasts were thought to indicate sexual experience, and could be damaging to a single woman's reputation. Many later medieval medical texts include cosmetic breast advice for young women – always on ways to reduce and firm, never to enlarge. There were numerous recipes (almost all based on ingredients with cooling and tightening properties) to stop maidens' breasts growing too large: anoint them with blood from the testicles of a castrated piglet, or with hemlock, or vinegar. Some texts also recommended binding, and there is some evidence that medieval women wore undergarments designed to make their breasts look smaller. In the twelfth century, Abbot Gilbert of Hoyland decried women who deceitfully tied and compressed their breasts, while the Romance of the Rose described young women encasing their breasts to make them look tiny and taut. A German verse, written around 1400, described how:

> Many a woman makes two bags for the breasts
> with them she roams the streets
> so that all the men look at her
> and see what beautiful breasts she has got;
> But whose breasts are too large
> makes tight pouches
> so it is not told in the city
> that she has such big breasts.[23]

The ideal man was tall, strong and well-proportioned, with pale skin. Fashions in hair varied: longer, curled locks were popular in much of Europe, but the handsome heroes of Icelandic sagas usually had short hair. Body hair was considered an important marker of masculinity, such that some men wore fake beards and (in contrast to female practice) very few shaved or plucked their hair.[24] It was widely assumed that women liked men with large penises, and the anonymous Spanish author of a fifteenth-century *Mirror of Coitus* claimed that 'From an experienced woman I learned the characteristics that women desire in men. These are: a good member, a large and hard penis, and an abundance of sperm.'[25] Medieval literature is littered with women obsessed with male genitals, including *The Blacksmith of Creil*'s wife. The blacksmith notices his young servant has an enormous penis, and knows that his wife would 'sooner have been dead and buried / than not secure herself a share'. So he tells her about it, claiming that 'I've never seen a larger member.' She pretends to be disgusted, but when her husband goes out (or so she thinks), she propositions the youth. At this point, the husband emerges from his hiding place to dismiss the servant and beat his wife.[26]

Courtship and Premarital Sex

Church teachings on premarital sex were straightforward: it was not acceptable to have sex before a marriage was formally solemnized by a priest, even if vows had been exchanged.[27] The poor could also face secular sanctions for engaging in premarital sex: lords could fine young peasant women for having sex before marriage (legerwite) or having a baby out of wedlock (childwite). In practice, such fines were collected inconsistently, with substantial variation both between manors and over time – often being shaped by the zealousness of particular bailiffs, or by the lord's pecuniary needs. In Wakefield, for example, every young woman in the manor was fined in 1316, either for being deflowered or for marrying without a licence, an act which almost certainly reveals a lot about the lord's financial situation, and nothing about the women's sexual behaviour.[28]

The evidence regarding illegitimate births and bridal pregnancy is somewhat more revealing, and strongly suggests that a sizeable number of couples did have sex before marriage. In 1466 the Venetian hospital of the Pietà claimed that it had received 460 infants – most of them, in all likelihood, the offspring of single women – left on its doorstep in the past year.[29] In England, the evidence of the earliest parish registers (dating from the sixteenth century) suggests that somewhere between 13 and 26 per cent of brides were pregnant when they married; there is no strong reason to suspect that this proportion was much lower prior to 1500.[30] Law codes can also shed some light on social norms. In Castile, men who repudiated their betrothed after sex could be punished with heavy fines, paying much larger sums than those who broke off an unconsummated engagement. And in many Castilian towns, if a man died his betrothed was allowed to keep the gifts he had given her only if they had had sex. These rules suggest that sex between betrothed couples was not unexpected, or even unusual, and only became problematic if the marriage did not go ahead.[31]

Indeed, it seems to have been widely assumed that young men would be sexually active before marriage: the Synod of Aachen (862) claimed that 'there is hardly any man who joined his wife in marriage as a virgin.' This was especially true at an elite level, to the extent that those who were not might be viewed with suspicion. William the Conqueror's alleged adolescent chastity apparently led to rumours that he was impotent.[32] University students were especially prone to sexual transgressions: the Parisian theologian Peter of Poitiers (c. 1130–c. 1205) suggested that their many vices were attributable to their being away from home, free from parental and neighbourly scrutiny – and so they did things they would not dare to do at home. Lengthy apprenticeships, which stopped young men from marrying, created similar problems; both men and masters felt that this led to bad behaviour, including the use of prostitutes. When Londoner Anthony Pontisbury was imprisoned for getting married, seven years into a nine-year apprenticeship, he defended his decision, claiming that the rules were 'contrary to the laws of God and causeth much fornication and adultery'.[33]

Although young women were thought to be at least as prone to lust as their male counterparts, they were held to very different standards and were supposed to remain virginal. It is possible that attitudes to premarital sex were partly shaped by class, so that it was more acceptable for a poor woman to be sexually experienced than a wealthy one. Theoretically at least,

heiresses in wardship who committed sexual indiscretions could be disin-
herited; other women had less to lose.[34] Nevertheless, a thirteenth-century
proverb warned, 'Give your cunt to the penis and lose out on marriage.'[35]
Witnesses in court cases often claimed that ordinary women were irre-
deemably wounded by sexual defamation. A man who testified in support
of Joan Sebar (who had been called 'a strong whore', and accused of having
sex in a doorway) claimed that he would be reluctant to marry a woman
who had faced such accusations. In 1408, in the diocese of Salisbury, Alice
Sauser claimed that William Roper had contracted marriage with her
using the words, 'I William take you as my wife, on account of the scandal
which you have endured, being pregnant by me.'[36]

Such claims of permanent reputational damage may sometimes have
been exaggerated in order to enhance a plaintiff's chances of winning her
case, but they highlighted the very real vulnerability of female sexual reputation, a vulnerability which men sometimes exploited in order to win the
hand of a seemingly unattainable woman. Elisabeth Badoer's father was
negotiating her marriage when Pirano Contarini (the illegitimate son of
a prominent Venetian nobleman) claimed that he had repeatedly slept
with her and that they were secretly married; he also produced a witness
who had seen him climbing in her window, and a batch of love letters. He
was seemingly attempting to win her hand by making himself the only
possible candidate, but a physical examination indicated that Elisabeth
was 'a virgin intact and immaculate'. Pirano was thus shown to be a liar,
and her reputation was restored. In a similar case, Boneto, a poor young
bellringer, fell for his master's daughter, Margarita. He was not allowed
to marry her, so he claimed to have had sex with her, and forced a ring
onto her finger. The father threw him out of the house, and he was ultimately ruled to have defamed her.[37] Such cases were not restricted to Italy:
in fifteenth-century London, William Markis defamed Alice Brigge by
accusing her of sleeping with other men. He was angry that she would
not marry him, and hoped to stop anyone else marrying her. His claims
apparently did deter other suitors, but she still refused him.[38]

Yet the gender difference was perhaps not as stark as is often assumed.
Although a man's unchastity was rarely (if ever) said to make him unmarriageable, plenty of women who had non-marital sex went on to marry.
Young men were warned to be careful about getting caught: Peter Idley's
fifteenth-century moral treatise *Instructions to His Son* warned young men
that 'blind bargains' made 'in dark corners' were liable 'to the consistory
after to be led'. Although stereotypes held that women had sex in order
to snare men, and most Church court cases did involve women trying to
make men keep their promises, this was not always the case. When, in

late fifteenth-century London, Margaret Isot and Thomas Wulley were caught fornicating and made to marry, it was Margaret who resisted, and Thomas who took her to court to oblige her to recognize their marriage.[39]

The situation was complicated by the complexities of the medieval marriage-making process. A marriage could be contracted without the involvement of a priest, simply by the exchange of vows, which could be made in either the present or the future tense. The former were immediately binding; the latter were reversible only until the couple had sex. All such contracts were supposed to be followed by banns and solemnization; to fail to complete this part of the process was a sin, and a couple could be summoned before the Church courts if they exchanged vows and consummated their union but did not have their union solemnized.[40] It was for this reason that the Paris couple Denis Petit and Jeanne Maillarde were both fined for clandestine marriage: they had been together for five years, and had a child, but had not formalized their partnership.[41]

Some couples seem to have deliberately exploited this ambiguity to form committed but non-marital relationships, such as those documented in late fifteenth-century records of the Paris ecclesiastical courts. Guillaume Baudry of Sucy-en-Brie, a forty-year-old tanner, admitted that he had maintained Cecilia la Bernadete, who was thirty years old, for at least a decade. They called each other husband and wife, and had promised to marry. They had no children; he insisted that if they had, he would have married her. The court made them both swear that they were free to marry, then betrothed them and ordered them to have their union solemnized. They were fined two gold ecus. Aimery Girard, a vineyard worker, was living with his partner Lawrence in Montmartre at the time of their court appearance. He had supported her for eight years, and they had five children together. When the judge suggested he should marry her, he said he did not want to, and denied that they had ever made vows.[42]

Such relationships were clearly atypical, and it may be that rates of non-marital cohabitation varied significantly over time and by place: there is, for example, considerably less evidence for this practice in the central Middle Ages. One likely reason for the scarcity of such unions is highlighted by a case cited in a thirteenth-century English legal treatise, which illustrates the extreme vulnerability of women who cohabited with men. Alice was the long-term mistress of James de Cordunville, but they married only two months before he died, and not in church. She pleaded with Bishop Hugh of Lincoln (1186–1200) to allow her to receive her dower, but the bishop knew her backstory and denied her claim.[43]

The bishop's actions were harsh, but in line with ecclesiastical policy, which insisted that marriages must be properly celebrated. The First

Statutes of Salisbury (1217–19) warned that marriages should be made in the presence of a priest and witnesses, not

> with laughter and ribaldry, not in taverns, with public drinking and eating together. Nor should anyone bind women's hands with a noose made of reed or any other material, be it cheap or expensive, so as to fornicate with them more freely, for fear that while he considers himself to be joking, he binds himself with the rites of marriage.[44]

Such injunctions were designed to make people treat the sacrament of marriage with due solemnity, but they also provided wise advice. Undoubtedly, many hastily made marriages were repented at leisure. Some couples could not even agree on whether they were married, and thus ended up in the ecclesiastical courts, with one party (usually, but not always, the woman) suing the other for breach of promise. One common problem seems to have been that a woman refused to have sex with her partner unless he agreed to marry her, leading him to make promises that he later regretted. When, in 1480s Paris, Tassine la Martine claimed breach of promise against Mathieu Coquillen, a neighbour testified that she heard Mathieu say 'I take you in marriage' after Tassine refused to have sex with him otherwise.[45]

In 1455 Lusanna, the widow of a linen-cloth manufacturer, took Giovanni di Ser Lodovico della Casa, a wealthy merchant from a prominent Florentine family, to court. It seems that the pair began their relationship while her husband was still alive. In 1453, four months after she was widowed, they contracted a clandestine marriage, after which they regularly spent the night together. Then, in 1455, Lusanna learnt that the man she believed to be her husband had contracted another marriage, with a fifteen-year-old named Marietta, prompting the court case. Giovanni admitted to a decade-long sexual relationship with Lusanna, but denied contracting marriage. He and his witnesses painted her as a promiscuous woman who had taken many lovers both during and after her marriage. Moreover, while he was young, handsome, virile and rich, Lusanna was old (she was actually of an age with Giovanni – they were both born around 1420), sterile and of vastly inferior rank. Therefore, it was ridiculous to suggest that he would ever have married a woman who was little better than a prostitute, to the great dishonour of his family. Although the court found in Lusanna's favour, Giovanni successfully appealed to Rome, and subsequent records name Marietta as his wife.[46]

Other cases came to court because a woman had been left pregnant. In 1350s York, a servant named Alice Harpham testified about her mistress's relationship with a man named Robert Middleton, which had taken place nearly a decade earlier. She reported that Middleton had refused to make a promise of marriage, because 'he wanted to determine wither they could have children before they exchanged vows.' But although he admitted to fathering his lover's son, Middleton later married another woman.[47] Similar cases were heard in courts across Europe. In 1470, Margaret, a Polish widow, claimed that Jacob, a peasant, came uninvited into her room one night; he promised to marry her, had sex with her and got her pregnant. But afterwards he refused to solemnize the marriage in church, so that she was obliged to seek legal recognition of their union.[48] A few years earlier, Barbara Lechinger of Eching (near Munich) sued Paulus, a servant, for breach of promise. She told the court that she had been an honest virgin until she met him, but after they exchanged vows she had sex with him, and later gave birth to a son, Stephanus, whose costs he refused to cover. Paulus denied that he was the child's father, claimed that Barbara had another lover, and insisted that he had not slept with her at the relevant time. After several weeks of legal proceedings, the court found in her favour, and Paulus was required to pay for the child.[49]

Men who were sued for breach of promise frequently alleged – probably truthfully in some cases – that they had been forced into marriage by angry relatives. In a case heard by the London Consistory Court in 1475, Agnes Wellys claimed that William Rote was refusing to honour their marriage vows, but he told a rather more complicated story. He said that, one day during the previous summer, his friend John Wellys had angrily accused him of having violated his daughter Agnes and threatened him: 'You will marry her, even if I have to force you.' When William denied having sex with Agnes and refused to comply, John drew his dagger; when William tried to escape, Agnes and her mother dragged him back into the house. John made repeated threats (of both violence and an appearance before the aldermen) before William gave in, and the couple exchanged vows in the presence of witnesses.[50]

In an equally dramatic fifteenth-century Italian case, Giacoma was found hiding in Ventura's room at night, and a marriage was immediately performed, with several witnesses dragged from their beds. Although her family said that he had taken his vows willingly, he claimed that the marriage was invalid because he had been 'forced into it against his will'; one witness said that the couple had to be pushed together to make them kiss.[51] Usually, when a man claimed to have been coerced, the woman's family was (allegedly) to blame, but for apprentices, masters might play a similar role. John Waryngton, who appeared in court in York in 1417, was apprenticed to the cordwainer John Bown. After tiring of Waryngton's sexual exploits, Bown extracted a promise from his apprentice that he would mend his ways – but then he found him in bed with Margaret Barker. Bown later confessed that he had made the couple engage vows, threatening to use force if Waryngton did not comply.[52]

In each of these cases it seems relatively clear what had happened, and why the couple needed a court to resolve their differences for them. Other cases are more ambiguous. Barbara, daughter of Conrad Tunmair, sued Johannes, son of Otto de Zayfheim, for breach of promise in April 1462. She claimed that they had exchanged promises, after which he had taken her virginity; he admitted that he had loved her and had slept with her, but denied promising to marry her. The court ruled that Barbara's accusations were unproven, and therefore Johannes only had to marry her if his conscience required him to (which, unsurprisingly, it seems not to have done), although he did have to compensate her for her lost virginity. But Barbara did not produce witnesses or contest the verdict. It seems possible that the former couple actually wanted a formal statement that they were not married, in order to allow them both to move on with their lives after the end of their relationship.[53]

A little over a century earlier, Maud Schipyn told the York consistory court that she had recently married Robert Smith. The testimony of Margaret Theker, a witness for the plaintiff, suggested that this was not a straightforward case of young love gone wrong. Margaret claimed to have seen Robert drag Maud into his cowhouse, where he attempted to have sex with her. Maud objected that 'Our goddes forbode that you should have the power to know me carnally unless you will marry me,' so he pledged that 'if I take anyone to be my wife I shall take you if you will yield to me.' After this, he 'took her in his arms and threw her to the ground in the cowhouse and knew her carnally'. If her testimony was accurate, then it seems likely that Maud was trying to make the best of a bad situation: having been raped, or at least coerced into sex, she then claimed to be married in order to save her reputation.[54]

Love Magic

All of these couples ended up in court because they had had sex, but in other relationships the big problem was that one party was not willing to go to bed with the other. In such circumstances – and if normal acts of courtship failed to have the desired effect – then a would-be lover might resort to magic, a force which many medieval people both believed in, and feared. It was widely assumed that men were more likely to use magic to initiate a sexual relationship, whereas women would use it to reinvigorate existing unions, although this was not always the case. Indeed, many churchmen seem to have viewed love magic as a peculiarly female act: drawing on an early medieval penitential, William of Montibus (d. 1213) suggested that penance was required 'if some woman has given either a fish which has died in her vagina, or bread which was made on her buttocks with blood, or menstrual blood to her husband to eat or drink so that his love will be more inflamed'. Similarly, a list of questions for penitents, copied out by a Yorkshire monk in the fifteenth century, asked only women 'Have yowe gyffune any drynke vnto your husbande to make hyme lystyar to occupye wt yowe?'[55]

Love magic typically involved common herbs or body parts and secretions, which the victim would unwittingly touch or ingest. Matteuccia di Francesco, executed for witchcraft at Todi in 1428, had aided numerous would-be lovers to begin or revive relationships. Many of her remedies were based on the horsetail plant and designed to be fed to the target, but she also made hair-based charms to be placed under the couple's bed.[56] A quarter of a century later, Filippa da Città della Pieve of Perugia was executed for witchcraft; her crimes included making a love potion from semen, her own menstrual blood, and a powerful herb which she harvested on a Thursday before sunrise while mouthing incantations. Using this and other magical procedures, she had seduced four men.[57] Other magical acts involved religious objects; for example, a would-be lover might kiss her target with a communion wafer in her mouth.[58] Caesarius of Heisterbach (c. 1180–c. 1240) told the cautionary tale of a priest who kept the host in his mouth after Mass, intending to kiss a woman who had previously rejected his advances, only to be prevented by divine intervention.[59]

The most sophisticated forms of love magic typically involved images of the beloved and the conjuring of demons, and were practised chiefly by educated men. A fifteenth-century German necromancer's manual, for example, instructed the would-be lover to draw an image of the woman and write the names of demons on various parts of the image, so that the corresponding parts of her body would be afflicted until she yielded to him. It was even possible to conjure demons to transport the woman to a magic circle, where the man could have his way with her. Those accused of using such magic were often priests such as William Netherstrete, whose case was tried in the Bishop of Ely's court in 1377. This chaplain was accused of using conjurations and incantations to make Katherine Molle, a married woman, commit adultery with him – a charge he denied.[60] A century later, a priest of Tournai tried to seduce a girl by drawing her image on a tile in charcoal; he then baptized the figure and sprinkled it with holy water. Next he made a wax image, which he also baptized, before reciting conjurations from a book which were supposed to invoke demons.[61]

Medieval people were uncomfortable with such acts not only because of their magical nature, but because they compelled people to have sex against their will. Love spells rarely sought to make the would-be lover more attractive, but instead to make the person of interest conform with his or her wishes.[62] This created the potential for inappropriate relationships, including those that crossed class boundaries, as well as giving women a disconcerting level of control over men. In the early 1480s a young Venetian nobleman called Domenico Contarini fell madly in love with Gratiosa, a poor Greek woman. She had won his affections using magic – specifically, a concoction made from a rooster's heart, wine, water and menstrual blood, mixed with flour and cooked to a powder, which she fed to Domenico. This unappealing-sounding potion 'rendered him insane and wild' so that he 'committed the most diverse and sad stupidities' and engaged in 'frequent and diligent copulation' with Gratiosa. Once she had snared her man, Gratiosa used more magic to keep him: one day she 'took from his navel some of that dust or material that collects there and mixed it with some of her own', adding this to wine which they then shared. On another occasion when they were in bed, she took a candle and used it to measure his penis, intending that it should be lit at Mass in the name of their love. The court was very clear that, as a victim of black magic, Domenico was excused from blame for his actions. Gratiosa was heavily punished, with a large fine, branding on the face and banishment from the city, with the added threat that her nose would be chopped off if she returned.[63]

Fortunately, there were things an individual who had been afflicted in this way could do to end the infatuation, besides seeking help from the Church, or the courts. Hildegard of Bingen recommended the leaves or roots of betony as a cure. The plant should be held in the hands and placed in the nostrils, under the tongue and feet, and left there until it felt hot. This should be repeated until the victim was 'released from the madness of love'.[64] Alternatively, the object of the obsession should pour wine three times over a sapphire, saying, 'I pour this wine, in its ardent powers, over you; just as God drew off your splendour, wayward angel, so may you draw away from me the lust of this ardent man.' The obsessed person must then drink this wine on three successive days, and their passion would fade.[65]

Lovesickness

Another potential consequence of romantic misadventure was lovesickness – which in the twenty-first century is usually classed as an emotion, but in the Middle Ages was seen as a potentially serious medical condition. A disease of both the body and mind, it was closely related to melancholia and was said to be potentially fatal. Its key symptoms included a pulse that fluctuated wildly when the beloved was mentioned, loss of appetite, insomnia and difficulty concentrating.[66] Despite its name, lovesickness was understood and treated in terms of sex. Thus Constantine the African's *Viaticum*, the text that brought lovesickness into the medical mainstream in the late eleventh century, includes a section on *eros*, a form of love which is also 'a disease touching the brain. For it is a great longing with intense sexual desire and affliction of the thoughts.' Such love is often caused by 'an intense natural need to expel a great excess of humours' – that is, to have sex. Alternatively, it may arise from the contemplation of beauty, which drives the soul into a form of madness as it seeks the fulfilment of its pleasure.[67] Bona Fortuna's *Treatise on the Viaticum*, written in early fourteenth-century Montpellier, attributed lovesickness to a combination of 'the beauty of a woman and the necessity of expelling superfluities'.[68] Some authorities saw lovesickness as a disease of the testicles, because it was related to coitus and seed, and because the cure was 'plasters or women . . . applied to the testicles'. Others thought it was a disease of the brain, but acknowledged that sex would cure the symptoms.[69]

The usual cure was a regimen to strengthen the body (with baths, good food and wine, and sleep) and distract the mind. The range of possible distractions was considerable: Constantine's suggestions included listening to music, reciting poems, spending time with good friends, looking at beautiful gardens or good-looking people, and drinking a moderate amount of wine (but not getting drunk). Bona Fortuna claimed that he had once caused a patient to be falsely accused of homicide, so that he would be obliged to go on the run and would be too concerned by his daily needs to think about his beloved. However, the best cure for lovesickness was sex – preferably within the bounds of marriage, but if this was not possible, then with other available women, perhaps prostitutes or enslaved women. Gerard of Berry, in his commentary on the *Viaticum* (*c.* 1200), recommended 'consorting with and embracing girls, sleeping with them repeatedly, and switching various ones'. He also suggested a sort of aversion therapy, in the form of old women relating 'many disparagements and the stinking dispositions of the desired thing'.[70]

Lovesickness was a disease to which rich young men were particularly prone; some cynical contemporaries suggested that this was because they had easy lives, and sufficient leisure time to practise the art of love.[71] But susceptibility to the disease was also thought to be related to complexion: men with hot complexions produced more seed, were consequently more desirous of sex, and were therefore most prone to lovesickness. Women could also suffer from lovesickness; indeed, they were sometimes considered more prone to it, 'on account of their weak hope and because they are more frequently stimulated to intercourse'. However, the differences between the male and female brain meant that lovesick females forgot their lovers more quickly, and were more easily cured.[72]

Lovesickness was much discussed by medical writers, and medieval literature is full of afflicted men. Marie de France's *Les deus amanz* features a young man whose love exhausts him so much that he dies.[73] John Gower's poem *The Lover's Confession* tells the story of a man who claims to be so lovesick that his only hope is death; eventually he is cured by Venus, who treats him with a cold ointment.[74] Several of Chaucer's characters suffer in this way, including the aristocratic Arcite and Palamon, whose love for and suffering over the unobtainable Emily is described in 'The Knight's Tale'.[75] Real-life cases, on the other hand, are hard to come by; we can only speculate about what this might tell us about both premarital sex and medical practice in medieval Europe.

What is certain is that courtship could be a challenging process for men and women alike: couples faced both social and familial pressure to make the right choices, and it could be hard to find a partner who liked you as much as you liked them. Once you had found the right person, it was advisable to take a trip up the aisle before going to bed with them, since premarital sex was fraught with risk. But for many people, the wedding was where the trouble began.

THREE

Sex within Marriage

W hile the medieval Church condemned premarital sex, it had a very different attitude to sex within marriage. The exchange of vows not only made it socially and morally acceptable for a couple to have sex; it also meant that they were actually required to do so. Indeed, intercourse played such an important part in medieval marriage that some authorities argued that a union was not truly valid without it.

Consummation

Around the year 1200 a debate raged over whether it was consent or consummation that created a marriage, with prominent voices on both sides of the debate. Ultimately, consent became the defining factor, for both practical reasons (since most people preferred to have sex in private, it was harder to prove than the public act of consent) and ideological ones (it was widely believed that Mary and Joseph's marriage was unconsummated, but how could a good Christian question that theirs was a valid union?)[1] Nevertheless, there is ample evidence that many people continued to see sex as a crucial part of the marriage process, without which the union was not properly complete. One late thirteenth-century Spanish law code went so far as to state that, if a groom died before the first kiss and consummation, his bride must return all gifts to his heirs. If he died between the kiss and the consummation, she kept half; only if the marriage had been consummated did she retain everything. If the bride died, all gifts must be returned whether or not they had kissed, but the groom kept everything if they had had intercourse.[2]

Indeed, sex was such an important part of the marriage-making process that the Sarum Missal (which contains the liturgy most commonly used in the pre-Reformation English Church) concluded that weddings should not take place at times (for example during Lent) when sex was prohibited. The same volume required the priest to bless the bedchamber and the bed in which the newlywed couple laid down, in preparation for the consummation of their union; such blessings often included invocations (involving crosses and holy water) to make the marriage bed fertile.[3] However, newlyweds were sometimes enjoined to observe the night of Tobias – that is, to refrain from sex on their wedding night.[4]

Both bride and groom were expected to have some idea of what to do when they were finally left alone. While evidence for medieval sex education is very limited, it seems that women usually advised their daughters: in fiction mothers are often called on to help newlywed couples who are having difficulty consummating their union, and a didactic manual from late medieval Italy, written in the voice of a mother speaking to her soon-to-be-married daughter, refers to earlier conversations about honest practices in love-making.[5] For educated men, some knowledge could be acquired from books – that is, from the dirty bits of classical literature, for example, rather than texts specifically designed for this purpose.[6] And in a largely rural society, in which true privacy was a rare commodity for all but the wealthiest, many young people must have seen both animals and people having sex long before they were old enough to experience it for themselves.

Although the groom might be a virgin, this was neither expected nor required, since the sexual purity of laymen was not especially valued. Bernard of Gordon, a professor of medicine at Montpellier, placed chastity tenth on a list of things a tutor should teach a young man, but first on a list of traits to be encouraged in girls.[7] On the other hand, it was expected that the bride would be a virgin on her wedding night, and the discovery that she was not could cause considerable upset. In one extreme case from early fifteenth-century Venice, Francesco di Vanzoni married Maria, and that evening the marriage was consummated. But the next morning the groom sent his bride home to her father, claiming that she was not a virgin and therefore the marriage was invalid. Although the pair were eventually reconciled, this was only achieved after a court case, during the course of which it was tacitly accepted that female virginity was a prerequisite for marriage.[8]

In a culture that placed such emphasis on the value of sexual purity, it is perhaps unsurprising that medical texts include considerable discussion about how to ascertain whether a woman was truly a virgin. The hymen, and the bleeding which accompanied its rupture, were central to medieval ideas about virginity. According to Nicholaus, a fifteenth-century Florentine physician, 'before defloration . . . the mouth of the womb is covered with a membrane woven with veins and arteries which are broken when she is deflowered and the woman bleeds.'[9] For the bride, the rupture of this membrane might cause pain, bleeding and swelling, which could be treated by bathing and the application of scented oils. In extreme cases, a wax plaster wrapped in wool on a reed should be inserted into the vagina, not to encourage healing of the broken follicles but to stop the cervix closing up.[10]

Such symptoms could provide important evidence of virginity: a bride who could be easily penetrated, and who did not bleed, would be viewed with suspicion. In particular, it was important to make sure that she was not simply having her period: the blood produced by a first sexual experience could be distinguished from menstrual blood because it was clearer, less copious, and was shed only at the moment of defloration, not before or after.[11] But medieval people were also well aware that the hymen could be ruptured in other ways (for example, with the fingers, or through injury), and that bleeding during sex could have a range of causes. It was thus no guarantee that a woman was previously intact, and truly a virgin.[12]

Consequently, numerous other virginity tests were developed. Many believed that virginity could be detected by behaviour: a virgin would have a modest gait, a downcast gaze and a sense of shame about sexual matters. Physical appearance was also important, as witness statements from the posthumous retrial of Joan of Arc (1456) reflected. Guilaume de la Chambre, a physician, testified on the basis of having seen her nearly naked that 'in so far as one can tell by the art of medicine, she was a virgin and intact', while Marguerite la Tourolde, who sheltered her, reported that 'I saw her several times in the bath and in the hot-room, and so far as I could see I believe that she was a virgin.' According to Froissart, it was the French custom that any prospective royal bride must be examined 'in a completely naked state' to confirm her virginity and her potential for childbearing.[13]

Breasts were of particular interest: large and loose breasts, as we have seen, were often taken as a sign of sexual experience, sufficiently reliable that at least one medieval bishop allegedly ordered nuns' breasts to be examined to see whether they remained pure.[14] Physiognomy suggested that other body parts were also worth examining. Michael Scotus, in his *Liber physonomie* (c. 1230), described a test which, unusually, worked for both sexes: touch the tip of the nose. In a virgin, the cartilage would be dense and whole, but after sex it would feel broken into parts. Another test was based on the belief that menstrual blood ascended through the body during coitus, making the veins swell and change colour. Consequently, swollen veins in a woman's left arm indicated lost virginity.[15]

Many physicians thought that examining urine (a common medieval diagnostic practice) was the most reliable way to detect virginity. A virgin could supposedly be identified by her thin, clear urine, which she passed in a slow, delicate fashion, because the passages of the womb and vulva were narrow (that the urinary passage and the vagina are the same thing was a seemingly common misconception). A non-virgin, on the other hand, would produce turbid urine, with sperm in the bottom of it.[16] Fumigation was another useful tool:

> if a woman is covered with a piece of cloth and fumigated with the best coal, if she is a virgin she does not perceive its odour through her mouth and nose; if she smells it, she is not a virgin . . . Upon fumigation with dock flowers, if she is a virgin she immediately becomes pale, and if not, her humour falls on the fire and other things are said about her.[17]

Astrology offered yet another method of investigation: according to the thirteenth-century astrologer Guido Bonatti, it was possible to read the moon and planets to establish not only whether a woman had lost her virginity, but exactly how she did so. If he was consulted on this subject, the astrologer had the responsibility to be honest, but not too honest. If the woman was a true virgin, he must say so; if she had had full intercourse, that too must be revealed. But Bonatti also recognized that virginity could be lost without the involvement of a penis. In such cases, he argued, the astrologer should simply say that the stars indicate that she is excused before her interrogator, otherwise it will be assumed that she has been with a man.[18]

Faced with such scrutiny, it is unsurprising that some women tried to hide their sexual experience. The *Trotula* (the most influential compendium of women's medicine in medieval Europe) includes several recipes for constrictive powders and ointments that could be placed in the vagina to make a woman seem like a virgin; one such preparation contained egg white mixed with the water in which pennyroyal and hot herbs had been cooked, and powders of blackberry or natron. Alternatively, a bride could spend the night before her wedding placing leeches into her vagina, taking care that they did not go in too far, 'so that blood comes out and is covered into a little clot. And thus the man will be deceived by the effusion of blood.'[19] Allegedly, this method was particularly favoured by brides of Naples.[20] The Italian surgeon William of Saliceto (*c.* 1210–*c.* 1277) suggested that a woman who wanted to fake virginity should wash her genitals, sit in a hot bath, rub on special ointments, and place in the vulva a dove's intestine filled with blood.[21]

The Marital Debt

Even once a couple had successfully negotiated their wedding night, they were still not free from ecclesiastical scrutiny, for the medieval church taught that couples must pay the marital debt – that is, that spouses had a religious obligation to have sex with each other on demand. This was an idea with biblical origins, specifically St Paul's statement that 'The wife does not have authority over her own body but yields it to her husband. In the same way, the husband does not have authority over his own body but yields it to his wife.'[22] It gained in importance during the twelfth century, as canon lawyers and theologians became increasingly interested in both marriage and marital sex, and eventually this debt (along with reproduction, fulfilling sexual desire and avoiding incontinence) became one of the four widely accepted reasons that justified marital intercourse. Some theologians even thought that sex for the sake of the marital debt (and for offspring) was without sin.[23]

Such was the importance of this debt that its fulfilment took precedence over many of the Church's other rules on sex. During the early Middle Ages, rules on sexual abstinence during penitential periods such as Lent had been taken extremely seriously. Then, in the mid-twelfth century, Gratian (one of the most influential canon lawyers of this period) made the ground-breaking pronouncement that such abstinence was contingent on the consent of both spouses, and Pope Alexander III (1159–81) ruled that it was a counsel, not an absolute requirement. Henceforth, if a husband asked his wife for sex on Good Friday, for example, she could grant his request; indeed, it might even be better for her to do so.[24] Refusing the marital debt became a matter for confession, and those who refused it without good reason were guilty of sin, although there was considerable discussion about exactly what constituted a good reason.

In his treatise on the marital debt, Francis de Plathea of Bologna (d. 1460) gave twelve factors that he considered to be valid reasons why a spouse might refuse the marital debt:

1   When the demander's rights are suspended owing
    to fornication
2   During the two months immediately after marriage
3   When rendering is seriously detrimental to health
4   When the demander is mad
5   When the husband cannot render without weakening
    his body
6   During menstruation

7 When a foetus would be endangered

8 In a holy place

9 On grounds of consanguinity (that is, the marriage is incestuous)

10 If the husband wants to commit sodomy

11 If the spouses are spiritually related (and therefore they should not have married)

12 If a pregnant wife is very close to her due date and believes rendering would endanger the child.[25]

However, these rules were not universally accepted; there was, for example, much debate about the rights and wrongs of sex during menstruation. Since medical theory suggested that sex at this time could produce deformed offspring, some authorities classed it as a mortal sin. But others were more concerned about the risk of adultery if a menstruating woman refused to have sex with her husband. Some argued that it was less serious for a man to ask his menstruating wife for sex (since he might do so in order to avoid adultery) than for her to approach him, since she would hardly be tempted to commit adultery at this time.[26] Sex during pregnancy was another cause for concern. Many pastoral manuals suggested that an expectant woman must pay the debt if she suspected that to refuse would lead her husband into a more serious vice. On the other hand, Jean Gerson taught that 'no spouse is held to pay the debt in notable and certain detriment to her body or to a foetus about to be born.'[27]

Yet even serious health concerns were not universally accepted as grounds for refusal. Some thinkers, including the German theologian John Nider (*c.* 1380–1438), thought that a healthy individual could withhold sex from a leprous spouse, and the disease was accepted as grounds to dissolve an unconsummated marriage. In 1437 Robert Place was granted a papal dispensation to marry the sister of his former fiancée, the first relationship having been unconsummated 'because she was a leper'. But many argued that a married couple must continue to cohabit and have sex even if one contracted leprosy. Around 1175 Pope Alexander III wrote to the Archbishop of Canterbury:

> Since man and wife are one flesh and ought not to live without each other, our command is that you should not delay in earnestly inducing the wives of husbands who are afflicted with leprosy, and the husbands of wives, to follow them, and minister to them with conjugal affection. If they cannot be induced to do this, you should strictly order both of them to remain continent for the rest

of their lives. And if they refuse to obey your command, you must excommunicate them.[28]

When Geert ten Starte, a merchant from the Hanseatic port of Kampen, was diagnosed with leprosy in the late 1460s, his wife, Fenne Bouster, wanted to leave him. In response, he commissioned a canon lawyer friend to write a tract 'On the Marriage of Lepers', which argued that she must continue to live with him, and perform her marital obligations, at least until he became so ill as to require hospitalization.[29]

Similarly, some authorities thought that sex in holy places could be justified – even though this was a significant cultural taboo, and would mean that the church in question would have to be reconsecrated. Berthold of Freiburg, for example, argued that if asked for sex in a holy place, a spouse should try to dissuade their partner. But if the sex was strictly necessary – in the sense that no unblessed place was available, and this was the only way to avoid a greater sin or to produce offspring – then asking was a minor sin, and complying was completely sinless.[30]

What, in practical terms, was the impact of the marital debt? It certainly did not mean that couples were allowed to have unlimited sex. Indeed, it arguably made marital relations a duty rather than an indulgence – thus reducing the pleasure, or even creating displeasure.[31] Theologians railed against men who loved their wives 'in adulterous fashion' (that is, with too much lustful enthusiasm); the Italian monk Giacomo Filippo Foresti (1434–1520) claimed that anyone 'who has loved his wife so ardently that he would have wanted to lie with her even if she had not been his wife . . . is said to have committed adultery inferentially'. William of Rennes, a thirteenth-century friar, criticized husbands who deliberately provoked lust (perhaps using their hands, or hot drinks) so that they could have sex more often.[32] Even the Ragusan humanist Benedetto Cotrugli (1416–1469), author of an advice book for merchants, warned men to 'take care not to encourage your wife's wantonness from the outset, because you may come to regret it. Engage in coitus with moderation, because this will encourage good behaviour in your wife, the most favourable circumstances for procreating children, and a more perfect and understanding love.'[33]

Cotrugli's assumption that a husband could control his wife's sexual behaviour raises interesting questions about the impact of the marital debt on gender relations, especially in a society that expected women to obey their husbands. In theory, it applied equally to both sexes, and Cotrugli's advice seems to reflect this. He thought that the husband must oblige not only when the wife explicitly asks for sex, but when she 'makes herself understood through certain signals', because women are usually 'more bashful than men' on this subject. In addition, a man must not scold a wife who does not ask for sex, and he should not ask persistently.[34] Some ecclesiastical sources acknowledged female needs, and *Handlyng Synne* (a popular Middle English devotional verse) even suggested that a man was responsible if his sexually unsatisfied wife committed adultery.

On the basis of such writings, some historians have argued that the marital debt was actually good for women, offering them both sexual satisfaction and equality within their marriage. In practice, marital sex was intimately entwined with power, and the obligation of wifely obedience surely outweighed any theoretical equality.[35] There was no concept of marital rape in medieval law, and discussions of the marital debt often took wifely subordination for granted. The Catalan friar Raymond of Peñafort (d. 1275) argued that a wife should comply with even semi-sinful requests, for in obeying her husband she was obeying God. The rule of life that Giovanni Dominici, an influential Dominican preacher, wrote for a well-born matron, Bartolomea degli Alberti, in 1403, indicated how a woman might make herself scarce at bedtime. Yet he also suggested that a wife was in some way excused when engaging in potentially sinful acts by her duty of obedience, where the husband was not.[36]

There were, however, some dissenting voices who recognized the problems women faced because of the marital debt, and questioned just how far female obedience should go. The popular preacher Bernardino of Siena (1380–1444) complained about the 'many unspeakable and incredible ways husbands abuse their wives . . . and although wives may be unhappy, nevertheless they agree to [sex] in whatever manner'. His discussion assumed that the husband would always be the petitioner, even the aggressor, in a manner that clearly challenged the apparent equality of the debt:

There is a great difference between the harassments and orders which oblige wives to render the debt and those which oblige husbands, because wives can expect more obvious harassments than husbands. There is a threefold reason for this. First, because women are more modest about seeking than men. Second, because such a petition is viler and more ignominious for a woman than a man. Whence from natural instinct and direction they have rather the condition of suffering and accepting than of exacting and exciting, and the condition of submission than of domination; and on that account the impudence of seeking smacks of greater impudence and is more unseemly in them than men. The third reason is that women are more under the rule of men than the converse.[37]

He rejected the idea that the husband's will was also God's will, and therefore thought that she should resist unnatural and sinful acts. Indeed, he went further: 'Just as no one of sane mind would say that a wife ought to obey her husband by having sex on the sacred altar or some holy spot, so neither ought he say that she should obey by having sex day and night and almost infinite times.'[38] But his ideas were not universally, or perhaps even widely, accepted. While clerical writers often required a woman to allow sex even if she was pregnant or menstruating, they were typically more sympathetic to male physiology as a justification for non-payment. For example, if a couple had just had sex and the man was not yet able to perform again, the Italian theologian Thomas Aquinas (1225–1274) thought that 'the wife has no right to ask again, and in doing so she behaves as a harlot rather than a wife.' Nor, many argued, was it a sin for a married man to render himself impotent, either temporarily or permanently, by fasting.[39]

Perhaps, for some especially devout women, there was a kind of pleasure in submission, in doing what society expected and considered the right thing for a good wife to do.[40] Many more women, we can only hope, were fortunate enough to marry decent men with whom they could have the sort of sexual relationship which took into consideration the wishes of both partners. Nevertheless, it is hard to escape the conclusion that the existence of the marital debt, in combination with contemporary ideas about gender roles and the eternal realities of biology, must have caused significant suffering to many women.

Chaste Marriage

Despite the importance of the marital debt, there was such a thing as a spiritual marriage – that is, a union in which the couple mutually agreed to give up sex for religious reasons. By the later Middle Ages, couples who agreed on a chaste marriage were supposed to take a public vow before a bishop, but episcopal registers include very few examples of this: a rare example comes from the archdiocese of York, where William de Sibbilton and his wife Isolde made such a vow in 1321. The scarcity of such pledges reflects the rarity of unions like this, but perhaps also the reluctance of couples who were living chastely to make a permanent commitment to do so. Once made, such vows were irreversible, and could not be commuted for something else (for example, fasting or almsgiving) because there was nothing better than chastity. If a couple made and then broke such a vow, any resultant offspring would be illegitimate; their actions would also have serious consequences for their eternal souls. Consequently, even the most pious and abstinent couple would be well-advised to think extremely carefully about formalizing their status.[41]

Sometimes one spouse sought a chaste marriage right from the start; in such cases, it was typically the wife who took the initiative, and she was usually a pious girl who had been married against her will, having wished to devote her life to God. Such requests were, understandably, not always greeted with enthusiasm: when Christina of Markyate (c. 1096– c. 1155) refused to consummate her marriage to a young nobleman called Beorhtred, he strongly resisted her efforts to talk him into a chaste marriage. She ran away, and eventually their union was annulled.[42] But other men proved more amenable. In early thirteenth-century Brabant, Mary of Oignies' parents hoped that marriage would cure her religious fervour, but her new husband, John, was receptive to the idea of abstinence. 'Out of a natural goodness', he not only supported his wife's holy practices, but embarked on his own life of chastity and charity.[43] Jeanne-Marie of Maillac and Robert of Silleyo, a noble couple from Touraine, married in the mid-fourteenth century; she reportedly told him of her desire for chastity before the wedding. On their wedding night she recited saints' lives until he agreed to pledge virginity. They cohabited for fourteen years, and adopted three orphans.[44]

For other couples, the desire for chastity emerged unexpectedly when one spouse had a life-changing religious experience. John Colombini (d. 1367), a fifty-something Sienese merchant, underwent a sudden conversion while reading the life of St Mary of Egypt. As a result, he and his much younger wife Biagia lived in total continence for eight years, before she freed him to live a life of itinerant poverty. James Oldo of Lodi (d. 1404) lived a frivolous life until he was 26. Then, one day, he lay down in the cave of the local church of the Holy Sepulchre, as a joke, to see if he was taller than Christ. Experiencing a sudden conversion (perhaps not unrelated to the death of his two young daughters from plague), he asked his wife, Catherine, to consent to a chaste marriage. His mother, concerned that his wife was too young to give up sex, urged him to be patient, and he waited seven years before becoming a Franciscan tertiary, and then a priest. But for the last three years of their marriage they lived chastely, despite sharing a bed.[45]

The majority of couples, however, vowed celibacy only towards the end of a long marriage, often when at least one of them was relatively elderly or ill. Hedwig of Silesia (d. 1243) convinced her husband to make a formal vow of chastity only after 28 years of marriage and six children. But throughout their marriage, they abstained on holy days, and as a consequence they often went eight weeks or more without sex, despite sharing a bed. Hedwig's story is not a wholly negative one: she seems to have had some influence over her husband, and for many years they lived a compromise which, if not wholly satisfactory to either party, at least allowed both of them something of what they wanted.[46]

Other cases highlight more strikingly the difficulties of living in a world in which marriage was for life, and in which married women had very little agency over their own bodies. Frances of Rome (d. 1440) and her husband, Lorenzo Ponziano (d. 1436), abstained for the last twelve years of their forty-year marriage, but for decades before this, Frances had suffered greatly: she was invariably ill after having sex, sometimes vomiting blood. Before having intercourse, she would drip molten grease or wax onto her skin. But still, on the orders of her confessor, she complied with the marital debt, bearing at least six children before her husband (by now an old man sickened by a period of exile) agreed to give up sex.[47]

The complex and emotionally draining negotiations that a married woman might have to undergo to secure a chaste marriage are documented most powerfully in the autobiography of the Norfolk mystic Margery Kempe (c. 1373–c. 1438). Married at twenty, for many years she had an unremarkable (and seemingly pleasurable) sexual relationship with her husband. Then, one night when she was in bed with her husband, she had a vision, after which 'paying the debt of matrimony was so abominable to her that she would rather, she thought, have eaten and drunk the ooze and muck in the gutter than consent to intercourse, except out of obedience'. For the next few years she frequently tried to persuade her husband that they should embark on a chaste marriage; they had, she argued, taken too much pleasure in their bodies, and should punish themselves by abstaining from sex. He agreed that this was a good plan in theory, but refused to implement it yet; he would do so only when God willed it. He continued to have sex with her, failing to notice that she had taken to wearing a hair shirt even in bed; she obeyed, albeit with much weeping and sorrow, and had several more children. Eventually, Christ intervened on Margery's behalf. One night John Kempe tried to instigate sex, but found himself unable even to touch his wife. A few weeks later, following a dramatic argument in the middle of a field, the couple agreed to abstain. Later, with her husband's consent and support, Margery took a vow of chastity before a bishop.[48]

Kempe's account provokes a great deal of sympathy in the modern reader, for whom it feels deeply uncomfortable that a woman should be obliged to continue having sex with her husband, even once the act has become repugnant to her. But John Kempe is not the villain of the piece, and Margery seems to have remained fond of him, despite their disagreements. After her vow, they continued to live together, separating only when slanderers claimed that 'they enjoyed their lust and pleasure as they did before.' Later, after a fall, John moved back in with Margery so that she could care for him.[49] And ultimately, he is presented as a good man: God tells Margery, 'I have given you the sort of man who would let you live chaste, he being alive and in good physical health.'[50] With hindsight, the doctrines of marital debt and indissoluble marriage must have made life intolerable for many men and women who felt obliged to have sex against their will, or found themselves trapped in a sexless marriage from which there was no (socially and ecclesiastically sanctioned) escape.

Frigidity, Impotence and Annulment

While some medieval couples chose not to have sex, others got married, only to find that they could not. Like chaste marriages, such cases are rarely documented, and we know about them only when one spouse decided to seek an annulment of their marriage. This happened very rarely: only ten requests for annulment due to impotence were made in Augsburg in 1350, and this was an unusually high number.[51] In the diocese of York, just six cases of annulment on grounds of sexual incompatibility are recorded for the whole of the fourteenth and fifteenth centuries.[52]

The typical annulment case involved a woman seeking a separation from her husband because he was impotent, and therefore their union remained unconsummated. Since she wished to have children, she wanted to have her first marriage declared invalid, and to be allowed to form a new relationship with a healthy man. This was, according to the Church, grounds for a marriage to be voided and, in contrast to other forms of separation, the healthy party could remarry. In 1317, for example, the marriage of a couple from Cerisy was invalidated on grounds of impotence: Thomassia, who was 'ample and apt for virile embraces', was granted a licence to marry again, but Thomas was forbidden to do so.[53]

Obtaining such a separation was not easy: a marriage could only be overturned if there was extremely clear evidence that it was necessary to do so. In particular, there was a great deal of concern about the potential for collusion between unhappily married couples, which was forbidden by canon law. John de Burgh, chancellor of Cambridge University in the 1380s, even suggested that a wife might use impotence magic on her own husband in order to escape an unhappy relationship. If so, her marriage could not be annulled, since her husband's problem was her fault.[54] In order to prevent such schemes, there were strict rules about when an annulment could be sought. The initial complaint should be made soon after the wedding, ideally within two months. But a separation would not be granted at this point: couples were often obliged to cohabit and attempt consummation for three years before receiving permission to part.[55]

The couple's own testimony was often supplemented by evidence from other witnesses. Sometimes a man's friends spoke on his behalf: in a case from 1470s Venice, for example, a priest recalled that he had once seen Niccolo having sex with two prostitutes, and had even agreed to feel his penis. In this way it was established that the member in question was 'erect just like the member of any other man', although the reason for the priest's presence at this gathering went unexplained.[56] More often, however, testimony was given by expert witnesses – usually 'wise matrons' – appointed by the courts. These women carried out physical examinations and watched as the man attempted to have sex, sometimes over a period of several days. Only if the man's member proved consistently useless were the couple allowed to separate.[57] Canon law also allowed 'expert and honest men' to inspect an allegedly impotent man, and the medical profession argued that physicians and surgeons should testify in such cases. In 1374, when Mable Cokes of Canterbury sought an annulment on the grounds of her husband's impotence, he was examined by five men.[58]

Impotence examinations usually involved efforts to increase bodily heat, by lighting fires and providing food and ale, as well as deliberate attempts to provoke sexual arousal. Some examinations may have been performed by prostitutes, since they often required interventions that would have been unfitting for a respectable woman to perform. For example, the female witnesses employed in a 1433 York case exposed their breasts and genitals and used explicit language in an attempt to arouse the husband.[59] In October 1441, Joan Savage recounted the impotence test she and several other women had performed on John Marche in the guildhall kitchen of the fraternity of St John:

> This witness and the rest of the women warmed [and] touched the said [John's] yard with their hands, embracing him around the neck and kissing him . . . [his member] was not able to rise nor stand but because of feebleness [was] at all times as if white, dead, empty skin down to its end . . . having scarcely the length and breadth of one of the fingers of this witness.[60]

Sometimes these examinations provided the evidence needed to end a failed marriage. In June 1462 Christian Höss of Freising found Katherina, his wife of sixteen years, in bed with another man, and sued her for adultery. She counter-claimed: they had, she said, cohabited for nine years,

An annulment case in a late 13th-century manuscript of Gratian's *Decretum*:
the wife and another woman pull aside the husband's robe to expose
his useless genitals (Walters MS.W. 133, f. 277).

but Christian was impotent. He admitted this, telling the court that he
had never had sex or even an erection, and his claims were backed up by
Sigismundus Boczkircher, a physician, who found that Christian was per
manently impotent due to physical problems. Consequently, the marriage
was annulled, leaving Katherina free to remarry.[61] But other couples underwent an extremely humiliating and public ordeal, only to find themselves
still married. In 1453, for example, the Kraków consistory court heard the
case of Stanislaw of Marsko and Margaret of Barczkow, a married couple
who had cohabited for three years – long enough to furnish proof of the
impediment of impotence that she claimed. However, an examination
found that he had 'a lively and functioning member; the blister [which it
had] has drained, and it is apparent that they can now seek to have children
or suffer the penalty of excommunication and incarceration'.[62]

The case of Katherine Barley vs William Barton provides a particularly
colourful account of the sort of scrutiny to which couples were subjected.
Over the course of several months in the early 1430s, thirteen deponents –
all local men and women of good standing, at least some of them known
to the couple – recounted their inspections of Barton to the Archbishop of
York's court, and all reported that he was able to perform. Emmota Garde,
a widow, examined his genitals and compared them favourably to those of
her late husband, by whom she had seven children. Matilda Leeke judged

his penis and testicles 'sufficient to serve and to please any honest woman'. Several men also scrutinized his erect penis during these examinations, including Robert Lincoln, a tailor, who felt William's 'manly yard, long and large enough to have carnal knowledge of any woman living'. John de Metelay admitted that William's penis was 'longer and larger' than his own. Katherine was also examined by women who judged that her breasts were not those of a virgin, and suggested that she might be pregnant. Her case was further undermined by her refusal to allow the women to 'inspect and touch ... [her] secret places', which was taken as a sign of guilt rather than modesty. Ultimately, this was the only English case in which a husband is known to have proved his potency.[63]

Men's reactions to accusations of impotence varied. Some readily acknowledged that they had a problem; others maintained that they were extremely virile, or claimed that they had a temporary complaint for which someone else was to blame. When Margareta Pschor told the consistorial court of Freising that her husband Fredericus was impotent, he countered that it was her fault that they had not had sex: she was disobedient to him, and he had used his well-proportioned (according to him) penis to have sex with other women. Consequently, the judge required them to cohabit and attempt consummation for another year before he would overturn their marriage.[64] Other men suggested that magic was involved. In 1490s Regensburg, Barbara had been married for eight weeks when she asked for her marriage to George to be nullified. He pointed out that he had fathered twelve children by his first wife, and claimed that Barbara had bewitched him. The judge found these arguments credible enough to require the couple to stay together for the next three years.[65] Sometimes, however, it was hard to find evidence to support such claims. An early thirteenth-century decretal discussed the case of a man who said he could have sex with women other than his wife, and thus suspected witchcraft – but his parish priest could not find anyone who would admit to having slept with him.[66]

Claiming bewitchment might help a man to save face, but it also reduced the likelihood that a marriage would be annulled, for there were considerable doubts over the legality of such proceedings. Some churchmen, including William of Pagula, believed that magical impotence was always impermanent, at least in theory, because the man could potentially be cured by the perpetrator. Robert Courson distinguished between cases in which a man had been made completely impotent (such spells being a permanent impediment to marriage) and those in which he had been bewitched for a fixed time, or with a particular woman. If a marriage was annulled due to bewitchment, he allowed only the woman to remarry

– and even then only after three years had passed, to be sure the problem was irreversible. Canon lawyers also disputed whether a couple who separated because of magic-related impotence, but who both remarried successfully, could (or should) be made to return to the original marriage. Some expressed concerns that, if this were to happen, they would simply find themselves bewitched again.[67]

The best cure for magical impotence was to make the perpetrator reverse the spell, as in an early thirteenth-century case in which a Parisian woman made her former boyfriend impotent by making an incantation over a closed lock and throwing it down a well. She threw the key into another well. Consequently, he could not consummate his marriage until both lock and key were retrieved, and the lock undone.[68] If the spell could not be reversed, then other cures could be tried; the English physician John of Gaddesden suggested drinking St John's wort, sprinkling the house with dog's blood, checking the house for magical objects, going to confession and wearing amulets.[69] Folk remedies were rather more amusing, at least to the onlooker: Roland of Benevento claimed to have heard that many women 'make their bewitched husbands hold his trousers on his head for a whole day and night . . . or they make the poor man stand naked all night under a stole when the weather is fair'.[70] A lucky few might benefit from divine intervention: in 1345 a miracle cured a young Pisan couple who suspected that their failure to consummate their marriage was due to bewitchment.[71]

Less fortunate men might resort to violence against their alleged attacker, sometimes with fatal results. In 1447 a Frenchman who believed he had been made impotent by a woman named Guillemmette tied her to a tree and was (or so he claimed) surprised to find her dead the next day; around the same time another Frenchman broke down a woman's door and beat her until she agreed to undo the spell she had put on him. She also died soon afterwards.[72] The courts treated women who performed such magic equally harshly. In 1324–5, Archbishop Auðfinnr of Bergen handled the case of Ragnhildr Tregagás, who was accused of making her ex-lover impotent with his new wife; she was sentenced to regular fasting for the rest of her life and required to undertake seven years' worth of pilgrimages to sites outside of Norway.[73] In 1390 two Parisian women, Margot de la Barre and Marion la Droiturière, were sentenced to burn for making Marion's ex-lover impotent with his new wife.[74]

Victims of magic were not the only ones to seek cures for their impotence, and there were many remedies that a couple required to cohabit for three years (or hoping to avoid a court appearance altogether) could try. Medical texts such as *The Mirror of Coitus* included numerous food-based remedies (such as cow's milk mixed with cinnamon) that were supposed to increase semen production and thus provoke sexual desire. Alternatively, there were many ointments and pastes to put on the penis, including burnt deer's tail mixed with ashes of old wine, or mustard seed ground with oil.[75] Witness depositions in annulment cases make clear the medieval tendency to link large genitalia with the ability to father children, and there were many medicines that claimed to enlarge the penis: chopped earthworms (or leeches) mixed with jujube oil, rubbed into the penis and left on overnight was just one example. Regular washing (several times a day) with warm sheep's milk or hot water and oil was supposed to achieve the same result.[76] Other sources suggested ways to make a man sexually aroused: he could read erotic stories, or his wife could dress provocatively. One Spanish text suggested that a man should 'imagine the act of coitus until the organs of sexual appetite begin to obey'.[77] And while magic could cause sexual problems, it could also cure them: a mid-thirteenth-century Castilian compilation of magical procedures suggested that impotence could be treated by making (at the auspicious astrological moment) wax images of the couple embracing, fumigating and bathing the images, and giving them to the man to carry.[78]

Remedies for impotence and non-consummation were almost entirely focused on men, and it is clear that sexual dysfunction was largely viewed as a male problem. Annulments granted due to a woman's inability to have sex were technically possible, but almost unheard of. The papal decretal *Fraternitatis* (1206) recorded the case of a woman granted an annulment because her vagina was too narrow to allow intercourse. Canon law recognized the existence of such 'closed women', but required them to undergo a physical examination in order to receive an annulment. If such a woman later remarried and consummated this second union, she could theoretically be obliged to return to her first husband, since this nullified the original annulment.[79] Pope Innocent III (1198–1216) permitted the dissolution of a marriage due to gross disparity in genital size, but others doubted that this was ever necessary. John of Freiberg thought not, and claimed to have been told by a wise woman that a man's penis was never so large that his bride could not accommodate it.[80]

Effectively, the Church condoned forced consummation. William of Rennes argued that a woman ought to be able to sustain a certain amount of violence, and Peter Chanter noted (albeit with some dismay) a case in which Pope Alexander III allowed a man to remarry after he had so damaged his wife on their wedding night that she was left permanently unable to have sex.[81] Gautier de Coincy's *Miracles of the Virgin Mary* tells the story of a young woman who was devoted to the Virgin Mary; when she was forced to marry, the Virgin promised to protect her, so that her husband would be unable to touch her virginity. For six months her husband tried to have sex with her, but 'found the passage so narrow that he could not breach it despite all his fighting'. Eventually, 'one night he felt his desire so hotly that, spurred on by the devil . . . [he] took a knife and in order to cool his great ardour he stuck the knife into nature's door so violently that she almost lost her entrails through the door of her jewel.' So seriously wounded that no doctor could cure her, she was bedbound until miraculously healed by the Virgin.[82] Given the circumstances of this supposed case, it is impossible to know whether this really happened, and the saintly intervention suggests that the reader was supposed to be repulsed by the husband's actions. Nevertheless, the infrequency with which such cases are recorded is surely due to the medieval perception that sex was something a man did to a woman – and therefore a woman was only considered incapable of having sex if her vagina was completely impenetrable by a penis.

Although few spouses were as horrifically incompatible as this mismatched pair, their story powerfully highlights the misery that marriage could cause, in a world in which personal preferences were rarely prioritized, premarital sex was fraught with risk, and ending a marriage was almost impossible. Of course, the majority of couples managed to negotiate the path from altar to grave without major incidents, and most must have had boringly ordinary sex lives. Yet even those fortunate couples who benefited from mutual attraction and shared sexual preferences could face challenges when it came to having, or trying not to have, children – as we shall see in the next chapter.

FOUR

Reproduction

For medieval people, sex was inextricably linked to reproduction – both because of religious ideas about the purpose of marriage, and because of the realities of life in a world without modern contraceptives. Yet this did not mean that men and women passively accepted their reproductive destinies, or that they lacked ideas about how to promote or prevent conception.

How to Conceive

Given how much misery marital sex seems to have caused and how convoluted it could prove to be in medieval Europe, it may come as a surprise to discover that both religious and especially medical authorities placed great value on sexual pleasure. For theologians, it existed in order to ensure that people (and animals) reproduced; if such pleasure did not exist, and humans were repulsed by sex, then they would not be willing to suffer the problems of pregnancy, childbirth and childrearing, which are essential for the continuation of the human race.[1] For medical writers, the connection between sexual pleasure and reproduction was even more marked, since orgasm was at the heart of both of the dominant theories of how conception occurred. The first suggested that both partners produced seed during orgasm and must therefore climax more or less simultaneously for conception to occur. The other suggested that conception could be compared to carpentry, with the male's seed forming an embryo out of the 'wood' (that is, the menstrual blood) provided by the female.[2] Although neither theory became totally dominant, there does seem to have been increasing awareness among physicians (based in part on female testimony) of the possibility that a woman might conceive without having an orgasm, and thus presumably without emitting seed.[3] Nevertheless, this preoccupation with seed meant that medical writers were rather more concerned with sexual pleasure (including female sexual pleasure) than we might expect.

How, then, should a married couple who wished to have children go about achieving their goal? Most authors expected the man to take the initiative: he should kiss, embrace and speak gentle words to his partner, before touching her breasts. Foreplay might also include fondling the area around the woman's genitals. The woman's eye movements and breathing, as well as her babbling speech, would indicate when she was ready for penetration. At this point the man should enter the woman; some sources suggested that he should spread ointments or even chewed peppers on his penis to cause her 'incredible delectation'. Position was also important, since it influenced the degree of pleasure experienced and the ability of the man's seed to remain in the woman's womb, and thus the odds of conception. The man should try not to ejaculate before the woman orgasmed, but once she had, he must do so as soon as possible.[4] Understanding of the anatomy of female sexual pleasure was patchy, and it is often claimed that the clitoris was not discovered (at least, not discovered by men) until the Renaissance; it is, however, worth noting that a 1425 treatise on uroscopy refers to something that 'lewd [that is, uneducated] folk' call 'the kykyre in the cont'.[5] It was widely believed that women experienced three sorts of pleasure during sex – from the motion of the man's seed, from the motion of her own seed, and from rubbing – which led some to argue that women enjoyed sex more than men. Moreover, since women were naturally cold, and male seed was hot, they also experienced pleasure because sex warmed the body.[6]

The exact manner in which a couple had sex was believed to significantly influence their chances of conception. There was some disagreement about whether the woman should be an active participant (in order to increase her pleasure), or whether it was best for her to lie still, since excessive movement could cause division of the seed, leading to birth defects.[7] What was certain was that she must lie on her back 'with her legs spread well apart and quite elevated so that the opening of the vulva is raised towards the thighs', so that the man's sperm would flow directly into her womb. Other positions hindered this process, which was one of the reasons for the Church's insistence that the missionary position was the correct position.[8] Having sex standing up meant that 'the seed is projected upwards and afterwards falls down', and if a couple had sex lying on their sides 'then the seed is pound in on one side of the womb and as a result is wasted and generation is prevented'.[9] Once a couple had had potentially effective intercourse, the woman must keep still, otherwise she would expel the seed from her womb. One text even suggested that the man should lie on top of the woman for at least an hour, in order to ensure that 'the seminal matter does not scatter and form a monster'.[10]

Key characteristics of their future offspring were also at stake, and having sex in the wrong way, or at the wrong time, could have serious consequences. Benedetto Cotrugli's conduct book for merchants included two important pieces of advice on when to have sex: 'be sure not to lie with a woman during her menstruation, because leprous children will result, nor after lunch, while food is being digested in your stomach, because you will have sickly children who will generally not live long.'[11] The best time was when the body was properly balanced: not too hot or cold, or too wet or dry, but in perfect harmony. Some doctors warned that if a couple had sex before digestion was complete, 'the foetus so conceived will be mentally defective, even if complete in its limbs – if not hydrocephalic or otherwise deformed.'[12] Very young parents were also likely to produce unhealthy offspring who would 'suffer much pain from physical debility'.[13]

Sex in an unconventional position could lead to physical disabilities, as in a case in which a man 'lying sideways on top of the woman during sexual intercourse caused the woman to produce a child with a curved spine and a lame foot, and the deformity was attributed to the irregular position'. Such issues could also be caused by strange sights or sounds. If a couple had sex during a storm, this could apparently kill the seed, preventing conception, or weaken it, leading to 'alien characteristics'. One woman who conceived under such circumstances supposedly gave birth to a toad.[14] Less dramatically, Hildegard of Bingen suggested that lunar cycles would affect the health of offspring: the waxing of the moon led to an increase in human blood, which produced strong semen, and this was therefore a good time for conception. As the moon waned, blood decreased, producing weak semen that would produce weak offspring. Furthermore, the point in this cycle at which a child was conceived could affect both its temperament and its future vulnerability to illness and accidents.[15]

A baby's sex was thought to be determined in part by the quality of its parents' seeds, with different couples and different life stages producing different sex ratios; some couples might only have children of one sex.[16] Medical authorities suggested various strategies that could increase the chance of having a child of a particular sex. Once again, positions could be important: after having sex, the woman should sleep on her right side to conceive a boy, and on her left side for a girl.[17] Jacopo of Forli's On the Generation of the Embryo, written in Padua around 1400, identified a range of factors that would be likely to produce a male child. Many related to the physical characteristics of the parents: a young man, for example, was more likely to father a son, and so was a man with warm testicles. External factors could also be significant: taking warm food or drink before sex made a male child more likely, as did north winds, a cold climate and certain celestial influences.[18] There were also medicines that could be used to influence an individual's complexion (that is, how hot, cold, wet or dry their body was) in order to shape their reproductive capabilities. The *Trotula* advised a woman who wanted to conceive a son to have her husband drink the powdered womb and vagina of a hare mixed with wine; she should drink wine mixed with powdered hare testicles. They should then have sex at the end of her period.[19]

This reference to the woman's period shows that, although medieval physicians did not fully understand the menstrual cycle, they did realize that it played an important role in reproduction. Medical advice on the best times to have sex was not entirely consistent, with some suggesting immediately after a woman's period had finished, and others the middle of her cycle. Nevertheless, the key principle was clear: a woman was 'cleansed' through menstruation, and this purgation of bad humours left her healthy, strong and more likely to conceive. Women who did not have their 'flowers' (as periods were sometimes colloquially called) were like trees that lacked flowers and thus did not produce fruit – that is, they were unable to conceive.[20]

As with most medieval health problems, female infertility was often explained in terms of unbalanced humours. The problem might well result from, or be indicated by, a lack of menstruation. Consequently, treatments were often designed to moderate a complexion that was too hot or too cold, and both men and women might be encouraged to eat foods that were supposed to encourage the production of seed.[21] Both sexes were cautioned not to do things that could cause excessive cooling of the reproductive organs or the seed, such as drinking too much cold water, which could be a direct cause of infertility.[22] One serious cause of female infertility was excessive warmth, which made the womb so hot that it burnt the semen. In such cases, the woman would also suffer from telltale symptoms including ulcers, spots, constant thirst and hair loss. A young woman with this problem could be treated with fumigations and pessaries, followed by regular sex, but those over thirty were considered so old as to be beyond help. Another potential problem was excessive humidity, which caused the womb to suffocate the semen. The relationship between the womb and the brain (they were believed to be connected by nerves) meant that such women would be constantly tearful and mentally distressed. The main treatment was frequent purgation (by means of pessaries) followed by regular sex.[23]

Alternatively, women who were unable to conceive might have a physiological issue: a smooth, slippery womb, wind or bad humours in the womb, pustules or warts on the womb's opening, and excessive closing of the womb's opening could all prevent semen entering, or staying in, the womb. If a woman's womb was torn in childbirth, it might subsequently be unable to retain sperm, preventing further pregnancies.[24] It was also recognized that women who were very thin or very fat might have difficulty conceiving, the latter because 'the flesh surrounding the orifice of the womb constricts it, and it does not permit the seed of the man to enter.' Women who were deemed too fat to conceive might be treated with a regimen of baths, designed to make them sweat and thus to lose weight.[25]

Some medical authorities also suggested a scrutiny of bleeding and vaginal secretions that seems reminiscent of modern fertility advice, although the rationale behind it was rather different. According to Albertus Magnus, menstruation was the key to fertility – and bleeding must occur at the right time, and be the right colour. If, after menstruation, a woman dreamt about sex and emitted 'a slight amount of sperm', this was a good sign that suggested conception was likely. After such a dream, she should masturbate until 'the sperm which has been in the pathway of the seminal vessels is emitted', to prepare her for sex. If 'the humour she emits during the pollution of her dream ... [was] mature, white and viscous', that was a good sign. If, on the other hand, she produced 'another humour, midway between water and sperm', this suggested that her seed was 'useless for generation'. When she had sex, she should produce some moisture 'rather resembling sweat in the genital area', but not too much.[26]

If it was accepted that a woman needed to produce seed in order to conceive, then one further explanation for infertility was a lack of sexual pleasure on the part of the woman. Consequently, medical texts often discussed aphrodisiacs and foreplay in the context of infertility. For example, John of Gaddesden prescribed herbs and ointments to prevent premature ejaculation, and suggested that the man 'should touch the woman with his hand on her genitals and breasts, and kiss her; and then know her'. This, he thought, would accelerate her climax, allowing her to conceive.[27] Some patients, however, could not be helped in this respect since, as Albertus Magnus acknowledged, 'certain women do not care for intercourse', regardless of technique.[28]

According to the priest and medical writer John Mirfield (d. 1407), 'when sterility occurs between married people, the males are accused by many people of not having suitable seed.'[29] Based on the emphasis on female problems in the surviving records, including recipe collections and case histories, it seems unlikely that male infertility was the automatic explanation when a couple had problems conceiving – in many cases, it would have been assumed that the woman was at fault. Nevertheless, contrary to popular belief, medieval people did not always blame reproductive

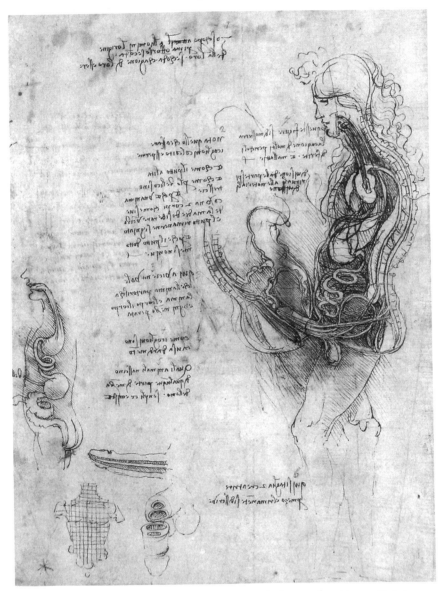

Leonardo da Vinci's drawing of intercourse (1492–4) illustrates the widespread belief that semen originated in the brain.

issues on the woman, and certainly recognized that men could also suffer from infertility.[30] Medical explanations for male infertility usually focused on three main problems: a lack of sexual desire (in which case his loins should be anointed with powders and oils, which were meant to increase his bodily heat), an inability to have an erection (which required different unguents), and defects of the seed (which were treated by a diet conducive to the production of semen, including onions and parsnips).[31] Physical injuries could also cause problems, for example if the veins behind a man's ears were cut (so he could not produce sperm), or if he was castrated, or the nerves in his genitals were injured.[32]

Discussions of male infertility often focused on sexual performance in a way that was not true for women.[33] Such problems were often linked to penis size: a very small penis could not send the seed far enough, but a very long penis meant that the generative spirit of the seed was weakened by the time it reached the end. It was important that a man chose a partner whose genitals were compatible with his own: a man with a short penis needed a small woman, whereas a man with a long penis should marry a big woman with long thighs.[34] Fortunately, if a couple who were already married turned out to be incompatible in this way, there were things they could do to tackle the problem, according to the French physician Bernard of Gordon (*fl.* 1270–1330):

> If it is because of shortness of the penis, then the woman's thighs should be lifted so the seed can fall into the depth of the natural field, or the penis should be magnified in this way: it should be beaten gently with rods and plastered with pitch ... If the sterility is because of the excessive length of the penis then the man or woman should hold the root of the penis tightly with his or her whole hand, both so that the whole penis is not put inside and so that the seed does not grow cold on the way.[35]

If a couple were unable to conceive, there were various ways in which they could determine who was at fault. Many such fertility tests involved sperm (which could be placed in water to see if it floated) or urine. Both sexes might pass urine on lettuce to see if it dried up, or in a pot of bran to see if worms appeared.[36] Other authorities thought that odour-based tests were the best way to determine whether a woman was fertile. These involved fumigating the womb with aromatics; if the smell rose to the woman's nose, then her passages were clear and she should be able to conceive. In another variation on this, peeled garlic was placed in the vulva overnight. A healthy woman would wake with the odour of garlic in her mouth and nose.[37]

Sometimes neither party was actually infertile, but rather the couple were in some way incompatible. Physicians noticed that sometimes a couple could not conceive together, but were able to reproduce with other people. Possible reasons for this included incompatible seeds (which corrupted each other), incompatible genitals and incompatible climaxes (that is, the man always came too quickly or the woman too slowly).[38] In other cases, an external factor, perhaps magic, was to blame. Alvaro Pelayo, a Franciscan friar writing around 1330, criticized women who 'with their magical songs and diabolical art impede others from having intercourse or generating offspring'. The physician Arnau of Vilanova also recognized magic as a common cause of female sterility, and said that it could only be cured if the spell was reversed.[39] Astrologers suggested that astrology could also influence human fertility, with Venus causing male infertility and certain stars causing both female sterility and male loss of libido.[40]

Infertility could also be interpreted as a manifestation of God's will; according to Hildegard of Bingen, 'it happens very often that, by the judgment of God, the power to beget is taken away from human beings.' Some chroniclers suggested that the failure of Emperor Henry v and his wife Matilda to produce offspring was attributable to his sins. Consequently, those who hoped to conceive often sought religious as well as medical advice. When Adeliza of Louvain, the second wife of Henry i of England, was trying to conceive, her spiritual advisor told her to be more penitent and to increase her almsgiving, in the hope that God would reward her with a son. Louis vii and Eleanor of Aquitaine conceived their second child after seeking counselling from Pope Eugenius iii, who made them sleep in a bed that he had personally prepared for them.[41]

Religious responses to infertility were not seen as an alternative to medicine, but were used in tandem; indeed, the boundary between the two was so indistinct that the well-respected physician Gilbertus Anglicus recorded what he claimed was a fail-proof method for treating infertility. It required the performance of a complex ritual by the prospective father, who must be at least twenty. On the vigil of the feast of John the Baptist, at the third hour, he must gather certain herbs while reciting the Lord's Prayer. He must then use their juices to write particular words (some biblical, some unintelligible) on a parchment amulet to be worn during sex, either by him or the woman, dependent on the sex of the child desired.[42]

Barren women often prayed to the Virgin Mary and her mother St Anne; the latter was their patron saint, due to the popular belief that she was herself unable to conceive without divine intervention. This focus on saints meant that pilgrimage, prayers and offerings were all popular strategies. At Walsingham, a Norfolk shrine dedicated to the Virgin, pilgrims could purchase small containers filled with holy water and a drop of the Virgin's milk, which were supposed to help with infertility, childbirth and lactation; both Anne of Bohemia and Margaret of Anjou went there to pray for an heir. In late eleventh-century Rouen, the shrine of St Catherine of Alexandria helped several childless couples, including Gislebert and his wife, who had been married for eighteen years when he made a vow to keep her vigils 'with fasting and watching'. Within a year his wife was pregnant.[43] Male saints might also help: in Bury St Edmunds, the monks led garlanded bulls (a symbol of fertility) in procession through the town, and presented female pilgrims to the saint's shrine in a spectacular public ritual intended to promote conception. When the offerings at Thomas Cantilupe's Hereford shrine were catalogued in 1307, they included 97 nightgowns from previously infertile women who had conceived after praying to St Thomas.[44] Childless women might also seek help from living holy men. Edward the Confessor cured a young wife who was suffering from both scrofula and sterility simply by touching her neck; within the year she was a perfectly healthy mother of twins.[45] A century later, a woman from Stamford gave birth to a son after St Gilbert of Sempringham slept in her bed, 'so that through his merits she might be found worthy to bear a son'.[46]

The complexities of individual experiences of infertility are illustrated by the story of Margherita and Francesco Datini, a mercantile couple from Prato who married in 1376. Francesco, who was considerably older than his wife, had at least one bastard, but they never had children together; it seems likely that at least one of their problems was the considerable amount of time they spent apart, as Francesco travelled for work. Over the years, the couple received a lot of advice from friends and family about possible remedies for their infertility. In 1395 Francesco's friend Dr Naddino Borattieri wrote to say that he believed Margherita's case to be similar to that of one of his patients, who suffered from 'pains every month before her purgation'; if so, he could cure her, as he had cured the other woman, who was now a mother of two. Margherita's sister Francesca and her husband Niccolò offered multiple suggestions. Relatively early in the marriage, Niccolò suggested a change of residence; he knew a Genoese couple who had been unable to conceive in their native city, but who started a family as soon as they moved to Tuscany. (This made sense given the belief that air and environment had a significant impact on individual health, with different locations being best suited to different complexions.) Later, Francesca heard about an extremely smelly poultice which, placed on the belly, had helped many women to conceive, and found a woman who could make one for Margherita. On another occasion Niccolò wrote on behalf of Francesca, sending a belt about which he reported:

> She says it is to be girded on by a boy who is still a virgin, saying first three Our Fathers and Hail Marys in honour of God and the Holy Trinity and St Catherine; and the letters written on the belt are to be placed on the belly, on the naked flesh ... But I, Niccolò,

think it would be better, in order to obtain what she wishes, if she fed three beggars on three Fridays, and did not harken to women's chatter.[47]

Although she never had a child, Margherita Datini was in one sense a fortunate woman: she seems to have been surrounded by people who were sympathetic to her plight and who did their best to help. Inevitably, some unscrupulous individuals exploited the despair of the childless. In 1326 a doctor named Antoni Imbert was accused of making fraudulent promises to the impotent and infertile; he made a considerable sum of money from desperate men and women in the small Provençal town of Draguignan before fleeing in the middle of the night. His treatments included medicines and baths, but also magical remedies. Among his victims was a woman named Raimunda Veranessa, who had consulted him on behalf of her daughter Roselina; he gave her a sheet for the marital bed, a veil for the daughter to wear, and a silk bag inscribed with thirteen letters, and said that the couple must have sex on Fridays. Bertranda, wife of Peire Gase, paid him a gold florin, for which she received an amulet with religious inscriptions, plus a drawing of the cross to be placed in her bed.[48] Unsurprisingly, none of these expensive items worked.

How Not to Conceive

While some medieval people tried desperately to conceive, others sought to prevent pregnancy. Inevitably, the Church was strongly opposed to any such efforts. If few clerics went as far as the English-born cardinal Robert of Courçon (d. 1219), who suggested that marriages should be invalidated if a couple used potions to avoid offspring, the ecclesiastical position was clear. Despite the Church's celebration of the celibacy of single people, for married couples even abstinence was wrong, since it interfered with God's plans for the perpetuation of the human race, and went against religious teachings on the purpose of marriage and the marital debt.[49] According to a set of English synodal statutes published in the 1320s, it was the job of the parish priest to 'frequently make public that a man when carnally knowing his wife or another woman ought to do nothing – nor should his wife do anything – on account of which conception of a foetus is impeded'.[50] He should then follow up on this in the confessional. Whereas early medieval penitentials have little to say about the avoidance of offspring, it is mentioned frequently in later medieval texts, with confessors required to ask both men and women whether they had (as John of Freiburg put it in his fourteenth-century manual on confession) 'brought about some impediment to avoid conceiving', and to impose the appropriate penance if this sin had been committed.[51]

Despite their best efforts, many medieval churchmen seem to have been convinced that the avoidance of conception was a widespread sin. John of Freiburg classed avoiding conception as a typical sin of the married, while William of Pagula (writing in 1320s Yorkshire) claimed that *coitus interruptus* was widely practised, and that 'many these days' did not consider it a sin. Alvarius Pelagius, a Galician canon lawyer, claimed that peasants avoided conception through abstinence.[52] Concern about contraceptive practices peaked in the early fourteenth century, when overpopulation was making life difficult for many people. But it is hard to tell whether this is because a lot of couples, faced with growing economic hardship, were successfully avoiding having children, or whether it was simply a moral panic.

Some clerics pondered the reasons why a couple might try to avoid pregnancy, and speculated on the methods they might use. In his treatise on confession (*c.* 1216), Thomas of Chobham wrote about women who sought to avoid the consequences of illicit sex or to avoid the pain of childbirth; at least one fourteenth-century text suggested that couples were mainly concerned to preserve the wife's beauty by avoiding frequent pregnancies. But other writers recognized that many of those who committed this sin did so because they were poor and desperate: the early fourteenth-century Dominican Peter de Palude, for example, mentioned men who did this 'in order not to have more children whom he cannot feed'. Pragmatism about such cases was perhaps behind the actions of those parish priests of thirteenth-century Passau, who allegedly made light of fornication by advising people to act 'with care', if not chastely. Peter Biller has even suggested that some parish priests may have given advice on contraception, since it was widely assumed that they would provide guidance on such unlikely topics as breastfeeding and childcare.[53]

If priests sometimes faced a conflict between the ideals of their Church and the day-to-day struggles of the poorer members of the flock, the situation was arguably even more complex for members of the medical profession. As Gentile da Foligno, an early fourteenth-century professor at Bologna, highlighted, there was a clear tension between the legal prohibition of abortion and the medical concern with 'the well-being of the patient'.[54] Several influential medical authorities identified circumstances in which it might be necessary to prevent conception. Avicenna, for example, acknowledged that a physician might need to prevent pregnancy 'in small women, in whom it would be dangerous to have childbirth on account of a diseased womb or from a weakness in the insides'.[55] Similarly,

Niccolò Falcucci's *Practica* (*c.* 1400) argued that contraceptives should be used if pregnancy might endanger the woman or foetus, for example if a woman had certain uterine conditions or a weak bladder that might rupture during birth, or if she was ill or constitutionally weak.[56]

Medical texts, especially those produced from around 1300 onwards, also included information about *how* pregnancy could be avoided. Some authors discussed the relationship between menstruation and fertility, although they understood this process in humoral rather than hormonal terms and offered conflicting advice. Thus Taddeo Alderotti, a thirteenth-century professor of medicine at Bologna, suggested couples who wanted to conceive should have sex during menstruation, but Peter of Palud, writing in early fourteenth-century Paris, thought that women could not conceive during their period.[57] Many of the suggested techniques focused on seed: given that pregnancy was thought to occur when the male and female seeds mixed, the best way to avoid pregnancy was to stop this happening, perhaps through abstinence or *coitus interruptus*. Other sources suggested putting slippery substances such as oil on the penis or in the vagina, so that the seed would run back out of the woman's body. Many medical experts suggested that a woman would not conceive if she moved about after sex – perhaps jumping up and down, running up and down stairs, or sneezing – because this would stop the seed being retained in the womb.[58]

One of the largest medieval collections of contraceptive techniques is to be found in Peter of Spain's *The Treasury of the Poor*, a text which is given added interest by the tantalizing possibility that its author may have been the man who was later (in 1276) elected Pope John XXI. Whatever the author's true identity, he assembled a whole host of remedies to reduce desire, from eating rhubarb (which 'takes away lasciviousness and suppresses the semen') to anointing the genitals with cedar pitch (which 'contracts the genitals in such a way that they become useless for coitus or procreation'). These may have been aimed at celibate clergymen, but they would also have helped couples who wanted to avoid pregnancy by not having sex. He also provided more than two dozen methods that are explicitly identified as contraceptives. These included herbal remedies (such as applying mint juice to the female genitals before sex) and animal amulets (such as carrying a piece of a mule's ear, or the small bone from a female donkey's vulva, or the testicles of a male weasel, or elephant dung). Most of these were sourced from other medical writings, although he did claim that 'a certain experienced woman told me that, annoyed at the frequency of childbirth, she ate a bee and did not conceive again.'[59] Although few (if any) of the animal-based remedies would actually have worked, other than by making an individual so repellent that no one wanted to have sex with them, most were firmly rooted in contemporary science. Some worked by altering the patient's humours; others were used in an attempt to transfer supposed qualities of an animal to the woman, in a way that made sense according to medieval theories of touch.[60]

Real-life examples of individuals who used contraception are extremely scarce, but it is hard to know whether this is because it was seldom used, or because people were simply not caught using it. A very rare reference to *coitus interruptus* is found in a mid-fifteenth-century Venetian incest case, in which it was noted that the father 'coming together with [his daughter], when he came to the moment of emitting sperm, withdrew his member and ejected semen between the thighs of the said Antonia because he said he did not wish to impregnate her'.[61] Other cases show women seeking help from other women in their attempts to avoid pregnancy. In the early fourteenth century, a single woman from the duchy of Savoy was fined because another woman had rested on her a piece of bone that was supposed to stop conception.[62] A century later, one of the accusations against Matteuccia di Francesco (who was executed as a witch in 1428) was the claim that she had provided Caterina Castello della Pieve with 'a remedy to prevent her becoming pregnant'. Caterina was having a secret relationship with a priest; she 'feared public rebuke and she did not want this news to reach the ears of her family'. The remedy prescribed was to burn the hoof of a she-mule, mix it with wine, and drink it while reciting particular words.[63]

An unusually detailed description of how and why one couple attempted to avoid pregnancy comes from Montaillou, where in the opening years of the fourteenth century Béatrice de Planissoles, a wealthy widow, had a two-year relationship with Pierre Clergue, the village priest. Testifying to the Inquisition, she recalled that she had asked him: 'What shall I do if I become pregnant by you? I shall be ashamed and lost.' Her lover shared her concern: he worried that his mistress's father would be unhappy if they had a child. Fortunately, Pierre had a special herb, which a man could wear to prevent conception. When they had sex, Pierre wrapped this herb in a small piece of linen, and made Béatrice wear it on a long cord around her neck. 'When Pierre Clergue wanted to know me carnally,' she recalled,

> he used to wear this herb wrapped up in a piece of linen, about an ounce long or wide, or about the size of the first joint of my little finger . . . I would put the 'herb' in his hand and then he himself would place it at the opening of my stomach, still with the cord

between my breasts. And that was how he used to unite himself carnally with me, and not otherwise.

How this was supposed to work is not entirely clear, but she seems to have believed that it stopped the seed 'curdling' to produce a foetus. However it functioned, it apparently produced the desired effect, since Béatrice did not conceive. It also gave Pierre a degree of control over his girlfriend: after they had intercourse, he always made her give the herb back to him, to stop her having sex with other men behind his back.[64]

Abortion is equally hard to trace. Unsurprisingly, the Church was strongly opposed, tending to view it as murder, and therefore as a mortal sin. However, the precise gravity of the crime, and the nature of the punishment required, was directly linked to the stage of pregnancy at which it took place. From a religious perspective, the key point was when the embryo acquired a soul, which was usually linked to the quickening.[65] It seems that a termination before this point was normally viewed as a sin that required penance, whereas the abortion of a fully formed foetus was homicide, and thus also a crime. This distinction occurred even in cases where the woman's life was at risk.[66] The exact punishment might also be influenced by the guilty woman's attitude to her crime. Rufinus, Bishop of Assisi (*fl.* 1157–79), argued that all abortive acts were homicides, but a woman who voluntarily confessed her guilt should receive penance rather than punishment.[67] The Church also concerned itself with, and punished, those who provided the means of abortion. For example, a statute from a clerical council held at Riez in 1285, and often repeated by similar gatherings in the region over the next century, pronounced that anyone who provided the poison that causes an abortion should be excommunicated. If the guilty party was a priest, he should be deprived of both his benefice and his clerical rank.[68]

Providing or having an abortion was also punishable under secular law, and there was an increased interest in women as perpetrators of abortion (and infanticide) in high medieval law codes. In England, the *Leges Henrici Primi* (a legal treatise written around 1115) required seven years' penance for murder for a woman who intentionally aborted a child, reduced to three years if less than forty days had passed and the child had not yet quickened. The late thirteenth-century legal treatise *Fleta* simply stated that a woman committed homicide if she destroyed a child using a potion or in any other way.[69] Continental law codes also included harsh punishments, especially for terminations carried out after the quickening. In mid-thirteenth-century Castile, *Las Siete Partidas* required the death penalty for a woman who deliberately caused a miscarriage, whether by drinking a potion, striking herself in the belly or another method. If she did this before the quickening occurred, she should be banished to some island for five years.[70] At around the same time, Valencia made homicidal manslaughter in the womb punishable by burning at the stake. In the early fourteenth century, the Sienese authorities imposed a large fine for the distribution or consumption of abortifacient beverages, whether or not they worked. A few decades later, the Piedmontese city of Biella decided to impose a large fine for abortions performed during the first two months of pregnancy (that is, before the quickening); after this, men were to be decapitated, women burnt.[71]

In reality, however, abortion was hard to prove, and consequently was rarely prosecuted. Most foetal homicide cases relate to assaults on pregnant women that led to miscarriage, and the woman was the claimant, not the criminal. For example, a study of court records from later medieval Savoy found only fifteen cases of abortion across two centuries; the majority of these involved pregnant women who were struck (either accidentally or deliberately) by men, and for whom the subsequent miscarriage was an additional trauma.[72] Furthermore, although many jurisdictions allowed death sentences in such cases, these were not always followed through. Among the death sentences commuted by the French crown was one given to a man who had tried to provoke a miscarriage by twisting a piece of household linen around his pregnant maidservant's belly.[73] In fifteenth-century Slavonia a prostitute named Dorothy was sentenced to death by drowning after she confessed to terminating two pregnancies, squashing the foetuses in her womb before expelling them. She was pardoned in response to the petition of the executioner, Valentine, who wanted to marry her.[74]

Identifying abortifacients in medieval medical texts is also difficult. A few authors were explicit about what they were addressing: writing in thirteenth-century Italy, William of Saliceto justified his discussion of contraception and abortion 'on account of the danger that comes to a woman because of a dangerous risk of conceiving on account of her health, debilities, or the extremity of her youth'.[75] More often, however, the authors of such texts provide remedies that promote menstruation. Some historians have assumed that this was a discreet way of saying they would cause an abortion. However, at least some of these recipes probably were genuinely designed to treat amenorrhoea, given that regular menstruation was thought necessary for female health, and therefore a woman who did not have periods might well seek a remedy for this problem, even if she did not want children. On the other hand, the dominance of humoral medicine meant that the remedies provided to a woman without periods and a woman with an unwanted pregnancy were often very similar. In many cases, the only difference between an abortifacient and a menstrual remedy could be the user's intent.

Surgical abortions are even harder to detect, and it seems likely that even basic procedures using domestic implements such as knitting needles were very rarely, if ever, attempted in the Middle Ages. By far the most common approaches seem to have been herbal remedies (usually taken in drinks) and physical trauma, especially punching in the stomach. Many remedies were designed to be administered by the woman herself, without recourse to medical help, and countless such procedures must have succeeded or failed without ever being recorded, or even widely known. In many of the cases that did reach the courts, however, other people were involved – often people who had a vested interest in terminating the woman's pregnancy. A letter of remission, dated 1447, tells the sad story of Jehanne Dusolier, a widow from Puy la Roque. When she fell pregnant, her lover, a priest named Raymond Robert, told her to take two mouthfuls of pulverized rue in wine for three days, since this was 'among the things in the world that overcome a child in the womb most effectively'. Later, he told her to add scabious and hard liquor, but she refused. Her sickly baby was born secretly; she baptised it before suffocating it and burying it in a stable.[76] In 1471, in the German town of Nördlingen, the town council investigated a case in which a madam forced a young prostitute named Els von Eystett to drink a homemade abortifacient potion, causing her to miscarry a male foetus of about twenty weeks' gestation. The authorities seem to have accepted that Els, who wept for her lost child, was one of the victims of this crime, but the perpetrator was banished.[77]

Medical practitioners of various sorts were also likely to be implicated. Sometimes, women turned to highly skilled medical practitioners, including physicians. In 1298 a Jewish doctor named Isaac, practising in Manosque (Provence), was accused of preparing an abortive potion for Uga, who was unmarried and pregnant, causing a stillbirth. He claimed this was untrue – he had seen Uga's mother with the child, which had died in infancy – and there were no reliable witnesses. He was nevertheless imprisoned and fined because he was unable to disprove the rumours (and perhaps because his status as a member of a religious minority made the relevant authorities less willing to give him the benefit of the doubt).[78] In other cases, remedies were obtained from less reputable individuals. When eighteen-year-old Jehanette found herself pregnant, she got a potion from a woman called Margot of the Large Arms. Two months later, she miscarried an 'apple-sized' foetus, 'whether by illness or otherwise', and was condemned for suffocating it.[79] In 1409 Aldelheit von Stutgarden, an undesirable German woman known as 'the limper', was expelled from the French town of Sélesat and banished across the Rhine for three years, having procured abortions for many respectable women by giving them roots or concoctions.[80]

In both of these cases, the women involved seem to have been open with each other about what was being handed over: the acknowledged aim was the termination of a pregnancy. Other patients claimed to be suffering from a medical condition that would require purgative treatments, rather than explicitly asking for an abortion. For example, in a court case heard in Brittany in 1464, Jehanna Gaudu discovered she was pregnant, and confided in her mother, Marie. Marie approached a neighbour who had suffered from serious stomach ulcers, claiming that her daughter was suffering from 'a similar disease'.[81] In a near-contemporary case, Katherine Armant, a young woman from Clermont l'Hérault (Languedoc), became pregnant while her fiancé was abroad. She, together with her fiancé's sister Jehanne and her brother-in-law, tried to salvage the engagement by ending the pregnancy. First they punched her in the stomach; when this failed to produce the desired effect, they consulted Guillem Masson, a physician, telling him that Katherine was suffering from a serious condition of the uterus. Then the brother-in-law went to see Pierre Dalton, an apothecary; he claimed to be representing a poor woman suffering from chronic constipation, and was given potions and wraps to purge her. Finally, the family consulted M. Étienne de Linas, a barber. He was initially hired, he claimed, to purge the vessels of her intimate parts, and so he bled her from the hands, feet and the 'veins of the mother'. Only after this too failed did the desperate family specifically ask him to provoke an abortion, at which point he provided various potions and powders.[82]

Given that they were largely private practices that could not be publicly acknowledged, it is inevitable that medieval contraception and abortion are poorly documented, and impossible to know how widely they were practised. On the one hand, the religious and cultural emphasis on the importance of parenthood – as a God-given gift, as a duty of married men and women to procreate, and as a natural role that conferred social standing and security, especially for women – perhaps meant that fewer people deliberately chose to remain childless in the Middle Ages than today. On the other hand, some medieval people undoubtedly found themselves in situations in which to avoid or terminate a pregnancy seemed to be their only option. It seems that the knowledge and means to do so were available at all levels of society, even if the efficacy of the available methods was far from guaranteed.

Sex and Pregnancy

Whether or not she wanted to be pregnant, how could a medieval woman know whether she had conceived? Although reliable testing was many centuries off, medical texts suggest that certain bodily signs could serve as early indicators of pregnancy. Immediately after she had sex, a woman might feel cold and experience leg pain, and she would emit little or no seed if the womb closed up. A few weeks on, she might miss her period, have a flushed face, or experience a constant desire for sex; she was also likely to have strange cravings (perhaps for earth, charcoal or certain fruits), because the retention of the menses produced venomous humours in the stomach, provoking a desire for unusual foods 'because similar seeks out similars'.[83] Benedetto Cotrugli, in his handbook for merchants, said that 'indications of pregnancy will start to appear ten days after conception, with headaches, restlessness, clouding of the vision, reactions to foods, loss of appetite' and so on.[84]

Sex during pregnancy was potentially problematic, in part because it was not motivated by the desire to conceive. This did not mean that conception was entirely ruled out, at least during the earliest stages of pregnancy: Albertus Magnus thought that women could conceive again, although sometimes a second conception would destroy the first. In this way, it was possible for a woman to carry her husband's child and her lover's at the same time, so that folk belief suggested that a woman who gave birth to twins must have had an affair. But since most women produced only one baby, it was hard to escape the suspicion that couples who had sex during pregnancy were motivated solely by lust.[85]

Indeed, some medical authorities suggested that pregnant women were especially lustful – a trait that separated them from the animals, since, other than the mare, the human female was the only species that would have sex while pregnant. Albertus Magnus explained that pregnant women wanted frequent sex because

> the sperm in pregnant women pours itself into the nerves and by its itching arouses pleasure. The women then seek after the rubbing caused by intercourse and ... take more pleasure in it than at any other time because of the drawing in of humour to the groin area.

Women who were expecting girls were particularly susceptible.[86] Nevertheless, it was thought that a pregnant wife sinned more than her husband would in seeking the marital debt, since she had more responsibility for the foetus.[87]

The primary issue, however, was not the couple's motivations for having sex, but the safety of their future offspring. In the early stages of pregnancy, the chief concern was that sex could cause the womb to reopen, so that the foetus would slip out of the body. As the pregnancy progressed and the baby grew, it could be damaged by 'excessive and frequent oppression and pounding', or its development could be 'polluted by excessive and wasted seed'.[88] When the woman's due date was near, there was a danger that sex would induce labour – or, as Albertus Magnus put it: 'the giving birth will be hastened along from this due to the movement of the womb, the rubbing caused by the intercourse, and the agitation of the head of the foetus.'[89]

Consequently, sex during pregnancy was deeply troubling to religious authorities. Hildegard of Bingen claimed that 'those who have intercourse with the pregnant are murderers', and suggested abstinence for the whole pregnancy.[90] Among the *exempla* (moral stories for inclusion in sermons) collected by Jacques de Vitry (d. 1240) was the story of a man who had sex with his wife after a visit to the tavern, and in doing so killed his own child. More generally, he complained about

> certain men who bother their pregnant wives when they are near childbirth, because the men do not want to and are unable to abstain from their pregnant wives for a short time. As a result, the child in the mother's womb is killed and deprived of baptism. Cursed be the desire which snatches the soul of its son from God.[91]

The gravity with which this problem was treated is reflected in theological writings that viewed pregnancy as sufficient grounds for deviation from norms which were normally rigidly upheld. Authorities including Jean Gerson and Francis de Plathea of Bologna (d. 1460), both of whom thought that refusing the marital debt was almost always a sin, agreed that a woman could refuse her husband sex towards the end of her pregnancy, if she feared for the life of her child.[92] Despite their usual insistence that there was only one proper way to have sex, some theologians were even willing to accept that a couple might have to adopt a non-missionary position (probably side-by-side) during the advanced stages of pregnancy, in order to protect the foetus.[93]

After childbirth, a couple should not resume sexual relations until the woman had been churched – that is, ceremonially repurified in a religious ceremony conducted by a priest, usually about a month after the delivery.[94] Such abstinence was required partly due to perceived uncleanness, but also for medical reasons: to allow the woman time to recover physically after the delivery, and to prevent pregnancy (it was thought that a child conceived during this period was likely to be deformed).[95] New mothers were also advised not to have sex while breastfeeding, because this would stir the blood and putrefy the milk.[96] Indeed, some Spanish law codes went so far as to banish and fine those who had sex with a wet nurse – a punishment equivalent to that for murder, since the corruption of her milk might cause the child's death.[97] Medieval people knew that lactation could affect fertility, but they also understood that it was not a foolproof method of contraception. Jewish authorities sometimes tackled this by allowing nursing women to use contraception, usually cervical sponges. Rabbi Tam (d. 1171), one of the leading French Jewish thinkers of his generation, went so far as to say that a nursing woman must use contraception to protect the life of her existing child, who depended on her for nourishment.[98] For the Christian authorities, on the other hand, such pragmatism was a step too far. Abstinence, they insisted, was the answer.

Reproduction is a topic that highlights both how much and how little has changed since the Middle Ages. On the one hand, the existence of fertility treatments, contraceptives and safe abortion have revolutionized both our attitudes to sex and our experiences of its consequences. And yet, two of the fundamental issues facing modern couples – how to get pregnant and how to deal with an unwanted pregnancy – were also experienced by countless medieval people. Only one group was (supposed to be) exempt from such concerns, and indeed from all sex-related problems, thanks to their adoption of a celibate lifestyle: the clergy.

FIVE

The Battle for Chastity

All medieval Christians were expected to go without sex sometimes, perhaps even for years at a stretch, but for one sector of society abstinence was a way of life. The clergy's adherence to a higher ideal excused them from the laity's duty of having sex and perpetuating the species in accordance with God's plan for humanity.

Why Celibacy?

The ideal of clerical celibacy is an old one, dating back to the early days of Christianity; from the late Roman period onwards, high-ranking clergymen (such as bishops) were not supposed to marry, and monks and nuns took vows of celibacy. Nevertheless, throughout the early Middle Ages most parish priests probably had wives, despite periodic attempts at reform. Only in the mid-eleventh century was there a major drive towards universal clerical celibacy, led by the papacy and enforced (with varying degrees of success) by the episcopate.[1]

This renewed interest in clerical sexual behaviour was linked to a wider ecclesiastical reform movement, which aimed to enforce clear boundaries between the clergy and the laity. Although this divide was created by ritual processes (especially ordination), it was reinforced by behaviour. Consequently, clerics were forbidden not only to have sex, but from engaging in other lay pursuits, such as frequenting taverns and going to war. There were also (not wholly unfounded) concerns about Church property, specifically that clerics would squander Church revenue on their women, and pass benefices down to their sons. Families drained not only a priest's financial resources, but his time: he would be distracted from his duties by his personal life. Rather than having a biological family, reformers argued, a priest should have spiritual kin: he was 'married' to his church, and a 'father' to his parishioners. Arguably, celibacy was also necessary to give priests the moral authority to enforce the Church's sexual teachings, and to act as role models to their spiritual offspring.[2]

At around the same time, there was also a new emphasis on the Eucharist, including transubstantiation (that is, the belief that the communion bread and wine turned into the actual body and blood of Christ when consecrated). Consequently, the Church became increasingly concerned about pollution: it seemed incredibly important for the priest to be unsullied when he celebrated Mass, and thus it was necessary to create a ritually pure clergy.[3] Sex was forbidden because it was unfitting to administer the sacraments with hands that had engaged in sexual acts: as the influential Italian reformer Peter Damian reminded priests, 'At the imposition of your hand, the Holy Spirit descends, and with it you touch the genitals of whores.'[4] The English preacher Thomas Agnellus (*fl.* 1183) attacked priests who go 'from a whore's bed to the table of the lord, from a place of pollution to a place of sanctification, from shameful contact with women to consecrating the sacrament of the flesh and blood of God', and denounced them as 'Christ-killers', as hateful as the Jews. Others made comparisons between a priest who had sex before celebrating Mass and one who vomited or defecated on the altar.[5]

Such was the obsession with clerical purity that merely avoiding sexual intercourse was not enough; priests were supposed to eschew all forms of sexual activity, even involuntary nocturnal emissions of semen. Such occurrences were particularly problematic if they had been provoked by a conscious action on the part of the polluted priest, such as engaging in immoral thoughts or getting drunk. If, however, there were no aggravating factors, these emissions could be excused as a necessary rebalancing of the humours, and the priest would be considered not culpable.[6] According to his biographer, the future Pope Celestine v (1294) was wrestling with this problem when he had a dream about a defecating donkey. In the dream, the Trinity urged him not to be repulsed by this unseemly act, since the beast had no choice. Celestine therefore decided that since his emission was, like the donkey's, caused by superfluity rather than sin, he could celebrate Mass.[7]

Despite the colourful rhetoric, and the best efforts of the ecclesiastical authorities, not everyone agreed that clerical marriage should be forbidden, especially in the century or so after clerical celibacy was introduced. Many claimed that priests had a right to have wives, and argued that denying them their right to marital intercourse would force them into unnatural vices, especially sodomy. As one married priest wrote, in around the year 1090:

You deny it is right to touch a woman's bed,
And to consummate the marriage rite in the bridal chamber.
It is the natural right of a man to enjoy his wife.
This is how we were all born and this is how we multiply,
This is how each generation follows the preceding one.[8]

Some priests bribed bishops to turn a blind eye so that they could keep their partners, while others turned to violence: in 1072 the Archbishop of Rouen had to flee a synod when the assembled clerics stoned him because he tried to take away their concubines.[9]

With time, however, the clergy seem to have become resigned to the ideal of clerical celibacy, even if not all priests managed to live by it; towards the end of the Middle Ages the main dissenting voices were heretics. In England, for example, the Twelve Conclusions (posted on the doors of Westminster Hall in 1395) argued that celibacy plus gluttony inevitably led to sodomy, and accused nuns of having abortions. Other Lollard tracts claimed that priests had illicit relations with married women and nuns, and murdered women who rejected their advances. Fifteenth-century heresy trials often featured individuals with unconventional views on clerical celibacy, such as William White, who admitted preaching that it made priests greedy and lecherous, and had himself taken a wife.[10] Judaism also offered an alternative version of religious leadership. Medieval rabbis were usually married men, and their wives were respected figures – to the extent that Eleazar ben Judah (d. 1232) wrote a poem about his wife Dulcia after she was murdered in 1196, in which he celebrated her learning and piety, and the active role she played in leading worship at the synagogue.[11]

Although much of the discussion about religious celibacy focused on men, religious women were also expected to avoid sex. Indeed, sex with a nun was a particularly serious offence, because it offended God, polluted holy places, and caused infamy and scandal. Moreover, it was incestuous, because nuns were married to Christ, and the man was therefore sleeping with his Father's wife. Consequently, when in 1395 Antonio Vianaro was tried for sex with a nun, having entered the Venetian convent of Santa Croce several times to have intercourse with Sister Ursia Tressa in her cell, he was accused of 'not considering how much injury he caused the Highest Creator by violating the Bride of Christ' and of 'committing wicked incest, fornication, adultery and sacrilege, not keeping God before his eyes'.[12] In fifteenth-century Italy, many city states passed increasingly strict laws against this offence: one typical set of statutes, introduced in Bologna in 1454, imposed the death penalty on a man who took or received a nun with sexual intent, while she was to spend the rest of her life in confinement on bread and water.[13] More rarely, but perhaps even more frighteningly, there was also the risk of divine punishment: Caesarius of Heisterbach claimed that when a cleric from Lower Utrecht (a friend of a friend) 'corrupted a veiled nun', Christ punished him by placing 'such a sign on his genitals, that it was a terror to all who could see or were told of it'.[14]

How to Be Celibate

Living up to the high standards that the Church imposed upon the clergy was difficult, not least because this group was widely believed to be unusually prone to sexual temptation; the Devil, wishing to undermine God's work, subjected them to greater temptation. When a woman complained to St Hugh, Bishop of Lincoln, about her husband's impotence, he allegedly quipped 'Let us make him a priest and the power will immediately be restored to him.'[15] Fortunately, however, there were many things that could make the burden of celibacy more manageable.

When St Hugh spoke about the trials faced by priests, he did so from personal experience. Before he became a bishop, Hugh was prior of the Carthusian house at Witham, Somerset, and immediately after his appointment to that position he reportedly experienced such terrible lust that 'the thorns of the flesh almost caused his physical death.' He resisted temptation with tears, confession and asceticism, but could only be cured by divine intervention. He had a dream in which St Basil cut into his bowels, extracted 'something resembling red hot cinders' and threw it away. After this, Hugh was completely free from sexual temptation.[16] It is important to note that such deliverance was not freely given: only those particularly favoured by God would receive help of this kind. Moreover, it was only granted to those who genuinely tried to remain celibate. Men such as Hugh were rewarded after fighting hard in their battle for chastity, a struggle which allowed the model priest to overcome an enemy and display military prowess without actually going to war.[17]

Nevertheless, a sizeable minority of the medieval clergy were saved by dreams and visions, some of them disturbingly violent. Gerald of Wales (*c.* 1146–*c.* 1223) recounted the story of a nun who became obsessed with a man whom she saw through a window, to the extent that he appeared frequently in her dreams, apparently wanting to have sex with her. One night she dreamt that she grabbed a scythe off the wall and chopped the man in half. A terrible smell woke her up; it returned whenever she recalled the dream, and in this way she was cured of lust.[18] Another nun arranged a secret assignation with a man, but when she tried to leave the church to go to the meeting, she found 'Christ hanging with outstretched arms on the cross' at each door. Fearing that the meeting was against God's will, she prayed before an image of the Virgin Mary, which promptly smacked her so hard on the jaw that she was found on the floor the next day, still in a deep swoon. Although this was a grievous blow, it delivered her from all temptation.[19] The Dominican preacher Étienne of Bourbon (c. 1180–1261) described how a friar struggling with lust had asked the Virgin Mary for help. As he slept, she appeared to him, dragged him by his hair and flayed him. In the morning he had new skin, and was no longer vulnerable to temptations of the flesh.[20]

Those who were not lucky enough to receive such a miracle sometimes decided to take matters into their own hands. William of Ashby, one of the first Franciscans in England, reportedly castrated himself in order to maintain his chastity, after which he had to obtain a papal dispensation to continue celebrating Mass.[21] This approach was not condoned by the Church, since it both damaged the physical integrity that was required of priests (this was an age in which a man with even a relatively minor physical defect, such as a missing finger, could not be ordained without a papal dispensation), and was in some sense seen as cheating. Nevertheless, papal records include occasional references to priests who had castrated themselves, and thus had to apply for permission to continue in office.[22] These men – physically and no doubt psychologically traumatized, but alive and able to carry on practising their vocation – were arguably the lucky ones. Others, including the canon of Bushmead who in 1282 'castrated himself with his own knife and died of the cut the same day', did not live to tell the tale.[23]

Unsurprisingly, most celibates preferred less drastic remedies. Texts aimed at nuns stressed the dangers of pregnancy and childbirth, to deter their readers from doing anything that might lead to conception.[24] Writings for and by male clerics were often deeply misogynistic, partly because men who were not allowed to have sex tried to convince themselves that women were so repulsive that they did not actually want to. Such contemplation was usually a private process, but occasionally an individual was forcibly confronted with the real physical shortcomings of the object of their desires. When a nun became fixated on St Gilbert of Sempringham (c. 1085–1189), he responded by preaching a sermon on the importance of resisting desire before removing his cloak, showing his repulsively emaciated body to the entire convent. This apparently solved the problem.[25]

Another common technique was to avoid temptation, for which reason most religious houses were single-sex institutions with strict rules about visitors. In 1234, for example, the monks of Bury St Edmunds were instructed not to have private meetings with any women (including close relatives); nor were they allowed to speak to nuns or other religious women, for fear of scandal. Some orders, such as the Carthusians, went even further, barring women from their monasteries altogether since no man could resist their 'caresses and ruses'.[26] There was also a lot of concern about adolescents in religious houses. When Hugh of Cluny founded the convent of Marcigny in around 1055, he forbade the entrance of women under twenty, since that was a lascivious age. Similarly, Lanfranc, Archbishop of Canterbury (1070–89), asked Abbot Anselm to pay special attention to his young nephew, a novice at Bec, because he was of an age when men are 'tormented by many and diverse titillations of the flesh, both inwardly and outwardly'. Others, such as Peter Abelard (1079–1142), expressed fears that young monks could pose a danger to older brethren, with whom they might form 'vice-prone' attachments.[27] Consequently, the behaviour of novices was closely scrutinized, to the extent that in some houses they were forbidden even to go to the latrine alone, instead being accompanied by the novice master and a third monk to act as a witness.[28]

The cloister was a place of relative safety, but many thousands of priests lived in a world full of temptation. Gerald of Wales recommended that a man who had vowed continence could live only with women who were closely related to him and thus were above suspicion, but even that was best avoided. It was also wise to avoid looking at women.[29] The saintly Robert de Béthune, Bishop of Hereford (1131–48),

> was wont never to fix his eyes on a woman. For he had read that he who so fixes his eyes is the abomination of the Lord. He nowhere presumed to sit or speak alone with a woman except in the presence of appointed companions, not even in confession or any secret matter.[30]

His successor at Hereford, Thomas Cantilupe (1275–82), similarly avoided female company. From his youth he would draw his hood over his face when a woman passed, and as bishop he refused even to meet with his own sisters. Contact with women was dangerous for two reasons: first, because a cleric might fall prey to lust, and second, because medieval optical theory suggested that gazing on an object would cause the onlooker to absorb some of the properties of that object – in this case, the sexual corruption inherent in all women.[31]

As well as removing sources of temptation, many tried to make their bodies less susceptible to lust. It was partly for this reason that regular phlebotomy, which was thought to reduce the amount of semen produced, was practised in most religious houses.[32] Diet was another very important consideration, since gluttony was thought to lead directly to lechery – especially for men. According to Gerald of Wales, 'since the stomach and the genitals are so close together, we ought to mortify the one in order that the other may not be wanton.' Overeating warmed the genitals, and also (once the excess food was digested) provided the raw material for the production of semen. A cleric who wanted to remain celibate would thus be well advised to eat and drink in moderation, and to subsist mainly on the cold foods that 'impede, repress and thicken semen and extinguish lust', such as fish, certain vegetables and cold water.[33]

The majority of religious men and women probably used such practices in moderation, being regularly bled and eating sensibly, and hoped that this would be enough to keep them chaste. The most devout, however, embarked on programmes of extreme devotion and asceticism that were intended to focus the mind on spiritual matters and to tame the body into complete submission. Some fasted almost to the point of starvation; this was one of the strategies adopted by Christina of Markyate (c. 1096–c. 1155) when she was tempted by Roger, the male hermit with whom she lived.[34] Immersion in cold water was another popular practice, especially among religious men, who believed that it would cool the heat of their bodies and thus suppress their sexual urges. At Rievaulx Abbey in Yorkshire, Abbot Aelred (d. 1167) had a special underground chamber, which filled with water from hidden streams, constructed for this purpose. When he was alone, he would 'immerse his whole body in the icy cold water, and so quench the heat in him of every vice'.[35] His contemporary Godric of Finchale (c. 1065– 1170) went even further. This hermit lived on roots and leaves, sometimes supplemented with excessively dry, rough and tasteless bread, and fasted for up to six days at a stretch. He chopped wood while wearing a hairshirt and a heavy mail tunic, slept on sackcloth with a stone for a pillow, and frequently threw himself naked into the brambles. On snowy nights, he would strip off and immerse himself in the River Wear, offering up tearful prayers and consoling himself with the thought that his earthly suffering was nothing compared to the torments he would experience in Hell.[36]

One final, unlikely response to the challenge of celibacy was bedsharing. From a modern perspective, the late medieval practice of senior clergymen sharing their chambers, and even their beds, with junior clerics in order to prove they were not guilty of sexual misconduct seems rather problematic, since this surely created an environment that was favourable to same-sex activity.[37] This, however, was a relatively low-risk strategy compared to the approach favoured by Robert of Arbrissel (c. 1045–1116), the unconventional founder of Fontevraud Abbey, who was allegedly in the habit of sharing his bed with his female followers. He apparently saw this as 'a new form of martyrdom', an ascetic practice through which he could demonstrate his ability to overcome temptation. But Abbot Geoffrey of Vendôme, the correspondent who recorded his unconventional behaviour, was understandably sceptical, warning him of the dangers of female company, and pointing out that no one was so secure in his faith as to be immune to falling into sin. Moreover, he cautioned, there was a serious risk of scandal: even if Robert did manage to avoid sin, many who heard the rumours would assume that he had failed to keep his vows.[38]

Those Who Failed

If Robert of Arbrissel's behaviour provoked rumours, many other religious men and women unambiguously failed to keep their vows. Few flouted the rules quite so blatantly as Jean de Heinsberg, Bishop of Liège (1419–56), who reportedly had 65 children.[39] But, according to one estimate based on records from around the turn of the sixteenth century, somewhere between 45 and 60 per cent of the clergy in Brabant were fined for sexual

A lewd hermit embraces a miller's wife, from a 14th-century Book of Hours (British Library Yates Thompson MS 13, f. 177).

offences at some point in their careers.[40] Despite the prohibition of clerical marriage, it is clear that many priests continued to have sex, and even to form long-term partnerships, long after the papacy forbade them to do so.

Attitudes to such relationships varied across Europe. In England celibacy had apparently become the norm even among the parish clergy by the thirteenth century. This did not mean that all clerics were celibate – a 1397 Hereford visitation in which 14 per cent of clerics were charged with sexual misdemeanours shows that a relatively high proportion were not – but this was nevertheless a significant shift from a world in which most were married.[41] The Register of Eudes Rigaud, Archbishop of Rouen (1248–75), which documents his many visitations and thus gives a detailed picture of clerical sexual conduct over a period of more than a quarter of a century, suggests a similar shift in attitudes. Priests were reasonably frequently accused of concubinage, or of having relationships with married women, but they were dealt with quite firmly by the ecclesiastical authorities. In January 1248 the deanery of Longueville was home to at least ten incontinent priests, several of whom had fathered children; at least two were guilty of adultery with married women. On this occasion they were rebuked and warned to mend their ways or face severe punishments.[42] But Archbishop Eudes also uncovered some truly scandalous behaviour. In November 1254 Richard, rector of Nesle, was summoned to respond to accusations of affairs with both his nephew's wife and his own sister; unable to prove his innocence, he was obliged to submit to an unknown punishment.[43] In January 1257 the Bishop of Lisieux was ordered to investigate (and if necessary punish) a canon who had allegedly participated in the brutal gang rape of a woman who was throttled so violently that she died shortly afterwards.[44]

In contrast, more relaxed attitudes to clerical concubinage prevailed in the south, and consequently the practice was seemingly more common. In fourteenth-century Italy, both Church authorities and lay people tended to turn a blind eye if priests were involved in consensual sexual relationships with single women, although this did not mean that priests' families were universally accepted. There were cases in which women lost their homes and access to their children on the basis of neighbours' testimony, while the children of priests were legally defined as the worst type of bastards, and could not be legitimized. There may also have been significant regional variations: in Bergamo, for example, references to concubines in clerics' wills were heavily veiled, whereas in Treviso some priests openly made their concubine their heir.[45]

In the Iberian Peninsula, where religious reformers were generally far more concerned with interfaith mixing, papal pronouncements on clerical celibacy were widely ignored until well into the fifteenth century.

Across the region, parishioners were used to seeing priests with long-term partners and children – men such as Pere de Quintana, the rector of Sant Vincenç de Maia, who lived with Ermesenda de Comba and their eight children, and Guillem Mul, a priest who cohabited with a woman named Ferrera for more than 25 years.[46] Some clerical couples even took marriage-like vows: the rector Jaume Ferrer and his concubine Jaçmeta swore on the Gospels, before the altar of his church and in the presence of witnesses, that they would never forsake each other, and he also pledged to provide for her.[47] Episcopal authorities sometimes fined priests for keeping concubines, even doing so repeatedly. Bernat Mola of Calonge and his concubine Berengaria Rotlana were penalized on at least five occasions between 1329 and 1345. Although Bernat did pay some fines, there was a pattern of officials reducing or pardoning them, and no evidence that more serious sanctions were ever imposed, or even threatened.[48] Overall, it is hard to avoid the impression that the authorities were not trying to eradicate concubinage, but simply to prevent flagrant misbehaviour while augmenting their own coffers. Moreover, clerical sexuality only seems to have provoked complaint from parishioners if it was in some way troublesome – if, for example, a priest took advantage of virgins or pursued married women. Concubines were widely accepted unless they behaved in an indecorous fashion or caused conflict in the community.

Even monks sometimes formed long-term relationships: at Sant Joan de les Fonts, the prior kept a woman named Ermesenda, and refused to comply when the bishop told him she must go. According to the other monks, the elderly pair spent much of their time reading in the kitchen.[49] This relationship was clearly about much more than sex: there is something rather touching about this image of a long-term couple keeping each other company in their old age. Some of the behaviour uncovered when William Alnwick, Bishop of Lincoln (1436–49), visited religious houses in his diocese was rather less heart-warming. Dorchester Abbey, near Oxford, was the subject of some particularly colourful accusations, although in some cases the monks involved were able to clear their name. In 1441 the problems went right to the top: the abbot was alleged to have at least five lovers, all of them married women, whom he supported with the goods of the house. Several of his subordinates were equally dissolute. Brother John Shrewesbury had been caught having sex with a woman in the bell-tower; 'in fear and fright', he hid her in a chest. Thomas Tewkesbury had a private chamber in which he played chess and entertained women, including his long-term mistress Margaret Heny. Walter Dorchester had impregnated two married women, and the husband of one had to be given a large pension to stop him killing Walter. The bishop forbade the canons, on pain of excommunication, to allow women into the abbey, and placed limits on their movements outside. But, despite these sanctions and the appointment of a new abbot, a 1445 visitation revealed similar problems.[50]

Religious women were also prone to sexual failings, with close relationships between holy women and their male spiritual advisors subject to particular scrutiny. At the end of the thirteenth century, Ida of Louvain's closeness to a Dominican friar led to rumours of pregnancy, which the Dominican chapter took seriously enough to send a medical expert to ascertain whether she was still a virgin. Since the said expert seemingly believed that it was possible to tell if a woman was pregnant simply by looking at her, the verdict was perhaps not wholly reliable.[51] Nuns were quite often accused of immoral conduct, and some convents were persistently problematic. Eudes Rigaud visited the priory of St Aubin in 1256, 1257, 1261 and 1263, and on each occasion found serious problems. Among the troublesome residents was Agnes of Pont, who was sent to the leper house at Rouen in 1256 as a punishment for arranging another nun's assignations, and providing her with an abortifacient potion – which apparently failed, since the woman concerned was pregnant with a chaplain's baby when she left the convent shortly afterwards. Alice of Rouen was temporarily deprived of the veil in 1256 because of her persistent fornication, but managed to give birth to at least three children (doing a penance imposed by her abbess on each occasion) before finally leaving the convent, and being forbidden to return, in the early 1260s.[52]

Similar problems were found in Italian convents. In the late 1360s Jentadona de Collionibus, a well-born nun, lived in her convent rooms with a canon of Bergamo Cathedral. According to witnesses, their relationship lasted for at least five years; they openly retired to bed together, and had three daughters, who were publicly acknowledged by their father and their maternal grandmother. Jentadona remained a nun until her death in 1387, and eventually became abbess of Santa Grata. At an episcopal visitation of the convent of San Blasio in 1420, several nuns reported that Sister Retorica de Padua was having a relationship with Johannes, the priest who served at their altar. Several nuns recalled waking up one night and realizing he was with Retorica in her dormitory bed, and one of the sisters testified that she had found them having sex on a chair in the kitchen. On that occasion the priest had fled wearing only his shirt. While Retorica admitted her guilt, her lover denied it – and despite her confession, there is no evidence that either was punished.[53]

Yet such colourful cases should not lead us to assume that such behaviour was the norm, or that it was condoned. Based on visitation records from mid-fifteenth-century Lincolnshire nunneries, Eileen Power estimated that approximately 5 per cent of nuns were guilty of immoral behaviour; the vast majority kept their lifelong vow of chastity. Eudes Rigaud's Register similarly suggests that more than 95 per cent of individuals who took religious vows remained celibate, or at least did not get caught breaking their vows.[54] Despite the popular stereotype of the naughty nun, records suggest that more monks than nuns were accused of sexual misconduct, and that there were differences in the nature of the relationships they formed. Nuns usually had liaisons with clerics, who were often the only men with whom they had any close contact, and were less likely to be accused of multiple relationships, whereas monks typically had relations with laywomen, and were often serial offenders.[55]

Moreover, nuns (and monks) who committed sexual sins could be harshly punished, especially if they were repeat offenders. A nun who absconded might be excommunicated until she made submission and returned to the nunnery; a repeat offender could be sent to a different house to do penance. Nuns could also be imprisoned within the convent, given penances (fasting, barefoot processions, beating, reciting particular devotions), excluded from chapter meetings and deprived of office.[56] The most problematic individuals could be permanently expelled: in 1346 the Archbishop of York told the prioress of Nunappleton not to receive back a nun called Margaret, who had left the convent pregnant, as she was a repeat offender who had done the same on multiple occasions.[57] Although poor leadership within institutions was often a problem, some took a harsher stance on sexual immorality than the bishop: in 1414 the prioress of Rothwell refused to comply with an episcopal mandate to receive back a nun called Joan, who by her own confession had lived with William Suffewyk for three years.[58]

Overall, however, it is hard to form an accurate picture of the sexual behaviour of the medieval clergy. Stories of blatantly immoral conduct have an innate appeal to both medieval onlookers and modern historians, and have consequently received a vastly disproportionate amount of attention. Much of our information about sexual behaviour comes from visitation records, which are inherently problematic sources. Since they largely report accusations, they were heavily shaped by jealousy, power struggles and other internal quarrels; consequently, at least some of the claims presented were entirely false. The increase in such visitations (and also in associated record-keeping) towards the end of the Middle Ages also gives a false impression that standards were declining; in reality, ever-present problems simply became better documented.

A further complication is the age-old tendency of the Church to try to cover up sexual scandal, a topic with which it has long been preoccupied.[59] Such concerns were surely behind Eudes Rigaud's decision to 'privately warn' the abbot of Valment to 'try to conduct himself in such a way that he might be able to restore his reputation, which had been somewhat impaired by the vice of incontinence'.[60] Similarly, in late fifteenth-century Paris, concern about the relationship between Georges Tastevya and his concubine Pierrette seems to have focused less on the fact that they were having sex, and more on the fact that their public rows ('after many words between them, she pulled out his testicles or pulled them so that blood flowed') caused scandal.[61] The obsession with scandal probably explains why cases of pregnant nuns and promiscuous monks are found in relatively large numbers, while same-sex relations and child abuse within institutions are rarely recorded. Perhaps this reflects real-life trends, but more likely it reflects the fact that internal misconduct could be hushed up, whereas a new baby or a band of angry husbands could not.

Certainly the case of Heinrich of Rheinfelden, a theologian suspected of making sexual advances to lay workers in Basel's Dominican monastery, contains uncomfortable echoes of more recent Church cover-ups. In 1416 the city council investigated rumours about his behaviour. Several witnesses were questioned, but as a cleric he was not obliged to answer to the secular authorities. Among the accusations against him were claims that he had exposed himself to workers, and asked others to do the same; touched a workman's penis, and asked the man to touch his; and encouraged workers to discuss their sexual exploits with women. The men had been reluctant to speak out against their superior, and no witness testified to intercourse (although there were obvious reasons not to, since this would lead to prosecution). The secular authorities decided there was clear evidence of 'sodomitical depravity', and presented their case to the bishop's court – but those who wanted a cover-up, claiming that the testimony of an 'honourable and pious man' must be believed, ultimately won. Heinrich left the city for a few years, but later returned and remained a member of the Dominican order.[62]

Cases such as Heinrich's reflect some of the more disturbing aspects of medieval clerical sexuality: the frequency with which unscrupulous clerics abused their privileged positions, for example, as well as the Church's willingness to hush up such failures for the sake of appearances. But, like many of the stories in this chapter, it is also a tale of human frailty, which reflects the tremendous suffering caused by a policy that demanded a level of sexual purity not easily achievable by mere mortals. Those who were not gifted with natural aptitude, or aided by divine intervention, were prone to fail, and the clergy were not alone in this. The laity, as we shall see in the next few chapters, had a similar tendency to fall short of the high standards demanded of them.

SIX

Immoral Behaviours

In a world in which sexual morality was such an important concept, many people must have found themselves engaging in immoral behaviours. Those who got caught doing so faced not only the disapproval of their peers, but the imposition of (sometimes harsh) punishments by the secular or ecclesiastical authorities.

Fornication

In 1300 John, son of Nicholas, and his girlfriend Julia Rede were publicly punished in Droitwich town centre. Both were repeat offenders, and both had confessed their sin, and so they were 'whipped once in the usual way through the market', even though she was pregnant.[1] Their offence was fornication (that is, sex between two unmarried people), which was generally seen as the least serious of the sins of the flesh – but, as they found out, this did not mean that it was treated lightly, or that it went unpunished. In 1495 alone, 66 men and 24 women were cited for fornication in the London Commissary Court.[2] Besides offending God, it caused social disorder and had consequences far beyond the individuals involved.[3] Young people who were caught having premarital sex were a source of great shame for their relatives, especially in the honour cultures of Catholic Southern Europe. When Giacomello Bono was tried for fornicating with Nicolina, the niece of a Venetian master craftsman, the court said that he acted 'in contempt of God and with dishonour for modesty, shame and clear contempt of Master Blasio, her uncle'. Such concerns were not limited to social elites; when Stegano Bucio and Caterina eloped in 1326, her mother and brother (both poor Slavic immigrants) brought the case to the authorities. And when Marco Menego had a relationship with Antonia, he acted 'not fearing God and holy justice and as a result not holding in awe the state and with contempt for modesty and manifest infamy . . . dishonouring and defaming Pasqualino, the father of the said

Antonia, and Cabrina her mother'. He was imprisoned for three months and required to pay a large fine.[4]

Similar concerns were at play in much of Scandinavia, where fornication was effectively treated as a property crime. As an infringement of the rights of the woman's kin, it was punishable by fines payable to them. A woman who committed this offence risked forfeiting her property, unless she was over eighteen, and having the relationship to protest at her family's failure to find her a husband. Nevertheless, the penalties were not always financial. On the Swedish island of Gotland, a law code of about 1220 stated that if a couple were caught fornicating, the man would be locked up, and his kin had to pay a fine. If they could not or would not do so, his hand and foot would be amputated.[5]

This was a particularly harsh system, but fornicators across Europe were subject to the sorts of corporal punishment dished out in the Droitwich case. There was also the risk that family members would take matters into their own hands. In thirteenth-century England, a distinguished knight named Godfrey de Millers crept into John the Briton's house in the middle of the night, hoping to have sex with his daughter Olive. But the girl, fearful for her reputation, had revealed the plan and Godfrey was violently assaulted, then hanged from a ceiling beam and castrated. This greatly angered Henry III, and those who took part in the attack were exiled – although the victim and her mother were later pardoned. On the king's order, it was proclaimed that 'no one should presume to mutilate the genitals of an adulterer, except in the case of his own wife.'[6]

Others escaped with financial sanctions, among them Fabian of Heilsberg, a student at the University of Kraków. In 1479 the university council fined him

> for a certain abominable deed, which he committed publicly in the presence of many students or lay persons. While he was taking a woman to the Vistula River, he touched and held her shamelessly and undressed her; once in the river he fondled the nude woman, thus scandalizing many students and lay persons.[7]

In the English manorial system, lords could demand legerwite, a payment for fornication that was mostly imposed on female villeins who had been convicted in the ecclesiastical courts. These courts imposed fines that were effectively paid by the lord (because these unfree peasants did not own their own property), and legerwite was a way of recouping his costs. It was most often demanded from young single women, thanks to both double standards and concerns about bastardy. In practice, it was quite rarely imposed: in the Lincolnshire village of Ingoldmells, there were fifteen payments between 1291 and 1315.[8]

Milder penances were given to fornicating couples who agreed to marry, which partly explains why so many cases ended with a wedding.[9] Thus John Esyngwald and Elizabeth Snawe of York, who were accused in February 1399, presented themselves as husband and wife and exchanged vows in court.[10] But not everyone who got together in this way lived happily ever after. Joan Chylde and Thomas Rote appeared in court in London in 1472, charged with fornication, and contracted marriage in the presence of the authorities; a year later she was back in court, suing him for breach of promise.[11] Other couples could not be persuaded to marry, but the man could still be made to take responsibility for his illegitimate offspring. In 1451 Gherem Borluut, a son of one of Ghent's patrician families, impregnated Lysbeth van der Steene, but when pressed to marry her he refused, because she was his social inferior. So the city aldermen ordered him to pay a lifelong annuity to her instead.[12]

Social concern about fornication is reflected by the steps people took to prevent it happening, and to ensure that it was punished when it did. In late medieval London constables and beadles could enter houses to arrest suspects, aiming to catch them in the act. Yet most of the allegations considered by the courts came from community members, who reported each other either directly to the court, or to the priest or churchwardens. One afternoon in August 1471 John Palmer went to Horne Tyler's house, where he found William Stevenes and Juliana Saunder having sex. She tried to buy his silence with a pair of hose, but he reported them to both Church and City officials. In Walthamstow, John Gosnell confronted Richard Heth 'because it was publicly said that Richard too suspiciously frequented the home' of Gosnell's neighbour Agnes Waltham. John wanted to know if Richard intended to marry her, and was told that the couple were indeed man and wife. This did not satisfy John, who insisted they must make public vows immediately.[13] Their interventions surely caused resentment, but Palmer and Gosnell were not sanctioned for interfering in their neighbours' sex lives. In contrast, those who allowed fornication to take place in their house could also find themselves in trouble. In 1491, Buckinghamshire couple John and Alice Godyng appeared in the Church court accused of allowing their son Thomas to have illicit sex with an unnamed woman. They denied this, purged themselves, and the case was dismissed, but many others were fined for similar offences.[14]

If the Godyng case reflects the expectation that parents should stop their unmarried children engaging in illicit relationships, employers also had responsibility for the sexual conduct of those who lived under their supervision. Female servants and enslaved women were a particular focus of concern, as illustrated by late thirteenth-century Venetian regulations that banned men from having sex with other men's slaves, and stated that servant women could be branded, whipped and banished for bringing a sexual partner into their master's house. Such punishments make clear that the chief concern was the woman's value to her master, not her safety.[15] The sex lives of apprentices were similarly closely scrutinized, and indentures often included clauses regulating sexual conduct. In theory, both boys and girls were bound not to commit fornication anywhere, but in practice female apprentices seem to have faced tighter controls than their male counterparts. In 1360s York, William of Lincoln was bound not to fornicate within his master's house, not with the daughter, wife or maidservant, or to visit brothels. But in London, just under a century later, Eleanor Fincham was bound not to commit fornication 'in any way at all'.[16]

Adultery

Medieval attitudes to adultery were, unsurprisingly, closely linked to medieval ideas about marriage, which gained considerable importance in the twelfth century when it was made a sacrament. This made insufficient regard for wedding vows a serious problem, and adultery something that demanded a serious response.[17] Consequently, it was an offence that was frequently punished: in 1495 alone, 220 men and eighty women were cited for adultery before the London Commissary Court. Even the wealthy were not spared scrutiny: those accused included high-status individuals such as Lewis Caerleon, a royal physician presented for adultery with his maidservant in 1491.[18] It was also an offence that could result in severe punishments, and not just for the couple involved. A woman named Marina was caned and banished from Gradec in 1432 for allowing adulterers to meet in her house.[19]

Under certain legal systems adultery was a capital crime, and some people were executed for having extramarital sex. The 1348 statute book of the German city of Zwickau includes an illustration of two adulterers bound face-to-face, impaled, and then buried alive. In this case it is unknown whether such punishments were actually carried out, and it is interesting (perhaps even suggestive) that the condemned pair are respectably tidy, whereas the executioners are wild-looking.[20] Cases in which the adultery was aggravated by another offence were probably most likely to lead to a death sentence. In late thirteenth-century Bologna, Floriana ran away with a man called Tegna. When her husband reclaimed her, her lover threatened him with a lance. Tegna was beheaded, because 'it is a foul thing and a bad example to commit adultery with other people's wives and because of it to want to blind their men.'[21] In Slavonic cities, death was the standard punishment until the fifteenth century, when it was reduced to banishment plus corporal punishment. In 1432 Margaret, a tailor's wife from Gradec, was bound on the 'horse' (a triangular torture device that could seriously damage the genitals), branded on the face with a hot iron, caned and expelled from the city. Her lover was given the same punishment, minus the branding.[22] Elsewhere, common punishments included castration and, for women, nose-slitting.[23]

Public beatings were a particularly common punishment, although they were not deemed suitable for all offenders. During the course of a late thirteenth-century Canterbury visitation, Thomas de Marynes, a married knight, was found to have several mistresses. One of the women, Agnes Soppestre (with whom he had had a nine-year relationship, and two children), was sentenced to 'be whipped five times through the marketplace and five times round the church in a chemise as is customary', but since it was 'not seemly for a knight to do public penance' her lover had to pay twenty marks to the local poor.[24] One punishment particularly associated with adultery was running, in which the guilty pair were stripped naked, tied together at the level of the genitals, and flogged through the streets. The surviving law codes that recommend this as a punishment (the majority of which date from the twelfth and thirteenth centuries, and from Spain and southern France) make clear that this should be the only penalty imposed on the couple. Moreover, while the public nature of the punishment made it both deeply humiliating to the guilty pair and an

'The Parade of the Adulterers', from *The Customs of Toulouse* (1296)
(Bibliothèque municipale d'Agen, MS 42, f. 39).

effective warning to others, it was not supposed to exclude people from normal social interactions within their communities.[25]

In contrast, some jurisdictions favoured ostracism, in the form of banishment, as a punishment. In 1413, for example, the bailiff of Beveren (East Flanders) banished Eleinne, wife of Jacques Martin, for a year because of her affair with Clais Lammyn. The authorities condemned her 'repudiation' of her husband, who was restored to honour at the request of 'several good people' in the village.[26] Prison was another possibility: in 1390, when a Venetian woman called Antonia committed adultery with a young painter, they were both sentenced to three months in jail.[27] In late fifteenth-century Ghent the punishment was supposed to be two weeks' imprisonment on bread and water, but enforcement seems to have been patchy, and most offenders probably did penance and paid a small fine.[28]

Indeed, from the thirteenth century onwards it was often possible to avoid public humiliation by paying a fine.[29] For example, a Provençal lawcode from the 1230s required all adulterers to undergo a nude beating through the town, or pay a 60 shilling fine.[30] The sums involved varied considerably, dependent on date, location and the details of the offence. In Orvieto (c. 1300), the standard fine was 200 libra, roughly a year's wages for a skilled mason. Yet Clara, a low-status single woman convicted of adultery with Berzono, a married public crier, was fined five times more, because she had supposedly used 'evil things and enchantments' on her lover.[31] As well as or instead of paying a fine, a woman could lose her dowry. This was standard practice in Venice from the 1360s, at which time increasing numbers of women were being punished for this offence.[32]

The existence of this female-specific punishment, in combination with the Venetian tendency to discuss adultery as if a wife was her husband's property, raises an important question about medieval attitudes: how far was there a gender-related double standard? Some legal approaches were certainly tilted in favour of the husband, to the extent that a few jurisdictions allowed a man to determine the fate of both his wife and her lover. Unsurprisingly, the wife's opinion was not sought if the circumstances were reversed. Others simply imposed distinctly unequal punishments. In Cuenca, an adulterous wife was to be flogged and run out of town, after which her husband could repudiate her and remarry (contrary to canon law), whereas an adulterous husband would only be flogged.[33] In thirteenth-century Scandinavia, the ecclesiastical authorities imposed fines for adultery – but a woman might forfeit all her property, whereas a husband only had to pay three marks to his wife for each lapse. In a particularly extreme case, under Danish law, only a woman could commit adultery. A husband who had sex with another woman was classed as a fornicator.[34]

Yet, contrary to popular belief, it was very rare for adulterous wives to be either murdered or sent to a convent. Although canon lawyers discussed at length the possibility of monastic enclosure as a punishment, the handful of real-life cases concerned high-born women who were also accused of killing (or at least trying to kill) their husbands.[35] Nor did canon law permit a husband to kill his adulterous wife or her lover, although a few secular law codes (most of them from the earlier half of our period, with notable examples from Norway and Spain) disagreed.[36] Even in the fifteenth-century Burgundian Netherlands – a cosmopolitan and relatively permissive society – adultery was seen as a source of humiliation and dishonour for the betrayed husband, and it therefore seemed understandable that he would want revenge. If he killed the lover, his uncontrollable anger might be cited as grounds for appeal against a sentence of death or banishment. The authorities were most likely to be sympathetic if there were aggravating factors such as a public scandal or an illegitimate child. If the wife's lover was a friend of the husband, that was also seen as a mitigating circumstance, as in the case of Ywain Voct. He and Jean were like brothers, but Jean betrayed his friend's trust by having a four-year affair with his wife. Eventually the deceitful pair ran away together, taking most of Ywain's moveable goods with them. In response, Ywain killed Jean. He was pardoned for his crime, and his honesty was contrasted with Jean's dishonesty.[37]

By the end of the Middle Ages, however, lost honour was rarely accepted as justification for murder. In France, truly spontaneous crimes of passion were sometimes pardoned, but there is no evidence that the authorities were particularly sympathetic to betrayed husbands. Even if letters of remission were granted, they usually replaced the death penalty with another serious punishment, rather than giving an absolute pardon. When, in 1456, Jehan de Punctis killed his wife Séguine, he claimed that his actions were justified by her frequent infidelities, and the striking resemblance between her daughter and one of her supposed lovers. The defence (supported by her mother and sister) responded that Séguine's adultery was unproven, but also emphasized the seriousness of uxoricide, especially when it was clearly premeditated and had deprived her children of a mother and killed her unborn baby. The court found against de Punctis, who was sentenced to death, and ordered Masses to be said for his victim's soul.[38] Four years later, Simon Šterk of Gradec was banished for two years because he cut off his wife's nose after she committed adultery. A few years after his return, Šterk was killed by his own lover's husband; the adultery was not considered to be a mitigating circumstance in the murder.[39]

Sampling of late medieval court records from northern France suggests that adulterous men, not women, were often the main target: in Arras (1328), five times as many men were fined for adultery, and in Tournai (1470) fourteen times as many men were punished. In late medieval Ghent, Bruges and Ypres, the ratio for adultery convictions was approximately 80:20 male to female.[40] The reasons behind these striking figures are complex, probably including a preference for dealing with female adultery privately to avoid shame, and the fact that fewer women wanted to (or dared to) commit adultery. However, it is also possible that courts genuinely found male adultery highly offensive. Contemporary ideas about marriage and gender suggested that men were supposed to set an example of sexual restraint, and to control their wives. Arguably, a married man who committed adultery sinned more than a married woman, because he should have been better able to resist temptation. If a man's wife strayed, he should have controlled her better, so he was more at fault than her.[41]

Surprisingly, male conduct was quite frequently blamed for women's extramarital relationships. The French theologian Jacques de Vitry (*c*. 1170–1240) wrote that much female adultery resulted from 'sadness and desperation' provoked by male drunkenness and violence. Such ideas had real-life impact: one father in the Massif Central negotiated a settlement in which his son-in-law's long absences from home were blamed for his daughter's infidelity.[42] Despite considerable concern that female adultery would leave husbands unwittingly raising other men's children, courts could be surprisingly lenient in their treatment of pregnant adulteresses. When Paolo, a Venetian carpenter, accused his wife Maria of having sex with many men, she was sentenced to four months in prison and lost her dowry. The Council of Forty nevertheless ruled that Paolo must raise the child his wife was expecting, since there was no firm evidence to contradict her assertion that it was his baby.[43]

Nor was male adultery necessarily condoned, or even empathized with. Philippe de Deux Vierges, lord of Montpeyroux, was sentenced to death for seducing a barber's wife, although this was subsequently reduced to a large fine. The barber's lawyer cited the lord's marriage to a beautiful woman who had borne him several children as an aggravating factor; there was no need for him to have a mistress and a wife.[44] Having an affair could seriously damage a man's reputation, as several cases from fifteenth-century London illustrate. When Thomas Hay was accused of adultery, witnesses reported that many people (not just his wife) turned against him, while William Boteler's rumour-mongering about John Stampe and Joan Folke left the 'status and good fame' of both parties 'greatly injured'. After Alexander Marchall was imprisoned for adultery, the executors of his wealthy father's will tried to block his inheritance, due to his serial philandering and other vices.[45]

This surprising near-equality between the sexes strengthened towards the end of the Middle Ages, as authorities increasingly promoted reconciliation. This new emphasis on forgiveness grew out of a firm belief in the indissolubility of marriage, plus an increasing recognition of the power of love, which was quite frequently mentioned in fifteenth-century adultery cases. When, for example, Angelo Vignati of Venice ran off with a builder's wife, the court noted that 'at that time Agnesina ... loved this Angelo and Angelo loved her.' Love was seen as a mitigating factor, but also as something that would pass, allowing the damaged marriage to be repaired.[46] As reconciliation rather than renunciation became the norm, public punishment became problematic: if the couple was going to stay married, it was arguably better to handle things discreetly, usually with a fine or simple penance. Some husbands even complained that the punishments given to their unfaithful wives were too harsh, such as the man from Toulouse who in 1398 objected to his wife being sentenced to running.[47]

When couples reconciled, they were often obliged to reach a formal settlement, which placed conditions on both parties. In December 1347, Bishop Hamo of Rochester handled the case of Henry Cook and his wife; they had separated because of her scolding, and his cruelty and repeated affairs. They swore to live amicably; he promised to treat her with marital affection, on pain of a severe penalty.[48] A century later, Jean and Maria Maupou of Avignon were reconciled after she confessed to a string of infidelities, as well as stealing money from her husband. She had to pledge to be a good wife, to serve her husband and not to betray his trust, but he had to treat her 'humanely, honestly, benignly and peacefully'. In Castile such documents had to include a promise from the husband that he would not harm his wife.[49]

Despite social and legal pressures, some couples could not be reconciled, and very occasionally adultery was cited as grounds to end a marriage. In 1496 the archdeacon of Buckingham's court granted Roger and Elizabeth Calaber a separation due to her adultery and drunkenness. Although this was not a divorce in the modern sense, and neither could remarry, they were freed from cohabitation and the marital debt.[50] Since such suits highlighted a man's embarrassing inability to control his wife, they were not casually pursued, and it was arguably more shameful still for a woman to initiate such a process. Only a brave few did so, among them Londoner Alice Hobbys. After learning that William, her husband of twenty years, was a serial adulterer and habitual user of prostitutes, she stopped paying the marital debt and started legal proceedings.[51]

Of course, many affairs remained concealed: as *Las Siete Partidas*, a mid-thirteenth-century Castilian law code, acknowledged, 'Men and women who commit adultery endeavour to do so secretly, as far as they are able, in order that it may not be known and cannot be proved.'[52] Some canon lawyers even argued that staying married was so important that a woman might justifiably conceal her affair, or her child's paternity, to avoid spousal violence and marital breakdown.[53] In some cases families may have colluded to conceal illicit relationships, perhaps especially those concerning high-status women: in late medieval Venice and Orvieto, for example, most of the women accused were from poor or middling families, although this may in part be because noblewomen's lives were so strictly controlled that it was virtually impossible for them to have extramarital sex.[54]

Not everyone was discreet: in London, Cecily Bower's troubles began with her own ill-advised boast that she had borne a priest's child with her husband's knowledge.[55] But most illicit relationships were revealed by a third party, often the betrayed spouse, who may have conducted their own investigations. It was, for example, believed that placing a lodestone under a woman's pillow would reveal the truth: if she was faithful, she would embrace her husband, but if not she would leap out of bed in fright. Another strategy was to place a piece of paper inscribed with the names of the Seven Sleepers between a sleeping woman's breasts, forcing her to name her lovers.[56] Alternatively, a suspicious spouse might emulate one Mrs Haslopp of Whitechapel, and take direct action. She seized a ladder, climbed up it, and looked into her husband's chamber, where he was in bed with his mistress.[57]

Some proceedings were triggered by pregnancy or suspicious behaviour; Agnes Johnson was accused of adultery with Roger Clerk in 1470 after she was seen drinking with him in a London tavern.[58] Others were 'notorious' (that is, there was widespread gossip about them), and so the authorities investigated, even trying to catch suspects in the act. In 1310 a burgher of Figeac complained to the Parlement de Paris that the abbot's bailiff had dragged him naked from his bed in the middle of the night, beaten him and locked him up. The bailiff defended his actions, saying that the burgher had been found naked in bed with a married woman, and Parlement accepted his account. It also upheld the judgement against a married man and a widow who had been dragged from her house, beaten, imprisoned and fined; they claimed to have been dining with the man's wife, but it was seemingly common knowledge that they had been having an affair for at least two years, despite repeated warnings.[59]

Some legal systems insisted on official testimony to avoid false and malicious accusations. In twelfth-century Agen, for example, an adulterous couple had to be caught in the act by the bailiff and two other officials, and could only be arrested if they were found naked, the man with his trousers down.[60] *Las Siete Partidas* also emphasized the necessity of proof, and allowed only close male relatives to accuse a woman of adultery, in order to prevent marriages being 'made the subject of scandal by the accusation of some strange man' when the family wanted to keep their dishonour quiet. Moreover, the code placed time limits on when an accusation could be made (within five years, unless force was involved), and added various other caveats. If a woman could prove that her husband had condoned or encouraged her adultery, then she and her lover had not committed a crime, and if a man allowed his adulterous wife back into his home and bed, then he was considered to have pardoned her and could not complain. If a man had sex with a woman who had concealed her marital status from him, she would be punished but he was not guilty; if a woman genuinely but falsely believed that her husband was dead and so remarried, she had not committed adultery.[61]

This last clause highlights the fact that although 'adultery' usually meant the same in the Middle Ages as it does today, definitions have shifted somewhat. In 1351, for example, a Provençal court dealt with Almodia, who, unhappy in her first marriage, had contracted another. Having no jurisdiction over bigamy, which was handled by the ecclesiastical courts, the court simply condemned her as an adulteress and gave her an unusually large fine. If she could not pay, she would be flogged through the streets and then permanently exiled, under pain of having her foot amputated.[62] Conversely, adultery was sometimes prosecuted as a different crime, usually abduction. In an early fourteenth-century case, Richard Mareschal was accused of kidnapping the wife of Stephen of Hereford, a capper, and stealing his goods. It is clear that the pair were actually having an affair: when Stephen went to the Winchester fair, his wife invited her lover over, and then hid him in a chest when the neighbours came to investigate. Richard was ultimately acquitted, because although the woman had left, there was no evidence that she had gone with her lover. Eventually (through the woman's pleading and 'ecclesiastical coercion') husband and wife were reconciled.[63]

Incest

If medieval approaches to adultery were complicated, attitudes to incest can seem downright contradictory. According to the English theologian William of Pagula (d. 1332), a man who masturbated should be told 'that in doing this he sins more than he would by having sexual relations with his mother or sister'.[64] Such pronouncements, along with a plethora of literary stories of accidental incest between long-lost relatives, have created the assumption that medieval people were untroubled by incest. On the other hand, according to Hostiensis, a leading thirteenth-century canon lawyer, incest was one of the worst sexual sins, nearly as grave an offence as sex with a nun, or priestly fornication.[65] John of Reading saw it as proof of post-Black Death social and moral chaos, claiming that 'in many places brothers took their sisters to wife', and even incest was considered 'as a game rather than a sin'.[66] Caesarius of Heisterbach used the story of a woman who gave birth to her son's child, but whose genuine penitence earnt her papal absolution, as proof of the marvel of God's kindness, which could forgive even the gravest sins.[67]

Incest was much more broadly defined in the Middle Ages than it is today, including the extended family but also the family of anyone with whom an individual had had sex, and their spiritual relations (that is, people connected through baptism).[68] The inclusion of so many non-blood relations strongly suggests that concern was not linked to the dangers of inbreeding, which are almost never mentioned by medieval writers. Instead, incest was seen chiefly as a spiritual issue, as an extreme form of lust, and was classified as a branch of that deadly sin. The key difficulty, then, was the risk that such relationships posed to the souls of those involved, and punishment therefore focused on contrition and penance. The gravity of the problem is reflected in the fact that incest was one of the few sins that could not be handled by a parish priest, but had to be referred on to the bishop, or even to the Roman Curia.[69]

Nevertheless, the evidence suggests that the rules were sometimes ignored or manipulated, at least in the case of marriages between distant relatives. Some even suspected the aristocracy of deliberately marrying distant relations, knowing that such unions would not be prevented, but could easily be annulled if necessary. This is not to say that society was completely untroubled by the rules. The man who, as he lay dying in 1462, fretted about his son's marriage, years earlier, within the prohibited degrees, was probably something of an anomaly. Nevertheless, in some jurisdictions, including England, most of the incest cases that ended up in court involved distantly related married couples who had presented themselves, wanting to ensure the validity of their union.[70] Bishop Trefnant's visitations of the parishes in the Hereford diocese, conducted in 1397, uncovered several such unions, all reported by parishioners. For example, in the small village of Brinsop, Thomas Simmonds and his wife Matilda were accused of 'cohabiting illegally', since Matilda had slept with his cousin in the fourth degree, Sir William, before her marriage.[71]

Fortunately for such couples, the ecclesiastical authorities were often willing to provide dispensations for those related in the third and fourth degrees of affinity. When Pope Alexander III (1159–81) considered the sheriff of Exeter's longstanding marriage, which was within the prohibited degrees, he decided that the union should be allowed to stand, on the grounds that 'it is more tolerable to leave some people married in contravention of the laws of man than to separate those who are legitimately married, in contravention of the laws of God.'[72] In 1351 the Bishop of Worcester remarried a couple who had married illicitly and without banns because the man was godfather to the woman's son by a previous marriage. Their defence was that it was a time of pestilence, and he knew no one else he could marry.[73] An aristocratic Icelandic couple, þorkleifur Björnsson and Ingveldur Helgadottír, who had married and had children despite being related in the fourth degree of consanguinity, received a papal dispensation in the 1470s, on the condition they confess to the Bishop of Skåholt and do penance.[74]

Nevertheless, many ecclesiastical writings (including theoretical legal discussions) seem strangely preoccupied with incest between distant relatives, to the exclusion of the relationships between close kin that would concern us today. This trend has led some historians to suggest that medieval people were untroubled by close incest, preferring to simply conceal it rather than shaming whole families. On the other hand, it could be that such relationships were so obviously taboo that there was no need for them to be interpreted by lawyers.[75] If third cousins married, there was some room for doubt: might it not be better to let their union stand, even if technically it broke the rules? But sex between siblings, for example, was so clearly wrong that there was no need to discuss it.

Certainly this seems to have been true in mid-fifteenth-century Cambrai and Brussels, where officials known as promoters were employed to catch incestuous couples – a task in which they were aided by rumour and denunciations, since local synodal statutes threatened lay people who concealed such relationships with excommunication. At least 150 cases came to court in this way: none related to siblings or first cousins (suggesting that those rules were widely understood), and most involved distantly related couples or those whose affinity was based on illicit intercourse. It seems that the rules on third- and fourth-degree relationships and non-blood ties were less widely understood, or perhaps less respected.[76]

Similarly, the fact that penitentials often ask broad questions about incest, but make detailed enquiries about sex with distant relatives, is revealing. Thus Robert of Flamborough asked:

> Have you slept with a blood relation? Say how many times, and
> what relation she was to you . . . Have you slept with two women

related to each other by blood? . . . Have you slept with women after male relatives of yours? . . . Have you slept with the mother of your godchild? With your own godmother? With your father's goddaughter? With your godfather's daughter?[77]

The structure of these questions suggests that people knew they should confess to nuclear family incest, but needed more guidance on less obviously problematic relationships. The existence of a hierarchy of sin is also reflected by the penances given. Late medieval Swedish synodal statutes, for example, listed first-degree incest among the most serious sins, requiring fifteen years of penance, whereas incest in the fourth degree needed a mere six.[78]

Further indication of social attitudes to incest comes from secular law codes, which often suggest harsh punishments. *Las Siete Partidas*, the law code promulgated by Alfonso x of Castile (r. 1252–84), described incest as 'a very great sin . . . committed by a man who knowingly lies with one of his female relatives within the fourth degree, or with a female related to him by affinity, the wife of a relation of his within the same degree'. The punishment for non-marital incest was death, whereas those who married within the prohibited degrees could face forfeiture of office/property, banishment and/or public scourging, dependent on social rank.[79] In Sweden first-degree incest (that is, a parent and child, or a parent and child both having a relationship with the same person) was one of the serious sexual crimes over which the secular authorities sought to assert their jurisdiction from the fourteenth century – a development that sometimes led to conflicts between secular and ecclesiastical authorities. In the 1490s, for example, Gudmund Gers, of the parish of Kemiö, confessed to incest with his stepdaughter, and was granted absolution, along with the necessary penance. But Gers claimed that he and his property were nevertheless being harassed by the secular authorities over this offence, and asked the local bishop to intervene on his behalf.[80]

Gers's offence was one that troubled medieval people much more than it would modern society: today a relationship between a man and his adult stepdaughter would be legal if distasteful, but in the fifteenth century Gers's marriage to the woman's mother created spiritual kinship between the pair, rendering the subsequent relationship deeply wrong. The adulterous relationship between Olav Steinsson and his sister-in-law, Hilda Petersdaughter, who were similarly related in the first degree by marriage, was problematic for the same reasons and was treated by the papal curia as an incest case, although in 1474 the pair were granted absolution. Nor is there any evidence that Steinsson was troubled by the secular authorities, who theoretically could have outlawed him and confiscated his property.[81]

Nevertheless, some of the tiny number of cases found in the surviving court records involve nuclear family incest of the sort that is still widely condemned. In Durham, the episcopal court of Richard Kellaw (1311–16) investigated two such cases. In the first, Isabella, wife of Nicholas Surteys, was accused of adultery and incest with her brother Thomas; the case had come to the attention of the authorities through public rumour.[82] In the other, Ranulph de Neville was cited to do penance, having been found guilty of incest and adultery with his married daughter, Anastasia de Fauconberg; when he failed to appear, he was excommunicated.[83] In the 1450s the Venetian authorities handled an incest case involving a goldworker and his daughter, 'a young girl and a virgin before she was deflowered'. He was sentenced to ten years in prison followed by perpetual banishment; if he returned, he would be beheaded.[84] Svein Igulsson of Stavanger, whose case was heard in Rome in 1476, had 'repeatedly by the act of incest and fornication had sex with his own daughter', about whom nothing is known. He was certainly imprisoned for a period and excommunicated, but ultimately received papal absolution for his crimes, and was dispensed to 'remain with his wife in order to render and claim the conjugal rights'.[85]

Incestuous relations often came to light when another, usually pregnancy-related, crime was uncovered. Jehan Faudier of Eu, Normandy, was executed in 1453, having admitted to the repeated rape of his daughter Marion. When she became pregnant, he and his wife forced her to take an abortifacient potion. His confession implicated his daughter, who was threatened with imprisonment over the abortion, although she later received a royal pardon.[86] Incest also appeared in infanticide cases, including two French examples in which the girls concerned received royal pardons. In 1382 Annette de Bousseau, a sixteen-year-old who was pregnant by her brother, threw her baby into a neighbouring garden. Denisette Bierarb, a fourteen-year-old impregnated by her stepfather, gave birth alone and drowned her baby in the privy, saying the words of baptism as she did so, in an attempt to hide her circumstances from her pregnant mother.[87] Although this unfortunate girl's attempt at concealment was doomed to fail, many more cases must have remained completely secret, or else been dealt with through the confessional, thus leaving no trace.

Bestiality

In contrast to the complexity of medieval ideas about incest, the verdict on bestiality was unambiguous, being determined by contemporary attitudes to animals. Christian thinkers typically saw sex as a field in which the distinction between humans and animals could (and should) be clearly emphasized. Reason set humans apart from the animals, and sex was dangerous because it caused them to lose reason – and therefore to become animal-like – but humans could set themselves apart in their manner of copulation. This meant having sex face-to-face, preferably in the missionary position, rather than face-to-back, which was bestial behaviour and therefore unfitting for humans. Albertus Magnus also suggested that, while animal sex was often 'loud and noisy', human sex should be quiet, because humans are 'discreet, rational, prudent, and bashful'.[88]

Even worse than having sex like an animal was having sex with an animal. This was explicitly forbidden in Leviticus 18:23, which stated that 'You shall not lie with any beast and defile yourself with it, neither shall any woman give herself to a beast to lie with it: it is perversion.' Nevertheless, in early medieval Europe bestiality was considered to be a relatively minor offence, roughly equivalent to masturbation – especially when it was committed by young bachelors, who did not have a legitimate outlet for their sexual urges. Then, over time, the gravity of the sin increased. By the eleventh century it was ranked as an unnatural act, alongside same-sex intercourse and masturbation; by the thirteenth it was widely considered to be the worst sexual sin a person could commit.[89]

Heightened disgust resulted in increased concerns about the blurring of human-animal boundaries, and a growing sense that they needed to be reinforced. Whereas earlier approaches had worked on the assumption that the animal involved was essentially an object, later medieval animals were more likely to be seen as lustful, willing participants in the act. Such concerns developed in parallel with (and were not unconnected to) fears about demonic sexuality, for demons occasionally appeared in animal form, usually as a dog or goat. There were also concerns that some animals could 'mingle with humanity and create offspring'. Consequently, bestial acts took on a new character of menace, becoming inextricably linked to heresy and the Devil.[90]

Growing repugnance inevitably led to increased efforts to punish offenders. In the eleventh century Norway introduced laws that forbade men to have sex with animals; anyone who did so 'destroys his rights as a Christian' and would be castrated and outlawed.[91] In thirteenth-century Castile, *Las Siete Partidas* punished bestiality by executing both the human and the animal involved – the latter because it was necessary 'to blot out the remembrance of the act' – while a Swedish law of 1442 stated that 'If the fiendishness should occur to a man to mix with a domestic animal or other senseless creature . . . they must not live upon the earth.'[92] The idea that the animal must also be punished was a common one, in both legal and confessional writings, and was repeatedly linked to the idea of memory. Thomas of Chobham (*c.* 1158–*c.* 1233) required a penitent who admitted to bestiality to do penance for fifteen years (twenty if married), in addition to going barefoot for life, never entering a church and permanently abstaining from fish, meat and intoxicants. But he also insisted that the animal involved must be killed, burnt and buried, to erase the memory of the offence.[93]

Despite heightened levels of concern, most medieval courts seem to have paid greater attention to same-sex acts, and records of real-life cases of bestiality are few and far between. A thirteenth-century Premonstratensian lay brother from Orte was convicted and buried alive, alongside the animals he had defiled.[94] Several fifteenth-century Majorcans were executed for bestiality, and in 1466 the Parlement de Paris condemned a man and sow to be burned for the same offence.[95] The Venetian court register includes the curious case of Simon, an artisan accused of having carnal relations with his goat. He claimed as extenuating circumstances that 'he had not been able to have sexual relations with a woman or masturbate for more than three years due to an accident.' He was examined by a team of physicians and surgeons, who found that he was able to have an erection, but 'he has a defect in his testicles which leaves him little sensation and as a result he can neither emit sperm nor be healed.' The judge also required two of the city's prostitutes to 'do numerous experiments' in order to test Simon's claims. He was labelled a sodomite, but the medical evidence meant that he escaped the death penalty. He was instead branded, beaten and lost a hand. The fate of the goat is unknown.[96]

The relative leniency extended to Simon reflected not only his physical handicaps, but the widespread belief that men had a biological need to have sex. If the only way a man could achieve release was by fornicating with his relatives or with his livestock, then it seemed, within the framework of medieval medicine, almost inevitable that he would do so. This did not mean that medieval people condoned such behaviour, as the vast numbers of people punished for having illicit sexual relations demonstrate; even less egregious acts, such as fornication or adultery, were sins, and must be condemned for the good of both the individuals involved and the communities in which they lived. Nor were these the only activities of which both society and the authorities disapproved, for this was a world in which there were many 'wrong' ways to have intercourse – including with a member of the same sex.

SEVEN

Defying Sexual Norms:
Positions and Partners

U ncovering sexual non-conformity in the Middle Ages can be a challenging and depressing task: prevailing attitudes meant that so-called deviant behaviour was often concealed, and when it was uncovered those involved usually ended up in court. Occasionally, however, potential evidence is found in surprising places.

Defining Deviance

Turkish workers restoring the Arap Mosque in Istanbul in 1913 broke through its wooden floor and discovered the remains of the medieval church of the Dominican Friars of Galata. Among the treasures they uncovered was a large medieval tombstone dedicated to the memory of two medieval English knights. The memorial shows the helmets of the two men, facing each other and touching at the visor, almost as if kissing; underneath, their shields are impaled (that is, slightly overlapped), just like those of a married couple. The two men were Sir William Neville and Sir John Clanvowe, and they died within days of each other in October 1391.

The close bond between the two men is further attested by the Westminster Abbey Chronicle, which claimed that Clanvowe's death

Caus[ed] to his companion on the march, Sir William Neville, for whom his love was no less than for himself, such inconsolable sorrow that he never took food again and two days afterward breathed his last . . . These two knights were men of high repute among the English, gentlemen of mettle and descended from illustrious families.[1]

Although unusual, the Istanbul tombstone is not unique. A late fourteenth-century memorial brass in the chapel of Merton College, Oxford, jointly commemorates John Bloxham and John Whytton, who are depicted side-by-side and with a shared inscription.[2] Wills provide further evidence for men requesting burial with or near to other men: the 1499 testament of William Jekkes, priest of Salle (Norfolk), requested his burial in that church, near to his friend and fellow priest Simon Bulleyne.[3] From a modern perspective these cases seem easy to interpret: surely only a couple would be buried and commemorated together? Yet caution is necessary. Medieval culture allowed for other forms of male intimacy that no longer exist, notably sworn brotherhood (a ritual process in which men took a religious oath).[4]

Similarly, much has been made of claims that Richard 1 of England shared a bed with his French counterpart – behaviour which, to the modern mind, is almost certain proof of a sexual relationship. Yet such an interpretation rests heavily on the projection of modern practices and perceptions onto the distant past. For high-status medieval men, bed-sharing often had more to do with politics than sex, and the same was true of other intimate gestures such as kissing and handholding. Such behaviours served as tokens of peace or reconciliation, and as demonstrations of alliance and favour. Consequently, while some men certainly did have sex with their male bedfellows, we cannot automatically assume that this was always the case.

The picture is further complicated by the fact that we tend to think of sodomy (if we use the word at all) in terms of sex between men. Medieval sodomy, on the other hand, was about acts rather than identities, and encompassed all forms of non-normative and/or non-reproductive sexual relations. It could be committed by two men, but also by a man and a woman, two women, or an individual. Essentially, sodomy was anything abnormal – an extremely broad category in a world in which 'normal' sex involved two people of the opposite sex copulating in the missionary position. Normal sex was something a man did to a woman in order to have children, and was therefore something that upheld gender norms and social order. Any deviations from this norm threatened to undermine both.

One of the most vehement medieval critics of sodomy was the Italian monk Peter Damian, who in 1049 wrote a long letter to Pope Leo ix. In it he railed against the increasingly common sin of sodomy and urged the pope to do something to tackle it, especially with regard to the clergy. He claimed that those who committed this sin were often allowed to be ordained or to remain in office, even though such a priest ruined his flock because he could not intercede with God on their behalf and was unfit to perform the sacraments. How could it be right, he demanded, that a priest who had sex with a nun should be deposed, but not one who had sex with a monk?[5] He claimed that there were 'four varieties of this criminal vice.

There are some who pollute themselves; there are others who befoul one another by mutually handling their genitals; others still who fornicate between the thighs; and others who do so from the rear.' He considered the last two to be graver sins than the first pair, with anal sex being the worst of all; group masturbation was worse than the solo variety.[6] He also claimed that a man's lust for another man was clearly unnatural, since animals did not act in this way. And yet, he complained, 'dissolute men have no fear of doing what dumb animals indeed abhor.'[7]

Peter Damian's focus on clerical sexuality meant that he was particularly preoccupied by men's behaviour, but other authorities provided much broader definitions and identified further 'unnatural' practices. According to the the thirteenth-century French friar William of Peraldus, sodomy could be committed 'in terms of the manner' (that is, in a forbidden position) or 'in terms of the substance, when someone sees to it or has consented that semen be spilled elsewhere than in the place allotted by nature.'[8] Thomas Aquinas' definition of 'unnatural vice' provided further details:

It may happen variously. First, outside intercourse when an orgasm is procured for the sake of venereal pleasure; this belongs to the sin of self-abuse, which some call unchaste softness. Second, by intercourse with a thing of another species, and this is called bestiality. Third, with a person of the same sex, male with male or female with female ... Fourth, if the natural style of intercourse is not observed, as regards the proper organ or according to other rather beastly and monstrous techniques.[9]

Many authors are infuriatingly vague about exactly what these 'beastly and monstrous techniques' might entail, but confessional writings can be used to reconstruct a provisional hierarchy of positions. In order of increasing wrongness, most agreed, were:

1 Woman on back, man on top (that is, the natural position)
2 Side by side
3 Sitting up
4 Standing
5 Woman on top
6 Like animals, with the man behind.[10]

The reasons why a couple had sex in an unnatural position were also important in determining the gravity of their sin. William of Rennes, a

'The Sins of Sodom', including same-sex relations and masturbation, are depicted unusually explicitly in this 14th-century picture Bible (British Library Egerton MS 1894, f. 11).

thirteenth-century theologian and canon lawyer, posed the question, 'Does a man sin mortally if he knows his wife not in the customary manner even though he performs the act in the proper orifice?'; to which his answer was yes, if he was merely seeking greater pleasure. If, however, the non-standard position was justified by illness or pregnancy, then it was not a mortal sin so long as there was no improper use of the genitals or spilling of seed – although abstinence was a better option.[11] Positions in which the woman went on top of the man inverted the gender hierarchy, and were also problematic in biological terms. This type of sex, it was argued, might prevent conception, since gravity would make the man's seed flow back out of the woman's womb. Anything that hindered procreation was, of course, inherently sinful.[12]

Such deviant acts had consequences not just for individuals, but for society as a whole. The *Practijke Criminele* (the standard treatise on criminal law and procedure in fifteenth-century Burgundian Flanders) classed sodomy as an offence against the state, and against both divine and public order.[13] According to the *Christenspiegel* (1485), a devotional book for laypeople written by the Franciscan observant Dietrich Kolde, the consequences of this sin included the Great Flood and a 5,000-year delay in the birth of Christ, as a result of God not wanting to expose His son to sodomites; he also claimed that all sodomites were killed on Christmas night. The punishments were still ongoing:

This is the sin, because of which God punishes the world every day
. . . God hates this sin more than all other sins . . . This sin takes
away all inwardness from a person and brings him to despair and
every kind of worldly harm, and God punishes this sin with an
early death and later with eternal death.[14]

Masturbation and Other Unnatural Acts

Tracing the history of masturbation is unsurprisingly difficult, given that it
is an overwhelmingly private practice. Compared to later centuries, it seems
to have provoked relatively little concern, at least in part because medieval
legal systems (both secular and ecclesiastical) were preoccupied with more
blatant flaunting of norms. Solitary vices, which were hard to uncover and
hard to prove, were more likely to be dealt with in the confessional, or by
the individual conscience.[15] This is not to suggest that medieval society
was unbothered by masturbation; indeed, some authorities even claimed
that it was worse than incest. As the Italian jurist Antonius de Butrio
(1338–1408) put it: 'If he has foully touched his own member so that he has
polluted himself and poured out his own semen, this sin is greater than if
he had lain with his own mother.'[16] Religious texts sometimes included
cautionary tales about self-pleasurers. The Flemish theologian Thomas de
Cantimpré (1201–1272) recounted several such stories, including one (supposedly shared with him by the Bishop of Lausanne) about a man who
reached between his legs to indulge in his usual vice and found a snake
in place of his penis.[17]

A particularly probing and frank approach to such activities is found
in Jean Gerson's *On the Confession of Masturbation*, which required the
confessor to ask detailed questions about solitary sexual activity. According
to this early fifteenth-century guide, the questioning might begin, 'Friend,
do you remember when you were young, about ten or twelve years old, if
your rod or virile member ever stood erect?' Anyone who replied in the
negative was clearly lying, since this happened to all youths, and must
therefore receive further warnings and questions; these should continue
until he admitted not only that he had sinned in this way, but how often
and for how long. Gerson was particularly concerned about teenage boys,
who he thought so prone to masturbation that the usual concerns about
giving people ideas did not apply here. (The association between masturbation and teenagers seems to have been a strong one, and not just for
boys. Albertus Magnus wrote that, from the age of fourteen, girls 'often
rub themselves with their fingers or other instruments'.[18]) Confessors,
parents and teachers must all warn the young against masturbation, and

drill into them the importance of confessing to such acts if they did occur. But, despite his preoccupation with youthful sin, Gerson also recognized that adults were susceptible to both committing and concealing this vice. Consequently, they too must be asked about it in confession.[19]

The exception to this confession-based approach was when masturbation occurred within the context of male-male sexual encounters that came to the attention of the authorities. At his early fourteenth-century trial, Arnaud de Verniolles testified that a youth called Guillaume Roux had asked him, 'Do you want me to show you what a man can do when he wants to have sex with another man but doesn't have the chance, so he can satisfy his own lust?' Guillaume added that he frequently took his penis in his own hand and rubbed it in order to satisfy his lust, and offered to show Arnaud how it was done. But the older man was uninterested, or so he claimed.[20] The level of legal interest in such activities varied considerably. In Venice, even at the height of the panic about male-male sex, there was little interest in prosecuting masturbation. Thus Andrea Coppo, a nobleman who in 1471 was accused 'of agitating his virile member most evilly in the presence of Marino, a goldworker', went unpunished once it was established that there had been no physical contact between the men.[21] But in late fourteenth-century Munich, Heinrich Schreiber was sentenced to death after confessing to mutual masturbation with several other men, and Johannes Rorer of Strasbourg, a bathhouse owner, was executed in 1400 for mutual masturbation with Heinzmann Hiltebrant, a carpenter.[22]

Overall, while there is plenty of evidence that the Church worried about masturbation, there is relatively little evidence that real medieval people pleasured themselves. The same is true of other forms of sexual experimentation, so that we can do little more than speculate about what went on in the average medieval bedroom. When doing so, we should remember that this was a world in which entire families lived in a single room, in which many couples shared a bed with their children, and in which buildings were often insubstantial enough to allow neighbours to peak through cracks in the walls; in other words, privacy was a rare commodity for all but the wealthiest members of society. These practicalities, along with the influence of hostile religious and social attitudes and a lack of exposure to the media through which we now gain much of our sexual knowledge, perhaps combined to make sexual experimentation less common than it (apparently) is today.

Nevertheless, it is clear that at least some people knew about the sort of sex that was very much not sanctioned by the Church. The fifteenth-century *Mirror of Coitus*, a vernacular medical treatise by an anonymous Catalan author, claimed that there are five ways to copulate. In the first way the man and the woman lie down together. In the second way they lie on their sides. The third way is seated. The fourth way is on their feet, and in the fifth way – which is the most common form of coitus – the woman lifts her legs and rests them on the man's buttocks and the two become tightly entwined.

He proceeded to describe no fewer than two dozen variations on these five basic positions, including 'the man lies down and the woman mounts him, resting her legs on his thighs' and 'the woman kneels face down on the bed and the man enters her from behind while embracing the sides of her buttocks.'[23]

But how far does this relatively obscure text reflect medieval attitudes and behaviour? Some astrologers argued that an individual's future sexual practices were determined by the position of the stars at the moment of his conception: for example, if Venus was in a certain position when a male was conceived, he would grow up to prefer sex with the woman on top.[24] This was probably the most commonly discussed non-missionary position, and even the Church allowed that there might be certain circumstances (including advanced pregnancy) that justified it. It was often presented in a humorous manner in literary texts such as 'The Monk's Punishment', a fourteenth-century German verse-story in which an ignorant young cleric receives his sexual initiation at the hands of a more experienced woman. The following morning, the worried monk asks his servant:

'I have often heard that when a man and a woman have been together, children are born. But tell me, by your faith, which of the two bears the child?' 'I will tell you everything,' replied the servant. 'It's the one underneath.' 'Woe is me', thought the monk, who was starting to realise the extent of his misfortune. 'Alas,' he said to himself, 'whatever can I do? What a disaster! I was the one underneath. I'm going to have a baby!'[25]

In mid-fifteenth-century Dijon, neighbours claimed to have seen Jeanne Saignant, a brothel-keeper, having sex standing up; she apparently also had a penchant for watching what was happening in the rooms of her house. The witnesses denounced her as the personification of lasciviousness and perversion, and professed to be scandalized by her behaviour. Still, unless they occurred within the context of prostitution (and overall there is very little evidence for prostitutes engaging in 'unnatural' acts), opposite-sex deviations from the officially sanctioned norms were extremely unlikely to end up in court.[26]

The one exception to this was anal sex, which was widely regarded as a particularly serious offence, and was thus harshly punished. A 1493 protocol from Fribourg referred to anal sex as 'the true sodomy, that is to say, from behind', and suspects of both sexes similarly seem to have viewed this as the most serious transgression.[27] The vast majority of court cases involving anal sex involved men, although several cases of such opposite-sex sodomy are recorded in late fifteenth-century Venice. In most, the husband was absolved, but in 1481 Giovanni Furlan, a fisherman, was beheaded and cremated for his 'frequent sodomy with his own wife'.[28] Testimonies against men accused of sex with other men sometimes included claims that the accused had also practised this vice with women. In 1482 the anonymous Florentine informant who accused Bartolomeo di Niccolò of sodomizing a young cleric reported that he had a wife, 'but she doesn't live with him because he used her from behind'. Another informer said that the wife of Benedetto Sapiti, a 'very great sodomite', had left him because she refused to let him sodomize her.[29]

Some practices that are now relatively common are very rarely mentioned in the Middle Ages, to the extent that we might reasonably assume that they were rarely practised – notably oral sex. It may be that this seemed especially repugnant to a society that associated the upper body with God and morality, whereas the lower body was linked to filth and sin. To bring the mouth into direct contact with the genitals was thus to sully an organ made for better things. On the other hand, interfemoral intercourse appears to have been far more popular (and continued to be so well into the early modern period).[30] It may have been used by opposite-sex couples as a form of contraception, but the surviving descriptions mostly relate to same-sex relations. According to the Italian philosopher Pietro d'Abano (*c.* 1257–1315), this was the favoured method of men who had sex with men, whom he describes as:

> those who exercise the wicked act of sodomy by rubbing the penis with the hand; others by rubbing between the thighs of boys, which is what most men do these days; and others by making friction around the anus and putting the penis in it the same way as it is placed in a woman's sexual parts.[31]

His claims are supported by the legal record. In 1357 the Venetian gondolier Nicoletus Marmanga and his apprentice Johannes Braganza were sentenced to death by burning for having intercourse 'against nature'.

According to Johannes's testimony, they had had sex more than twenty times; on each occasion Nicoletus had 'shoved his member between his thighs from in front' until he ejaculated.[32] In fifteenth-century Venice, Benedicto, a government herald, admitted having had interfemoral intercourse with a Saracen many times, many years ago.[33]

The records from the fourteenth-century trial of Arnaud of Verniolles hint at one possible reason why some men had sex in this way. He allegedly believed that sex between men was only a serious sin if 'a man lay on top of another man like a woman or committed the sin through the rear', and while he confessed to interfemoral sex with several men, he fiercely denied that he had ever engaged in anal sex. The testimony of one of his sexual partners, a sixteen-year-old student named Guillaume Roux, who described how Arnaud had, on several occasions, 'thrust his penis between the speaker's thighs', provided support for his claims.[34]

Men with Men

Although such cases demonstrated that there were numerous ways in which two men could have sex, medical and religious authorities were chiefly preoccupied with anal intercourse. According to medical theorists, there were two key reasons why certain men enjoyed this practice. The first explanation was biological: some men had physical defects that made them especially prone to this vice. Most men enjoyed sex with women because it provoked the expulsion of superfluities via the pores in their penis, but in some men these openings were obstructed. Consequently, their superfluities were expelled through anal pores, and rubbing these gave them pleasure. There was, most experts held, no cure for these unfortunate individuals.

The second, much larger category consisted of those who had no physical abnormalities, but became habituated to sinful practices as young men.[35] Bernardino of Siena (1380–1444), a popular Italian preacher, was convinced that sodomites were not born, but made, with parents often to blame. He warned that many boys knew about sodomy by the age of seven, and were already predisposed to it by the time they reached puberty. Some learnt from fathers who were themselves sodomites, others from overhearing casual 'chatter about sodomy and lewdness'. As boys grew older and began to experiment, parents tended to take a boys-will-be-boys attitude, rather than intervening and making them confess. Indeed, some exacerbated the problem by dressing their sons in immodest clothing that made them more appealing to sodomites, so that they were in danger of being raped in the streets. In Bernardino's view, mothers who dressed up their sons in order to satisfy their own vanity were effectively pimps; he further suggested that some parents were happy to let powerful men sodomize their sons, so long as they received money and favours in return, while others kept quiet because they feared scandal. While some of those defiled in their youth later rejected this sin, others became life-long sodomites who justified their behaviour by saying that all the leading men did the same. Once a youth had taken to this vice, only force could cure him, and a man who was still a sodomite by his early thirties was a lost cause.[36]

To Bernardino, as to many of his contemporaries, a man who was of marriageable age and unhampered by ill health or holy orders, but who remained unwed, was automatically suspect. In 1421 the Florentine government went so far as to ban unmarried men between thirty and fifty years old from holding civic office, almost certainly in an attempt to promote marriage and to bar sodomites from such roles.[37] A man's appearance could also raise suspicions that he was a sexual deviant. Orderic Vitalis (1075–*c.* 1142) claimed that William II's court was full of 'foul catamites' who 'shamelessly gave themselves up to the filth of sodomy'; they 'ridiculed the counsels of priests and persisted in their barbarous way of life and style of dress'.[38] A few decades later, Alain de Lille (*c.* 1128–1202) criticized those unnatural men who favoured 'womanish adornments', styling their hair, shaving off their beards, and wearing tight tunics and shoes.[39] According to physiognomers, physical characteristics could also identify sodomites. A black circle around the pupils and a small, slightly stub nose with an incision in the lower part running towards the tip of the nose were both supposed to indicate a tendency to deviant sexual practices. In addition, the effeminate (that is, the passive partner) was 'drooping-eyed and knock-kneed; his head hangs at his right shoulder; his hands are carried upturned and flabby; and as he walks he either wags his loins or else holds them rigid by effort; and he casts a furtive glance around.'[40]

While there is no clear evidence to suggest that this sort of theory was used to identify and persecute sodomites, there was a strong sense that their actions needed to be punished, both for the good of the individual (it was wise to try to prevent young males becoming habituated, and to make sinners repent in order that they might be saved) and for the sake of society as a whole. For one thing, sex between men threatened gender norms. Until the mid-twelfth century, close bonds between men had often been depicted without much awkwardness or embarrassment, but after this there was a growing need to emphasize that their connection was not erotic, but spiritual.[41] At the same time, loving (and wanting to have sex with) women developed into a key part of male identity; a man who seemed uninterested in the opposite sex would automatically be suspected of sodomy, and not seen as a proper man. The love triangle (in which two men fall for the same woman) became one of the few acceptable ways of depicting male intimacy, with the friends' interest in the woman proving they were not sodomites.[42] Fears grew that men's loyalty to each other could undermine their loyalty to Church and state; by placing suspicion on male intimacy as sexual, loyalties could be redirected to their proper focus.[43]

The case against sodomy was also a practical one, especially during the post-Black Death demographic crisis, when many regions needed high birth rates to increase their depleted populations: this vice was, some argued, the reason for Tuscany's demographic crisis.[44] Sodomy was seen as an internal enemy to be beaten; it threatened the natural order of things, as ordained by God and upheld by the secular and ecclesiastical authorities, and thus repressing it helped to maintain social order and political control.[45] The thirteenth-century Spanish law code *Las Siete Partidas* explained that male-male sex must be prevented because

> it is something which causes great grief to God, and a bad reputation results therefrom, not only to those guilty of it but also to the land where it is permitted . . . Every man should avoid this offence, because many evils arise from it, and contempt and ill fame attach to the person who commits it. For on account of offences of this kind Our Lord God sends hunger, pestilence, tempests, and innumerable other evils on the country where they are committed.[46]

In a law passed in 1418, the Florentine government stated its desire to 'root out the vice of the sodomites and Gomorrhans, contrary to nature itself, for which the anger of the omnipotent God is incited in terrible judgements not only against the sons of man, but against the country and against inanimate objects'. The 1436 sentence of a sodomite from the same city explained that punishment was necessary: 'In this way the city and its upright citizens may be freed from all commotion, wars ended, plague abolished, enemy plots curbed, and cities turned toward good government and praiseworthy conduct.'[47] Around the same time, the Venetian authorities ordered a crackdown on sodomy on the city's ships, fearing that the sin might lead God to destroy their fleets; the city was terrified that it might share the fate of Sodom and Gomorrah.[48]

Such hysteria was fuelled by religious rhetoric. The German abbess Hildegard of Bingen provided a particularly vivid explanation of why sodomy was a problem:

If a man is together with a woman during his ejaculation of semen, he will pour his semen into the right place, similar to someone putting cooked food from a pot into a dish so that it can be eaten. If, however, he is not with a woman but with another being that is contrary to him in nature, he sordidly ejaculates his semen into the wrong place, similar to someone taking cooked food from a pot and pouring it onto the floor.[49]

Some theologians, such as the French Dominican William of Peraldus thought that it was wrong even to speak of sodomy; an anonymous fifteenth-century sermon went further, and said that 'one should not even think of this sin.' It was widely believed that even demons felt shame when confronted with sodomy.[50] But others believed that, as Jean Gerson put it in his apologetic introduction to his treatise on masturbation and sodomy, 'the obscenity of the subject matter and the words' were justified by the need to teach remedies.[51] In the late 1420s Bernardino of Siena preached a series of sermons against sodomy in several major Italian cities. He spoke at a time when attitudes to men who had sex with men were hardening: the authorities (especially in Italy) were increasingly keen to punish them, and prosecution rates were high. In a Lenten sermon delivered in Florence in 1424, he exhorted his audience: 'Whenever you hear sodomy mentioned, each and every one of you spit on the ground and clear your mouth out well.' And, with a noise that 'sounded like thunder', the crowd spat on the floor.[52]

Although attitudes to male-male sex were consistently hostile throughout our period, the intensity and impact of this hostility varied over time and by region. In the broadest terms, legal efforts against sodomy increased towards the end of the Middle Ages, and were most intense in the south of Europe. The English displayed a striking lack of interest in this vice: there was no secular law against it until the reign of Henry VIII, and only a handful of cases appeared in the ecclesiastical courts. The lack of prosecutions was matched by a lack of high-profile accusations. For example, although many chroniclers openly disapproved of the relationship between Edward II and his probable lover Piers Gaveston, only one explicitly claimed that their relationship was sexual.[53]

Elsewhere there were very few accusations of sodomy at a popular level before the late thirteenth century, when several regions subject to Roman civil law (including parts of Italy and Portugal) prescribed death by burning for convicted sodomites. The earliest known execution of a male sodomite in the Holy Roman Empire was in 1277, when Rudolf I of Habsburg, king of the Romans, sentenced a lord of Hapisperch to burn for committing the 'sodomitical vice'.[54] Many towns north of the Alps experienced their first sodomy prosecutions during the fifteenth century; for example Hermann von Hohenlandenberg, a Zurich nobleman of poor reputation, was sentenced to death in 1431 for having sex with several male adolescents. The numbers of prosecutions in these regions were far lower than in Italy, although northern cases were far more likely to lead to the death penalty. In Basel there were only eight legal proceedings relating to sodomy (or attempted sodomy) between 1399 and 1449. Five of the 388 death sentences issued by the council of Zurich during the fifteenth century were for same-sex acts, and 26 sodomites were executed in Brussels during the same period.[55]

Hardening attitudes may have been linked to wider political and social upheaval, which led to an increased preoccupation with the regulation of public morality; the Black Death, which was sometimes viewed as a divine punishment for sin, may also have fuelled concerns about sexual deviancy.[56] Nevertheless, levels of prosecution and punishment were not consistent over time, and some cities experienced relatively short-lived panics provoked by particular events. In the summer of 1484, for example, a secret committee of thirteen 'clever gentlemen' was entrusted with investigating 'the unspeakable dumb sin' in Cologne. The investigation was sparked by a priest's report to the city council; he claimed that a dying musician had confessed to committing sodomy with 'a rich and respectable man'. The council took spiritual advice, and was warned to keep quiet: investigations would only give other young men ideas, and risk conflict within the city. But they decided to set caution aside, and soon the committee members began to interrogate priests. A few refused to reveal the secrets of the confessional; others claimed to know nothing on this matter. Some, however, admitted that they had heard similar confessions – from both men and women – and several expressed their belief that sodomy was a growing problem in the city. The committee also received information from anonymous denouncers and from young men who claimed to have been the target of attempted assaults by high-profile men.[57]

Particular cities and regions (including Bruges and Venice) were more persistently focuses for concern, but nowhere was so strongly associated with sodomy as Florence, to the extent that in Germany sodomites were often known as 'Florenzers'.[58] How far this reputation was deserved is largely unknowable, but men who had sex with men were certainly pursued with great enthusiasm by the city authorities. In 1325 they issued a set of statutes that prescribed castration for a man who sodomized a boy, and allowed local people to beat foreigners caught abusing youths without fear of punishment. Even composing or singing songs about sodomy became punishable by a small fine. In 1365 the law was changed to allow sodomites to be burnt to death, although conviction rates remained low for the next few decades, with most relating to rape, child abuse or serial offenders.[59] In the fifteenth century attitudes hardened, and Florence's ruling class came to see sodomy (by which they chiefly meant male-male sex) as one of the most serious problems facing the city. In 1432 the Office of the Night, a judiciary magistracy solely dedicated to this crime, was set up. It operated until 1502, and over these seven decades around 17,000 individuals were incriminated at least once (since first offences were not usually punishable by death, there was a high level of repeat offending). Nearly 3,000 were convicted, at a time when the population of Florence was only around 40,000.[60] Other Italian cities had similar institutions: in Venice a special subcommittee of the main criminal court was dedicated to apprehending sodomites, while Lucca had the Officers of Decency. But the prosecution rates were much lower: only 268 men were convicted in the much larger city of Venice between 1426 and 1500, and just eight sodomites were executed in Ferrara between 1440 and 1520.[61]

The Office of the Night was comprised of laymen, who had to be married citizens over 45 – a requirement that was presumably meant to ensure that the officials themselves would not practise (or even be sympathetic to) this vice. Inevitably, however, many Night Officers did have sodomites in their families, and some would themselves be accused. Bernardo di Taddeo Lorini, an official in 1484–5, was named and absolved in 1476 and again in 1487. When, in 1496, he was accused for a third time, the 65-year-old patrician sent his son to confess on his behalf, and to beg the officials to do what they could to salvage his reputation.[62]

Unsurprisingly, given that both formal accusations and anonymous tip-offs were allowed, false allegations were a frequent problem. This was also a problem in the Dutch Netherlands, where in 1473 Jehanne Sey and Katerine van der Leene both made false accusations of sodomy against their husbands, hoping that this would end their unhappy marriages. Their (apparently unrelated) schemes backfired, and both women were themselves punished for lying.[63] Many doubtful claims were simply ignored, although those who made them could be punished: in 1496 a boy who lied about his employer was whipped through the city, including in the master's neighbourhood.[64] Self-denunciation was also possible, and if followed by a confession and names of partners it led to immunity from prosecution. Consequently some men repeatedly accused themselves, although few went so far as Bartolomeo di Folco. He denounced himself so many times (collecting a reward for denouncing his partners each time) that in 1488 he was given a public flogging and banished for ten years.[65]

A conviction required a confession, clear evidence in the form of multiple eyewitnesses, and/or multiple testimonies that the suspect's behaviour was common knowledge. The officials could impose serious punishments (including exile), but there were limits to their powers: they had to transfer a case to the professional judges if it involved certain acts (for example, men who committed sodomy 'in an unusual and horrible fashion, that is, with damage to the anus of their partners') or if the death penalty was required. The majority of cases were punished by fines, even for repeat offenders, and the death penalty was typically only imposed for a fifth offence, and for over eighteens. This dependence on fines rather than execution may reflect the contemporary sense that death was too harsh a punishment, especially given how many families were affected – and it was probably not irrelevant that Florence was facing a serious financial crisis.[66]

Sentences were also determined by the precise role an individual had played in the sexual act for which they were convicted. Florentine (and many other) laws made clear distinctions between active and passive partners: the former committed a crime whereas the latter merely allowed it to be committed on him.[67] In Venice, from the mid-1440s onwards, the active partner was often executed, while the passive received corporal punishment, detention and/or exile. For example, when six Venetian sodomites were denounced to the Council of Ten (one of the Republic's main governing bodies) in 1474, the two active participants were beheaded and their remains burnt. Of the four passive partners, a ten-year-old boy was sentenced to lashing; an eighteen-year-old barber to lashing, five years' banishment and the loss of his nose; two others were sentenced to three years' banishment *in absentia*, having fled.[68] This case also highlights another trend: an underage suspect who had not actively solicited sex, had been the passive partner and could arguably be seen as a victim, was likely to go unpunished, or to be punished less severely.[69] Indeed, until the mid-1420s Venice did not prosecute minors for sodomy, which led some parents to denounce their young sons, in the hope that they would be brought into line before they were old enough to face serious punishment. Later on, the law was revised to allow youths to be punished at the discretion of the authorities.[70]

The Florentine evidence suggests that the dominant form of male-male sexual activity (at least among those who were detected by the authorities) was an 'active' adult with a 'passive' adolescent: 90 per cent of passive partners for whom age is given were under eighteen, while 82.5 per cent of active partners were over eighteen. There was, perhaps, a parallel with local marriage practices, in which men of around thirty typically married women over a decade younger. Strikingly few of the adolescents who are recorded as passive partners later turn up in an active role, seemingly contradicting medical and religious theories about boys being turned into life-long deviants, and many men who had sex with men also had sex with women. The handful of men who did turn into habitual passives, taking on a feminine, subordinate role even when they were decades past their teens, undermined masculine ideals and were harshly punished. Salvi Panuzzi was 63 when he was arrested in 1496; he admitted to a long history of same-sex relations, during which he had been sodomized by several youths. Only his prominence in the city saved him from the death penalty, and he was instead sentenced to life imprisonment in the insane ward of the local jail.[71]

Such age-based patterns surely help to explain why preachers such as Bernardino of Siena were so concerned about the corruption of young boys: while the reasons for our repugnance have shifted, modern society would be equally concerned about many of the relationships recorded in the court records, which would now be seen as abuse by predatory adult males. Certainly some medieval parents were deeply concerned by their sons' entanglements. When Martino Martini found his son Marco's lover in the house, he punished him severely and took away his slippers, which were presumably a gift from the boyfriend. In 1495 a widow named Maria Angelica begged the Night Officers to arrest her son, Niccolò, and to 'put a little fear into him', because every night he went out with a man who sodomized him, and she could not prevent it.[72] But some parents were accused of pimping for their sons. In 1481 Cipriano, a doublet maker, was denounced twice for prostituting his son Giuliano, taking money from his lovers and letting them have sex in his house.[73]

On the basis of the legal evidence (which, we should remember, only tells us who got caught), most male-male sex in fifteenth-century Florence took the form of casual encounters outside the domestic sphere. The records contain many references to sex in public places such as the fields outside the city, doorways and stables, while fencing and dancing schools were particularly associated with such behaviour. Certain taverns and streets (often those linked to prostitution) crop up frequently. The Via tra' Pelliccini, for example, was sufficiently associated with sodomy that the Night Watch sent a constable there one evening in 1482 'to investigate and arrest such men who usually frequent this place around this hour in order to engage in the vice of sodomy'. They apprehended the notorious sodomite Jacopo di Niccolò Panuzzi when he propositioned the constable.[74] In the last two decades of the fifteenth century, at least fifty men and boys who worked in the shops on the Ponte Vecchio were implicated. There are also references to group sex, and it was seemingly not unusual for friends to share a boy; in one exceptional case from 1469, a youth reported that eight men had taken it in turns to sodomize him in a shed behind the cathedral.[75]

Although most cases seem to relate to casual sex or brief liaisons, the courts did uncover a few long-term relationships. Salvestro di Niccolò Alamanni and Jacopo d'Amerigo da Verrazzano were arrested in 1404, but their affair had begun two years earlier, when Salvestro was a 36-year-old husband and father, and Jacopo was seventeen. They had had sex in various friends' houses and at the bank where Salvestro worked; the older man had given his lover cash and expensive clothes, and confessed that he liked him better than his wife. Both were punished with large fines and several years' banishment (to different cities), and barred from public office.[76] When Michele di Bruno da Prulli and Carlo di Berardo d'Antonio were accused in 1497, they had been in a committed relationship for several years; according to Michele's sentence he had been 'seized by love' and had 'kept him as his wife and in place of a wife'. The two men had even exchanged an oath on the Gospels to remain faithful to each other.[77]

Only rarely do the legal records allow us to reconstruct a detailed picture of an individual's sex life, but the case of Arnaud of Verniolles, who was tried for sodomy and heresy in 1323–4, is a particularly intriguing one. Posing as a priest (when he was actually a thirty-something subdeacon), he had sex with a series of youths. Guillaume Roux, a sixteen-year-old student at Pamiers, testified that Arnaud had told him that 'if a man plays with another, and because of the warmth of their bodies semen flows, it is not as grave a sin as if a man carnally knows a woman; because, he said, nature demands this and a man is made healthier as a result.' Guillaume was sceptical, but Arnaud untruthfully insisted that this was included in canon law. They subsequently had interfemoral intercourse on five or more occasions; sometimes Arnaud had to use force to get his way, and he also offered bribes in the form of cash and gifts.[78] Guillaume Bernard, a fifteen-year-old student who was invited back to Arnaud's house after meeting him at Mass, told a very similar tale, in which the reluctant youth was repeatedly persuaded to have sex with the older man.[79] Eighteen-year-old student Guillaume Boyer also met Arnaud at church, and went back to his house, where they had sex with the maid and another woman. They then went to lunch (where they talked about sex, which seems to have been Arnaud's only topic of conversation). But when the older man hugged and kissed him, Boyer told him to leave him alone.[80]

All three youths stressed their reluctance to have sex with Arnaud – quite possibly because this was the truth, or perhaps because they wanted to avoid, or at least minimize, punishment. Arnaud himself, however, was apparently happy to discuss his sexual history with his cellmate Pierre Recort, a Carmelite friar. Recort reported that he had not only admitted his guilt and reasserted his unorthodox beliefs about the gravity of the sin, but boasted about participating in orgies involving several young students. He additionally claimed that the bishop would have difficulty dealing with all the sodomites in Pamiers, since there were at least 3,000 of them.[81]

Arnaud's own testimony revealed that his first sexual experience had taken place when he was himself a student of only ten or twelve years old. One night, the older boy with whom he shared a bed had raped him; Arnaud was too ashamed to tell anyone what had happened. As a young man, he had slept with women, but had been taken ill after having sex with a prostitute; fearing he had contracted leprosy from her, he had given up sex with women. His descriptions of his more recent sexual activities closely matched those of the other witnesses, although he claimed that they had been enthusiastic participants. He also confirmed his unorthodox opinions, and described other sexual encounters, implicating several other men.[82] At a distance of several centuries it is hard to judge whether Arnaud was a deeply damaged man, a sexual predator or something in between, but the contemporary verdict was clear: he was a hardened sodomite, and thus deserving of harsh punishment. He was sentenced to life imprisonment in chains and perpetual fasting on bread and water.

Women with Women

If relationships between men were usually conducted in secrecy, sex between women was almost invisible, to the extent that such relationships were hardly ever mentioned.[83] When churchmen fulminated against sodomites, they were usually talking about men; secular authorities used the sodomy laws to prosecute men who had sex with men. Indeed, women who had sex with women effectively did not exist as a legal category in medieval Europe, and very few law codes refer specifically to such individuals. A rare exception comes from late thirteenth-century Orléans, where a law code made a clear distinction between male and female sodomites:

> He who is proved to be a sodomite must lose his testicles. And if he does it a second time, he must lose his member [that is, his penis]. And if he does it a third time, he must be burned. A woman who does this shall lose her member [contemporary meaning unclear] each time, and on the third must be burned.[84]

People knew that women could have sex with other women, and they knew that this was a bad thing to do. According to Peter Abelard, such women were 'against the order of nature, which created women's genitals for the use of men and not so women could cohabit with women'.[85] But many people, living in a world in which sex equalled the penetration of a woman's vagina by a man's penis, seemed rather confused about exactly *how* it was done. At the end of the thirteenth century, when Ugolino Martini spoke to a woman who professed to be interested in another woman, his response was 'Unlucky you, how can you be interested in women?', and she had to explain how it worked.[86]

In an echo of the handling of male relationships, there was a strong tendency to see female-female sexual activity in terms of passive/active roles, with the one who took the male role committing the more serious offence. Hildegard of Bingen wrote that 'a woman who takes up devilish ways and plays a male role in copulating with another woman is most vile', although she also considered that both women had 'impudently usurped a right that was not theirs', rendering them 'transformed and contempt-ible'.[87] The Italian legist Cino da Pistoia (1270–1336/7) wrote of 'women who exercise their lust on other women and pursue them like men', while a legal gloss written by Bartholomew of Soliceto (*c.* 1400) prescribed the death penalty for a woman who defiled another woman.[88] Medical writers had little to say on this subject, but authorities including Avicenna and William of Saliceto suggested that some women had fleshy growths, perhaps caused by a difficult childbirth or an abscess in the womb, which grew out of the womb like a penis, and could be used to have sex with other women.[89]

If theoretical discussion of female-female sex was limited, evidence for real women who engaged in such activities is even rarer: for the whole of the Middle Ages we know of fewer than two dozen women whom extant sources explicitly identify in this way, all of whom were punished (mostly by execution) for their sexual behaviour. Whereas male sodomy period-ically became the focus of major crackdowns, in the course of which large numbers of men would be investigated and punished, equivalent cam-paigns against women were unheard of. The largest prosecutions occurred in the South Netherlands: five women who were probably female sodom-ites were burnt to death in Ghent in 1374, and six female sodomites were burnt on a single day in Bruges in 1482/3.[90]

The earliest evidence of female-female sexual relations in medieval Europe comes from Bologna, where in 1295 the civic court investigated a woman named Guercia for sodomy with other women. Her accuser claimed that she was 'a public and well-known sodomite', who had sex with women and performed illicit magic in her house next to the town ditch. According to Ugolino Martini, one evening at a small gathering he and Guercia discussed their mutual interest in a widow; when he asked her how she could be interested in women, she showed him a number of silk instruments, of varying sizes but all equipped with silk testicles, which allowed her to have sex like a man. When the judge sent for Guercia, she could not be found; she was nevertheless sentenced to banishment, with the vast sum of 500 Bolognese pounds to be paid if she dared to return. Her punishment was relatively mild compared to the standard punishment imposed on male sodomites in Bologna at this time: death by burning. Even more striking is the fact that Guercia's behaviour was apparently widely gossiped about, and she made little effort to conceal it, but no one did anything about it: only after an anonymous notification to the podestà's court created a legal obligation for the authorities to investigate did they do so.[91]

Guercia's use of a dildo-like device is intriguing, and raises the possibility that sex between women was most likely to be punished if it involved women acting in a masculine fashion, in particular if it involved a penis substitute. A similar object features in the case of Katherina Hetzeldorfer, who was tried in Speyer in 1477. She had a two-year relationship with a woman whom she initially claimed was her sister, but eventually confessed was her lover. Besides her long-term involvement with this woman (who does not appear in the trial records, and had probably fled the city), she was also accused of making advances to at least two other women, both of whom testified against her in court. Else Muter, a married woman, confessed that she had once had sex with Katherina, who came to her house one day when her husband was out and, by force and argument, 'tried to seduce her and to have her manly will with her'. Having sex with Katherina, she said, was like having sex with a man: she saw and felt what appeared to be a large penis, 'as big as half an arm . . . like a horn and pointed in front and wide behind', which apparently produced semen 'so much that it is beyond measure, that one could grab it with a full hand', as well as urine. Another woman admitted that she had 'committed an act of knavery' with Katherina on three occasions. Both women claimed to be the victim of a hoax: the accused looked, dressed and behaved like a man (which might make a modern reader wonder about Katherina's gender identity, though no one can form any definitive claim based on the evidence available, and so I have followed the pronouns used in the medieval court documentation), and even managed to perpetuate this deception during intercourse. Both were sentenced to banishment 10 miles outside the city – a relatively mild punishment which suggests that the authorities accepted their claims to have been duped.

Katherina explained that 'she did it at first with one finger, thereafter with two, and then with three, and at last with the piece of wood that she held between her legs.' Later, she 'made an instrument with a piece of red leather, at the front filled with cotton, and a wooden stick stuck into it, and made a hole through the wooden stick, put a string through, and tied it round'; this was the 'penis' that Else Muter felt, and which she used to have sex with each of the women mentioned at her trial. Although it is unclear exactly what Katherina was tried for (her crime is never actually named), her behaviour challenged too many sexual and gender norms to be overlooked. She was a cross-dresser, at a time when the authorities in Speyer were especially concerned by such behaviour. Not only did she commit sodomy by having sex with women, but she did so in a way that usurped the male role. She was sentenced to death by drowning.[92]

The verdicts in this trial echo the idea that the woman who took the active role was more culpable for the offence, and deserved to be punished more harshly. Other cases followed the same pattern. Jehanne Seraes, who confessed to having committed 'buggery . . . in the manner of a man', was sentenced to burn in Ghent in 1422.[93] Twelve years later, in the same city, Marie de Valmerbeke and her daughter Belle were sentenced to burn for committing 'the sin against nature'. But their servant, Margarete Scoucx, was exiled for ten years, the court seemingly having concluded that her employers had taken advantage of her.[94] Of course, it is hard to know whether women who claimed to have been passive victims of unnatural predators were truly unwilling participants in their crime: in the circumstances, it would be understandable if some individuals deliberately presented themselves in this way. A 1405 letter of pardon from the French royal register deals with a sexual relationship between Jehanne and Laurence, two married women. Both were prosecuted, and both were imprisoned, but Laurence appealed: Jehanne had initiated the relationship, had 'climbed on her as a man does a woman', and then attacked her with a knife when she tried to end a relationship. By presenting herself as the 'woman' in the relationship, and as someone who had been led astray but who repented, she could be viewed as someone who needed penance, but not serious punishment – and since the king reduced her sentence to six months in prison, after which her name would be cleared, it seems that the authorities agreed.[95]

Of course, it is entirely possible that this emphasis on masculine behaviour and the use of penis substitutes helped many female couples to go unnoticed, at least by the relevant authorities. But the potential evidence is sparse, fragmentary and extremely difficult to read. For example, an unusual little memorial brass in a Sussex parish church has sometimes

Memorial brass of Elizabeth Etchingham (d. 1452) and Agnes Oxenbridge (d. 1480), the Church of the Assumption of Blessed Mary and St Nicholas, Etchingham.

been interpreted as evidence of a lesbian relationship. The women represented, Elizabeth Etchingham (d. 1452) and Agnes Oxenbridge (d. 1480), were both born into local gentry families in the 1420s; they probably knew each other from childhood, and there is no evidence that either woman married. The two women are depicted on a joint brass, facing each other and looking directly into each other's eyes — a form and design usually reserved for married couples. It was presumably commissioned by, or at least approved by, their brothers (who were the heads of their respective families at the time of Agnes's death), and it is intriguing that they were willing to show the pair in a manner suggesting affection and intimacy. Moreover, although The Assumption of Blessed Mary and St Nicholas, Etchingham, was Elizabeth's family church, Agnes presumably requested to be buried there, rather than in her family mausoleum at Brede – and this too must have been authorized by both families. Their story is an intriguing one, and it is tempting to read the brass as evidence for a lasting love affair, a pleasing counterpart to the unhappy endings found in the court records. But ultimately it is impossible to know whether they had a sexual relationship – whether they were 'lesbians' in the modern sense of the word – or whether theirs was the deeply significant, but chaste, friendship of a pair of spinsters.[96]

Yet, while the true nature of many individual relationships remains unknowable, it is clear that large numbers of people in medieval Europe both experienced and acted on same-sex attraction. Such behaviour was treated very differently to how it is today (at least in much of the world), and it was also understood very differently, within a wider framework of deviant behaviours. Such conceptual variations meant that, whether by having the wrong kinds of intercourse, or by having relations with the wrong people, there were many ways of defying medieval sexual norms. In the next chapter, we will explore another contentious set of issues: religion and the race-based taboos that placed even more constraints on the sexual freedoms of medieval people.

EIGHT

Defying Sexual Norms:
Religion and Race

S exuality was not the only characteristic on which medieval people
judged their peers: religion and race also formed the basis of many
negative perceptions, and sometimes these hostile attitudes combined
to form more complicated prejudices.

Racial Stereotypes

In the late twelfth century the churchman Gerald of Wales made three
visits to Ireland. These trips inspired his book *The History and Topography
of Ireland*, in which he described the Irish as 'a filthy people, wallowing in
vice'. They were prone to incest, and in particular men tended to 'debauch'
(though not necessarily to marry) their widowed sisters-in-law.[1] Despite
his close personal ties to the country, he was equally negative about the
people of Wales, and similarly used their sexual behaviour as evidence for
their primitive nature. The Welsh, he claimed, had lost first Troy and then
Britain because of their fondness for sodomy; although they had since
given up this practice, they were still 'sunk in sin', and frequently guilty of
rape and adultery, among other things. They also practised incest, often
marrying within the forbidden degrees – supposedly in order to end family
quarrels, or because they refused to marry beneath their rank. They had a
custom of buying young girls from their families, 'not in the first instance
with a view to marry them, but just to live with them'.[2]

Gerald was far from unique in his fondness for race-based sexual
stereotypes, or in using them as a way to attack foreigners. In 1376
Parliament petitioned Edward III of England to banish Lombard bankers
from England, in part because they had supposedly introduced to England
'the too horrible vice that is not to be named'.[3] In Felix Hemmerli's *On
Matrimony* (1456), a German cleric who had visited Rome authoritatively
condemned Italians as sodomites.[4] Late fifteenth-century German
humanists were particularly keen to include stereotypical slurs about

Mediterranean sexual depravity in their work, as in this poem composed by a member of the Regensburg circle in the 1490s:

> You Italian shit-shot licker of arses,
> . . . you jump boys: in your impious embraces
> You go coddling bristling hairy hollows.
> Cannot shame, poor man, keep you from pretending
> To be sober: intoxicated jerkoff,
> Flaccid cock-sucked pathic [passive] and masturbator.

The Crusades inevitably provoked considerable discussion in Western sources of the people who lived in the Holy Land, most of it hostile. From the First Crusade (1096–9) onwards, descriptions of the Islamic world emphasized sexual behaviour that was repugnant to Christians. A text that purported to be an appeal from the Eastern emperor for help in the Holy Land, but which was almost certainly a forgery written in the West shortly before the First Crusade, claimed that infidels forcibly circumcised Christian youths, and ravished virgins and matrons. They forced mothers and daughters to witness each other's rape, and made them sing lewd songs as they watched. Worst of all, they sodomized men of all ranks, including clerics; they had even killed a bishop in this way. Jacques de Vitry, Bishop of Acre (1216–28), claimed that Muslims were not only enthusiastic sodomites, they also had sex with animals. William of Ada, another thirteenth-century chronicler of the Crusades, claimed that Islam 'not only allowed but also approved and encouraged' all sexual acts, and therefore the Saracens had 'innumerable' prostitutes, both male and female, in addition to a tendency to satiate their lust with misguided Christian boys.[5] In 1268–9, when the papacy launched a Crusade against the Muslim colony of Lucera (in northern Apulia), Cardinal Eudes of Châteauroux preached against the sexual excesses of the infidels, which included raping virgins and forcing Christian women to become their concubines.[6] Such descriptions of depravity were designed to anger European men, and thus to persuade them to take the cross.

While many accounts focused on negative sexual behaviours, other authors stereotyped on the basis of physical characteristics. In the anonymous Occitan poem 'While along a bank', the narrator spies an ugly pig-girl, whose breasts 'were so big that she looked English'.[7] In a late fifteenth-century comic tale, a woman's pubic hair (which was 'abundant, and very long, as is common among Dutch women') is mistaken for a cow's tail.[8] The Venetian merchant Marco Polo's comments on the repulsive women of Zanzibar, who had breasts 'four times as big as those of other women', reflected the tendency of European writers to make particularly outrageous comments about the bodies and behaviour of non-white, non-Christian, and/or non-European peoples.[9] Polo (1254–1324) recorded his voyages in the Far East in *The Travels*, which is full of stories of polygamy, nudity and unbridled lust. Among the idolaters of Kamul, he claimed, it was considered good manners for a man to lend his wife to guests, and in Tibet virgins were virtually unmarriageable, being assumed to have displeased the idols. Consequently, parents encouraged foreign visitors to have sex with their daughters.[10] Polo was particularly impressed by the prostitutes of Kinsai (now known as Hangzhou), who were 'highly proficient and accomplished in the uses of endearments and caresses, so that foreigners who have once enjoyed them remain utterly beside themselves and so captivated by their sweetness and charm that they can never forget them'.[11]

A near-contemporaneous work, *The Book of Marvels and Travels*, presents a host of similar stories, supposedly gathered by Sir John Mandeville, a knight from St Albans who spent three decades travelling the world before writing down his recollections in the late 1350s. Although this framework is probably fictional, and there is no evidence that Mandeville was a real person, the text was based on a wide range of sources, intended as a serious work of non-fiction, and was widely translated and circulated in Europe throughout the later Middle Ages. It includes numerous claims

The male inhabitants of the Island of Crues were afflicted with enormous genitals, according to this 15th-century copy of *Mandeville's Travels* (British Library Harley MS 3954, f. 32).

about the sexual beliefs and behaviours of exotic peoples: the Greeks apparently believed 'that fornication isn't a deadly sin but a natural thing', while Islamic countries practised polygamy and allowed divorce.[12] Further afield, on Hormuz (an island in the Persian Gulf), it was so hot that 'men's bollocks hang down to their shins', and mixed-sex naked bathing was the norm.[13] In Cathay, men had as many as one hundred wives, and could marry anyone except their own mothers and daughters; elsewhere in China groups of ten or twelve men shared houses and wives, seemingly unbothered by the uncertain paternity of their offspring.[14] On one of the Indonesian islands lived a race of hermaphrodites, able to use either their male or female genitals at will.[15]

Such travel narratives emphasized the eroticism of the exotic – a tendency that was also found in medical and literary sources, perhaps especially in relation to Black people. Black Africans were extremely rare in twelfth-century Europe, but they began to feature prominently in learned Christian culture from around this time. Writing in the 1250s, Albertus Magnus described Black women in terms of their greater bodily heat, the special qualities of their milk, and their excessive lust. Black characters also feature in courtly literature, and here too they are often defined by their sexual behaviour. For example, the characters in Heinrich von Neustadt's *Apollonius von Tyrlant* (c. 1300) include Palmina, a beautiful Black queen who boasts of the special sexual delights provided by women of her kind, and Glorant, a Black tyrant who claims to have raped hundreds of Christian women. But in the fifteenth century, with the arrival of increasing numbers of enslaved Africans, attitudes to the sexuality of non-white people changed. Rather than focus on individuals who were high-born and exciting, literary texts foregrounded the figure of the greedy, lustful and grotesque slave. For example, Masuccio Guardati's *Novellino* (1460s) includes the story of a Christian woman driven by 'perverse lust' to have an affair with her Black slave, a hideous dwarf with a huge penis. When another slave discovers the pair in bed together, she is so horrified that she kills them.[16]

Of course, European Catholics were not unique in their fascination with the sexual behaviour of people who were different from them; indeed, they were themselves the focus of very similar stories by non-Christian writers. Usuma bin Munqidh (d. 1188), a Syrian poet and diplomat, considered them remarkably lacking in any sense of honour and jealousy; the men were quite happy for their wives to have male friends. He told the story of a husband who came home to find his wife in bed with another man, and demanded to know what was going on:

'I was tired', replied the man, 'and so I came in to rest.'

'And how do you come to be in my bed?'

'I found the bed made up, and lay down to sleep.'

'And this woman slept with you, I suppose?'

'The bed', he replied, 'is hers. How could I prevent her getting into her own bed?'

'I swear if you do it again, I shall take you to court!'

Bin Munqidh was baffled by this man's muted reaction. He also claimed that Westerners bathed naked in public bathhouses, and reported a story supposedly told to him by Salim, a bathhouse employee. One day a Frankish knight came to the bathhouse, whipped off Salim's loincloth, and saw that he had shaved off his pubic hair. Full of admiration, the man insisted that Salim shave both him and his wife in the same way.[17]

Imad al-Din (1125–1201), Saladin's secretary, recorded the arrival of three hundred 'licentious harlots', who travelled to the Middle East to offer sexual services to Crusaders. He describes at length the activities they engaged in, offering lists of metaphors for sex (the women 'gave the birds a place to peck at with their beaks ... caught lizard after lizard in their holes ... guided pens to inkwells'). He also claims that they had unconventional ideas: 'among the Franks a woman who gives herself to a celibate man commits no sin, and her justification is even greater in the case of a priest, if chaste men in dire need find relief in enjoying her.' The men of Saladin's army were baffled and repulsed by this, although some foolish individuals still slipped away to visit them.[18]

Reflections on sexual differences between races are also found in Jewish sources. A thirteenth-century French rabbi expressed concerns that Jewish women would be attracted to Christian men:

for he thrusts inside her a long time because of the foreskin ... When an uncircumcised man sleeps with her and then resolves to return to his home, she brazenly grasps him, holding on to his genitals, and says to him, 'Come back, make love to me'. This is because of the pleasure that she finds in intercourse with him, from the sinews of his testicles – sinews of iron – and from his ejaculation – that of a horse – which he shoots like an arrow into her womb.

Circumcised Jews, he suggested, not only gave their wives less pleasure, but were often too tired for sex, because they worked so hard in Gentile lands.[19] The Toledan poet Todros ben Judah Halevi Abulafia dismissed the Christian woman as unclean and 'so ignorant of intercourse she knows nothing', but praised the female Muslim as charming, beautiful and sexually adept.[20]

Non-Christian travellers also described exotic peoples in terms that recall the accounts by Marco Polo and Sir John Mandeville. The fourteenth-century Moroccan scholar Ibn Battutah, for example, claimed that the women of Dawlat Abad 'have in intercourse a deliciousness and a knowledge of erotic movements beyond that of other women'. He spent over a year in the Maldives, where the diet (dominated by fish and coco-palm) apparently had 'an amazing and unparalleled effect in sexual intercourse', so that 'the people of these islands perform wonders in this respect.' During his visit, he himself had four wives plus several concubines, and visited each of them every day.[21]

Sex and the Jews

While the sexual practices of other peoples were surely not as exotic as these fantasies suggested, some of medieval Europe's religious minorities did have distinctive ideas and behaviours that set them apart from their Christian neighbours. Medieval Jews, especially those living in the north of Europe, were typically less impressed by celibacy and virginity than their Christian contemporaries.[22] According to an anonymous thirteenth-century Spanish kabbalist: 'If we were to say that intercourse is repulsive, then we blaspheme God who made the genitals . . . Marital intercourse, under proper circumstances, is an exalted matter.'[23] Marriage was seen in an extremely positive light and reproduction was a powerful ideal, to the extent that some texts even compared childless individuals to a dead person.[24] Maimonides (c. 1135–1204), one of the most influential medieval Torah scholars, rejected celibacy as a permitted form of asceticism for the especially devout, arguing that marriage and children were required even of a religious man.[25]

Unsurprisingly, then, Jewish teaching placed great emphasis on the importance of marital sex, and Jewish law forbade a spouse to unilaterally abstain: a husband or wife who did so was considered rebellious, and a woman who refused to have sex with her husband would forfeit some of her financial rights if they divorced. In theory, even mutually agreed abstinence was not permissible.[26] Sexual pleasure within marriage was often considered to be a good thing, since it helped to avoid extramarital temptation and increased the likelihood of conception. According to Rabbi Elezear of Worms (1176–1238), a man 'should avoid looking at other women and have sex with one's wife with the greatest passion because she guards him from sin'. During marital intercourse, he 'should give her pleasure and embrace her and kiss her . . . arouse her with caresses and with all manner of embracing in order to fulfil his desire and hers so that he doesn't think of another, but only of her'. *Sefer Hasidim* (an influential Hebrew treatise, written in Germany around 1200) encouraged wives to dress in such a way as to inflame their husbands' lust, and advised men that they should ensure that their wives orgasmed first, so that they would conceive sons. Other authorities advised couples to have sex in the missionary position, since this was most pleasurable for the woman, and therefore most likely to lead to conception.[27]

Despite the importance of marital sex, there were clear limits on how it should be performed. A man should not have sex with his wife against her will, while drunk or depressed, if he planned to divorce her, or while thinking of another woman. In twelfth-century Provence, Rabbi Abraham ben David thought that a husband should consider his wife's wishes, and refrain from doing things she did not like. Sex between a couple who hated each other was, he argued, 'like harlotry and not marital relations'.[28] Excessive lust was also suspect, because, as the Spanish scholar Abraham Ibn Ezra (*c.* 1092–*c.* 1163) argued, sex for reasons of procreation or health was a necessity, but sex purely for the sake of desire was animal-like. According to Maimonides, laws against illicit sex were designed to prevent 'an intense lust for sexual intercourse and for constant preoccupation with it', and the ultimate aim was the dulling of desire through a monogamous marital relationship.

Maimonides was also one of several medieval Jewish authorities to see circumcision as a way of reducing lust; he seems to have believed that the foreskin is highly innervated, and thus generates intense sexual pleasure. Removing it would therefore reduce the problem.[29] Similarly, Isaac ben Yedaiah, a late thirteenth-century French rabbi, thought that Jewish men were protected from lechery, because the circumcised man climaxed quickly and rarely gave pleasure to his wife.[30] Despite giving advice on enhancing sexual pleasure, Eleazar of Worms also ordered that a man should not look at '[his wife's] clothes, her face, the jutting out of her breasts, and her genitals'.[31] And while some Jewish authorities suggested that nursing mothers should use cervical sponges because another pregnancy would threaten the health of the existing child, this did not reflect a wider acceptance of contraception.[32] In twelfth-century France, Joseph Bekhor Shor complained about 'those whose only concern is their own pleasure', who used *coitus interruptus* to avoid offspring.[33]

There was also considerable concern about sexual purity. Leviticus requires that any man who has experienced an emission of semen must wash before entering the Temple, just as a woman must undergo ritual immersion after menstruation or childbirth. In the Middle Ages, male impurity was increasingly linked not to sex but to nocturnal emissions. Consequently, pious men would try to avoid such pollutions; *Sefer Hasidim* includes the story of a man who, when his wife was ritually impure, would sleep in an uncomfortable chair or read the Torah all night to avoid having an emission. Although Ra'aviah (1160–1235) complained that only the most pious men washed before attending synagogue, and greater emphasis was often placed on encouraging men to avoid impure thoughts, ritual bathing before Yom Kippur (in order to counteract male impurity due to nocturnal emissions) did become an expected practice by the end of the Middle Ages.[34]

Menstruation (which was divided into two phases, the days of bleeding, and the seven 'white' days afterwards) was also strictly regulated. Absence from the synagogue was only required during a woman's period, but ritual bathing and the resumption of sexual relations were only supposed to happen after the 'white' days. The observance of these rules seems to have become more widespread during the later Middle Ages: in late eleventh- to early twelfth-century Ashkenaz (that is, the Jewish communities of northern France and Germany), highly observant women stopped attending the synagogue during menstruation, and this became standard practice by the thirteenth century.[35] At the same time, the rules about postnatal sex became increasingly strict, with the period of abstinence extended from one to six weeks. Christians and Jews alike saw the Jewish insistence on avoiding sex during menstruation as a defining difference between the two peoples. The French theologian Peter of Poitiers (c. 1130–1215) thought that 'the Jews are rarely defiled by the stain of leprosy because they do not approach menstruating women.' Eleazar of Worms warned that sex with a menstruating wife would produce leprous offspring, and lower the Jews to the station of their Christian neighbours, 'for non-Jews have sexual relations with their wives while they are menstruating, as insects do, and that is why they are sent to Hell'. The pejorative term for Christian men was 'bo'alei niddot' (those who have sex with impure women). Sexual purity mattered because it was a way to set Jews and Christians apart.[36]

There was also considerable concern about non-marital sexuality. Hebrew verse from thirteenth-century Castile, including the poems of Todros ben Judah Halevi, depicts illicit relations among wealthy Jews, and a sermon of Rabbi Todros ben Joseph Halevi Abulafia (the poet's uncle) exhorted Jews to give up their bad habits, including leering at and propositioning women. Jewish authorities tried to regulate and improve the behaviour of their communities, and rabbis were often asked for advice on intimate problems. Among the cases handled by Rabbi Nissim of Gerona (1320–1376) was that of a wife who refused to have sex with her husband, saying she could not bear to be with him in bed. Another involved a woman who objected to her husband's insistence on masturbation, which she found painful. She thought he did this because he was impotent, but then he threw her out of the house, acquired a mistress, and fathered a daughter.[37]

Like Christians, medieval Jews were required to atone for their sins, through penances such as fasting, lashings and charitable deeds. Sins that involved men having inappropriate sexual contact with a woman (such as adultery, or sex with a menstruating woman) required the most substantial penances. *Sefer Hasidim* suggested that, during the winter, a male adulterer should immerse himself in a frozen river, and in the summer he should sit on an ant hill.[38] Strictly speaking, Jewish law did not forbid sexual relations between single people, but in practice medieval rabbis tried to impose controls. In the thirteenth century Rabbi Meir of Rothenberg ruled that a betrothed couple must not cohabit, since they were not allowed to have sex; around the same time, a Jewish couple from Navarre were fined for having premarital relations.[39] Similarly, efforts were made to prevent polygamy: in eleventh-century Ashkenaz a ban was placed on any man who took a second wife. Some Spanish Jews did practise polygamy, but fines intended to prevent abandonment of wives also reduced polygamy as a side-effect, and the practice was probably never widespread.[40]

Divorce was sometimes permitted and could be initiated by either sex, although it was considerably easier for men. Meir of Rothenberg opposed easy divorce and required extremely solid proof. When he heard on appeal the case of a man who claimed to have seen his wife with a young man on several occasions, and once to have heard them breathing heavily behind a wall, he pointed out that this was not conclusive evidence of adultery.[41] *Sefer Hasidim* only allowed a man to divorce his wife for serious reasons, including the woman being a 'harlot'.[42] In a thirteenth-century case in London, an adulterous wife was told that her husband should divorce her; she should not receive the money that was usually owed to a Jewish woman on the termination of her marriage.[43] Although arranged marriages were common, there was some scepticism about the wisdom of such arrangements. *Sefer Hasidim* suggested that a father would be morally accountable if he married his daughter to a man she did not love and she subsequently committed adultery; for similar reasons, a son should also be allowed to choose his wife. But the key concern seems to have been the social impact of promiscuity, rather than personal happiness.[44]

Interfaith Relationships

While relationships between two members of the same faith often provoked disapproval, arguably the most problematic unions were those that
crossed religious boundaries. Christian efforts to prevent intermarriage
with members of non-Christian faiths, especially Jews, dated back to at
least the mid-fourth century, and rules against such unions were reiterated
throughout the early Middle Ages. From the twelfth century onwards,
interfaith relations became an increasing concern, and both ecclesiastical and secular authorities introduced new legal prohibitions. Those who
flouted canon law and married Jews could be excommunicated; in theory,
this was also a capital crime under secular law. More often, the Jewish
spouse would be expected to convert, otherwise the marriage would be
nullified and the couple forced to separate. Non-marital relations could
also be harshly punished.[45]

Such issues were of particular concern in (although not limited to) the
Crusader kingdoms, where Christian warriors came into contact with the
native Muslim population, and in Iberia, which had sizeable Muslim and
Jewish populations until the late fifteenth-century expulsions. In the Holy
Land, the Council of Nablus (1120) tried to prevent interfaith relations –
although frequent complaints about the licentiousness of Crusaders, and
the fact that female Muslim captives were often used as prostitutes, raise
questions about the efficacy of these new laws.[46] According to the Council,
if a Christian man had consensual sex with a Muslim woman, he should
be castrated and she should lose her nose; the rape of Saracen women was
punishable by castration and/or enslavement. If a Christian woman had
consensual sex with a Muslim man, both were to receive the same punishments as adulterers; if she was raped, she should not be punished, but
he should be castrated. Saracens of either sex who dressed like Europeans
were to be punished by enslavement, to prevent accidental sexual mixing.
From the twelfth century onwards, Iberian authorities took a similarly
strict approach to sexual mixing, especially for cases in which a Christian
woman was caught having sex with a non-Christian partner. The standard
punishment for this was execution, although the laws were not consistently
enforced, and death sentences were not always implemented.[47]

Concerns that the indistinguishability of Muslims and Jews might lead
to sexual relationships with Christians were not limited to these regions,
but existed across Europe. Consequently, Catholic authorities repeatedly
ruled that non-Christians must wear clothing or symbols that distinguished them from Christians. At the Fourth Lateran Council (1215) it
was noted that 'it sometimes happens that by mistake Christians join with

Jewish or Saracen women, and Saracens or Jews with Christian women'; to prevent 'such a damnable mixing ... under the excuse of a mistake of this kind', non-Christians must wear distinctive clothing.[48] This requirement was frequently restated in subsequent centuries. Juan I of Aragon issued a letter in 1393 stressing the need for Jews to wear identifying badges, and ordering that if a Jew was found having sex with a Christian woman, both should be burnt to death. This pronouncement was probably triggered by the case of Saltell Gracia, a Jew of Barcelona, who in the week the letter was issued was tried for 'promenading in Christian dress and under guise of that dress having sex with Christian women'.[49] For similar reasons, a 1443 ruling required Venetian Jews to wear a yellow mark on their breast.[50]

Why were the authorities so keen to stop Christians having sex with Muslims and Jews? Throughout the Middle Ages, the key problem with mixed marriages seems to have been religion, not race, since Crusaders were free to marry both Syrian and Armenian Christians, as well as converts from Islam.[51] In Iberia, at least until the fifteenth century (when attitudes to non-Christians hardened considerably), Christians were able to marry converts from other faiths, and the offspring of these mixed unions were viewed as unquestionably Christian.[52] In fifteenth-century Italy there are several recorded cases of Jewish women converting to Christianity to marry a man of that faith; although this often provoked familial disapproval, the state sometimes intervened to ensure that the bride received her dowry. When, for example, Ricca, a Jewish widow from Spello, decided to marry Bartolomeo, a Christian merchant, she was baptised, along with her young daughter from her first marriage. This so infuriated Aleuccio da Pesaro, her father-in-law, that he refused to return her dowry, so the authorities raided his bank and seized the sum he owed her, ultimately leading to his ruin.[53]

The civic authorities supported Ricca's marriage because she had converted; had she tried to keep her own faith, her new relationship would have met with a very different response. According to Alfonso X of Castile (*r.* 1252–84): 'Since Christians who commit adultery with married women deserve death, how much more so do Jews who lie with Christian women, for these are spiritually espoused to Our Lord Jesus Christ by virtue of the faith and baptism they received in his name.' Christian women were the spiritual wives and daughters of God, who was like a paterfamilias with rights over his family, and his honour was tied up in their behaviour. Because Jews and Muslims were not baptised, they were excluded from this group, but if they had had sexual contact with it, they created a fleshly kinship that dishonoured spiritual kinship. The cases which caused greatest concern often seem to have been those in which non-Christian men had sex with Christian prostitutes: because sex created affinity, this connected not only the people having sex, but the wider community. Consequently, these women became the focus of collective anxiety about interfaith sex.[54]

Relations that dishonoured God in this way could be seen as sacrilege: this was the offence for which Zacharias, a Venetian Jew tried in 1442 for an affair with a Christian friend's daughter, was prosecuted.[55] They could also provoke divine anger against entire populations. The Valencian friar Vincent Ferrer (1350–1419) claimed that Christian men nowadays 'want to taste everything: Muslims and Jews, animals, men with men; there is no limit'. Proper segregation must be achieved, and all improper contacts prevented, in order to protect the city and its inhabitants from God's wrath. In 1415 he preached a sermon in Zarazoga, in which he claimed that many men unwittingly raised as their own children who were actually the product of their wives' adultery with Muslims and Jews; citizens must act, or God would send plague. This led Christian vigilantes to search the city for predatory non-Christians, resulting in numerous sex-related charges against Muslims and Jews.[56]

Concerns about sexual mixing were also related to questions of identity and power. Christians across Europe, but perhaps especially in Iberia, frequently defined themselves against non-Christians; sexual behaviours and the maintenance of boundaries were an important part of this. Medieval ideas about sex (in particular, the tendency to see sex as something that a man did to a woman), gender and honour meant that the gender of the people involved was key. Christian men who had relations with minority women could, in some sense, be seen to reinforce hierarchies, by subjugating them to their will. Relationships between Christian women and non-Christian men, on the other hand, dishonoured families, and threatened patriarchal authority and Christian rule. Indeed, medieval men of all religions argued that their women should not have sex with men of other faiths, because this led to apostasy and was a form of submission.[57]

Another key issue was children. In theory, the offspring of a mixed union were automatically deemed to be fully Christian and should be raised accordingly, but it was widely recognized that the reality was rather more complicated. Thomas Aquinas thought that interfaith marriage was a bad idea because one of the purposes of marriage was to produce good Christian children; if a couple had different faiths, they would each want to bring up their offspring in their own religion, leading to conflict.[58] If a couple were not married, then things could get even messier, and Christian authorities sometimes seized children in order to ensure that they were raised in the correct faith. For example, on his deathbed in 1401, Antoni

Safàbrego confessed to an affair with a Muslim woman named Axa. She was now dead, but the authorities seized her son Mahomet from her widower and sent him to be raised as a Christian. Even more troubling, from a Christian perspective, were the offspring of non-Christian sex workers, who would surely not be baptised, meaning that the father would be responsible for the damnation of his child's soul.[59]

Unsurprisingly then, some interfaith relations were harshly punished, especially in cases where non-Christian men were accused of sex with Christian women. Jaume II of Aragon ruled in 1311 that Muhammed, who had been accused of trying to have sex with a Christian prostitute, should be burnt at the stake as an example to others of his faith.[60] In the same year, Prima Garsón fled Daroca due to rumours that she was involved with a Muslim man named Ali. He was executed, only for a subsequent medical examination to suggest that she was still a virgin. Others survived only by paying huge fines, among them the eighteen Muslim men from the Vall d'Uxó who were condemned to death for having sex with a Christian prostitute in a field, but whose sentence was remitted on payment of 4,120 Barcelona sous.[61] In fifteenth-century Venice, Leo, a Jewish doctor, raped and then had a relationship with the fifteen-year-old daughter of his friend Giovanni, a Christian sailor. After their liaison was discovered, Leo was tortured until he confessed, and subsequently sentenced to a year in jail and a 100 ducat fine.[62] Others were punished by dismemberment: a Jewish physician in mid-fourteenth-century Manosque accused of making unwanted sexual advances to a Christian patient was sentenced to have his penis chopped off. This unusually harsh punishment was almost certainly linked to his religion.[63]

Despite the possibility of such sentences, some people managed to escape serious censure. Sometimes this was achieved through conversion: one of the physicians of Alfonso V of Portugal was baptised after being accused of sex with a Christian woman.[64] But a change of religion was not always required; some people (and not just high-status individuals) paid only small fines. Thus in 1294 a Muslim woman of Navarre was fined a mere 30 shillings for sex with a Christian man, while in the port of Sétubal, Ali and Muhammad received pardons for adultery with Christian wives, in return for payment of a fine. In 1486 a Muslim woman from Santarém who committed adultery with a Christian man became a fugitive, but after her Muslim husband forgave her 'sin and error', she was punished with the fine she would probably have received if both she and her lover had been Christians.[65]

Some couples even managed to forge lasting unions. In a very rare case from the mid-1260s, Goig de Palafols, a wealthy Jewish woman who may have lent money to the crown, petitioned King Jaume I for an extension of his previously granted permission to live with her Christian lover, Guillemó, whom she had brought 'into her house, her living quarters, and her bedchamber'. The couple were 'burning in their love for each other', and the impending expiration of their licence made them feel like 'a thief whom the lord has ordered to be hanged'. Unfortunately the outcome of this petition, which would have protected them from Jewish authorities as much as Christian ones, is unknown.[66] In 1298 Abulfacem, a Jew of Murcia, and his Muslim concubine Axona were arrested; they appealed to the king, who ruled that, since neither was a Christian, they should be allowed to cohabit.[67] In 1499, two years after the expulsion of Muslims and Jews from Portugal, Diogo Pires and his wife Isabel de Goïs sought a royal pardon. Diogo was born a Muslim, and before his conversion had entered into a relationship with Isabel, which produced a child. Then, in 1483, he converted to Christianity and the couple married, with the consent of her family. They had five surviving children. They made their petition because they had broken the law by having sex before his conversion, but it seems unlikely that the authorities were actively seeking such cases at this time, and the pardon was readily granted. It therefore seems possible that they feared neighbours would denounce them, and took pre-emptive action. If so, this might indicate that popular attitudes could be stricter than legal ones, and that peer pressure could be as significant a factor in preventing mixed relationships as fear of the law.[68]

Given that our knowledge about such couples comes almost entirely from legal records, it is hard to know what ordinary people thought about sexual mixing, but the monks of Rueda were clearly untroubled by such sensitivities. In 1356 they received a royal grant of the profits from the sale of any Muslim woman within the abbey's domains who had been enslaved for having sex with Christian men. The grant was revoked the following year, when it was discovered that the monks themselves had been sleeping with the women, and pocketing the resultant revenues.[69] On the other hand, two cases involving Christian prostitutes suggest that, while people were happy to work and socialize with non-Christians, they recognized that sexual relationships with them were taboo. In 1304 Alicsén de Tolba, a prostitute, visited a Valencian shepherds' camp, where a Muslim shepherd named Aytola was persuaded by a friend to pretend he was a Christian in order to have sex with her. When Alicsén realized that her client was circumcised, she denounced both men to the authorities, claiming that their deception was to 'the dishonour of God and of the Catholic faith and of Christianity'. Around the same time, visitors to a tavern in Benimahabet noted that Christians, Muslim converts to Christianity, and Muslims all drank and gambled together, but only Christians were allowed to have sex with the prostitutes who were also present.[70]

Popular concern was intensified by ongoing conflict between Christian and Islamic regions of Iberia, which included raids on the border between Castile and Granada, and by piracy. It has been estimated that, in any given year, at least 2,000 Aragonese Christians were being held captive in Iberia or North Africa, most of them permanently and in terrible conditions. Christians were particularly concerned about the sexual exploitation and conversion of female captives, and Christian women who died rather than have sex with Muslim captors were viewed as martyrs. Among the women celebrated in this way was a group of nuns, captured from the convent of Santa Clara in 1298, who were killed by Muslim raiders when they refused to surrender their virginity.[71] Jewish communities also worried about this threat: the late thirteenth-century Toledan Rabbi Asher ben Yehiel, for example, wrote about Leah, a young Jewish woman captured by raiders, who converted to Islam and married a Muslim.[72]

Jewish concerns about women like Leah were linked to the faith's opposition to mixed marriages, which was as vehement as that of Christians. According to Maimonides, 'it is in these matters that the Omnipresent one has sanctified us and separated us from the heathens, namely in matters of forbidden unions and forbidden foods.' Rabbi Nahmanides (1194–1270) wrote that 'whoever goes astray with Gentile women desecrates the covenant of Abraham', and Rabbi Asher ben Yehiel (*c.* 1250–1327) ruled that any Jewish man who practised 'harlotry with the daughter of a foreign God' should be expelled from the Jewish community. Other Jews had a responsibility to denounce such men.[73] A 1418 meeting of Jewish delegates at Forlì (Italy) complained that sexual relationships between Jews and Christians threatened to weaken the fabric and moral integrity of Jewish society. The meeting was also concerned by the offspring of mixed relationships for, like their Christian counterparts, medieval Jews worried that these children would be raised in the wrong faith.[74] As Rabbi Todros ben Joseph Abulafia put it, 'Jews, who are a holy people, must not profane their seed in the womb of a Gentile woman, thereby gathering offspring for idolatry.'[75]

Such attitudes were reflected in Jewish practice, including an unusual early fourteenth-century German case in which Rabbi Alexander Zuslin accepted a woman's complaint that her husband had sex with a Gentile woman as grounds for divorce.[76] Some community members in fourteenth-century Castile wanted to ban prostitution, but others successfully argued that Jewish prostitutes were needed to stop Jewish men 'mix[ing] the holy seed with Gentile women'.[77] In practice, many Jewish communities lived by the same gendered double-standards as Christians, with men able to have sex with women of other faiths relatively uncensured; admonitions against sex with Gentile woman (especially servants and concubines) remained necessary throughout the Middle Ages. In 1236 Rabbi Moses of Coucy visited Spain and chastised the Jews there for their bad behaviour; his visit coincided with an earthquake that was widely seen as a sign from God, and he claimed that, as a consequence, there was a 'sending away of many Gentile women'.[78] In Toledo the problem was sufficiently widespread that in 1281 the Jewish community issued a formal ban on men who kept Muslim concubines, but it had little impact and was soon relaxed.[79] In late medieval Umbria, where the Jewish population was small, scattered and unstable, young Jewish men often seem to have had premarital relationships with Christian girls. In 1480 Venturello da Bevagna, a merchant's son from Spoleto, was 'courting Catalina', a local beauty, and seemingly meeting her quite openly. A few years later he married Stella, the daughter of a Jewish banker from Bologna.[80]

Meir of Rothenburg even claimed to have heard of French cases in which Jewish women were allowed to marry Gentiles, but he strongly disapproved of such arrangements, claiming that they were made 'merely in order to gratify her carnal desires'.[81] Jewish women who had non-marital sex with non-Jews were usually treated harshly, receiving corporal punishment, exile or death.[82] In 1319 a Jewish official wrote to Rabbi Asher asking for permission to punish a Jewish woman from Segovia who had given birth to two children by a Christian man (one had died, the other been taken by the Christian authorities) by cutting off her nose.[83] In 1356 Oro de Par, a Jewish woman from Zaragoza, had sex with both Christian and Muslim men; the Jewish authorities asked the king to have her disfigured and exiled, saying they were afraid to act alone in case of retaliatory violence by her Christian lovers. In another case from Zaragoza, a Jewish woman was murdered by her brothers because she was pregnant by a Christian.[84]

Classical Islamic jurisprudence allowed Muslim men to marry women of other faiths, but not the reverse. In reality, neither was feasible in medieval Europe, where Muslims were subject to Christian rule. The Segovian scholar Yçe de Gebir's ruling (in his 1462 work *Breviario Sunni*) that 'whether men or women, they shall not sleep with nor marry infidels' was typical of late medieval Iberian Islamic thought. Ordinary Muslims seem to have shared his view, and sometimes took action to enforce sexual segregation, as in 1444, when a group of Muslims who found a Jew in the brothel in the Muslim quarter in Huesca dragged him naked into the street.[85]

In practice, like their Christian and Jewish counterparts, Muslims were especially preoccupied by female behaviour, to the extent that the late fourteenth-century mufti Ibn Miqlash told his co-religionists to emigrate to Muslim lands, because they could not properly protect the chastity of their women under Christian rule.[86] By both religion and gender, Muslim women who had sex with non-Muslims were particularly vulnerable. They could be executed for sex with Christian men, but this was often commuted to enslavement by the crown – a punishment that could not be imposed on Christians and Jews – with the accuser receiving a portion of the sale price. Although some Muslim women were accused by profit-seeking Christians or by their own sexual partners, they were vulnerable not just because of Christian hostility, but because of the honour culture within which they lived.[87] A Muslim woman who had sex with a non-Muslim man would likely be punished by both the Islamic and Christian authorities, probably by stoning or whipping under Muslim law, and by enslavement under the Christian system. Some Muslims denounced their own women to the Christian authorities for transgressive sex, and the self-governing Muslim community in Valencia purchased royal confirmation of its privilege that whenever a Muslim woman was found guilty of sex with a non-Muslim, the death penalty would be imposed on her without possibility of monetary remission. Crown registers include numerous cases of Muslim women convicted of sexual offences and sentenced to death, flogging or enslavement by their co-religionists. Amiri, a Muslim woman living in Zaragoza at the beginning of the fourteenth century, was twice caught having sex with non-Muslims. Her community intervened on her behalf, preventing her enslavement, and she promised not to reoffend. But then she was found with a Jewish man; the two communities came to blows, 'wishing to kill each other over her'. She was convicted and sold into slavery, with the proceeds divided between the crown and the informer who denounced her.[88]

Heretics

In the early twelfth century Guibert, abbot of Nogent, described a heretical sect near Soissons. Its members had unorthodox beliefs: they were nominally Christian, but were distinguished from the rest of the population by their refusal to accept key Catholic doctrines. Moreover, or so he claimed, they had extremely unusual views on sex, condemning both marriage and procreation. Most scandalously of all, they met 'in underground vaults and hidden cellars', where 'as soon as the candles are extinguished, they shout "chaos!"'... and everyone has intercourse with the first person who happens to be at hand' – of whatever sex. Any children born as a product of these orgies were ritually killed and made into bread, which was consumed 'as a sort of sacrament'.[89] Surprisingly, this orgiastic sect was not a one-off, and similar stories can be found throughout the Middle Ages. Around two centuries later, for example, John of Viktring came across a group of Austrian heretics who met in dark caves after midnight; there they held religious rituals, but also engaged in feasting, dancing and sex. This, they said, was the state of paradise in which Adam and Eve lived before the Fall.[90]

Claims that religious deviants also engaged in sexual deviancy dated back at least to Roman times, when early Christian converts were accused of participating in incestuous orgies and worshipping the genitals of their spiritual leaders.[91] From the twelfth century onwards the Inquisition, a group of Catholic institutions specifically set up to deal with heresy, seized on this tradition and characterized heretics as sexual deviants with strange ideas and a particular penchant for orgies. Such claims stemmed from the idea that heretics were hypocrites (because they preached one thing but did another), and from a (possibly deliberate) misinterpretation of the common heretical belief that it was possible to obtain a state of sin-free perfection, which allowed the supposedly perfect individual to indulge in all sorts of sin without consequence.[92] They were frequently accused of having eccentric ideas. In early eleventh-century Italy, the heresiarch Gerald told Bishop Aribert of Milan: 'We esteem virginity above all else, although we have wives . . . No one knows his wife carnally, but carefully treats her as his mother or sister.' The bishop asked how the human race would perpetuate itself if everyone remained a virgin, to which Gerald replied that once humanity was free of corruption it would reproduce sinlessly, like bees.[93]

At least some Cathars apparently taught that marital sex was a sin; indeed, it could even be considered worse than sex with a stranger, since it (hopefully) happened more often and therefore caused greater shame.[94] In 1245–6 the Inquisition extracted confessions on this subject from several Cathars in Toulouse. Peire Farcias saw the body as an unfortunate reminder of the Fall, for it was steeped in corruption and was the prison of the soul. He also believed that 'Matrimony, as an encouragement to procreate and so to the making of more flesh, was therefore nothing but prostitution; the only true marriage was that of the soul with God.' Consequently, he had not slept with his wife Ayma for two years, even though she did not share his beliefs.[95] Peire Alboara of Laurace, an ex-Cathar, confessed that he had once believed that sex with his wife was as sinful as sex with other women.[96] Other sources claimed that Cathars did not eat meat, cheese or eggs, because they were 'begotten of coition', although it may actually have been because they believed in the transmigration of souls to warm-blooded creatures, which would explain why they did eat fish.[97]

Accused heretics allegedly continued to make unorthodox assertions throughout the later Middle Ages. In 1339 three men who were arrested in Constance made the troubling claim that sex on the altar was as meritorious as the consecration of the host.[98] In 1434 Master Werner, a schoolteacher from Ulm, recanted the 'evil articles' taught to him by a heretic, which had led him to visit a brothel, even though he was married.[99] In fifteenth-century Norfolk, William Colyn said that he would rather touch a woman's private parts than the host; he also believed that all women should be held in common and marriage abolished.[100] Elsewhere, dissenters expressed offensive views about the sexuality of Christ and the saints. William, a heretic interrogated in Lübeck in 1402, claimed that Christ fornicated with Mary Magdalene, and the Virgin Mary with John the Evangelist.[101]

The Catholic Church was particularly keen to highlight cases in which heretics preached high-minded ideals, but failed to live up to them. For example, Bernard Gui, a Dominican Inquisitor writing in the 1320s, claimed,

> The Waldenses praise continence to their believers, yet they admit that burning passion must be satisfied ... They declare that it is better to satisfy passion by any means, however shameful, than to be tempted within the heart. This, however, they keep very secret lest they fall into disrepute with their believers.[102]

In addition, heretical leaders were frequently accused of spreading their ideas through seduction, and of sexually exploiting their followers. Tanchelm, a twelfth-century radical preacher from the Low Countries, was stated to have 'spread his errors by way of matrons and harlots, whose intimacies, confidential conversation and private couch he was most willing to enjoy'. One chronicler alleged that he was 'so incontinent and beastly that he violated girls in the presence of their mothers and wives in the sight of their husbands, asserting that this was a spiritual act'. At around the same time, the charismatic preacher Henry of Lausanne supposedly surrounded himself with women and adolescent boys, and encouraged them to touch him intimately, so that they 'publicly proclaimed that they had never touched a man of such strength, such humanity, such power'; he was also accused of being 'wholly given over to sensuality' and of having an affair with a knight's wife.[103] A fourteenth-century German heretic allegedly taught three women about the Trinity by having them strip naked before having intercourse with each in turn.[104] Such accusations may, in some cases, have been true, but most were probably rooted in deliberate misinterpretations of ministry to women and in centuries-old stereotypes of nonconformist leaders as tricksters who seduced vulnerable people into sin under the guise of sharing religious ideas.

Even when alleged heretics confessed to unorthodox beliefs or behaviour, it is unwise to take their statements at face value: many did so only when tortured or after several months in prison.[105] The impact of such practices is particularly clear in the trials of the Knights Templar, held across Europe in 1307–11. The members of this religious order were charged with religious offences (including heresy and blasphemy), but also with sexual crimes. There were suggestions that, although the Templar rule threatened sodomites with expulsion from the order or life imprisonment, in reality members were actively encouraged to have sex with each other, and young recruits were sexually exploited by older brothers. Very few Templars admitted that they had personally committed such acts, but many testified that permission to do so was given, or made accusations against other members of the order. In Poitiers, for example, Raymond of Narbonne said he had been told that sex with women was more sinful than sex with men, although he had never acted on this. Brother Stephen claimed that Brother Paul had tried to 'corrupt and pollute him with that abhorrent sin'; he had responded by breaking his jaw, and an official rebuked him for refusing Paul's request. In Paris, John Torteville confessed to having sex with a brother named William. However, it is worth noting that the vast majority of confessions were obtained in regions where torture was used; witness statements from countries that did not employ such tactics, including England, were decidedly tamer. There is also some evidence that, in certain trials, witnesses were hand-picked and possibly coached in what to say. Overall, there is no reason to think that Templars were any more prone to sodomy than any other religious order, and both accusations and confessions were clearly shaped by contemporary ideas about how heretics behaved.[106]

The testimonies of alleged Cathars from the small French village of Montaillou, recorded in the early fourteenth century, are also illuminating. Some of the villagers did confess the sorts of ideas and behaviours that a medieval inquisitor expected of a heretic. Pierre Clergue, the priest, had at least a dozen mistresses, and when a woman upbraided him for sleeping with a married woman, he supposedly replied 'One woman's just like another. The sin is the same, whether she is married or not. Which is as much as to say that there is no sin about it at all.'[107] Overall, however, there was a distinct lack of the outrageous attitudes and practices found in the more scurrilous accounts. Many residents do seem to have taken a relaxed attitude to irregular unions, but perhaps not for religious reasons; non-Cathars seem to have fornicated just as much as Cathars, and concubinage was a common practice in other parts of the Pyrenees that were untroubled by heresy.[108] The views of Guillaume Bélibaste, the Cathar holy man of Morella, seem to have been fairly representative. He asserted that 'It amounts to the same and the sin is the same, to know one's wife carnally or to do the same with a concubine'; it was, however, best to live with one woman who ran your house, since having mistresses led to bastards and poverty. He was also strongly opposed to incest.[109]

Even in the Middle Ages some more moderate writers were sceptical about the lurid claims that emerged from inquisitorial processes. The friar Giacomo Capelli, writing around 1240, said that the Cathars were chaste, the rumours of fornication and orgies were untrue, and those who sinned were dealt with harshly.[110] That so many heretics, across such a wide geographical range and over a period of several centuries, were accused of and confessed to such similar beliefs is almost certainly evidence not of coherent and interconnected belief systems, but rather the product of inquisitorial imaginations, with testimonies shaped by existing ideas and leading questions.[111]

Sex with Demons

Sex with people of other races and faiths was seriously offensive to medieval sensibilities, but perhaps the ultimate transgression was to have intercourse with a demon. Fears that such relationships were possible hardened into a firm conviction that demons could have sex with humans during the twelfth century, so that by the mid-thirteenth century the chronicler Caesarius of Heisterbach could write, 'There is nothing wonderful that demons should make love to a woman.' Nor was this unsophisticated fantasy: there was a great deal of serious discussion in learned circles about exactly how this worked. It was generally agreed that demons did not have bodies, or gender, and that they could not experience sexual pleasure. They could, however, assume sexed bodies to seduce humans, appearing as an incubus (that is, apparently male) or a succubus (seemingly female). Two groups were thought to be particularly vulnerable: women (because their souls were more impressionable), and those who were committed to the religious life, including the clergy.[112]

Women who had sexual intercourse with demons might be harshly punished: Angèle de la Barthe was burnt to death at Toulouse in 1275, having been found guilty of having sex with an incubus over a period of several years.[113] Other women received spiritual remedies for their problem. On a visit to Aquitaine, Bernard of Clairvaux (d. 1153) met 'a pitiable woman possessed of a wanton demon, an incubus, who for six years abused her and treated her with incredible lust'; the saint saved her by giving her one of his staffs to place in her bed, and then excommunicating the demon, so that it could not approach any woman.[114] Stephen of Bourbon, a thirteenth-century Dominican inquisitor, related the story of a female mystic who committed the sin of spiritual pride. One night, as she contemplated her own excellence, a beautiful king and his entourage appeared in her room, claiming to be Christ and his apostles. The next night, the man came alone and seduced her, swearing her to secrecy. He subsequently appeared in various guises (including as a knight, a cleric and a peasant), until the woman eventually realized that he was a demon, and rushed to confession.[115]

Not every woman who became the recipient of demonic sexual advances succumbed to them, even when the persecution lasted for years. The pious widow Ermine of Rheims (c. 1347–1396) lived as a religious recluse for the last three years of her life, and every night she was visited by demons, who left her covered in wounds and subjected her to sexual temptation. One appeared in the form of her dead husband, got into bed and snuggled up to her before falling asleep. On several occasions she awoke to find male demons in her room, exposing their genitals to tempt her into sin, although she always hid her face and resisted. Another demon predicted that her confessor would seduce her; yet another kissed her and lifted her into bed, so that she had 'a very ugly dream'. One particularly trying night, a pair of demons in the form of a beautiful young couple had sex in her chamber, to encourage her 'to take evil pleasure in fleshly sin'. One of them taunted her that, despite all her piety, she would go to Hell, so she might as well enjoy herself first. Ermine's struggles with demons were particularly extreme, but they were not unique. The Italian mystic Frances of Rome (1384–1440) had nightly visions of naked demons of both sexes engaging in sodomitic orgies as she lay in bed next to her husband.[116]

Nor were the afflicted solely women, and clerical writers recorded stories of similarly troubled holy men. Gerald of Wales recounted the case of a young monk who had lost his virginity to a demon: whenever the monk tried to pray, 'an evil spirit approaches him, places its hands on his genital organs, and does not stop rubbing his body with its own until he is so agitated that he is polluted by an emission of semen.'[117] Giordano da Bergamo, author of *An Inquiry into Witches* (c. 1420), recounted the story of a hermit who lived near Lake Garda. The holy man was seduced by a beautiful girl and had sex with her. Afterwards, the 'girl' taunted the hermit: 'Look what you've done! I'm not a girl or a woman, in fact, but the Devil!' and promptly disappeared. This evil being had extracted so much semen that the hermit's body completely dried out, and he died within the month.[118]

According to the theorists, demons could not only have sex with humans, they could impregnate them. Sometimes such conceptions were mere trickery: women swelled as if pregnant, but then 'they detumenesced, with only the emission of a great windiness'.[119] But sex with a demon could occasionally lead to a real pregnancy. Since demons did not produce semen, they had to steal it; to do this, they would take the form of a succubus and gather it from a human male. The succubus would then turn into an incubus, and impregnate a woman with the stolen seed. Alternatively, according to the fifteenth-century Castilian theologian Alonso Tostado, a demon could gather up the semen emitted when a man masturbated, and use it to impregnate a woman. Although a man might not intend this to happen, he was still to blame for the consequences of his sinful act.[120]

Both methods were problematic, because the child's paternity could not be known, but the use of stolen semen did at least mean that the children of such unions were human, and could be saved. Nevertheless, when such offspring appear in the records, it is usually because they are behaving in ways that reflect their dubious origins. Guichard, Bishop of Troyes (1298–1314), was supposedly the son of an incubus and a human woman, and was himself tried for sorcery in 1308.[121] Stories also circulated of demonic descent in the female line. According to legend, the Angevin kings of England were descended from Mélusine, a beautiful countess of Anjou whose true identity – she was the daughter of Satan – was revealed when she vanished out of a window rather than stay to the end of the Mass. Such ancestry, many thought, explained why Henry II and his sons were such wicked men.[122]

For much of the Middle Ages people who had sex with demons were presented as victims: they were assaulted, or tricked, or at least pestered into submission. But towards the end of the period things began to change, as prosecutions for 'maleficia' (black magic), which had previously been extremely rare, became increasingly common, especially in Italy and Switzerland. In many cases, they seem to have developed out of campaigns against heretics, with inquisitors claiming to have uncovered groups who engaged in orgy-based Devil-worship. The *Errores Gazariorum*, probably written within the circle of the Lausanne inquisitors in the late 1430s, includes one of the earliest descriptions of the witches' sabbath, a gathering that included orgies: 'a man with a woman, or a man with another man, or sometimes a father with his daughter, a son with his mother, a brother with his sister and a horse, without any respect for the natural order.' This all took place in the dark.[123] The influence of such texts is apparent in confessions such as the one extracted from a young Swiss man named Aymonet Maugetaz, in 1438. He testified that, after worshipping the Devil, everyone present would 'copulate with each other in the manner of dogs'. He had himself participated in such an orgy, having sex with a woman he had not met before.[124]

Towards the end of the century the persecution of witches intensified, and texts such as Heinrich Kramer's *Hammer of the Witches* (1486) increasingly stressed the intimate personal bond between a witch (who was almost always a lustful female) and her demon, a bond that was often intensified by sex.[125] Girolamo Visconti, a Milanese Dominican writing around 1460, claimed that witches lured people into their sect with the promise of handsome youths and beautiful women; once recruited, they were assigned a demon with which they had frequent intercourse.[126] The earliest known example of such sex comes from Ireland, where Lady Alice Kyteler was investigated for sorcery and witchcraft in 1324. Among the charges against her was the claim that 'the said lady had a certain demon as incubus, by whom she permitted herself to be known carnally'; her servant Petronilla (who was subsequently burnt to death) confessed that she had watched as 'the apparition had intercourse with Alice'. As a high-status woman, Alice was able to evade punishment by fleeing to England. But many of the women accused of witchcraft in the fifteenth century were marginal figures.[127] Jordana de Baulmes, who was tried in Lausanne in 1477, confessed that, years before she participated in satanic orgies, she had left her husband and borne two illegitimate children. Martiale Espaza, who in 1491 confessed to having sex with a demon called Robin, had a similarly complex sexual history.[128] In 1495 nine poor women were burnt as witches in Rifreddo, Piedmont. Several of the victims confessed to sex with demons, including Giovanna Mottossa, although she had not enjoyed the experience very much, since the creature's penis was 'as cold as ice'.[129]

Although such stories seem like the ultimate proof of medieval credulity, scholarly interest in demonic sex may actually have arisen out of scepticism. From the early thirteenth century, angelology and demonology were studied as serious sciences: rather than simply accepting that these beings were real, scholars sought proof of their existence. Perhaps inevitably this led instead to a growing sense of doubt. But men and women who confessed to sex with demons – and especially women who were penetrated and impregnated and exhausted by such beings – seemed to provide conclusive proof that they did exist, thus upholding an important article of the Christian faith. Moreover, they reinforced the widespread belief that deviation from sexual norms was displeasing to God, and detrimental to society's well-being.

For these reasons, sexual misbehaviour, whatever form it took, was something that needed to be controlled. And yet the medieval authorities were well aware that this was easier said than done; if very few people were tempted by a demon, and only a relatively small minority had the opportunity to form a relationship with a person of a different religion, lapses into fornication, adultery or sodomy were far more common. The need to avoid the transgressions detailed in the last three chapters led many people to believe that it was necessary to provide a less sinful outlet for male desires, and thus shaped medieval attitudes to prostitution.

NINE

Prostitution

Prostitution has often been described as the oldest profession, and it was certainly well established in medieval Europe. Equally firmly entrenched were the complex and varied attitudes which sex work continues to provoke, ranging from sympathy to pragmatism to outright hostility, and everything in between.

Religious Ideas

In *The Treasure of the City of Ladies*, Christine de Pizan (1364–c. 1430) discussed the conduct of various groups of women – including prostitutes, or, as she called them, 'women who are foolish and loose and lead disorderly lives, although there is nothing more abominable'. The life of a sex worker puzzled her: how, she asked, 'can she tolerate indecency and living, drinking and eating entirely among men more vile than swine – men who strike her, drag her about and threaten her, and by whom she is always in danger of being killed?' This woman was 'sunk in sin' and must repent, but God (and, if necessary, a magistrate) would help and protect her. Good people would pity her, and help her find honest work.[1]

Christine de Pizan's attitude, at once judgemental and sympathetic, may seem contradictory, but her words reflect medieval society's ambivalence about women who had sex for money. In part, this uncertainty was fuelled by linguistic issues: there was no direct equivalent of our word 'prostitute', and arguably no direct equivalent of the concept. In particular, there was no clear line between a prostitute and a promiscuous woman; they were called by the same names, and motivated by the same uncontrollable female lust, so that whether or not they took money was a minor detail. A 'common woman' was one who slept with many men, usually but not always for payment, and any woman who was not obviously under the control of one man risked being labelled as such.[2] Thomas of Chobham's definitions of the word 'meretrix' (perhaps best translated as 'whore' rather than 'prostitute') included 'a woman who makes herself available to the lust of many men' and 'a woman who sells her depravity in public'.[3] The flexibility of the term is probably illustrated by the fact that forty Exeter women (about 1 per cent of the female population) were accused of being whores in 1324.[4]

From St Augustine onwards, ecclesiastical discussions of prostitution suggested that it was a necessary evil in an imperfect world. Medieval attitudes to prostitutes are perhaps most closely comparable to medieval attitudes to Jewish usurers: their existence was incompatible with Church teachings, and discomforted many, but they were tolerated because their services were socially useful. Male biology meant that a man might need to have non-marital sex, and it was better that he do so with a prostitute than with an honest woman or – worse still – another man. As the Dominican preacher Giordano of Pisa (*c.* 1255–1311) explained:

God always loathes the greater evils, and from every evil that he tolerates he always retrieves a greater good ... And so an evil is suffered in order to preserve a greater good, and sometimes more than one good. Now do you see the prostitutes of the cities being tolerated? This is a great evil, and if we avoided it, yes, we would be taking away a great benefit, in that there would be more adultery, more sodomy, which would be much worse.[5]

This is not to say that the Church was comfortable with the existence of prostitution, and three issues were the cause of especial angst. One problem was that prostitutes had sex with many unknown people, and thus could not be sure if a client was 'a husband, an excommunicate, a priest, a monk, a Jew, a father or brother or relative of a person with whom they had previously slept'. Consequently, it had to be assumed that they committed adultery, incest and other forms of 'impurity and wantonness' on a regular basis.[6] There was also considerable concern about the financial implications of prostitution. Most authorities agreed that a prostitute earned her money through her bodily labour, and was therefore entitled to keep it. If, on the other hand, a woman profited from deceit – for example wearing make-up – her claim was less secure. Such earnings should really be given to the Church, although the clergy must be wary of the scandal this might cause.[7]

This caveat highlighted another key concern: on what terms should churchmen interact with, and minister to, prostitutes? Bishop Maurice de Sully of Paris (d. 1196) would not allow the prostitutes of Paris to fund a window for his cathedral, in case he seemed to condone their life, and

Thomas of Chobham argued that they should not make offerings at the altar during Mass, 'lest they carry with them the stench of the brothel to the perfume of the sacrifice'. He also argued that prostitutes should not be allowed to take communion, although they should be permitted to confess. But 'If prostitutes . . . come to do penance, priests should make clear their baseness to them so that they understand how much they have offended God by selling their bodies . . . to the service of the Devil.' It should also be stressed that their actions had endangered many others.[8]

These words seem cruel, but were based on the belief that sex workers, like all humans, were sinners. Consequently, the kindest thing a priest could do for them was to highlight the repugnance of their sin, thus making them repent and offering a chance of salvation. There was some recognition that the gravity of this sin varied; indeed, it was widely recognized that many women were forced into prostitution by poverty, and often argued that this lessened their sin. Thomas of Chobham judged that a woman who slept around purely for pleasure was worse than one who did so out of need. Ultimately, however, there was a strong sense that every woman who sold sex could, and should, mend her ways; if she did so, her past should be forgiven. Saints such as the Desert Harlots (who abandoned their debauched lives for asceticism) and Mary Magdalene (a repentant prostitute who became one of Jesus' most important followers) offered models of how this could be achieved.[9]

Inspired by such thinking, convents for repentant prostitutes (many of them dedicated to Mary Magdalene) were established across Europe from the thirteenth century. Their exact purpose and character varied from institution to institution: some were temporary shelters where women could be rehabilitated then married, but others functioned like conventional religious houses. The Avignon house for repentant prostitutes was founded in the 1330s by Guibert du Val, Bishop of Narbonne; its first building was small and dark, like a prison, and located on the very outskirts of the city, but it was soon improved and enlarged. By 1376 there were forty women in residence; they had to be under the age of 25 at the time of entry, and many of them seem to have stayed for decades. They lived a life of penance, with lots of fasting, contemplation, devotion and manual labour, and very little talking or contact with the outside world.[10] Other institutions, such as the Paris Convent of the Filles-Dieu, seem to have functioned chiefly as retirement homes for former prostitutes who had reached the end of their working lives. These elderly women (most of them were at least thirty) lived like nuns and supported themselves chiefly by begging, which was seen as an appropriate activity for those who had already been sullied by their work.[11]

Repentant prostitutes were also seen as a fitting focus for individual charity: because poverty was thought to be one of the main reasons why women engaged in sex work, it was assumed that improving their financial circumstances would enable them to stop sinning. According to Pope Innocent III, men who married reformed prostitutes did a good work that counted towards the remission of their own sins.[12] In Nuremberg such marriages were actively encouraged, and craftsmen could receive citizenship in return for marrying a prostitute from the civic brothel.[13] More commonly, organizations and individuals gave money to allow women to give up sex work. Some Avignonese confraternities offered dowries to prostitutes who wished to renounce their trade and marry, and the secular authorities provided similar aid. In 1429, for example, they gave Adrienne, a poor woman willing to leave her life of sin, three gold florins from the estate of a wealthy merchant. Individuals also left money in their wills. In 1315 Rostain de Vallobrègue left money to be distributed to the 'sinful women' of Avignon every Good Friday; a century later, Cristina, wife of a Venetian dyer, bequeathed 25 ducats to liberate a 'sinner' who was working in the public brothel because of misfortune, but wished to leave it for a better life in divine matrimony. Acts of charity to poor girls, such as leaving money for their dowries, may have been intended as pre-emptive efforts to prevent prostitution.[14]

Rules and Regulations

If ecclesiastical attitudes to prostitution were often idealistic and impractical, urban authorities generally took a more pragmatic stance. In the twelfth and thirteenth centuries the emphasis was firmly on expulsion, an approach typified by the early thirteenth-century statutes of Carcassonne, which baldly stated: 'Public prostitutes are to be put outside the walls of Carcassonne.'[15] Then things began to change. The earliest surviving reference to the creation of an authorized red-light district comes from Montpellier, where in 1285 the Carreria Calida ('Hot Street') in the suburb of Villanova was assigned to the town's prostitutes, who were given the protection of the king and court, and could no longer be expelled.[16] Over the next few decades, numerous cities (including Dijon, Nuremberg and Munich) followed suit and founded municipal brothels, or established areas (sometimes streets, sometimes walled and gated enclosures) where prostitutes were allowed to live and work, under the regulation and supervision of public officials.[17]

The reasons for this shift are unclear but, like most things that happened in the fourteenth century, it has often been linked to the Black

Death. High male mortality possibly made it harder for women to marry, and the economic difficulties resulting from the pandemic may have made cash-strapped urban authorities keen to profit from prostitution, but this was also a time when wider attitudes to sexual morality were changing. There was increased fear of sodomy (a crime which, it was widely believed, men were more likely to commit if they were unable to have sex with a woman), and growing concern that prostitutes could corrupt good women. As a 1337 statute from Lacaune put it, 'One diseased ewe infects the whole flock.'[18] Similar sentiments were expressed in the 1355 statues of the Florentine podestà:

> To extirpate the evils and sins which might enter the city of Florence stemming from the indecency of whoring women who circulate continuously through the city, for which reason in the city are committed shameful acts, behaviour and many sins, for which God is angered and the honour of the city is mocked.[19]

Such thinking seems to have been especially prevalent in the honour cultures of Southern Europe, where towns were particularly keen to enclose their prostitutes.[20]

Nevertheless, municipal brothels were not universally adopted, and cities including Paris and Cologne instead recognized privately run brothels, allowing them to operate in certain areas of the city.[21] England was another significant anomaly. There was a semi-official brothel district in Southwark, on the south bank of the Thames. Those who worked there were governed by a set of customs that banned troublesome behaviours such as supporting lovers, harassing potential customers in the street, spinning and wearing aprons. Unusually, it was also stipulated that brothels must be run by men. By the end of the fifteenth century there were also municipal brothels in the port towns of Sandwich and Southampton. The former was run by a married couple, and had four resident prostitutes; the regulations required that the women pay 16d a week for bed and board, and banned the keepers from beating them or overcharging them for ale.[22]

These exceptions apart, most English towns and cities continued to focus on punishment and expulsion. In the City of London, women convicted of bawdry or whoring were punished on an ascending scale, encompassing hair shaving, public processions and the pillory, and were banished for a third offence.[23] A 1344 Bristol ordinance barred lepers and prostitutes from living within the city walls, and from 1467 Leicester required burgesses to report any brothel, prostitute or procuress to the courts so they could be expelled.[24] Nevertheless, conviction rates were astonishingly low: in the (admittedly incomplete) records of the London Commissary Court, 377 women were charged with prostitution between 1471 and 1515, but only ten confessed, and conviction rates for pimping were even lower. The experiences of Mariona Wood, who was first cited for prostitution in 1479, seem typical. She appeared regularly through the 1480s, charged variously with fornication, adultery, prostitution and pimping, but the city courts never punished her. The ecclesiastical court excommunicated her but could not enforce the sentence.[25] Similar patterns were found across the country, and we might reasonably wonder whether some authorities really wanted to prevent prostitution, or simply to share in the profits. In Winchelsea, one of the Cinque Ports, whores were simply required to pay a quarterly penalty of 6s 8d, which was effectively a licensing fee.[26]

Whichever approach a city chose, it was ultimately doomed to failure, and thus illicit sex work was a problem for urban authorities across Europe. While some brothel-keepers ran large, professional operations, many worked part-time and on a very small scale, often in domestic settings. In Exeter, for example, seventeen women were listed as brothel-keepers between 1373 and 1393; they all had other jobs. In York, Medard Leonard and his wife were charged: 'They keep common bawdry in their house between whoever wants to commit adultery or fornication. And also they keep a common whore in their house for the desire of whoever wants to take her.' This was not, however, Leonard's primary profession, since he was also a goldsmith.[27] Many women sold sex on a casual basis, among them Marion de la Court, a linen-weaver who lived in late fourteenth-century Paris. She was perpetually hard up, and was forced to commit multiple thefts by her boyfriend, who also seems to have been her pimp. Around the same time, Marion la Liourde cohabited with a pastry chef and serial thief who passed as her husband; she worked as a prostitute in the Cité.[28] Like the two Marions, many of the women who sold sex in this way were older and in long-term relationships. The women punished for engaging in prostitution in fifteenth-century Gradec included several married women such as Margaret, wife of Lacko the Shoemaker.[29]

Fourteenth-century Prague had two civic brothels, but there were frequent complaints about unlicensed brothels. In the parish of St Gallen, for example, Wenceslaus Lopata ran one from his house, to the scandal of his neighbours. Ludwig Coiata, the parish priest of St John of the Rocks, was similarly accused of keeping numerous prostitutes in his house and allowing all manner of men to visit them, 'all of which neighbours and people passing by stumble upon and are scandalised'.[30] Women often solicited in taverns, such as the notorious Bell in Warwick Lane, London.

In 1485 the innkeeper was charged with 'keeping whoredom in his house' by 'harbouring suspected women', and the ostler was accused of fornication. Fourteen years later Joan Blond, the tapster, was charged as a whore, and Agnes Thurston, another employee, as a bawd.[31] In Nantes a decree of 1494 noted that in several bathhouses 'poor girls abandoned their bodies to a great number of strangers', while an earlier set of Sienese statutes complained that 'in the public baths horrible and mortal sins are committed.' In many cities, this problem was addressed by restricting access to these buildings: in thirteenth-century Marseilles, for example, prostitutes were only allowed to bathe on Mondays.[32] In 1487 Strasbourg additionally forbade any former prostitute to work as a bathhouse attendant unless she had unquestionably mended her ways.[33]

Other women worked entirely in the streets, where their clients were often men too poor or too tight to pay the official rates: in fifteenth-century London a priest paid 'Prone Joan who lives with Spanish Nell' 4d for their first encounter, and gave her cake and beer for the second.[34] Streetwalkers were seen as the lowest of the low, and were often women who had been expelled from the municipal brothel for being too old, ill or disorderly to work. They thus had few other options, despite facing serious punishments if they were caught.[35] Particular districts became associated with this sort of prostitution. In Ghent, for example, sex workers touted for business within the recesses of the city walls; a 1330 ordinance forbidding single women to sit there was clearly an attempt to prevent this.[36] A surprising amount of soliciting seems to have taken place in and around churches: in medieval Paris 'filles de vie' were often arrested in and around Notre Dame, and several of the women presented for prostitution in fifteenth-century York lived in rented properties in St Andrew's churchyard.[37] Few cases, however, were as outrageous as that of the young Florentine noble who in 1445 was convicted of sacrilege after fornicating under the organ in the church of San Barnaba with a 'poor little prostitute' named Margarita.[38]

Across Europe, sumptuary laws were used to stigmatize prostitutes, although the mere existence of these rules implicitly recognized the women as a permanent feature of urban life. A striped hood was one common sign of prostitution, but some towns chose their own symbols. In fourteenth-century Avignon prostitutes were banned from wearing coats, silk veils, amber rosaries and gold rings, under penalty of fines and confiscation. When the rules were tightened in the fifteenth century, they were required to wear a four-finger-wide dark or white cloth on the left arm. Sex workers in fourteenth-century Caustres were obliged to wear a man's hat and a scarlet belt. In Venice their identifying symbol, worn on the rare occasions they were allowed out in public, was a yellow scarf. Such distinctive attire helped clients to identify prostitutes, and stopped honest women being propositioned.[39]

In addition to regional variations in practice, there were also shifts in attitude over time. Outbreaks of disease often triggered campaigns against prostitution, since they heightened awareness of both the moral and medical dangers of sex. A crackdown on disorderly houses in Ipswich began during the 1465 plague outbreak, and in 1470 (following another serious outbreak) there was an order for the expulsion of all 'harlots and bawds'.[40] The personal opinions of those in charge were another important factor. In 1473 there was a substantial increase in prosecutions in London; the Great Chronicle recorded that the new mayor, William Hampton, 'did diligent and sharp correction upon Venus' servants, and caused them to be garnished and attired with ray [striped] hoods, and to be shown about the city with their minstrelsy before them by many and sundry market days'.[41] Other officials could be persuaded to turn a blind eye: in 1344 the beadle of Farringdon Without was accused of taking bribes from local prostitutes 'to protect them in their practices'.[42] Similar misconduct probably explains repeated attempts to stop Venetian officials associating with prostitutes, including prohibitions on eating, drinking or sleeping with them, and on accepting gifts, including flowers.[43] At the very end of the Middle Ages an increased level of religiosity in urban government led some authorities (especially in Germany) to take a tougher approach to prostitution – foreshadowing the Reformation years, when brothels became the ultimate symbol of medieval corruption and were shut down.[44]

In the Middle Ages, as today, sex was often seen as an urban commodity, to the extent that Humbert of Romans (d. 1277) suggested that illicit sex among peasants was explained by the lack of prostitutes in villages.[45] Nevertheless, there are occasional references to women selling sex in rural areas, and to attempts to regulate this. Women living in settlements on major transport routes (such the Essex village of Ingatestone, on the main road between London and Colchester) were particularly likely to engage in prostitution, but brothels were even found in the tiny hill towns of the Languedoc. 'The house of Peter Rascacii' was the authorized brothel in Uzès in 1326, while Lacaune allowed 'public immoral women' to live in 'the street of France' in 1337. Back in England, a woman known as Little Agnes was repeatedly presented in the late fifteenth-century manorial court of Battle Abbey for procuring and keeping a 'suspect house'.[46]

Life in the Brothel

While efforts to control prostitution were driven by negative stereotypes, some accounts of life inside a medieval brothel were extremely
romanticized. Antonio Beccadelli's *L'ermafrodito* (1425), dedicated to the
banker and politician Cosimo de' Medici, praises the 'pleasant bordello'
in Florence, where 'You will meet the sweet Elena, the blonde Matilde
. . . You will see Gianetta followed by her little dog . . . Then will come
Clodia with her naked painted breasts, Clodia a girl whose caresses are
priceless . . .'[47] The women thus idealized were clearly attractive young
girls, and throughout the Middle Ages the stereotypical prostitute was a
young, single woman. Many of the women working in municipal brothels
probably did fit into this category: in late medieval Dijon most prostitutes
began working in their late teens and few seem to have stayed in public
brothels past the age of thirty; in Avignon the women were supposed to
be under 25 and pretty.[48]

To add to their appeal, many brothels functioned as mock-courtly
spaces, with feasting, drinking and dancing. They were often given names
drawn from love poetry, and the rooms were showily decorated and lav-
ishly heated. The women were well dressed in fine fabrics and expensive
accessories, and clients were encouraged to buy food and drink and to play
board games.[49] When 'Le Paon', a large Sluis brothel, was inventoried
in 1396, the goods and chattels owned by the recently deceased madam,
Bette Caens, were worth £450; they included some very expensive clothes,
such as a scarlet cloak lined with squirrel fur, and 25 wimples, which were
probably worn by the prostitutes. The building (which was rented) had
hot baths, a well-equipped kitchen, and at least six bedrooms spread over
three floors – although the fact that all but one of these rooms contained
several beds raises the intriguing possibility that sex in a brothel was not
necessarily a private activity.[50]

But behind the fantasy lay a less palatable reality: in many establishments the furniture was hired, and the clothing second-hand. Even in the
best houses, the pleasure-seeking ladies were really working women who
were hired by the half-hour, often because they were compelled to do so.
The Book of the Knight of the Tower, a late fourteenth-century advice book
for women, claimed that 'many of the women of the brothel do their sin
only because of poverty, or because they were deceived by bad counsel of
bawds and evil women.'[51] Evidence from fifteenth-century Dijon seems
to support this assertion, since the vast majority of women who appeared
in court charged with prostitution claimed to have been forced into the
profession either by people or by personal circumstances.[52]

'The Prodigal Son at the Brothel', drawn in Alsace in 1469
(Getty Museum, MS Ludwig XV 9 (83.MR179), f. 106).

Persuading women into prostitution was viewed as a typically female sin, with particular hatred being reserved for women who prostituted their own daughters. According to the Slovenian *Law Book of Ilok*, a woman who led her daughter into prostitution should be punished in the same way as a woman who killed her illegitimate child – that is, she should be burnt – because both were a form of murder.[53] Several such cases were tried in late medieval London, including those of Juliana Colson, a widow who forced her daughter 'to go at night to the stews side and return the next day', and Katherine the Dutchwoman, who beat her daughter to make her go to the home of 'a certain Lombard' who later impregnated her.[54]

Other women apparently made a profession out of luring young, vulnerable girls into prostitution. In 1298 a Bolognese woman named Blonda accused her neighbour, Meglior, of being a well-known pimp who 'steals small girls and has them corrupted of their virginity for money'; the alleged victims included Blonda's young daughter, Dulce, although several neighbours testified that these claims were malicious falsehoods.[55] In 1385 Elizabeth Moring, a married woman, appeared before the borough court of London accused of being 'a common prostitute and common procuress'. According to the testimony of Joan, her servant, Elizabeth pretended to be an embroideress, and took in young women as her apprentices in this craft. Once they were bound to her, she 'incited' them to have sex with numerous men; she took their earnings and encouraged them to steal valuable items from their clients, which she then sold on. She was placed in the pillory before being expelled from the capital.[56]

Newcomers to the city were particularly vulnerable to such trickery. Joan Rawlins grew up in a Herefordshire village; as a young woman she decided to go to London to work as a servant. A tailor called John Barton offered to take her, and to find her 'good and honest service'. When they arrived in the city, he left her at a waterman's house near the Southwark stews, and went to find a bawd with whom to place her. Realizing she was in danger, the girl begged the waterman's wife for help. Barton turned out to have previous convictions for selling girls into prostitution; he was imprisoned in Newgate, then paraded through the streets to the pillory, and finally banished from the city.[57] It was probably not a coincidence that so many prostitutes were immigrants to the city in which they worked. A 1438 census by the Florentine Office of Decency, for example, found that only one of the 71 prostitutes working in the brothel district was a native of the city. The largest groups were (in order) from the Netherlands, Germany, northern Italy (mainly Venice), France and Slavonia. In Palermo, most of the women were Spanish.[58]

Other women ended up as prostitutes through circumstance. Some made unfortunate life choices, including Catherine, the wife of a Beaucaire boatman, who eloped with her lover 'out of madness'. He was a riverman and a pimp, and she ended up in the municipal brothel in Avignon.[59] Others were the victim of horrific crimes. Constanza was a young girl who moved from the countryside to work as a servant in Florence in the 1490s. Then she was 'assaulted, violated and sodomized' by 'many brutes, who shared her among themselves'; as a direct result she lost her job, and ended up working out of the Buco, a notorious tavern.[60] The limited options available to 'ruined' women are illustrated by the story of Sancha Bolea, who 'became by chance a wayward woman, because a man there, in Zaragoza, took my maidenhood and dishonoured me, and I was on the verge of going to the brothels'. Instead, in 1460, she entered into a contract with Juan de Madrid:

> In order to have some goods and not end up in the brothels, I have decided to come and live with you and serve you of my own free will. And I begged and asked you to take me into your house as housekeeper or servant, to stay with you and sleep with you, and to do with my body as you wish.

He paid her 200 sueldos to make her his concubine, which was arguably a better fate than the alternative, but which still left her in a dishonourable and precarious position.[61]

In some places a woman could be labelled as a prostitute purely on the strength of her sexual reputation. A woman's status as a prostitute in twelfth- and thirteenth-century Castile was established by notoriety, or by the number of men she had lain with; the critical number was usually five, but could be as low as two or three. In some towns a suspected prostitute could try to prove her innocence by undergoing an ordeal in which she carried a heated iron rod for nine paces. If her hands were not healed after three days, she would be considered guilty.[62] Elsewhere a woman could be ruled a prostitute based solely on the testimony of several witnesses of good repute. In 1400 Selvaggia, a married Florentine woman in her mid-forties, was accused of selling sex by neighbours who claimed that her reputation was that of a public prostitute, because men entered her house at all hours. Vanni di Miglore had argued with one of her regular visitors, a slippermaker; when he reproached the man for his behaviour, he was told 'I will screw who I please' and Selvaggia swore at him. Margherita claimed to have looked through the window of Selvaggia's house and seen her naked in bed with various men. The accused protested her innocence, but the judge ruled that she 'granted her body in lust for pecuniary gain' and should therefore to be treated as a prostitute.[63]

Equally disturbingly, women who sold sex outside of the officially sanctioned establishments could be forced into these institutions. From the 1470s, for example, the brothel-keepers in the Bavarian town of Nördlingen could take charge of itinerant prostitutes who stayed longer than three days in a tavern.[64] Some women were seized on even flimsier grounds, among them Elsa Stecklin of Merano, who in 1471 was processed to the brothel because she was found eating and drinking with a man in a dubious inn. Elsa protested her innocence, claiming that one Heinrich Stier was taking revenge on her because she refused to 'fulfil his will' (presumably she meant that she had refused to have sex with him).[65] The outcome of her case is unknown, but some women were rehabilitated: in 1480 Margret Pewrlein of Bolzano successfully petitioned the archduke of Austria to restore her honour after she was institutionalized on the mayor's orders, despite her protestations of innocence.[66] Others, knowing that they were about to face such humiliation, took a heartbreakingly stoical approach. When Catherine, a 26-year-old woman from Dijon, realized that the ducal archers wanted to carry her off to the brothel, she went there herself 'to avoid having them lead me there shamefully . . . and so the neighbours will not be scandalized'.[67]

The economic transactions that took place when women entered brothels are rarely visible to us, but a set of contracts from fourteenth-century Italy reveal the terms on which women were employed. In 1338 Ranaldo di Nicolò, keeper of the Perugia brothel, recruited five new women for his establishment; all of them agreed to contracts that obliged them to work at the brothel for a fixed term (of between one to three years), during which time he would take all their earnings, in return for covering their living expenses and giving them a small amount of clothing and other goods. The exact terms of the agreements varied slightly, probably in relation to the perceived vulnerability and marketability of the individual women, but all of them were employed on deeply unfavourable terms.[68] One hundred and fifty years later, Bernardino Fede recruited a girl named Sandra to the Florence brothel for a mere three florins – approximately the cost of a good donkey, and much lower than her purchase price had she been an enslaved woman.[69]

Such contracts put a woman entirely under the control of the brothel-keeper, who was usually a woman: most (but by no means all) 'matrons' were unmarried, foreign and poor, and many were former prostitutes. Some towns favoured male managers, especially towards the end of the Middle Ages, but male pimps were often seen as violence-prone wastrels who lived off women rather than providing for them.[70] In reality, brothel-keepers of both sexes were prone to mistreating their workers, as demonstrated by a 1471 criminal investigation into Lienhart Fryermut's mismanagement of the Nördlingen brothel. The problems came to light when one of the prostitutes, Els von Eystett, was forced to have an abortion, prompting gossip that the authorities decided to probe. They discovered that almost all of the women had been sold into the brothel and were heavily in debt to Fryermut. Several complained that they were regularly beaten and forced to see clients at inappropriate times (including on holy days and during their periods); they were also badly dressed, overcharged for basic necessities such as food and drink, and barely allowed to leave the brothel, even to go to church. Both Fryermut and his partner Barbara Tarschenfeindin were banished from the city, and the following year the city introduced new rules designed to protect prostitutes from financial exploitation and physical abuse.[71]

Given that several of the women suggested that their treatment in this house was unusually harsh, and compared it unfavourably to other brothels they had worked in, it was likely that many establishments were less problematic. Nevertheless, there was increasing concern about the mistreatment of prostitutes towards the end of the Middle Ages, in particular about trafficking and exploitative working conditions, and new regulations were introduced in an effort to tackle these problems and to enable women who wished to repent to do so. Men such as Peter Scheffner, who in 1480 was interrogated by the Augsburg city council on suspicion of trafficking, could face substantial penalties.[72]

Even by the standards of a society that allowed husbands to beat their wives, parents to beat their children, and employers to beat their servants and apprentices, prostitutes were unusually vulnerable to violence. In many cities brothel-keepers were allowed to physically punish women, and could request that they be imprisoned, usually for debt. This meant that many women experienced regular beatings, and only if they were subjected to extreme violence could they object. Marina, a Venetian prostitute, was frequently beaten by her pimp until October 1452, when he was fined by the Office of Decency for attacking her with a piece of wood, leaving her so bloody and swollen that she was unrecognizable. Fights between women were also a problem: in 1458 alone there were at least three serious scuffles in the Ferrara brothel. In one of these incidents a woman hit another with a club, and in another a woman named Caterina threw a chair at her colleague Agnese, hitting her in the face and splitting her lip.[73]

Sex workers were also attacked by clients, even though several cities introduced laws designed to prevent this. In the French market town of

Castelnaudry, for example, it was ruled that any attacker would be hoisted over a pole in front of the public house. Any client who injured a Genoese prostitute had to pay her medical costs, and to compensate her manager if she could not work.[74] In 1484 Giacomo Priuli, a Venetian noble, was banished for eight years for beating a prostitute and forcing her to commit sodomy.[75] The authorities also took seriously cases in which prostitutes (or their associates) were murdered by their clients. In 1299 the Oxford coroner held an inquest into the death of Margery de Hereford, recording that she was stabbed to death by a client, an unknown clerk, when she asked him for her fee. The man had got away.[76] Forty years later, the London coroner investigated the death of Alice Warde: 'on the preceding Sunday, at dusk, Geoffrey le Perler, a groom . . . came to the rent where Alice was living, intending to find Emma de Brakkele, a harlot, and to lie with her, but failing to find her, a quarrel arose between the said Geoffrey and Alice.' He stabbed her with his knife, killing her almost instantly.[77]

Another of the physical risks faced by the medieval sex worker is highlighted by a case from 1450s Dijon, in which a law clerk had sex with Jeanne de la Fontaine in the town's brothel. According to the court records: 'He had his pleasure of her and kept her under him about an hour; and he so wore her out and worked her so hard that she could do no more, and she dropped down beside the bed because this working overdistressed her so.'[78] From a medieval medical perspective, the unfortunate Jeanne was not just an assault victim, but living proof of the dangers of too much sex, which was probably seen as a greater risk to prostitutes than contagious disease. It was believed that, in very young prostitutes, too much sex might delay the onset of menstruation.[79] Even those who were past puberty would experience (perhaps not entirely unwelcome) physical consequences, according to the Norman philosopher William of Conches (c. 1090–c. 1154):

> On the inside the womb is hairy, in order that it retains the semen better . . . As a result of frequent lovemaking, a prostitute's womb is covered in slime, with the hairs, which are meant to retain the semen, covered up: hence in the manner of oiled marble it instantly rejects what it receives.[80]

Besides facing numerous physical risks, medieval prostitutes also had to deal with more general hostility. Many regulations (such as those passed by Duke Amadeus VIII of Turin in 1430) specifically stated that they must live as far as possible from decent women; when, despite such rules, people were forced into proximity with sex workers, they were prone to object.[81] In the late fifteenth century Caterina Muccingrifi, an assistant at the Hospital of Santa Maria Nuova, Florence, complained to Lorenzo the Magnificent that the institution was frequently visited by prostitutes, creating an unpleasant environment for the female staff and patients.[82] Neighbours often complained to the authorities about brothels and prostitutes. In fourteenth-century Prague there was much grumbling about one of the civic brothels:

> a place . . . in which public games of ball and dice are played on feast days and others; daily, year round, a place in which public and communal access to a brothel is had, and it is said about the same that in that place there is never a year when two or more men are not killed.[83]

In late medieval London, The Pye at Queenhithe attracted 'many strumpets and pimps' and the neighbours wanted it closed at night. In York in 1483 'the whole Parish of St Martin in Micklegate came before my lord the mayor and complained of Margery Gray, otherwise called Cherrylips, that she was a woman ill disposed of her body to whom ill-disposed men resort to the annoyance of her neighbours.'[84]

Some people took more direct action. A group of men broke into Joan Upholdstere's London house in 1366, claiming that she was 'a woman of evil condition [who] received men of ill fame', and they were members of a watch trying to catch her in the act. They were acquitted.[85] In fifteenth-century Zurich there were cases in which women suspected of prostitution were assaulted, or their houses attacked, including doors smeared with excrement.[86] But such efforts did not always achieve the desired effect. In 1398 the neighbours of Angela, a married Florentine woman, offered her a basket of bread a week to stop working as a prostitute, but she turned it down, as she earned more than they were offering her.[87] Seventy years earlier, in Manosque, a man attempted to expel a suspected prostitute from his street, but she retaliated by casting a spell to make him impotent, and thus alienated him from his wife.[88]

Nevertheless, there is some evidence that some sex workers did manage to integrate themselves into the communities in which they lived and worked. Isabella Wakefield of York first appeared in court in 1402, when she was a trainee seamstress suing her former lover for breach of promise; she was subsequently charged with sexual offences (ranging from fornication with a priest to 'keeping immorality in her house') at least nine times, and apparently operated as a prostitute until she was well into her forties. Nevertheless, she was repeatedly able to find compurgators to testify to her good character, even when the court demanded twelve, rather than the usual six. She was clearly a woman with respectable friends, and not a marginal figure.[89] Wills provide similar evidence. The 1494 will of Alice Stapeldon, a convicted brothel-keeper from Suffolk, included bequests to female friends and to various charitable causes – that is, her legacies were those of a typical well-born woman.[90] In Venice, Helena left money to the confraternity of the Holy Apostles, on the condition that they attended her funeral and prayed for her soul. It is unclear whether she was a member, but it is striking that the guildswomen were willing to associate with a known madam. On the other hand, she lacked the female networks that are usually revealed by women's wills.[91]

The mere fact that these women made wills is significant, since it demonstrates that there were no formal limits on their legal capacity. Evidence for prostitutes who went on to marry or who gave evidence in court is similarly suggestive, although the latter was rare, and usually happened only if their professional expertise was needed, perhaps in an impotence case.[92] The role of prostitutes in public festivities was similarly ambiguous. Although their participation has sometimes been seen as evidence for inclusion, they were often invited not despite but because of their profession. In Sicily, for example, they played a prominent part in the 22 July procession in honour of their patron saint Mary Magdalene. They were also involved in the *palio*, an annual race held in many Italian cities, which was supposed to be run by horses and donkeys, but which sometimes included races for Jews and prostitutes. During sieges, the routes were altered so that female participants ran along the ramparts with their skirts raised. It is hard to see such activities as anything other than an opportunity to humiliate women.[93]

The Clients

Medieval attitudes to men who used prostitutes were also somewhat contradictory. On the one hand, the existence of the civic brothels reflected a widespread recognition of male sexual needs, and seemed to suggest that it was acceptable to satisfy these needs by visiting a prostitute. There was also a strong tendency to suggest that any fault lay with the woman who had tempted the man, rather than the man who was tempted; this was all the more true if the prostitute was particularly beautiful, because this increased the difficulty of resistance.[94] On the other hand, medieval writers often expressed disapproval of brothelgoers. According to Andreas Capellanus, author of a twelfth-century treatise *On Love*, sex with a prostitute was 'a most foul pursuit . . . and a man loses his good name because of it'.[95] The father of the celebrated Burgundian knight Jacques de Lalaing (1421–1453) told him not to frequent prostitutes, who could cost a man both his soul and his physical strength, but to seek the love of noble ladies.[96] The French Dominican friar Humbert of Romans (*c.* 1200–1277) claimed that some young men had sex with servants because they were too embarrassed to use prostitutes – but he still thought that the blame for such encounters lay with the woman.[97]

However, the brothels were not equally accessible to all men, since most jurisdictions banned under-age youths, married men, priests and non-Christians from visiting them.[98] In parts of Iberia, Muslims and Jews could theoretically be executed for having sex with a Christian prostitute, although this was rarely enforced. Ali Valente of Elvas, for example, was fined and exiled for nine months for having sex with several prostitutes who worked from his shop, while Luís Eares, a Christian pimp who hired a Christian prostitute to a Muslim man in Faro for 'a pair of shoes and other things' was pardoned.[99]

Priests who used prostitutes also offended medieval sensibilities, but despite (or perhaps because of) the Church's insistence on celibacy, cities with large numbers of clerics became centres of prostitution. The trade thrived in Avignon, especially during the Avignon Papacy (1309–78), inspiring a popular saying which claimed that one could not cross the city bridge without encountering two monks, two donkeys and a whore. During this period there were two official brothel districts, the Bourg Gighonghan and the Bourg Nerf, plus several other 'good houses'; a partial census conducted in 1371 revealed unusually high numbers of single women living in the city.[100] Numerous clerics got into trouble in fourteenth-century Prague for visiting prostitutes, including Wenceslaus of Zap, who was fined after admitting to the archdeacon that 'he occasionally commingled at night with a public woman and first thing in the morning after paying, he dismissed her.'[101] In late medieval York some women actually seem to have specialized in catering to a clerical clientele: Margaret Phillips, for example, was presented with five different clergymen, while Elizabeth Frewe and Joan Scryvener were both summoned in 1424 for acting as procuress for clerics.[102]

While many people seem to have accepted that, in the words of one fifteenth-century English pastoral handbook, 'There are many that commit fornication with strumpets, because they have no wives', there was considerable disapproval of married men who went to brothels.[103] When, in 1429, a French royal sergeant found a married man in a brothel, he reportedly exclaimed; 'You have your wife and children and it is not for your kind to be in a brothel. By Saint George, I will take you to prison.'[104] In late fifteenth-century London, Alice Hobby's successful suit for separation from her husband William, a royal surgeon, highlighted his frequent brothel visits. Two of her witnesses, both medical men, recalled remonstrating with him after catching him in bed with a prostitute; Richard Chambyr admitted that he 'marvelled' at his friend's conduct.[105] It was, nevertheless, hard to prevent such behaviour, and when a pair of masons were charged with stabbing another customer in a Dijon brothel at Pentecost 1466, the court record noted that 'although they are married men and have their wives in the city', they were regular brothelgoers.[106] In fourteenth-century Manosque only one married man, Peyre Chaunelli, was prosecuted for using prostitutes, and it seems that this case was pursued because they had sex near the ovens in his bakery, which were visible public spaces. The woman concerned, the madam of the town brothel, was not charged, even though prostitutes were supposed to turn away married men or face adultery charges.[107]

It also seems to have been accepted that many male travellers would use brothels. In Venice, for example, the establishment of an officially sanctioned red-light district was deemed necessary 'because of the multitude of people entering and leaving our city'. It was probably not a coincidence that it was located in the Rialto, the focus of mercantile activity in the city.[108] Soldiers were another obvious clientele. One English chronicler claimed that the prostitutes who followed Richard I's army during the Third Crusade did so much business that they lived better than the French king's brother. Frequent attempts were made to get rid of them, since Crusaders were supposed to abstain, and defeats were often blamed on sexual misconduct.[109] But the problem refused to go away. In 1414 General Quartermaster Erhard Facher complained that his soldiers were visiting prostitutes in Constance bathhouses.[110] Later medieval regulations for English and French armies also tried to prohibit camp followers, although the main concern seems to have been with the rivalries caused by personal concubines, rather than with prostitution more generally. Late fifteenth-century English soldiers certainly frequented the brothel near the rue des Wez, Dieppe.[111]

Given the clear link between brothels and men away from home, it is unsurprising that apprentices and students also featured prominently among the visitors to such establishments. For these young men, visits to prostitutes provided a sexual outlet, an opportunity for male bonding, and a way to demonstrate one's masculinity – but they were also a good way to get into trouble. For this reason, apprenticeship contracts often included prohibitions against going to taverns, gambling and using prostitutes.[112] Universities similarly tried to control their students' behaviour, by placing strict limits on female visitors or (as in the case of fifteenth-century

Oxford and Cambridge) by expelling 'bawds, whores and incontinent women' from their cities.[113] Nevertheless, authorities across Europe struggled to deal with the problems that ensued when large numbers of young men found themselves away from home for the first time, and with ready access to the sex trade. According to Jacques de Vitry, writing about late twelfth-century Paris, some of that city's brothels were located on the lower floors of lecture buildings in the Street of Straw. The road had to be closed at night because prostitutes were plying their trade there, even committing their 'horrible filth' on the masters' chairs, and the women tried to draw students into their houses, calling them sodomites if they declined. The problem was still ongoing some three centuries later, when a group of students were expelled from the Sorbonne for bringing a prostitute into the university. At Montpellier, the university regulations specifically forbade first years from hiring prostitutes for the feasts given by new students.[114] The authorities there presumably hoped to avoid incidents like the one in which three Kraków University students were fined 'because of the violence they committed in a public and infamous brothel by beating the women, robbing some of the women's things such as their purses'.[115]

While the Kraków case provides further evidence of the threat men posed to female sex workers, violence in the brothel was also a risk for clients. In 1464 Cunrat, a bathhouse worker, got into a fight when Peter Zeiner and his companions stopped him entering a Zurich brothel. A few years later in the same city, a similar argument between Hanns Hellrigel and Mathis Sträler escalated and Hellrigel was stabbed.[116] Some of these incidents proved fatal: in May 1360 Maffeo Granella died after a fight in a Venetian brothel, which began when he hit one of the prostitutes.[117]

Male and Gender Non-conforming Prostitutes

Despite the consistent assumption that a prostitute was a woman who had sex with men, clients and pimps were not the only men involved in the medieval sex trade. While the majority of medieval sex workers probably were female, we should not conclude that only women sold sex; rather, legal and ideological frameworks made female prostitutes more visible in the surviving records. Only women lived and worked in civic-regulated brothels, and the law prosecuted women who sold sex as prostitutes. Men who bought or sold sex from other men were treated as sodomites, and records of sodomy very rarely tell us whether money changed hands, probably because this seemed like a minor detail if the sin against nature had been committed. In mid-fifteenth-century Florence, for example, Bindella's husband, a baker, was accused of sodomy; she complained that he had spent all their money on boys. Unfortunately, it is unclear whether she was referring to male prostitutes, or to gifts given during less explicitly transactional relationships.[118] And if it is hard to find evidence of men paying for sex with other men, women who paid for sex are even less visible.

Two important cases serve as a reminder that medieval prostitution was not just about men paying for sex with women. (As in the case of Katherina Hetzeldorfer, it is impossible to know for certain how individuals in these circumstances identified; although I have followed the pronouns used by the court records, it should be remembered that these are hostile sources which may not reflect the preferences of the individuals concerned.) In 1354 one Rolandino Ronchaia appeared in court in Venice. Although Rolandino had breasts and looked very feminine, he had been raised male and married a woman. The marriage failed, partly because of Rolandino's impotence (he had a penis and testicles, but had never had an erection), and then his wife died of plague. The new widower moved to Padua to live with a relative, where he had sex with another guest – taking the female role. Rolandino then returned to Venice as Rolandina, and worked as a female prostitute around the Rialto, having sex with 'an infinite number of men'. At the trial it was claimed that both clients and other prostitutes believed Rolandina was a woman; the court record states that

> He deceived them in the following manner – namely when they were on his body he hid as much as possible his member . . . and took the member [of the other] and put it in his rear parts and stayed with this until they emitted sperm giving them every delight as do true prostitutes.

On the evidence of both physical characteristics and behaviour, it seems likely that Ronchaia was intersex or transgender, and identified as a woman. In the eyes of the court, however, Ronchaia's penis made him a man whose chief offence was having sex with other men; consequently, he was tried as a sodomite and burnt to death.[119]

Ronchaia's story is an extremely unusual one, but it is not unique. One Sunday night in December 1394 the secular authorities in London arrested one 'John Rykener, calling [themselves] Eleanor, having been detected in women's clothing' in a public toilet, 'committing that detestable, unmentionable and ignominious vice' – that is, sodomy. John Britby, who was arrested with Rykener, testified that he had met the accused, dressed as a woman, in the street; assuming therefore that this person was a woman, he had asked 'as he would a woman if he could commit a libidinous act with her'. Rykener asked for money, Britby agreed to pay, and they went together to the public conveniences where they were arrested. Rykener corroborated Britby's account and was also asked about his sexual history. He confessed that a whore named Anna 'first taught him to practise this detestable vice in the manner of a woman'. Another woman, Elizabeth Brouderer, a bawd, dressed him in women's clothing and gave him the name Eleanor. After this, he posed as a woman to have sex with a priest, and then spent five weeks living as a woman in Oxford, working as an embroideress and having sex with 'three unsuspecting scholars'. Travelling around Oxfordshire and Buckinghamshire before returning to London, Rykener continued to have sex for money with both men and women – sometimes presenting as John, sometimes as Eleanor. He confessed that 'he often had sex as a man with many nuns and also had sex as a man with many women both married and otherwise ... many priests had committed that vice with him as a woman.'[120]

For various reasons the Rykener case is a particularly difficult one to interpret. The exact nature of the offence is never specified, the outcome of the case is unknown, and there is no indication that a formal legal process was underway. Prostitution was not normally a matter for the mayor's court (where this case was apparently heard), and in fourteenth-century England sodomy would usually have been tried in the ecclesiastical courts. It has even been suggested that Rykener was not a real person, and that the whole episode is actually a complex political satire about Richard II.[121] Even if we take these events at face value, it is hard to know how to interpret them. Today, we might describe Rykener as a transvestite, but medieval people tended to see cross-dressing as a gender transgression rather than in terms of sexual orientation. That Rykener had sex with both men and women might mean that he was a bisexual man, but this category did not formally exist in the Middle Ages. Alternatively, that Rykener not only had sex as a woman but lived as Eleanor for prolonged periods might indicate that this was an individual who would today identify as non-binary, or transgender.

In both cases, their sexual partners claimed to have been taken in by a deliberate deception, but it is hard to know whether this was indeed the case, given that the alternative was to identify oneself as a willing sodomite and face punishment. Perhaps the most we can confidently say is that both of these individuals were seen by the medieval authorities as men who had engaged in deviant sex in return for money, and who therefore needed to be punished; today we would certainly view them very differently.

More broadly, however, the sex trade has changed little since the Middle Ages. Many of the debates that divided medieval societies remain relevant today; we still can't agree whether it is best to legalize prostitution or to suppress it, and sex workers are still widely stereotyped as either victims or criminals. The mistreatment of those who work in this industry is equally persistent: many of these cases of violence and trafficking could easily have happened in the twenty-first century, demonstrating that some of the worst aspects of human behaviour have changed little over the years. Sadly, this impression is only reinforced in the next chapter, as we turn our attention to the problem of sexual violence.

TEN

Sexual Violence

Despite the common assumption that medieval authorities did not take sex crimes seriously, the surviving legal records tell a different story. Extensive documentation attests both to the existence of numerous laws against sexual assault and rape, and to the fact that offences of this kind were frequently heard by medieval courts.

Sexual Assault

Among the offences widely punished by the authorities was non-consensual sexual touching. From the late eleventh century the acts forbidden by Castilian law codes included pulling a man's hair, beard or genitals, and wrestling a woman to the ground as if to rape her. The punishments (usually floggings or fines) could be substantial: in Miranda de Ebro, anyone who made a lascivious attack on a married man was fined nearly ten times the penalty for a straightforward assault.[1] Such penalties were not limited to the Iberian peninsula: in late medieval Gotland, fines were imposed for touching a woman against her will, with the largest sums required for touching above the knee. If, however, 'you touch her higher up, then it is a shameless touch, and it is called a fool's touch; then no fine is payable; most want it when it gets that far.'[2]

Cutting or removing a woman's clothes was also widely treated as a crime. In Cuenca, cutting off a woman's skirts, which stripped her of her honour as well as her clothes, was punished with a large fine and possible banishment. It was also one of several Spanish towns in which a man who removed a woman's clothes or stole them from a bathing house received the same fine as a murderer – unless she was a prostitute, a distinction which makes clear that it was a crime which was as much about sex as property.[3] Even if a woman's clothes were removed during a more serious attack, this action could still be punished as a significant crime. In fifteenth-century Florence, Choccho of Toro attacked a young virgin named Martha, stripping her naked before beating and raping her. He was fined 90 Florentine pounds for the rape, 120 for the assault, and 40 for removing her clothes.[4]

Many sexual assault victims were, like Martha, people who were in some way vulnerable, usually due to their youth and/or social status. For example, when a committee was appointed to investigate the problem of sodomy in Cologne in 1484, one of the cases they considered concerned the late Johann Greeffroide, a city councillor. He was alleged to have touched both a servant and a young apprentice in a sexual manner, only desisting in his attack on the former when the man defended himself with a knife.[5] Five decades earlier, in the same town, a young apprentice complained to the council about the salt measurers' guild, saying that they 'threw him down and rubbed his member in salt'. They did not deny this, but said it was an old custom performed upon anyone coming aboard a ship laden with salt. They were required to swear an oath to end this practice.[6]

The punishments imposed on the perpetrators of such crimes varied considerably. In two cases from fourteenth-century Ghent, sexual offenders were treated quite leniently. Laureins Rabau was assaulting Callekin Van Laerne 'immorally above and below' when she pulled out a knife and used it to defend herself. He complained to the magistrates, seeking compensation for his injuries, but his claim was rejected on the grounds that he had got what he deserved. He did, however, escape punishment for attacking the teenager. Willem Clappaert was required to undertake a pilgrimage and pay damages for a horrific attack in which he put glowing tongs between Beele Baert's legs, tried to get at her genitals, and then opened the tongs, making two wounds. The court record notes that this penalty was imposed as a warning against such behaviour, but the fine was actually very low in comparison to other injury cases.[7] In contrast, Fantino da Pesaro, a young Venetian noble, was sentenced to a year in jail in chains for kissing and groping Marta, a servant, in the cathedral of San Marco in 1436; the location of his offence made it sacrilegious, and thus particularly problematic.[8] Men found guilty of indecent exposure in fourteenth-century Nuremberg could be banished from the city: one Rosenlacher was expelled for two years (on pain of losing his hand) after he exposed himself in the marketplace in 1307. Forty years later, Ulrich the pursemaker was banished for five years for showing his 'tool' to ladies.[9]

In a majority of the documented cases, the perpetrator was male, but, as recognized by many of the laws on sexual touching, women could also commit sexual assaults. In the Shropshire peace sessions of 1405, Isabel, wife of Ievan Gronowessone, was accused along with her daughters Joan and Petronilla: they 'lay in ambush in the field at Ightfield and they made assault on Roger de Pulesdon and held the same Roger and tied him with a cord around his neck and cut off his testicles', before using his horse to flee the scene of the crime. Their motivation and their punishment are both unknown.[10]

Rape

The medieval terminology relating to rape is vague: many of the rape cases that appear in the court records were actually forced marriages, abductions, elopements, or even attempts to cover up the adultery of married women.[11] According to the ecclesiastical definition, as set out by Gratian in the mid-twelfth century, the crime of *raptus* had four key elements: unlawful coitus, the abduction of a woman from her father's house, the use of violence, and no marriage agreement between victim and attacker. There was no such thing as marital rape, because marriage equalled consent.[12] Although rape (in the modern sense) was recognized across Europe as a crime, and one which should be tried in the secular courts, there was some dispute over whether it was a property crime against the woman's father or husband, or whether it was a violent sexual crime against the woman herself.[13] In late thirteenth-century Castile, *Las Siete Partidas* stated that men who used force to carry off virgins, nuns or honourable widows committed 'a very great offense and act of wickedness' due to the violence against her person, and the dishonour against her family; the resultant accusation to the magistrate was to be made by the woman's relatives.[14] Medieval English law similarly linked rape and abduction, with the common issue being the theft of a woman from her father or husband. The key legislation on this subject, the Westminster Statutes of 1275 and 1285, blurred the boundary between the two offences, and *raptus* was increasingly treated as a form of trespass, with cases brought to court by the male relative.[15]

In theory, many jurisdictions allowed rapists to be punished with death, but in practice this happened very rarely. No Englishman is known to have been executed for rape in the later Middle Ages, and although rapists could be buried alive or decapitated under German law, records show that the usual punishments were blinding, prison, or marriage to the victim.[16] Moreover, not all rape victims were equal before the law: most legal systems considered (either officially or in practice) the victim's marital status and social position. The *Sachsenspiegel*, a widely circulated and highly influential German law code, acknowledged that 'a man may commit rape with a common woman or his concubine and therefore receive the death penalty if he sleeps with her without her consent', but legal recognition that prostitutes and those who had been sexually involved with their rapists could also be victims was not widespread.[17] In some places, the rape of a married woman was viewed as a particular problem, since it dishonoured her husband and stole his property: in Cuenca the rape of a single woman was punished with a large fine and banishment, but the rape of a wife was punishable by burning.[18] Most legal systems, however, viewed the rape of a virgin as a more serious crime. According to the thirteenth-century English jurist Henry Bracton, since rape took a virgin's 'member', her rapist should also lose his member; a non-virgin could be raped, but the crime (and therefore the punishment) was less serious.[19]

In practice, it is clear that courts viewed attacks on very young women as particularly repugnant, and were most likely to convict in such cases. In January 1337, in a rare example of a man being executed for rape, a French tailor named Jean Agnes was dragged through the streets and hanged. He had raped two twelve-year-old apprentices employed by his kinsman, and his punishment surely reflected the victims' youth, and the fact that they were in his family's care, as well as their lost virginity.[20] On the other hand, the fact that a woman was not a virgin could be used to justify a lesser punishment. In thirteenth-century England, Hugh fitz Henry de Alkyndown raped a woman named Emma. The jury found him guilty, but argued that since she was not a virgin, he should not be mutilated; the justices upheld their conclusion, and he was sent to prison.[21]

For any woman, whatever her sexual and marital status, rape was a difficult crime to prosecute, and it was necessary to follow established procedure to bring a case. In thirteenth-century Bologna, rape charges could be initiated either by a straightforward accusation (by the victim or her representative) or by an inquisition (initiated by parish officials, or by a potentially anonymous notification supported by witnesses). Making an accusation involved using a specific formula, and was a relatively inexpensive process. If the accused did not come to court, he had committed contumacy, and was considered to have admitted his guilt. But the burden of proof fell to the victim, and producing witnesses and guarantors could be expensive and difficult.[22] From the twelfth century onwards there was a new emphasis on the need for proof that the woman had not consented; this meant that victims increasingly had to undergo physical examinations. In thirteenth-century Normandy, for example, the chief justice was supposed to have 'the girl and her injuries examined by good women and trustworthy matrons, who know how to discern the injuries of rape'.[23] Such examinations needed to uncover clear evidence of full penetration for the assault to be considered as a rape. For this reason, Jean Feuchre, a fifteenth-century Parisian accused of multiple rapes of the same woman, repeatedly insisted that during each of their sexual encounters he 'controlled myself and threw my semen' (that is, he did not ejaculate inside her body); if she was not a virgin, then another man must be to blame.[24]

Most legal systems also required formulaic behaviours during and immediately after the rape; failure to do these things could determine the punishment given (in Ghent, for example, a rapist could be beheaded only if his victim had called for help), or even whether a case was heard.[25] According to the *Coutumes de Beauvoir* (1283): 'Rape is when someone has carnal intercourse with a woman by force against her will and when she does what she can to defend herself.' The law book of Mühlhausen, written in early thirteenth-century Thuringia, required that

> If a man lies with a woman without her consent and against her will, and she does not want this, she shall defend herself with clamour, and afterwards she shall immediately declare it with torn clothes and with hand-wringing and with tears and with dishevelled hair. And having these four things presented everyone shall follow her to the judge, wherever she may find him.[26]

The required actions are illustrated in several fourteenth-century manuscripts of the *Sachsenspiegel*. In these drawings, women are presented as victims deserving of justice, because they resist attack (by pulling away, or by pulling the attacker's hair), make gestures of mourning, and testify in court (displaying the disordered hair and torn clothing that proved the truth of their claims).[27] In many Iberian towns women were also expected to display self-inflicted scratches on their cheeks, and in Old Castile, unless the victim could be physically proven to have lost her virginity in the attack, she was also required to cast aside her headdress and to demonstrate her humiliation by grovelling on the ground. Scratching was a traditional act of mourning, appropriate for lost chastity and honour, but such public humiliation was probably also intended to deter false accusations.[28]

In the face of such complex requirements, it is somewhat unsurprising that very few rape cases reached court, and even fewer received substantial punishments. During a typical 25-year period in the fourteenth century, the court of St Martin des Champs in Paris heard only six rape cases: one led to a death sentence, but in the other cases the perpetrator either disappeared or was absolved.[29] Equally inevitable is the reluctance of some woman to initiate legal proceedings, as happened in 1376, when Jan Van der Berghe was accused of raping Adelise Van Crabbingen of Ghent. She had cried for help and her friends rescued her. But, despite the bailiff's urging her to, she declined to press charges.[30]

Women's attitudes must have been influenced by the numerous occasions on which rapists either received token punishments, or escaped justice altogether. William Swayn, a mid-fifteenth-century cleric presented before the English criminal courts as a 'common rapist', was accused of the violent rape of at least five women; his attacks were committed 'with force and arms', and usually involved house-breaking. He was also described as 'a common ambusher of ways where women walk about their business'. But he was discharged with the help of six sureties (that is, people who would guarantee his good behaviour).[31] His case was far from unique. In Bologna, in 1286, a servant named Divitia was accosted in the street by a man called Rolandino, who claimed to be a friend of her brother-in-law and to be looking for a servant. He took her to his house, where he attempted to rape her in a stable; she fought him off, fled, and was assisted – injured, weeping and with her hair loose – by two clerics. Nevertheless, the court decided she had not provided sufficient evidence, and so Rolandino went unpunished.[32] A century later, in Normandy, Bertin Quenet and another man broke into the house of Alicia Hoquet, a widow, and raped her. He was fined five sous: one of the smallest fines that year. She was fined fifteen sous, for allowing the men to have carnal knowledge of her.[33] It is hard to avoid the conclusion that courts were extremely reluctant to convict men for sexual offences, and even less inclined to impose the harshest penalties.

Such hesitance persisted even in the face of the epidemic of rape and gang rape that afflicted fifteenth-century Dijon: at least 125 rapes took place in the city between 1436 and 1486, although the true figure was probably much higher. Many of these attacks involved considerable brutality, such as one in which a pregnant woman was dragged through the snow. The men involved were mostly young, unmarried journeymen or bourgeois sons, in their late teens or early twenties, and with no previous record of delinquent behaviour. Participation seemingly had little impact on the perpetrators' careers or reputation, and a man apparently had to participate in multiple attacks before he would be banished even temporarily. It is estimated that around half of young men in the town participated, so that it became almost a rite of passage, a way for youths to assert their masculinity by dominating women and challenging authority. Many attacks were clearly motivated by resentment: a weaver's son told Jacquetta, a 22-year-old maid, 'I have a right to go at you just like the others'; two journeymen masons shouted at a girl of good reputation, the sixteen-year-old niece of the viscount-mayor, in the street, 'We are going to fuck you, we can fuck you just as well as the others'; and a pregnant widow, a priest's servant, was told, 'We will have our share just like the priests.'[34]

Many of the women raped in the Dijon attacks were in some way vulnerable: they were poor, or widowed, or their husbands were away. In this they were typical of medieval rape victims, who were often low status or otherwise disadvantaged. Such women were arguably rendered vulnerable by the attitudes of men such as Andreas Capellanus, who advised that the love of a peasant woman was best obtained through 'rough embraces'; 'at least some compulsion' would likely be needed to make such a woman comply with a man's desires – although it is unclear how seriously this advice was meant.[35] In practical terms, high-status women were often better protected (and controlled) by their families; they were probably also less likely to press charges, preferring to (or being made to) keep quiet for the sake of the family honour.[36]

Servants, on the other hand, were particularly vulnerable and found it extremely hard to secure justice. In 1346 Zanino Sanuto, a Venetian nobleman, raped his mother's servant, but the Forty refused to rule on his case, so he was effectively let off. In the same city, Caterina was raped by Tomaso Bembo when she was a young servant in his father's house, and only reported the crime after she had left service and married. The Forty voted to prosecute him, but then fined him only twenty ducats – effectively a slap on the wrist.[37] In thirteenth-century Old Castile an unnamed female domestic brought a rape suit against her employer, a regional governor named Martin Ferrandes. He fled, and appealed to a higher court. There his peers not only threw out the case, but advised that others like it should not be considered.[38]

If female servants were often considered fair game, the position of enslaved women was even worse: for them, forced sex with the master could not be prosecuted as rape. In Valencia, a Black woman named Leonor was enslaved in the household of Louis Almenara. She reported that 'seeing himself as her lord and seeing that she could not contradict him, he took "love" from her whenever he willed, knowing her carnally one and many times.' The sex was clearly coerced. Leonor was, however, relatively fortunate in the sense that her master openly acknowledged their daughter; had he disowned the child, she would not have been allowed to bring a paternity claim. Equally disturbing is the case of Caterina, an enslaved woman in 1450s Florence. She was raped by a man named Francesco, who broke into her master's house and attacked her. In this case, the rapist was punished, for the work she had missed – that is, in reparation for the damage to the master, not to her.[39]

Another serious issue was the perception that women were rendered vulnerable by their behaviour. Christine de Pizan wrote:

It angers and upsets me when men claim that women want to be raped and that, even though a woman may verbally rebuff a man, she won't in fact mind if he does force himself upon her. I can scarcely believe that it could give women any pleasure to be treated in such a vile way.[40]

Yet she also suggested that women should wear modest clothing, avoiding low necklines and tight garments that gave the wrong impression to 'foolish men'.[41] Many conduct books, which were often presented as maternal advice to a young daughter, went further and warned women that they must protect themselves from assault, by gaining a reputation for chastity, being careful in male company, and staying at home.[42] Among the women raped in fifteenth-century Dijon were a woman who had left her husband, a carpenter's wife who was attacked 'because she is bawdy and laughs a lot', and several women who went out in the evening when it was not 'the hour for women to go about the city'.[43] In 1377 Wouter van Pudenbrouz was accused of trying to rape Bette Skevers, with whom he had been drinking in a Ghent tavern. The bailiff who handled the case 'thought that he could prove no other force than that he may have hit her with his fists, and they were a pair of noisy drunks anyway'.[44] The idea that some women are 'asking for it' clearly has a long history.

Doubts about female honesty were reinforced by medical ideas about conception, which suggested that a woman had to release seed in order to become pregnant, and that this seed was only released when she experienced sexual pleasure. This led to considerable debate about whether a woman could fall pregnant as a result of rape; did a pregnancy prove that the encounter was actually consensual? A fifteenth-century training lecture given at the London Inns of Court argued that

In an appeal of rape it is a good plea to abate the writ that she is pregnant by the same rape, because that proves her consent. It was said by the counsel of Bishop Nevil of York that although the body consents nevertheless the mind does not; to which the justices said that their authority extended only to the body and not the mind.[45]

This logic was applied to the case of Joan, a thirty-year-old woman who accused one E of rape; she had a child, which she said was his. 'It was said that this was a wonder because a child could not be engendered without the will of both,' and therefore he was found not guilty.[46] But many people questioned whether this was really true. The Norman philosopher William of Conches pointed out that there are 'women who were raped, who have suffered violence despite their wailing, and have still conceived. It seems that they never experienced delight in the act,' although he also concluded that such cases must reflect the ability of the body to consent, even when the mind does not.[47] The twelfth-century Spanish-Arab physician Ibn Rušd was similarly troubled by this problem, which he claimed to have discussed with many women: 'they replied that many were impregnated without emitting seed, and even if intercourse did not give them pleasure.' The handful of cases in which pregnant women successfully pleaded rape suggests that the impossibility of conceiving in this way was not universally accepted.[48]

If this debate offends modern sensibilities, the medieval tendency to see a marriage between rapist and victim as a satisfactory outcome to a trial is equally problematic.[49] Such unions were rare, but they could and did happen. Bonaiuxina was watching sheep in the countryside near Bologna when Fulcherus tried to have sex with her, threatening to kill her if she did not comply; she subsequently accused him of attempted rape. But twelve days later they both appeared before the judge, having agreed to marry, and the case was dropped.[50] Similarly, in 1340s Venice, Zanio Viscia raped Francesca, a trainee dressmaker; the court sentenced him to pay a fine, spend six months in prison, or marry her. The couple married.[51]

While there is no clear evidence that women were ever legally required to marry their rapists, some individuals may have felt obliged to do so in order to escape the ostracism experienced by many rape victims. In December 1483 Jeanette, a young woman from Dijon who had served her locksmith master well for two years, was gang-raped, after which 'out of fear, no-one dares receive the said Jeanette, even her former master'. In

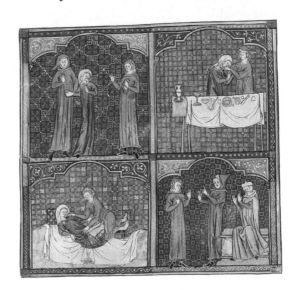

In this narrative from an early 14th-century copy of Gratian's *Decretum*, a man invites a girl to dinner, rapes her, and then forces her father to agree to their marriage (Fitzwilliam Museum, Cambridge, MS 262, f. 137r).

the same city, Jehanne, a fifteen-year-old servant, was fetching wine for her mistress one evening when she was violently raped by a stranger; after this, she ended up leaving service and was pursued by numerous young men for casual sex.[52] Not all rape victims ended up as social pariahs: Lisbette de Cousmakere, a Ghent burgher's widow who was kidnapped and gang-raped in 1375, was remarried by 1386. Clearly factors beyond the mere fact of having been raped – probably including her previous social standing – shaped a woman's prospects in the aftermath of an attack.[53] Somewhat distastefully, a victim's future could also be shaped by whether her attacker was wealthy enough to pay her off. In 1488 Thomas Shelley, a London mercer and former churchwarden, raped a neighbour's servant; in compensation, he gave her the relatively large sum of £40 for a dowry.[54]

In some cases the marriage option may have been exploited by people who wanted to ensure that a wedding took place. In 1464 Jehan Feuchre, a 28-year-old Parisian dressmaker, was accused of the rape and 'deflower-ing' of Denise, a teenage servant. He was imprisoned for two weeks, but after his second interrogation he agreed to marry Denise. It seems likely that she was pregnant, and that her father and godfather had brought the case in an attempt to secure this outcome.[55] But such strategizing was not without risk. In February 1287 a single woman named Domina Umelta accused Azo of rape. Both were from the same village near Bologna, and after he had raped her he took her away from her father's house, saying, 'I do not have a wife and now I take you as my wife.' On Azo's part, at least, the whole episode seems to have been staged in an attempt to force her father to agree to a marriage. If this was his plan, it went badly awry, for he was banished *in absentia*, to face a penalty of decapitation if he was ever caught.[56]

Inevitably, some women were found to have made false accusations. In 1202 Agnes Tredegold of Lincolnshire accused William de Smethefeld of rape, and the case came to trial. He defended himself by claiming that 'then and before and after she was his bedfellow'. The inquiry found that she had made this claim because William had pledged himself to another woman, and he was acquitted.[57] Agnes's fate is unknown, but women who lied were often punished, sometimes harshly. In the Spanish city of Soria, a woman found to have made a false accusation was fined roughly half of what she might have received in compensation, or jailed.[58] Ennesot la Brissete of Paris accused Angelot Burde of rape in 1340, but a physical examination found she was still a virgin. Consequently, the accusation was judged slanderous and Ennesot was herself fined.[59]

Such cases seemed to reinforce medieval stereotypes about female untrustworthiness, but they also reflected the perceived gravity of the crime: it was no small thing to accuse a man of rape. Indeed, despite the troublingly dismissive treatment of many victims, there is substantial evidence to suggest that sexual violence was taken seriously. Rape victims sometimes benefited from miracles, especially when the horror of the crime was exacerbated by the fact that it occurred in a church. Writing around 1200, Gerald of Wales reported two cases in which miraculously animated statues physically attacked a would-be assailant, preventing a rape.[60] Another dramatic intervention was performed by St Malachy, Archbishop of Armagh (1094–1148), who saved a praying woman from the barbarian who intended to rape her. Invoking the saint did not scare off the attacker, but then 'a poisonous bloated animal, a loathsome toad, was seen crawling out from between the woman's thighs', and the terrified man ran away.[61]

On a more practical level, rape during war was often used by chroniclers to suggest the evil of the opposite side. Thus Froissart claimed that the foreign captains left in France after 1360 'defiled many damsels', and accused the Bretons of 'ravishing' the wives and daughters of their Castilian opponents in 1385. In contrast, the chivalric English stepped in to prevent the 'defouling' of women by merciless French soldiers.[62] University regulations threatened heavy punishments for students who committed rape: in thirteenth-century Paris they faced excommunication, and in Copenhagen rape was one of the crimes that led to the loss of university privileges.[63] And men who took the law into their own hands and sought revenge against the attacker of a female relative might receive a sympathetic response from the authorities. In mid-fifteenth-century Burgundy, Guillaume Doille, a priest, broke into Claude Millet's house while her husband was away. 'Feigning to impersonate' her spouse, he was 'on the verge of knowing her carnally' when she woke up, and fled into the town, 'hurrying and crying as much as she could'. Three years later, having failed to achieve legal redress, her brother and two other kinsmen murdered the priest; the pardon they received for their crime cited the attack on Claude.[64] Of course, the reason why rape was felt in this case to justify murder is unclear: did the pardon reflect sympathy for the woman, or for the men whose property had been assaulted?

Like prostitution, rape was often viewed as a woman's issue, and cases of male rape were very rare, or at least very rarely reported. In a very late medieval German case, Jakob the Dandy and Kruysgin Wyncoeffer met in a public toilet. Wyncoeffer took Jakob (who seems to have been quite young, and/or possibly mentally handicapped) home with him, laid him on a bed, and had anal sex with him. Jakob protested that this hurt him, and threatened to 'shout out so that the neighbours will hear'. Afterwards he told several people what had happened, complaining that his leg and bottom were sore; a female neighbour claimed to have seen part of the attack through a hole in the wall, after hearing a loud noise.[65] The outcome of this particular case is unknown, but in general sexual attacks on men seem to have been taken more seriously – probably because they were sodomy, and therefore a crime against nature rather than a straightforward act of violence and/or theft.

Child Abuse

Whereas the modern legal system makes a clear distinction between the rape of an adult and a sexual attack on a minor, medieval law did not. In England, which was not atypical, a specific law concerning the rape of minors was not introduced until 1576.[66] But this should not be taken as evidence that medieval people were undisturbed by paedophilia; most surely agreed with the English poet John Gower (d. 1408) that a man who had sex with a young girl was 'unnatural in body and a villain in soul'.[67] While very few cases made it to court, it does seem that legal authorities took sexual attacks on children particularly seriously, and were often willing to impose harsh penalties. The rapist of a nine-year-old Venetian girl, for example, was sentenced to have his eyes removed, in addition to payment of a 100-ducat fine for his victim's dowry, and perpetual banishment from the city.[68] In 1333 Jacqueline la Cyrière was accused of luring ten-year-old Jeannette Bille-heuse into her house in the Marais district of Paris, where she gave her a 'vile green potion', and helped a Lombard soldier to rape the screaming girl. Afterwards she threatened to kill her if she told anyone. The case came to court, and the girl was examined by two matrons, who testified that she had been 'deflowered, wounded, tortured, and cruelly mutilated'. Jacqueline was sentenced to burn, although there is no mention of the soldier, who may have fled.[69]

Although the perpetrators of such offences were harshly punished, the authorities made few concessions to their young victims. Courts quite frequently decided that a child's evidence was insufficient to secure a conviction: in 1287 the case against John of Windsor collapsed because his victim – his ward Idonea, whom he attacked when she was under seven – failed to provide sufficient details about the timing of the assault, and about any resultant bleeding.[70] Thirty years later, the man who raped a young Londoner called Joan was acquitted partly because minor variations in the two testimonies she gave were deemed to have undermined her claim.[71] In addition, even very young girls were subjected to physical examinations in order to provide the proof of lost virginity that might secure a conviction. In late fourteenth-century Barcelona a group of 'mid-wives or women' examined two nine-year-olds who had been repeatedly raped; they found that Úrsula was not a virgin and showed signs of rape, while Isabel had certainly been penetrated by a man, but they could not determine when because 'the nature' had dried.[72]

Despite such thorough investigations, the medieval tendency to understand rape in terms of virginity produced some extremely disturbing verdicts. In late thirteenth-century Herefordshire, seven-year-old Agnes was minding her father's sheep when Hugh fitz Thomas le Renur came along and violently threw her to the ground. He squeezed her so hard that she bled from her nose and mouth. Yet when the case came to court, the jurors said that, because she was so young, he was able to penetrate her but not to break her maidenhood. Therefore, she had not been raped. Her attacker was required only to pay a small fine for the trespass he committed by beating her.[73] Equally unsettling is the clear reluctance to see child prostitutes as victims, as illustrated by a fifteenth-century Venetian case. Both Clara di Corfu and Marieta di Verona were under twelve, and too young to have full sexual intercourse with their clients; they instead practised an unspecified 'form of sodomy'. Despite being underage, the girls were treated not as victims but criminals, and were banished from Venice for five years – while the men involved went unpunished.[74]

Nor did youth provide immunity from accusations that the victim was actually a liar who had made the whole thing up. At the 1256 Hampshire Eyre, John Jordan was cleared of raping a ten-year-old girl after she admitted that a woman had forced her to make the accusation.[75] In other cases, parents were accused of making false allegations for their own benefit. In 1423 a Londoner named John Moleneux made a bond with Jerome Bragdini, a Venetian merchant, that neither he nor his daughter Agnes would bring further pleas against the Italian on the pretext of 'rape, trespass or injury done to her'. Moleneux owed Bragdini money, and allegedly used the accusation to avoid paying it.[76] Other cases are harder to interpret. William Barbour was a 76-year-old priest responsible for providing religious instruction to dozens of young Londoners, among them seven-year-old Elizabeth Garrard. Then the girl's father, 'of his crafty and malicious mind', accused Barbour of molesting the girl and took him before the sheriffs. The priest was acquitted, but then the father instigated further legal action against the priest, who sought for the case to be considered by the king's chancery.[77] Was the priest falsely accused, or was the father desperately seeking justice for a child who had been the victim of a terrible crime? At a distance of half a millennium, it is impossible to know where our sympathies should lie.

Court cases involving the assault of young boys are even rarer than those involving young girls, a statistic that probably reflects legal approaches to sodomy, and gendered attitudes to rape and the importance of virginity, rather than the frequency with which such crimes occurred. In late medieval Venice, for example, the increase in prosecutions for sodomy was accompanied by growing concern about men who assaulted very young boys. In a mid-fourteenth-century case, the death penalty was imposed: Niccolò, a servant who lured a ten-year-old schoolboy into a back room and raped him, was burnt alive. A century later, in 1467, the city introduced a law that required surgeons and barbers to report anyone treated for damage caused by anal sex; it made specific reference to young boys injured in this way.[78]

There was also some concern about teachers who had sex with their students, although there is insufficient evidence to determine whether this was a common problem. In 1444 the Venetian authorities expressed concern about performing arts schools that remained open after dark, 'because it might lead some of these youths to commit prohibited deeds', and banned this. It was also ruled that teaching must be done in public halls, not private rooms.[79] There was a lack of university regulations against same-sex activity (in contrast to considerable concern about relationships with women) – but that did not necessarily mean that it did not happen, or that it was condoned. In July 1491 Richard Edmund, a fellow of Merton College, Oxford, was accused of 'inciting and provoking various and different youths to the sin against nature . . . unto the greatest peril of your soul and the immense scandal of our college'; his 'nocturnal prowling', visits to 'suspect spots within the university' and habit of 'laying outside the college suspiciously' were also cited against him. After an extremely discreet investigation into his conduct, he was found guilty and expelled by the other fellows, but allowed to stay until Christmas 'for the honour of the college'. By the following February he had left the college, but was still living in Oxford.[80]

Given the depth of the medieval Church's involvement in education, which gave many priests ready access to young boys, it is perhaps unsurprising that much of the recorded abuse (and undoubtedly much that went unrecorded) took place in its institutions. Two cases handled by Bishop William Alnwick of Lincoln typify the ecclesiastical approach. During his 1438 visitation of Markby Priory, Alnwick was told that 'secular youths do lie in the dormitory among the canons, and some with canons in the same beds.' He did nothing. Two years later, however, John Dey's abuse of choristers at the Collegiate Church of St Mary in the Newarke was so well-attested that the bishop was forced to act, depriving the man of his clerical positions.[81] The case of Johannes Stocker, a cathedral chaplain in Basel, provides similarly damning evidence. In 1475 he confessed to having 'florenced' Johannes Müller, a young choirboy who lodged with him, fourteen times; he implied that he had done so because such acts were more acceptable to his peers than sex with women, and insisted that this was a consensual relationship. The youth disagreed, claiming to have experienced substantial pain and bleeding after the priest raped him. Only because Müller made a formal complaint (despite the best efforts of Stocker and another canon to dissuade him from doing so) did the case come to court, where the episcopal official sentenced the priest to perpetual imprisonment. But Stocker was a man with powerful friends, who supported his successful appeal, and his sentence was commuted to a fine, deposition from all benefices and perpetual exile. There were rumours that this was not his first offence – a teacher had warned Müller about Stocker's past involvement with at least two other boys – and one suspects that it was not his last.[82]

Many similar cases must have been hushed up in the same way; as Dyan Elliott has shown, the medieval Church often turned a blind eye to clerical abuse, prioritizing the preservation of the organization's reputation over the safety of children. Recent scandals involving the Catholic Church (and other religious organizations) have proven that this is not just a historical problem. Despite some clear improvements, there are some similarly uncomfortable continuities in the handling of sexual assault and rape. Like us, our forebears were troubled by sexual violence, but they also shared our tendency to handle it badly.

ELEVEN

Sex in Culture

While sex is often an important part of our lived experiences, in both positive and negative ways, it also plays a significant role in our cultural lives. Whether as a source of drama, humour or pleasure (or sometimes all three at once), it features prominently in the written, spoken and visual arts of the past.

Literature

As anyone who has read *The Canterbury Tales* or *The Decameron* knows, sex appears frequently in medieval literature, usually in the form of bawdy tales featuring relatively ordinary characters, from the middling or lower ranks, in domestic settings. Many find humour in the notion of a world turned upside down, linking sexual obscenity with resistance to authority, for example in stories of married women who commit adultery and disobey their husbands. The vast majority revolve around stereotypical characters and situations, such as the elderly husband and the young wife, yoked together in a mismatched marriage.

Several of *The Canterbury Tales* feature such unions, including 'The Miller's Tale', in which a rich old carpenter is cuckolded by his young wife, Alison. She convinces her husband that a second flood is imminent so that she can have sex with their lodger.[1] In 'The Merchant's Tale', January, an elderly knight, marries the teenage May, hoping both for children and a legitimate outlet for his sexual desires. He is so taken with his young bride that, on their wedding night, he hurries their guests away, takes potions to enhance his performance, and demands they go to bed. Then January goes blind, and May starts an affair with a squire called Damian, with whom she has sex in a tree, in the presence of her unseeing husband.[2] *The Decameron* features similar stories, including one of an elderly judge whose young wife is kidnapped by pirates. When she is reunited with her husband, she declares that he should have realized that young women need 'a thing they're too modest to give a name to'. Since the pirate provides this thing, she decides that she prefers her captor to her spouse.[3]

The husbands in these stories are fools, but they are far from being the stupidest men in medieval literature. That title may well be held by Lacarise, the husband in a Dutch tale of adultery, whose wife, Machtelt, and her priestly lover manage to convince him that he is dead. They then wrap him in a shroud, through which he sees them having sex. When Lacarise protests, the priest reminds him that corpses are supposed to lie still with their eyes shut, and the simple-minded man obeys.[4] The husband in 'The Peekabo Priest' is equally gullible. In this fabliau, a priest looks through a keyhole and sees a peasant couple eating a meal. But he claims he can see them having sex; if the husband doesn't believe him, he should go outside and see for himself. Locking himself in with the wife, the priest lays her over the table and has sex with her. When the man objects, the priest insists that he is experiencing the same illusion – and the husband believes him.[5]

Other husbands are mocked for their almost unbelievable naivety. In a story from *The One Hundred New Tales* (written for Philip the Good, Duke of Burgundy, in the late 1450s), a gentleman's wife gives birth on their wedding night. He exclaims, 'if she does that each time I do it, how am I possibly going to feed this household?', and never has sex again.[6] Others can't even work out what to do, among them 'The Silly Chevalier'. After a year of marriage, his wife remains a virgin because, although he is in the habit of 'hugging her, while in the nude', he is too stupid 'to know how cunts should be approached / or maidenheads may best be broached'. Eventually the desperate wife seeks her mother's advice, and the older woman shows her son-in-law her own genitals to help him understand what he must do.[7] In a similar story the wife eventually feigns illness, and her physician teaches her husband how to cure her. When she recovers, the foolish man laments that he did not cure his late parents in the same way.[8]

If men are often presented as fools, women are depicted as lust-crazed beings who are obsessed with male genitals. In 'A Talk of Ten Wives on Their Husbands' Ware', the title characters complain in graphic detail about their husbands' penises; one, for example, claims that her partner's 'penis peeps out before / Like a maggot'.[9] The wife of 'The Fisherman of Pont-sur-Seine' denies her husband's claim that she is only with him for the sex, but when he claims to have cut off his penis (and shows her one he has removed from a corpse), she is ready to leave him.[10] Arguably this husband is one of the lucky ones: at least his wife wants to have sex with him, unlike the man whose wife tries to betray him with his friend, an innkeeper who is endowed with both 'the most finely crafted, handsome, and thickest member in the whole region' and remarkable sexual stamina. Unbeknown to her, her spouse has arranged to take the innkeeper's place, and so she has an extremely disappointing night.[11] Other texts stereotype women as willing to take any opportunity to have sex, with a particularly egregious example involving a grief-stricken widow. When she encounters a knight who claims to have killed his love 'by fucking', she begs him to kill her too, and they have sex on her husband's grave. Soon the woman has forgotten her husband, complaining: 'You call this fucking? / You'll sooner wear yourself out bucking / than finish me off at this rate.'[12]

In literature, at least, the only group that can rival women in their lustfulness are the clergy: medieval writings are full of priests, monks and nuns who behave in a highly inappropriate manner. High jinks in religious houses feature prominently, as in two stories from *The Decameron*. In the first, a young monk picks up 'a ravishing girl', brings her back to his cell for sex, and then leaves her there. The abbot goes to investigate, wanting to avoid a scandal, but then decides that 'it's only common sense to grab a good thing when the good lord sends it', and has sex with her himself. Later, the two men smuggle the girl off the premises – although the narrator suggests that they often brought her back.[13] In this world, nuns are equally lustful and duplicitous, as the tale of Masetto illustrates. This handsome young gardener gets a job in a convent by pretending to be a deaf-mute; he hopes to seduce some nuns. Soon he overhears two young nuns discussing their desire to have sex; they cook up a plan to try it with the gardener, since he can't tell on them. Soon, all of the nuns are sleeping with Masetto – even the abbess, who keeps him in her cell for several days at a time. Despite struggling to keep up with the insatiable nuns, Masetto remains in their employ until he is an old man, and fathers 'a large number of baby monks and nuns'.[14]

Such liaisons are not always without consequence. In fifteenth-century English poems such as 'Jankin, the clerical seducer' and 'A night with a holy-water clerk', in which a naive maiden is seduced by a cleric, only to find herself pregnant and alone, it is the woman who pays the price for a clergyman's sexual adventuring.[15] But sometimes philandering clerics get their comeuppance. In a Dutch story, a friar who impregnates a 'fair maiden of good family' is befriended by the Devil, who has a scheme to prevent scandal: he will painlessly remove the priest's genitals, after which the friar will preach a sermon on slander, ending by exposing himself to demonstrate his innocence. As he does so, the Devil 'restores the friar's Father Confessor to its original place, harder and more rigid than it had even been before', so that the people curse and spit at him, and he is obliged to flee.[16] In other tales, priests are physically harmed, castrated or even murdered. In the German tale of 'The Three Monks of Colmar', the titular characters pester a female penitent for sex. She allows them to visit her home, where she has prepared a very hot bath. At the necessary moment, her husband makes an appearance. Each friar in turn leaps into the bath to hide, and is scalded to death.[17]

Much of the humour in obscene literature is derived from such trickery. Among the wives featured in *The Decameron* are Tessa, who convinces her husband that the sound he can hear is not her lover knocking on the door, but a phantom cat, and Petronella, who hides her paramour in a barrel when her husband comes home unexpectedly, claiming that the man is simply inspecting the container before buying it.[18] Disguise is another common motif: *The One Hundred New Tales* include the story of a Scotsman who lived for fourteen years in Rome, disguised as a laundress, so that he could have sex with women, and was found out (and punished) only when one of his conquests told her father about him.[19]

Stories in which would-be lovers have sex with the wrong person (either deliberately, or through genuine cases of mistaken identity) are also commonplace. In *The Decameron*, a clergyman tries to seduce a chaste widow named Piccarda. Eventually she invites him to her house, where she tricks him into sleeping with her extremely ugly maid, Eggyolk. Then she sends for the local bishop and shows him the couple in bed. The distraught cleric has to do penance, and urchins taunt him in the streets. Eggyolk, on the other hand, is delighted to receive a chemise as a reward for her assistance, and the bishop expresses his strong approval of Piccarda's scheme.[20] Elsewhere, as in Chaucer's 'The Reeve's Tale', dark bedchambers provide cover for sexual shenanigans: in this story an extremely unpleasant miller gets his comeuppance when two mischievous students stay the night in his house. They manage (by tricks including moving the furniture around the bedroom) to have sex with the miller's wife and daughter, before one of them accidentally ends up in bed with the miller, causing a fight.

Medieval authors also delighted in constructing elaborate euphemisms for sex and the genitals, many of them involving animals. In 'The Squirrel', an extremely innocent fifteen-year-old girl meets a young man named Robin, who approaches her with his erect penis in his hand. She asks what he is holding; he claims that it is a squirrel, and invites her to stroke it. He tells her that the squirrel likes to eat walnuts, which saddens her because she ate some yesterday, but has none left. He reassures her that the squirrel can get the nuts from her stomach, which he can access 'par vostre con'. So they have sex, which is described in great detail: the girl cheers on the squirrel as it hunts for its nuts, and eventually the animal feels queasy and vomits copiously inside her.[21] Others employ the language of construction. In *The One Hundred New Tales*, a knight convinces a miller's foolish wife that her private parts are falling off; the only solution is to hammer them back on as quickly and as frequently as possible. On several occasions the knight uses his 'special tool' to perform this task. Then her husband finds out and responds by visiting the knight's wife, offering to use his own special tool to look for a lost ring. It takes several goes, but eventually he finds it. When the knight's wife tells him what happened, he realizes that the miller has had his revenge.[22]

Elsewhere, sex is described in medical terms, as in the story of a monk who wants to have sex with a young wife, and realizes that he will only achieve this by deception. So he pretends to have a sore finger, and claims that it can only be cured in one way: he must 'insert my ailing finger into the secret recesses of an honest woman . . . and let it remain there for a reasonable length of time'. Although his profession does not allow him to do this, she insists that he must, and that she will help him. When they repair to bed, 'He lifted up her undergarments and, instead of his finger, inserted his hard, stiff staff.' When she asks why his finger is so large, he explains that it is swollen because of his illness; when she queries that 'sensation' she feels, he says that the boil on his finger has just burst. His cure gives her so much pleasure that she insists he must return to her if he has any more finger problems.[23]

To the modern reader, one of the most striking features of medieval literature is the frequent discussion of genitals. When a Norman peasant is granted 'The Four Wishes of St Martin', his wife persuades him to let her make one of them:

> I wish that you may be endowed,
> By God, with pricks in every place –
> And may you have nor eye nor face
> Nor head nor arm nor side nor foot
> On which a prick has not been put.

Immediately his 'whole body was a mass of pricks', to the delight of his wife, who hopes that he will now be able to satisfy her. He retaliates by wishing that she 'may have as many cunts / As I have pricks', and the woman is immediately covered with 'cunts of every kind' – hairless and bushy, 'virginal and splayed', 'cunts well used and cunts well made / and little cunts, cunts big as bowls'. Now they are both unhappy, so the peasant asks: 'for him no pricks, for her no cunts'. But now the foolish pair have no genitals at all, and so their final wish is to be made as they were before: 'a prick for you, a cunt for me', as the wife puts it. The verse is supposed to illustrate the foolishness of trusting a woman's judgement.[24]

Even more bizarre are the stories in which genitals feature as stand-alone characters, capable of independent thought, speech and movement. In 'The Tournament of Nuns', a fifteenth-century German-language verse, a knight and his penis have an argument, which ends with the man castrating himself. The knight is scorned by women, and spends the rest of his life as a hermit; the penis takes refuge in a convent, where the nuns take turns to have sex with it, leading to fierce rivalries. Eventually the abbess decides they must compete in a tournament to win the penis, but the contest descends into a brawl, in the course of which it is stolen. In 'The Rose Thorn', a beautiful young virgin bathes daily in her garden, as the poem's male narrator spies on her. One day a magic root that bestows speech somehow comes into contact with her vulva; it complains of feeling underappreciated, and so the lady and her genitals part company. But when the suitor finds that he cannot have sex with his love, he rejects her, and the community mocks 'the cuntless woman'. Meanwhile, the vulva offers itself to a young man, but he mistakes it for a toad, and kicks it away. Eventually the vulva returns to the lady, and the narrator helps by 'nailing' it back into place.[25] These stories (like the genital-themed badges discussed below) are perhaps intended to present sex as a natural force that is not fully under human control.

There are also a few extremely explicit verses that discuss sexual organs in graphic detail, and which are particularly hard to interpret. Dafydd ap Gwilym's 'The Penis', written in mid-fourteenth-century Wales, is both a complaint about that organ's unruly nature ('It is difficult to keep you under control'), and a boast of sexual prowess ('You are longer than a big man's thigh').[26] Gwerful Mechain's 'The Female Genitals' (*c.* 1480) is a counterpart to Gwilym's poem, but without the personal boasting; moreover, it is written by a woman from a female perspective. She describes 'the place where children are conceived' in lurid terms:

> . . . I declare, the quim is fair,
> Circle of broad-edged lips,
> It is a valley longer than a spoon or a hand,
> A ditch to hold a penis two hands long . . .[27]

Such writings are not necessarily intended to be erotic, and some are seemingly deliberately anti-erotic; it is probable that they were designed to shock by flaunting standard conventions of restraint in discussing sexual matters. Indeed, pornography in the modern sense (that is, material produced with the specific aim of provoking sexual arousal) does not seem to have existed in the Middle Ages. Nevertheless, it is obviously dangerous to assume that readers did not find any sexual content erotic. Some historians have even argued that we should look beyond literature and consider whether sources such as court records – which discussed topics such as impotence, often in graphic detail – may have served as voyeuristic erotica for the lawyers and clerks who had access to them.[28]

In the light of such debates, it is especially tricky to interpret the pastourelle, a poetic form that emerged in the twelfth century, and which (on the basis of the surviving texts) was particularly popular in France. The basic narrative of all these poems is that a well-born man is riding along in the countryside when he spies an attractive woman, usually a shepherdess. Typically, she is a virgin, which is a significant part of her appeal. The man tries to seduce her with gifts and loving words; sometimes he is successful, but often she resists. In these versions, she often explains that she already has a fiancé, who is usually called Robin. Sometimes this is enough to put him off; in others, Robin (and other shepherds) comes to her rescue, or she escapes through her own cunning. But in numerous examples the horseman rapes the woman, who ultimately enjoys the experience. The narrator of 'In May, at dawn, when flowers spring up' sees a shepherdess who is 'just what I like' and tries to seduce her:

> When I saw my prayer got me nothing
> I laid her on the ground right away.
> I lifted up her shirt
> And saw her flesh so white
> That I was all the more eager.
> I did the trick to her –
> She didn't try to stop me,
> But frankly wanted it.

As he rides off, having 'had my way with the shepherdess', she begs him to come back often.[29] The young girl in 'When I see the fresh flower' is similarly reluctant, and has to be forced to the ground:

> When I had taken her virginity,
> She got up on her feet;
> She cried aloud,
> 'I got away from you!
> It's thirteen years since I was born,
> As I well know;

I've never spent a morning
That I've enjoyed so much.'[30]

In these poems, rape is the almost inevitable result of an encounter between a rich man and a poor woman, and they are arguably as much about power and social status as sex. Indeed, it is hard to determine what, if anything, they tell us about medieval attitudes to real-life rapes; to read them as evidence for a lack of concern about sexual violence may be as foolish as arguing that the contemporary popularity of murder mysteries reflects our own indifference to violent death. The emphasis on female sexual pleasure might suggest that medieval readers were more concerned about consent than we might assume, that in order to enjoy such a work they needed to feel that they were reading about a consensual encounter, rather than a violent crime. Nevertheless, it is hard to escape the conclusion that these poems deliberately presented rape as a form of sexual fantasy, reinforcing the notion that all women secretly want to be raped, and thus offered erotic pleasure to at least some men.[31]

In addition to having different ideas about erotica and sexual fantasy, medieval minds do not necessarily seem to have made a clear division between the decent and the obscene in the way that we tend to do today. In many medieval manuscripts, bawdy verses can be found alongside saints' lives and fables: MS Harley 2253 (an early fourteenth-century manuscript now in the British Library) includes the fabliau 'The Three Women Who Found a Penis' only a page away from a collection of the sayings of St Bernard, and such juxtapositions are not atypical.[32] Obscene tales are often included in collections of *exempla*, which were illustrative stories used by clergy in their sermons as a way to capture the attention and ensure the understanding of their congregation. One oft-repeated tale focused on a couple who had sex in church (in defiance of the Church's rules against intercourse in holy places), and were then unable to separate; consequently, they were discovered in this deeply embarrassing position, and publicly shamed.[33] It is impossible to know how often these stories were used, especially as opinions differed on their appropriateness: Robert of Basevorn, author of an early fourteenth-century manual on *The Form of Preaching*, argued that it could be useful to 'add something jocular which will give pleasure when the listeners are bored', whereas John Mirk's *Festial* complained about priests who tell tales of 'ribawdye'.[34] Either way, the mere existence of such writings highlights the complexities of medieval attitudes to the interrelationship between sex and religion – complexities which become even more apparent when we turn our attention to the subject of art.

Art

San Pedro de Cervatos, a twelfth-century church in a tiny village on the edge of the Cantabrian mountains, is decorated with numerous obscene carvings. The sculptures include male and female exhibitionists, proudly displaying their oversized genitals; couples having sex in various positions; male masturbation; a woman showing her breasts; a megaphallic man with his penis in his mouth; animals having sex; and possible male-male anal sex. These images, most of which feature on the corbel table on the outside of the church, are interspersed with representations of animals, monsters, acrobats and drinking men.[35] While the scale of the obscenity on this particular church is extremely unusual, the decoration of medieval churches with lewd carvings was not. Indeed, this church is one of a small cluster in northern Spain that are decorated with such sculptures; there are other notable examples at Santa Marta del Cerro and Frómista.[36] Sheela-na-gigs, which are carvings of naked female exhibitionists, feature on churches across the British Isles, as well as in parts of France and Spain. These women, who are often grotesque figures, crouch or sit with their legs open, displaying their oversized genitals. Some gesture at or touch their pudenda; others (including a particularly well-preserved example at Kilpeck, Herefordshire) pull apart their labia in such a way as to make the vaginal opening more visible.[37]

Such images offend modern sensibilities; representations of sex and nudity are, to us, almost inherently erotic, and it seems deeply inappropriate that they should appear in a holy place. Why did medieval people think differently? Contrary to popular belief, such carvings are almost certainly not evidence of either paganism or popular fertility cults – not least because they were commissioned by the clergy, and were found not just in rural parish churches but also in the urban cathedrals that were the most potent and up-to-date symbols of Christian belief. It is, however, possible that some carvings, especially those on the outside of churches, had protective functions, being designed to threaten and repulse both human enemies and evil forces. The fact that similar images were often used on secular buildings, including fortifications, gatehouses and bridges, seems to support this theory. In Milan, for example, a twelfth-century relief on the Porta Tosa showed a semi-naked woman shaving her pubic hair, while the fourteenth-century gates at Semur-en-Auxois (Burgundy) featured a male exhibitionist. Michael Camille found dozens of what he called 'sexualised bum-bearers' with visible penises on civic buildings such as the Maison d'Adam in Angers and the Maison de la Reine Blanche in Bourges, where they served as imposing symbols of masculine power.[38]

Twelfth-century sheela-na-gig on the Church of St Mary and St David, Kilpeck.

It is also important to recognize that, from a medieval perspective, nude images in churches could be used to convey decidedly non-erotic meanings. It seems deeply unlikely, for example, that many people were aroused by the naked Hell-bound sinners who feature prominently in many doom paintings. Exhibitionist figures on churches should perhaps be understood in a similar way, as a tool of moral instruction and an illustration of what not to do. Carvings of entwined couples having sex, for example, may be a representation of the popular story of the couple who had sex in church and became stuck together; if so, they were probably commissioned as didactic representations of punishment and shame, intended to remind churchgoers of the consequences of sexual sin.[39] Female figures, including the Sheelas, may allude to the sin and pain associated with childbirth. Other curious church furnishings may have been targeted at particular audiences. A fifteenth-century roof boss of 'The Drunkenness of Noah', which shows him with his genitals exposed and clearly visible, was located above the monks' choir at Norwich Cathedral, and probably served as a warning against homoerotic gazing. Similarly, a misericord at Lancaster Priory, which seemingly shows a masturbating angel, was surely designed as a warning to the brethren, for if an angel could be thus tempted, how much more vulnerable were they?[40]

Such carvings also remind us that medieval Christians did not necessarily separate devotion and eroticism in the same way as we do. People would have been extremely familiar with nearly naked images of Adam and Eve, whether painted onto the walls of their parish church or decorating luxurious objects such as Jan van Eyck's Ghent Altarpiece (1432) – on which the portraits are so detailed that they include individually painted pubic hairs.[41] Depictions of Christ, especially those produced towards the end of the period, often have surprisingly ostentatious genitals, while the Virgin Mary frequently has one completely exposed breast. Historians have so far been unable to agree whether these individuals were such obviously blameless holy figures that they simply could not be seen in a sexual way (especially in a world that did not necessarily see nudity as sexual), or whether they were deliberately gendered and sexualized in response to the medieval desire to humanize the divine.[42]

The debate is further complicated by the fact that, while medieval discussions of sexual sin (in, for example, penitentials) certainly recognized that visual stimulation could provoke desire, they focused on the dangers of real bodies, rather than the potential risks of artistic representations. This would seem to suggest that objects and images were really not seen in an erotic light, however implausible our pornography-obsessed society may find that. On the other hand, there was a surprising amount of interest in the crucifix as an object of erotic interest for both sexes, and the pious both gazed at and touched representations of the naked Christ on the cross. This could go too far: St Bernardino of Siena denounced a devotee who had 'sensually and repulsively polluted and defiled himself' in worship. Yet it was often encouraged or even deliberately exploited. An undated and anonymous, but certainly late medieval, pastoral letter to the Dominican nuns of Unterlinden encouraged them to 'Imagine the Lord to yourself as he was naked before the cross, when he had disrobed for your sake, so that he might rest before you naked.' At Meaux Abbey in Yorkshire, the monks somewhat cynically calculated that female pilgrims would be attracted by a 'beautiful image' of Christ on the cross, and had one sculpted from a live nude model.[43]

From a religious perspective, one of the main problems with nudity in art was its association with paganism and idolatry. This connection had its roots in late Roman Christianity and it persisted into the later Middle Ages, through stories such as Pygmalion and depictions of pagans worshipping naked idols. It could also be used as a way to dehumanize marginal groups, such as foreigners and the poor.[44] In manuscripts of the Alexander Romance (a fictional retelling of the life of Alexander the Great), the various barbarians and monstrous races he encounters are mostly naked, and sometimes depicted in compromising positions – in contrast to the well-dressed and decorous hero and his followers.[45] In the *Très riches heures*, a devotional book commissioned by Jean, Duc de Berry, which was only part-finished by 1416 (the year in which the three leading artists, the brothers Pol, Jean and Herman de Limbourg, as well as the patron himself, all died), both male and female peasants are depicted in a state of semi-undress, with bare legs. In the miniature depicting *February*, three individuals warm themselves before a fire. One, a fine lady, lifts her skirts slightly, showing only a little hose-encased leg. Beside her, a peasant couple raise their smocks well above their knees, so that their genitals are clearly exposed. Some readers may have found these images erotic, but (like the pastourelles) they were about power and status as much as sex.[46]

Perhaps the most intriguing element of many medieval manuscripts are the images added around the edge of the text. These marginalia (the purpose of which remains uncertain, despite much speculation, and which rarely have any clear link to the words) are usually quirkily humorous, with popular motifs including rabbits going hunting and knights fighting snails. Many of them are surprisingly risqué. One particularly striking example is the fourteenth-century Paris manuscript of a poem called *The Romance of the Rose*, which was produced by a married couple, Richard and Jeanne de Montbaston. The margins are scattered with images of copulation and

Detail of marginalia of nuns handling penises, from a 14th-century Paris manuscript of *The Romance of the Rose*, produced by Richard and Jeanne de Montbaston.

phalluses, the latter both attached to men and independent of them. There is a sequence of miniatures in which a nun engages in an illicit relationship, which includes graphic depictions of her sexual encounters, as well as a pair in which nuns are presented with phalluses and pick them from trees.[47] This last image, the phallus tree, was a relatively widespread motif that appeared in wall paintings at the Fonti dell'Abbondanza in Massa Marittima, Tuscany, and at Schloss Lichtenberg, above the village of Montechiaro in the region of Alto Adige, and on objects including a German trinket box and a fourteenth-century Dutch badge.[48]

Although there is very little evidence of objections to such imagery, we should be extremely cautious about suggesting that reactions to potentially erotic art were uniform across Europe and throughout the Middle Ages. Despite the prevalence of obscenity, it was not used indiscriminately, and manuscript art could be surprisingly reticent, so that the images that accompany texts are often much tamer than the words they illustrate.[49] In particular, the various ways in which sexual subjects are illustrated in medical texts hint at well-defined registers of appropriateness. Sex is frequently mentioned in regimens (guides to healthy living that were often read by non-specialists), but the pictures are usually rather coy representations of a couple in bed; it is rare for such images to show more than head and shoulders, and possibly a glimpse of breast.[50] Only in texts aimed at medical professionals do we routinely find graphic depictions of physical complaints, including images of genital sores and diseases of the female breast.[51] Treatments are also shown: in a fifteenth-century manuscript of John of Arderne's *Liber medicinarum*, for example, there is a marginal drawing of a scalpel hovering over a sore on a disembodied penis.[52]

Moreover, attitudes seem to have shifted in the fifteenth century, possibly due to changing living practices: a growth in the popularity of bed-hangings and separate sleeping quarters created more privacy, which meant that seeing other adults naked became more unusual. Consequently the naked body became less visible, and more erotic.[53] In some this seems to have produced a new sense of prudishness, leading them to damage or erase explicit images; for example, the thirteenth-century Oscott Psalter includes many nude male figures whose genitals have been carefully rubbed out, probably towards the end of the Middle Ages.[54] On the other hand, the contemporaneous increase in silent, private reading helped to popularize erotic art and salacious reading. Texts such as *Les cents nouvelles nouvelles* were written specifically for this purpose, and by the late fifteenth century private devotional works often included vivid representations of human sexuality.[55] Images of Bathsheba in her bath were especially popular: Books of Hours made for the French nobleman Guyot II Le Peley

Jean Bourdichon, *Bathsheba Bathing*, 1498–9, miniature from the Hours of Louis XII (Getty Museum, MS 79 (2003.105)).

(in the early 1480s) and the French king Louis XII (in the late 1490s) both include full-frontal nudes (complete with bared breasts and visible genitals) of this biblical temptress.[56]

Books were not the only domestic objects that were decorated with nudes and sexual images: a late fourteenth-century earthenware plate found in Aardenburg (Flanders) is decorated with a phallus, and phallus-shaped drinking glasses survive from both Germany and the Netherlands.[57] Among a set of fifteenth-century stove tiles from the Slovakian town of Banská Bystrica, most of them decorated with patterns or religious images, is one that shows a couple having sex, with the man's penis clearly visible. Since it was on display in a semi-public area of the mayor's house, it was presumably not intended to arouse, so perhaps it is an instructive image of sin, or represents a popular story.[58] Some personal seals also featured imagery and words that we would now consider offensive. A seal matrix of about 1300, found in Derbyshire, shows a penis penetrating a vulva, apparently a pun on the name of the owner, James Tibblecock. A near-contemporary matrix that belonged to a man named Jean Grunard is held by the British Museum. It features three erect phalluses and the legend 'FOCATOUT' ('fucks everyone'), which seems to have been his nickname.[59] Since such objects survive in very small numbers, it is hard to know how we should interpret them: was it perfectly normal and acceptable to display crude words and images in one's house or one's correspondence, or was this an unusual choice that would have been viewed as vulgar by the majority of medieval people?

In contrast, significant numbers of obscene lead-tin badges survive; the material of which they were made and the quantities in which they have been found suggest that they were quite commonly worn, and by ordinary people.[60] At least eight such badges have been recovered from the banks of the River Thames, including a fourteenth-century vulva pendant (the labia inscribed 'con por amours': a pun on 'as for love'/'cunt for love'), a large phallus in an ornate purse, and three ships with crews of phalluses.[61] Far greater numbers have survived from the Netherlands and Flanders, almost all of them dating from the decades around 1400. A few show people having sex (often as other people, or animals, look on) or displaying their private parts, but most feature disembodied genitals.[62]

The purpose of these badges is mysterious; indeed, we do not even know whether they were openly displayed, or worn secretly on underclothes.[63] Many seem to mock pilgrims (especially those who saw their journeys as an opportunity for sexual adventure) and popular piety. It is almost certain that a badge found in Bruges, which depicts three phalluses carrying a crowned vulva on a bier, would have recalled a religious procession for any medieval person who saw it.[64] Some include captions: one fourteenth-century example has a phallus on legs approaching a similarly limbed vulva, with the inscription 'PINTELIN' ('Penis, go in!'), an injunction that seems to support the theory that these were good-luck charms, worn by young men to advertise their virility and sexual availability, and thus to help attract the opposite sex. Alternatively, they may have served as fertility amulets, or as protection against the Evil Eye.[65] Or maybe they simply appealed to those with a bawdy sense of humour – as, presumably, did the numerous surviving English dress accessories that alluded to, rather than explicitly depicting, sex. These include numerous cockerel broochs, the animal being a common symbol for the penis, and 'cock' being a slang term for that organ by about 1300.[66]

Archaeological excavations in Norway have revealed numerous sticks and bones covered with thirteenth-century runic carvings, including sexual messages. One stick found in Bergen was carved with the message 'Ugly is the cunt, may the penis pour for it'; another read 'The gentlewoman let loose for her lover – still she is a virgin for folk'; and a third said 'Rannveig the Red, you shall fuck her. It is supposed to be bigger than a man's prick and smaller than a horse's prick.' The carving on a cow's rib from Oslo included the claim 'Óli is unwiped and fucked in the arse.'[67] Late fifteenth-century graffiti from the Caestertgroeve chalk mines (on the Dutch-Belgian border) includes an image of a man buggering a dog.[68] The urge to scrawl crude pictures and messages on any available surface is clearly not a new one.

Popular Culture

Swearing

Throughout the Middle Ages the written word and the visual arts were largely the preserve of the social elites, those who were wealthy enough and educated enough to pay for and make use of such commodities, which probably provides one explanation for why many aspects of medieval culture were apparently unregulated. The spoken word, on the other hand, was accessible to all, and thus the relevant authorities made efforts to control its use, giving us a glimpse of less elevated attitudes to obscene language and behaviour in the process. Swearing, in particular, was taken very seriously, as one of the sins of the tongue – and especially if the person doing the swearing was female. Thus the late fourteenth-century conduct book for young brides known as *Le ménagier de Paris* included a warning that women should not speak of vulgar things, including their private parts.[69] One late fourteenth-century anatomical text suggested that men might refer to the 'balloc coddis' (the scrotum), but by 'wommen it is ycallid a purs for curtesie'; similarly, 'men callen [the penis] a ters but for curtesie wymmen callen it a yerde.'[70] In fourteenth-century Ghent, Goessin Van Peelkem completed a pilgrimage on behalf of his sister, who had used disgraceful words 'unbecoming for a respectable woman to speak', while Kateline Van der Ellen went on her own pilgrimage for the same offence.[71]

The records do not tell us which words these women said, but the worst medieval curses were religious ones, ranging from the relatively mild ('By my faith!') to graphic references to God's or Christ's body parts. These freshly wounded Christ each time they were used, and consequently swearing could be punished both on earth – St Louis IX of France report-edly required swearers to be branded on the face and placed in the stocks – and in the afterlife.[72] On the other hand, several words that we would now hesitate to say, at least in polite company, were spoken quite casually in the Middle Ages. For most of this period, the verb 'to fuck' usually meant 'to strike' or 'to beat', as in the archaic name for a kestrel: a wind-fucker. This is almost certainly the sense in which it was used in personal names. In the 1280s King Edward I had a horseman called 'Fuckebeggar', whose name surely derived from the Anglo-Norman surname Butevilein ('Strike the churl') rather than from his sexual proclivities. His contempor-aries Simon Fukkebotere and William Smallfuk of Ipswich were surely named after their occupations – the former name referring to the making of butter, and the latter to a type of sail.[73] Roger Fuckbythenavele, who failed to appear before the Chester county court in the early fourteenth century, poses more of a puzzle: his name may mean 'strike on the belly' (perhaps he was a brawler?), although it has been argued that it could refer to either his extreme sexual naivety or to an illicit sexual practice.[74] The Paris tax roll of 1292 includes men named Guillaume Fout-Vielle ('fucks the old woman'), Jehan Fout-en-Paille ('fucks-in-the-straw') and Renodet Fout-Oe ('fucks the goose').[75] The Bristol field known as 'Fockynggrove' (mentioned in a royal charter of 1373) may well have been a place associated with sexual assignations. But the earliest certain use of fuck in the modern sense seems to come from the 1475 poem 'Fleas, Flies and Friars', in which a coded passage reads 'They [the friars] are not in Heaven because they fuck the women of Ely.'[76]

Even more striking to the modern reader is the medieval use of 'cunt'. The meaning of this word has not changed – then as now, it referred to the female genitals – but its use has become considerably more restricted. In the fifteenth century it was used as a technical term, as in a Middle English medical text which states that 'In wymmen þe necke of þe bladdre is schort, and is maad fast to the cunte.' It also featured in place names such as Cuntelowe (Warwickshire, 1221) and Cuntewellewang (Lincolnshire, 1317), although some of these may have referred to topographical features, or derived from an unrelated Danish personal name. In other cases, the sexual meaning is unquestionable, notably in the common English street name 'Gropecuntlane': this is first recorded in Oxford in the 1230s, and occurs in more than a dozen towns between then and the end of the Middle Ages. Even in a world in which 'cunt' had not yet become the obscene term it is today, it is still hard for us to understand how a word with this meaning could be used in such a matter-of-fact way. Such usages, along with other crude street names (such as Shiteborrowlane and Pissing Alley) and place names (including the Derbyshire villages Balloklaw and Ballocþorn), suggest an approach to body parts and functions that was very different to our own.[77]

Even more surprising are the various instances of personal names including this word. English examples include Godewin Clawcuncte (1066), Simon Sitbithecunte (1167), Gunoka Cunteles (1219), John Fillecunt (1246), Robert Clevecunt (1302) and Bele Wydecunthe (1320), while in late thirteenth-century Paris there was a man named Jehan Condore ('Golden Cunt').[78] The apparent disappearance of cunt-based personal names after the early fourteenth century suggests that the word started to become more taboo, if still not downright offensive, towards the end of the Middle Ages. Euphemistic phonetic disguises, especially 'queynte', are used by several authors, including Chaucer, whose Wife of Bath also refers to her genitals as her 'thinge' and her 'bele chose'.[79] Both male and female genitals could be referred to as the 'taile', and consequently 'tailing' referred to sexual intercourse.[80] There were also various colloquial names for the penis. Some remain in use, so that this Middle English pun still makes sense today:

> I have a gentle [that is, noble] cock . . .
> And every night he percheth him
> In mine lady's chamber.[81]

Others, including 'pillock', 'pintle', 'limb' and 'yard', have fallen out of use or changed their meaning. Similarly, various medieval terms for sex have since disappeared, so that a man is no longer likely to 'sard', 'swive' or 'occupy' a woman. Nor do modern couples 'jape' with each other.[82]

Insults

While obscene language was apparently used much more freely in medieval Europe than it is today, sexual insults were far more offensive, to the extent that they were potentially a matter for the courts. To be considered actionable, an insult needed to be demonstrably untrue or reveal something that it was not necessary to disclose. There was a clear public interest case for revealing dishonesty or prostitution, for example, but revelations of bastardy and cuckoldry were less clear cut. In most legal systems, cases could be brought directly by the plaintiff, or instigated by the authorities, often in response to a complaint. Whose jurisdiction slander fell under varied by time and place: in England, such cases were heard in both ecclesiastical and secular authorities up to the end of the fourteenth century; after this they were restricted to the Church courts. In late medieval Bologna, they were heard in the criminal court of the *podestà* (the city's chief judge).[83] The number of cases fluctuated over time and from place to place, but were never very high. In the Italian town of Todi, for example, there were forty convictions for defamation between the years 1275 and 1280.[84]

There was, seemingly, no clear distinction between the insults used by the elites and by ordinary people: the language of insult was classless.[85] Nor, despite contemporary perceptions that scolding was a female crime, were women disproportionately prone to using insulting language. There was, however, a clear division of insults by gender, with female victims usually accused of sexual immorality. For example, in a 1492 argument between two married women, one accused the other: 'You're the greatest whore in Bologna and my father took you many times in the stables and was your pimp.' Fifty years earlier, another woman was accused of exchanging sex for luxury goods: 'Whore, you've been with courtiers and many others, and they've made for you a headdress of black velvet, and a pair of red velvet shoes.' Occasionally, such claims were accompanied by threats, as in a 1394 case in which a man told a woman and her daughter: 'Whores, I shall drag you to the brothel where you used to live. I've had you a hundred times in the brothel and shall do so again.'[86]

Insults directed at men often attacked their honesty, such as 'You're a robber and you rob all day', rather than their sexual behaviour. But men were sometimes taunted about their mother's sexuality: in a society preoccupied with legitimacy, to be called 'bastard' or 'son of a bitch' was a serious insult.[87] Other slanders focused on a man's alleged inability to control his female relatives. In a 1357 argument between two Bologna men, one challenged the other to 'Look to your wife and sister, who are getting themselves fucked by friars and priests.' In 1371 a man who jibed, 'You're the friars' pimp', earned the retort, 'I've never pimped except for your wife.'[88] On the rare occasions when men were sexually slandered, the insults typically focused on deviant practices, as in a 1361 insult against a Bolognese judge: 'Bloody bugger! Go and bugger someone: that's what you do all the time, you Florentine bugger. I've been with your mother over 100 times.'[89]

Sexual slander could lead to a citation before the courts for fornication, which forced people who had been unjustly slandered to respond with a defamation case. Offended parties had to clear themselves through compurgation.[90] In 1464 Margaret Hancoke, a married woman, was falsely accused of committing adultery with a priest. She purged herself before the Wells Consistory Court with the support of nine 'honest women neighbours', and the official 'declared her legitimately purged and wrongly defamed and restored her to her good fame'.[91] On the other hand, to pursue a defamation case when one had been justly accused was a risky strategy. During the course of a defamation suit heard in the diocese of Canterbury in 1418, Eleanor Ward admitted that she had indeed had sex with Robert Coting, and her case was therefore postponed to the next session, for further consideration.[92]

Claims that insults had seriously damaged the offended party's reputation were common. In 1334 Thomas was charged with calling Alice Daunce of Stainforth a whore, causing her to be accused before the Church courts and to lose money.[93] During the course of an argument in 1496, a man said to John Streme's wife (in the presence of Streme, his mother-in-law and two other men) 'Thow hast had a childe by a prest.' When he later begged her pardon, she replied, 'thow art never abyll to make me amendys.'[94] In 1459 Alderman Vincent Zoetaert of Nieuwpoort was pardoned by the Duke of Burgundy for the murder of Gerard Rossin. Rossin had repeatedly insulted his killer, including calling him 'false son of a whore'. The pardon acknowledged that these insults had seriously harmed Zoetaart, who had previously been a 'peaceable man of good repute'.[95]

Ideally, however, justice would be left to the courts, who usually imposed small fines for defamation, although a 1345 Liège ordinance ruled that those who refused to pay up after insulting a fellow citizen could be banished. Alternatively, slanderers might be sentenced to experience public humiliation for themselves. In fourteenth-century Eijsden, near Liège, customary law required women who called each other whores to walk a set route through the city, carrying a special stone shaped like a sharp tongue.[96] In 1495 John of Glogów called his fellow student Valentine of Rybitwy 'a sodomite and traitor [that is, to the faith] who does not have the right to call himself a good and honest person' in front of members of the canon law dormitory at the University of Kraków. The university authorities ruled that John must spend an hour publicly retracting his accusations in front of the same audience, on pain of excommunication; he was also required to pay a three-florin fine.[97]

Occasionally, if the accusations were particularly offensive, or if there were aggravating circumstances, a more serious punishment could be given. The German law code *Schwabenspiegel* (*c.* 1275) stated that those who defamed someone as 'a sodomite' or for bestiality should be broken on the wheel.[98] In Ghent, at the very end of the fifteenth century, Pierre Lancedonc accused Jehan Hanneman of bestiality with a mare; Jehan was interrogated three times, repeatedly insisting on his innocence, before Pierre was banished for fifty years. A few years earlier, Cornelis van der Poorten, a servant and tavern worker, posted handwritten letters at the stock exchange in Bruges, in which he accused two aldermen, and the people of the city, of sodomy. He then fled to Tournai, but the accused men persuaded their counterparts in that city to pursue the case, and Poorten soon confessed to both slander and sodomy. The gravity of his accusations and of his own crimes called for serious punishment, especially given recent political unrest in the city, so Poorten was beheaded.[99]

Most slander cases began with offensive words spoken in temper, but door-scorning was also a problem, at least in fifteenth-century Bologna. In 1420, for example, two men from Ferrera fixed horns (the sign of a cuckold) and phallic images on the door of Bonino the halter-maker; they did this in the middle of the night, shouting out 'indecent and filthy' words, to the dishonour of Bonino and his family. Six years later, a tailor twice decorated Vinciquerra Oselli's house with paper models of male and female genitals, 'to the great damage and shame' of the Oselli family. Then, in 1435, a group of men attached a letter to the door of Antonio and Caterina de Lino's house, calling him a cuckold and accusing him of acting as her pimp. They also put up indecent drawings and three pairs of horns. In 1454 Bologna introduced a statute against such behaviour.[100] On each occasion, the perpetrators were apparently driven by a hatred of sexual misconduct, rather than a personal grudge against their target, and felt justified in making public accusations.

Celebrations and Performance

As well as policing what people said to each other, the medieval authorities also tried to prevent obscene behaviour in public; they were concerned that obscene performances and celebrations would lead to social disorder and immoral conduct. Unsurprisingly, clerics were particularly vocal in their condemnation of these activities, although the frequency of their complaints must raise doubts about their impact. Bernard of Clairvaux, for example, condemned tumblers and jugglers, as well as theatre, 'which excites lust with feminine and lascivious wrigglings and represents wanton acts'. The obscene 'theatrical games' held by minor clergy in the days after Christmas were denounced by authorities including Pope Innocent III and Bishop Robert Grosseteste of Lincoln (1235–53), but the Feast of Fools was widely celebrated on 1 January throughout the Middle Ages; the festivities held at Notre Dame de Paris included the singing of lewd songs and the making of crude gestures.[101] Celebrations held on other feast days were similarly problematic. At the turn of the fifteenth century Jean Gerson complained about

> the most filthy corruption of boys and youths by shameful nude images, which are offered for sale in the very temples and on holy days . . . to which Christian children – oh horrible shame – are introduced by impious mothers or sluttish maidservants, and the senseless laughter of damnable fathers, even to the most obscene songs, gestures and behaviours and to many other abominations, even in the churches, in holy places and on holy days.[102]

Such complaints might seem to suggest that this was a world in which bawdy popular culture was reined in by clerical disapproval, but the reality was more complicated. In Easter week 1282, John, the parish priest of Inverkeithing in Fife, Scotland, persuaded a group of young girls to follow him as he sang and danced, incited them to lust with filthy language, and held aloft images of human genitals. He may have intended this as some sort of fertility ritual, but the community (especially the girls' mothers) was unimpressed, and remonstrated with him. Although there is no evidence that the Church acted against him, the chronicler who recorded the incident noted approvingly that John was stabbed to death shortly afterwards, receiving his comeuppance for his unconventional and inappropriate celebrations.[103]

This troubling incident occurred at a time of year that, despite its religious significance, was strongly associated with public obscenity. Carnival was widely celebrated in the build-up to Lent from the thirteenth century onwards, and often featured extremely rowdy behaviour. Consequently, many town regulations forbade problematic rituals (ranging from cross-dressing to throwing unmarried women in the river) and behaviour (a 1468 Nuremberg ordinance required the constabulary to stop revellers using 'bawdy words and obscene gestures', especially in front of genteel ladies), although these rules had a limited effect on would-be troublemakers. During Mardi Gras 1483, the journeymen blacksmiths of Soest in Westphalia covered one of their number in straw and tied to his front something that 'hung down very improperly and indecently', as the town council put it. In 1488, during the week after Ash Wednesday, the Nuremberg executive councillors ordered the supervisor of the craftsmen to identify the individual who had 'carried a disgraceful, lewd man-made member' through the town. And in 1491 two hatters in Nördlingen were cited for lewd behaviour in the streets: one of the men had dressed as a woman, and the pair had performed 'unchaste acts in front of the people' – that is, simulated sex.[104]

Another strange (to the modern mind) conflation of the religious and the obscene is found in mystery plays – religious dramas that were widely performed in late medieval towns, being organized by the guilds (associations of merchants and craftsmen) and performed in the streets for the whole community to watch. Although these plays feature lots of bad behaviour, marital tension and disobedient wives, there is surprisingly little sexual content. Nevertheless, some of the plays do contain moral messages. The N-Town play on 'The Woman Taken in Adultery', in which the offending woman is saved from a humiliating ordeal by Jesus, who declares 'If thou ask mercy, I never say nay', offers such a strong message of forgiveness that Christ almost seems to be condoning the sinner's behaviour.[105]

The representation of the Virgin Mary in these performances is particularly striking: despite the widespread veneration of Mary, and the fact that her sexual purity was one of her defining characteristics, all of the major English collections of biblical dramas include a comical episode in which the elderly and impotent Joseph accuses the pregnant Mary of adultery. These scenes echo popular tales of aged cuckolds and their much younger wives, but the joke is upended: Mary is beyond suspicion, and therefore Joseph is funny not because he is too trusting, but because he doubts.[106] The N-Town plays, which were probably written and performed in late fifteenth-century East Anglia, are particularly curious in this respect, because they make Mary the focus of obscene humour. There are lurid claims about her sex life (her alleged partners include Joseph, the Angel Gabriel and various local men); she is called sexual names ('quene', 'scowte' and so on) and threatened with sexual violence. In 'The Marriage of Mary and Joseph' there is a contest to win her hand, which involves much phallic and fertility symbolism, including discussion of Joseph's 'rodde'. In 'Joseph's Doubt', Mary tries to convince her husband that she is pregnant by the Holy Trinity, but he refuses to believe that God would 'jape so' with a human woman. In the Nativity Pageant she undergoes two gynaecological examinations at the hands of midwives who doubt her virginity, but the questions continue even after Jesus' birth. In 'The Trial of Mary and Joseph', her alleged transgressions are described in graphic detail. She is mocked like any other adulteress, threatened with facial mutilation, and obliged to drink a potentially poisonous potion to prove her innocence. Rather than being offended by jokes about the Virgin's sexuality, late medieval Christians seem to have been amused by them, and even found in them a strange kind of hope.[107]

In many ways these mystery plays nicely sum up the complexities and contradictions of medieval attitudes to sexuality. Many of these literary and artistic representations are surprisingly light-hearted and remain entertaining even today, although some are so bizarre that we are arguably laughing at medieval people, rather than with them. And it is hard to reconcile the seeming open-mindedness of this world in which you might walk down Gropecuntlane on your way to a church decorated with obscene sculptures, with its tendency to repress natural desires, and to punish those who failed to do so. Perhaps we can conclude only that, when it came to sex, medieval people were as confusing – and confused – as we are.

Conclusion

Although it is often said that history is written by the victors, in the case of the history of sex the truth is rather more complex. Much of what we know about the sex lives of real medieval people comes from sources that tell us about problems either anticipated or real. While medieval society presumably consisted largely of people with unremarkable sex lives, happily married couples and successfully celibate priests, for example, do not tend to make much of an impression on the historical record. Consequently, the picture of medieval sex and sexuality painted in this book is, if anything, perhaps somewhat bleaker than the truth. Nevertheless, the manner in which medieval sex and sexuality are portrayed in modern popular culture is largely inaccurate: for the most part, such depictions either reflect the very worst of medieval society, or have absolutely no grounding in the facts. Just like today, medieval sexual experiences could be horrifically violent or extremely funny, but most fell somewhere in between.

Insofar as sex in the Middle Ages was just like sex today, it was because, above all, medieval ideas and experiences were as varied and complicated as ours – and because sex has always had a tendency to cause problems. While death by celibacy is no longer a common fate, health issues such as STDs and impotence are still widely experienced. People still have unwanted pregnancies, and struggle to access the contraception and abortions they need; others face the heartbreak of infertility. Despite significant recent advances in LGBT rights in many countries, prejudice on the basis of sexuality is still widespread. Clerical sexuality remains the subject of considerable scrutiny, not least because of the Roman Catholic Church's continued adherence to the policy of mandatory celibacy. Debate continues to rage over how far this requirement is to blame for numerous recent scandals concerning same-sex relations and child sexual abuse, and about whether it would be best to abandon it altogether, and to allow priests to marry.

Even more striking is the extent to which much of the world continues to fetishize virginity, especially in women. In early 2020 a *Sunday Times* investigation found that there were at least 22 clinics offering hymenoplasty operations in London alone, many of them attracting clients from across the world, chiefly young women who were desperate to pass themselves off as virgins on their wedding night.[1] In the USA, abstinence-only sex education is mandated in several states, and purity pledges (in which girls promise to abstain from sex until marriage) are common in many evangelical Christian communities.[2] The value of female sexual purity is also emphasized by the fast-growing Trad Wife movement, which suggests that a promiscuous woman is less likely to secure a husband – and that once a woman has a ring on her finger, she should submit to her husband's wishes in all areas of married life.[3]

Across the world, sexual violence also remains a common problem – as was powerfully revealed by the #MeToo movement, which developed in response to the numerous accusations of rape and sexual abuse against the American film producer Harvey Weinstein that emerged in late 2017. According to the most recent National Survey of Sexual Attitudes and Lifestyles (conducted in Britain in 2010–12), 9.8 per cent of women and 1.4 per cent of men have experienced completed non-volitional sex; the equivalent figures for attempted non-volitional sex were 19.4 per cent and 4.7 per cent, respectively.[4] Nor are contemporary approaches to rape necessarily more enlightened or effective than those of our medieval counterparts. Across Europe most rapes still go unreported, and even for cases that do make it to court, conviction rates are extremely low. The gang rapists who plagued fifteenth-century Dijon were surely the medieval equivalent of the twenty-first-century Incels, for whom the inability to have the sex to which they feel entitled has provided justification for various acts of terrorism. Nor is one of the most horrifying medieval responses to rape – requiring the victim to marry her attacker – a solution found only in the distant past. Morocco repealed article 475, under which a rapist who married his victim was no longer liable for his crime (except under exceptional circumstances), as recently as 2014, after the suicide of sixteen-year-old Amina El-Filali. She had been raped by a family friend, and then forced to marry him as the result of an agreement between the two families.[5] Around the world, rape continues to be used as a weapon of war – and not just, as David Cameron apparently believed, by Islamic terrorists.[6]

If, therefore, there is a lesson to be learned from studying sex and sexuality in medieval Europe, it is certainly not that we are inherently superior to our distant ancestors. Indeed, even in comparing contemporary sexual behaviour to that of our forebears, we are doing nothing new.

In his memoirs, the Benedictine monk Guibert of Nogent (*c.* 1055–1124) bemoaned the 'wretched and progressive decline' in moral standards that had taken place since his parents' youth. Women had become more flirtatious, and showed off their bodies in tight-fitting clothes; married and single people of both sexes not only took lovers, but flaunted them, and were ashamed if people thought they were without paramours. 'In this and in other similar ways,' he complained, 'the modern world corrupts and is corrupted, pouring its evil ideas upon some, whilst the filth spreads to infinity like a hideous epidemic.'[7] One dreads to think what he would have to say about the way we live now.

REFERENCES

Introduction

1 Andrew Elliott, *Medievalism, Politics, and Mass Media: Appropriating the Middle Ages in the Twenty-first Century* (Cambridge, 2017), p. 195.

2 Shiloh Carroll, *Medievalism in 'A Song of Ice and Fire' and 'Game of Thrones'* (Cambridge, 2018), pp. 85–106, 140–84; Torben Gebhardt, 'Homosexuality in Television Medievalism', in *The Middle Ages on Television: Critical Essays*, ed. Meriem Pagès and Karolyn Kinane (Jefferson, NC, 2015), pp. 197–214; Rachael Brown, 'George R. R. Martin on Sex, Fantasy and "A Dance with Dragons"', *The Atlantic* (11 July 2011).

3 Amy Burge, 'Do Knights Still Rescue Damsels in Distress? Reimagining the Medieval in Mills and Boon Historical Romance', in *The Female Figure in Contemporary Historical Fiction*, ed. K. Cooper and E. Short (London, 2012), pp. 95–114.

4 Alain Boureau, *The Lord's First Night: The Myth of the Droit de Cuissage*, trans. Lydia Cochrane (Chicago, IL, 1998).

5 Michael Sharp, 'Remaking Medieval Heroism: Nationalism and Sexuality in *Braveheart*', *Florilegium*, XV (1998), pp. 251–66.

6 Albrecht Classen, *The Medieval Chastity Belt: A Myth-making Process* (Basingstoke, 2007), pp. 16–146.

7 Louise D'Arcens, *Comic Medievalisms: Laughing at the Middle Ages* (Woodbridge, 2014), pp. 127–8.

8 Ruth Mazo Karras, *Sexuality in Medieval Europe*, 3rd edn (Abingdon, 2017), pp. 4–6.

9 Karma Lochrie, *Heterosyncrasies: Female Sexuality When Normal Wasn't* (Minneapolis, MN, 2005), pp. xiii–xxiv.

1 Guiding Principles

1 Roger Rosewell, *Medieval Wall Paintings* (Woodbridge, 2008), pp. 35, 142.

2 Pierre Payer, *The Bridling of Desire: Views of Sex in the Later Middle Ages* (Toronto, 1993), pp. 20–21.

3 Conor McCarthy, ed., *Love, Sex and Marriage in the Middle Ages: A Sourcebook* (London, 2004), p. 157.

4 Alastair Minnis, *From Eden to Eternity: Creations of Paradise in the Later Middle Ages* (Philadelphia, PA, 2016), p. 41.

5 Paul Delany, 'Constantinus Africanus' *De Coitu*: A Translation', *Chaucer Review*, 4 (1969), p. 56.

6 Pierre Payer, *The Bridling of Desire: Views of Sex in the Later Middle Ages*
   (Toronto, 1993), p. 39.
7 Minnis, *From Eden to Eternity*, pp. 42–6; Payer, *Bridling of Desire*, pp. 33–4.
8 Margaret Berger, trans., *Hildegard of Bingen: On Natural Philosophy and
   Medicine* (Cambridge, 1999), p. 39; Minnis, *From Eden to Eternity*, p. 35.
9 Payer, *Bridling of Desire*, p. 45.
10 Ibid., p. 54.
11 Kim Phillips, 'Gender and Sexuality', in *The Routledge History of Medieval
   Christianity, 1050–1500*, ed. Robert Swanson (Abingdon, 2015), p. 312.
12 John Shinners and William Dohar, eds, *Pastors and the Care of Souls
   in Medieval England* (Notre Dame, IN, 1998), p. 135.
13 Edward Goulburn and Henry Symonds, eds, *The Life, Letters and Sermons
   of Bishop Herbert of Losigna*, 2 vols (Oxford, 1878), vol. II, pp. 352–7.
14 McCarthy, ed., *Love, Sex and Marriage*, p. 157.
15 Michelle Sauer, *Gender in Medieval Culture* (London, 2015), p. 47.
16 McCarthy, ed., *Love, Sex and Marriage*, p. 158.
17 Gerald of Wales, *The Jewel of the Church*, ed. John Hagen (Leiden, 1979),
   pp. 177–8.
18 Clarissa Atkinson, 'Precious Balsam in a Fragile Glass: The Ideology of
   Virginity in the Later Middle Ages', *Journal of Family History*, 8 (1983),
   pp. 131–43; Irven Resnick, 'Peter Damian on the Restoration of Virginity:
   A Problem for Medieval Theology', *Journal of Theological Studies*, XXXX/1
   (1988), pp. 125–34; Patricia Cullum, 'Give Me Chastity: Masculinity and
   Attitudes to Chastity and Celibacy in the Middle Ages', *Gender and
   History*, 25 (2013), pp. 225–40.
19 Barry Windeatt, ed., *The Book of Margery Kempe* (London, 1985), p. 88.
20 Thomas Tentler, *Sin and Confession on the Eve of the Reformation*
   (Princeton, NJ, 1977), pp. 166–7, 225.
21 Peter Biller, 'Birth-control in the Thirteenth and Early Fourteenth
   Centuries', *Past and Present*, XCIV/1 (1982), p. 10.
22 Siegfried Wenzel, ed., *Fasciculus Morum: A Fourteenth-century Preacher's
   Handbook* (London, 1989), pp. 688–701.
23 Ibid., pp. 648–66.
24 Ibid., pp. 668–9.
25 Ibid., pp. 676–83.
26 Ibid., pp. 682–9.
27 Ibid., pp. 708–15.
28 Ibid., pp. 706–7, 714–15, 726–31.
29 Goulburn and Symonds, *Herbert of Losigna*, I, pp. 103–5.
30 Robert Bartlett, *Why Can the Dead Do Such Great Things? Saints and
   Worshippers from the Martyrs to the Reformation* (Princeton, NJ, 2012), p. 202.
31 Charles Wood, 'The Doctor's Dilemma: Sin, Salvation and the Menstrual
   Cycle in Medieval Thought', *Speculum*, 56 (1981), p. 717.
32 Ibid., pp. 720–25.
33 Bartlett, *Why Can the Dead*, pp. 203–4, 535–40; Jacobus de Voragine,
   The Golden Legend, trans. William Granger Ryan (Princeton, NJ, 2012),
   pp. 101–4.
34 Jane Tibbetts Schulenberg, 'The Heroics of Virginity: Brides of Christ
   and Sacrificial Mutilation', in *Women in the Middle Ages and the Renaissance*, ed. Mary Beth Rose (Syracuse, NY, 1986), pp. 47–9.
35 Voragine, *The Golden Legend*, pp. 288, 328; Dyan Elliott, *Spiritual Marriage:*

Sexual Abstinence in Medieval Wedlock (Princeton, NJ, 1993), pp. 113–31.

36 Katherine Harvey, 'Episcopal Virginity in Medieval England', *Journal of the History of Sexuality*, XXVI/2 (2017), pp. 273–93.

37 Gonzalo de Berceo, *Miracles of Our Lady*, trans. Richard Mount and Annette Cash (Lexington, KY, 1997), pp. 32–5.

38 Ibid., pp. 49–53, 98–108.

39 Voragine, *The Golden Legend*, pp. 374–85.

40 Susan Haskins, *Mary Magdalene: The Essential History* (London, 1993), pp. 134–228, especially pp. 134–7.

41 Carole Rawcliffe, *Medicine and Society in Later Medieval England* (Stroud, 1995), pp. 172–4.

42 Albertus Magnus, *On Animals: A Medieval Summa Zoologica*, trans. Kenneth Mitchell and Irven Resnick, 2 vols (Baltimore, MD, 1999), vol. I, p. 216. Thomas Laqueur, *Making Sex: Body and Gender from the Greeks to Freud* (London, 1990), is the classic (if flawed) account of the one-body model.

43 Alexandra Barratt, ed., *The Knowing of Woman's Kind in Childing: A Middle English Version of Material Derived from the 'Trotula' and Other Sources* (Turnhout, 2001), ll. 40–51.

44 Monica Green, ed. and trans., *The Trotula* (Philadelphia, PA, 2001), p. 66.

45 Rawcliffe, *Medicine and Society*, pp. 172–5.

46 Delany, 'Constantinus Africanus' *De Coitu*', pp. 56, 62.

47 Danielle Jacquart and Claude Thomasset, *Sexuality and Medicine in the Middle Ages* (Oxford, 1998), p. 41.

48 Helen Rodnite Lemay, ed., *Women's Secrets* (New York, 1992), pp. 146–7.

49 Jacquart and Thomasset, *Sexuality and Medicine*, pp. 53–6.

50 Ibid., p. 60.

51 Lemay, ed., *Women's Secrets*, p. 147.

52 Albertus Magnus, *On Animals*, II, pp. 1227–8.

53 Jacquart and Thomasset, *Sexuality and Medicine*, pp. 55–6.

54 Luke Demaitre, *Medieval Medicine: The Art of Healing, from Head to Toe* (Santa Barbara, CA, 2013), p. 310.

55 Delany, 'Constantinus Africanus' *De Coitu*', p. 59.

56 Caroline Proctor, 'Between Medicine and Morals: Sex in the Regimens of Maino de Maineri', in *Medieval Sexuality: A Casebook*, ed. April Harper and Caroline Proctor (London, 2008), p. 118.

57 Enrique Montero Cartelle, ed., *Liber Minor de Coitu* (Valladolid, 1987), p. 78.

58 Lemay, ed., *Women's Secrets*, pp. 70, 127.

59 Joan Cadden, 'Western Medicine and Natural Philosophy', in *Handbook of Medieval Sexuality*, ed. Vern Bullough and James Brundage (New York, 1996), pp. 66–7.

60 Joan Cadden, *Meanings of Sex Difference in the Middle Ages: Medicine, Science and Culture* (Cambridge, 1993), p. 275.

61 Green, ed., *Trotula*, pp. 71–2.

62 Elisabeth van Houts, *Married Life in the Middle Ages, 900–1300* (Oxford, 2019), p. 47.

63 Jacquart and Thomasset, *Sexuality and Medicine*, p. 176.

64 Green, ed., *Trotula*, pp. 72, 91.

65 Laurinda Dixon, *Perilous Chastity: Women and Illness in Pre-Enlightenment Art and Medicine* (Ithaca, NY, 1995), pp. 25–38.

66 Jacquart and Thomasset, *Sexuality and Medicine*, p. 176.
67 Joseph Ziegler, *Medicine and Religion, c. 1300: The Case of Arnau de Vilanova* (Oxford, 1998), p. 264.
68 Cartelle, ed., *Liber Minor de Coitu*, pp. 56, 68.
69 Margaret Berger, trans., *Hildegard of Bingen: On Natural Philosophy and Medicine* (Cambridge, 1999), pp. 63–5.
70 Shulamith Shahar, *Growing Old in the Middle Ages* (London, 1997), pp. 40, 77–9.
71 John of Salisbury, *Historia Pontificalis*, ed. Marjorie Chibnall (Oxford, 1986), pp. 12–15.
72 Rosemary Horrox, ed. and trans., *The Black Death* (Manchester, 1994), pp. 163, 175–6.
73 Carole Rawcliffe, *Urban Bodies: Communal Health in Late Medieval English Towns and Cities* (Woodbridge, 2013), p. 109.
74 John Gillingham, 'Richard I and the Science of War in the Middle Ages', in *Anglo-Norman Warfare*, ed. Matthew Strickland (Woodbridge, 1992), p. 203.
75 Steven Bednarski, *A Poisoned Past: The Life and Times of Margarida de Portu, a Fourteenth-century Accused Poisoner* (Toronto, 2014), p. 146.
76 Ibid., pp. 42–3, 47.
77 Emmanuel Le Roy Ladurie, *Montaillou*, trans. Barbara Bray (Harmondsworth, 1980), p. 145.
78 Carole Rawcliffe, *Leprosy in Medieval England* (Woodbridge, 2006), pp. 84–5.
79 Ruth Mazo Karras, *Common Women: Prostitution and Sexuality in Medieval England* (Oxford, 1996), p. 40; Rawcliffe, *Urban Bodies*, p. 113.
80 Rawcliffe, *Leprosy*, pp. 82–3.
81 Ibid., p. 207; Green, ed., *Trotula*, p. 95.
82 J. D. Oriel, *The Scars of Venus: A History of Venereology* (Berlin, 1994), p. 10.
83 David Nirenberg, 'Conversion, Sex and Segregation: Jews and Christians in Medieval Spain', *American Historical Review*, CVII (2002), p. 1070.
84 Shinners and Dohar, eds, *Pastors and the Care of Souls*, pp. 143–5.
85 Ibid., pp. 177–80; Thomas Tentler, *Sin and Confession on the Eve of the Reformation* (Princeton, NJ, 1977), pp. 93–5, 100–101.
86 Michael Haren, 'The Interrogatories for Officials, Lawyers and Secular Estates of the *Memoriale Presbiterorum*', in *Handling Sin: Confession in the Middle Ages*, ed. Peter Biller and A. J. Minnis (York, 1998), pp. 123–63.
87 Robert of Flamborough, *Liber Poenitentialis*, ed. J. J. Francis Firth (Toronto, 1971), pp. 195–7.
88 Pierre Payer, 'Sex and Confession in the Thirteenth Century', in *Sex in the Middle Ages*, ed. Joyce Salisbury (New York, 1991), p. 127; Dyan Elliott, *The Corrupter of Boys: Sodomy, Scandal and the Medieval Clergy* (Philadelphia, PA, 2000), p. 123.
89 Tentler, *Sin and Confession*, p. 120.
90 Shinners and Dohar, eds, *Pastors and the Care of Souls*, p. 182; Payer, 'Sex and Confession', p. 131.
91 John McNeill and Helena Garner, trans., *Medieval Handbooks of Penance* (New York, 1938), pp. 355, 358; Shinners and Dohar, eds, *Pastors and the Care of Souls*, pp. 185–6.
92 Payer, 'Sex and Confession', p. 136.
93 Mia Korpiola, 'Rethinking Incest and Heinous Sexual Crime: Changing Boundaries of Secular and Ecclesiastical Jurisdiction in Late Medieval

Sweden', in *Boundaries of the Law*, ed. Anthony Musson (Farnham, 2005), p. 107.

94 Haren, '*Memoriale Presbiterorum*', pp. 123–63; Katherine Harvey, 'Food, Drink and the Bishop in Medieval England', *Viator*, 46 (2015), pp. 169, 173.

95 Beth Alison Barr, 'Three's a Crowd: Wives, Husbands and Priests in the Late Medieval Confessional', in *A Companion to Pastoral Care in the Late Middle Ages (1200–1500)*, ed. Ronald Stansbury (Leiden, 2010), pp. 232–3.

96 Ibid., pp. 217–20.

97 Shinners and Dohar, eds, *Pastors and the Care of Souls*, pp. 177–80.

98 Tentler, *Sin and Confession*, pp. 93–5.

99 Jacqueline Murray, 'Gendered Souls in Sexed Bodies: The Male Construction of Female Sexuality in Some Medieval Confessors' Manuals', in *Handling Sin*, ed. Biller and Minnis, pp. 83–7.

100 Bronach Kane, *Popular Memory and Gender in Medieval England* (Woodbridge, 2019), p. 39.

101 Barr, 'Three's a Crowd', p. 229.

102 Dyan Elliott, *Fallen Bodies: Pollution, Sexuality and Demonology in the Middle Ages* (Philadelphia, PA, 1999), p. 24.

103 Tentler, *Sin and Confession*, pp. 82–3; F. M. Powicke and C. R. Cheney, eds, *Councils and Synods, with Other Documents Relating to the English Church*, II: AD 1205–1313, 2 vols (Oxford, 1964), vol. I, p. 72.

104 Barr, 'Three's a Crowd', pp. 213, 227.

105 Barbara Hanawalt, *The Wealth of Wives: Women, Law and Economy in Late Medieval London* (Oxford, 2007), p. 45.

106 James Brundage, 'Playing by the Rules: Sexual Behaviour and Legal Norms in Medieval Europe', in *Desire and Discipline: Sex and Sexuality in the Premodern West*, ed. Jacqueline Murray and Konrad Eisenbichler (Toronto, 1996), p. 32.

107 Brundage, 'Playing by the Rules', pp. 27–8.

108 Shinners and Dohar, eds, *Pastors and the Care of Souls*, p. 292.

109 Martin Ingram, *Carnal Knowledge: Regulating Sex in England, 1470–1600* (Cambridge, 2017), pp. 106–8.

110 Brundage, 'Playing by the Rules', p. 33.

111 Ingram, *Carnal Knowledge*, pp. 108–10.

112 Walter Prevenier, 'The Notions of Honour and Adultery in the Fifteenth-century Burgundian Netherlands', in *Comparative Perspectives on History and Historians*, ed. David Nicholas, Bernard Bachrach and James Murray (Kalamazoo, MN, 2012), p. 267.

113 Guido Ruggiero, *The Boundaries of Eros* (Oxford, 1985), p. 5.

114 Shannon McSheffrey, ed. and trans., *Love and Marriage in Late Medieval London* (Kalamazoo, MI, 1995), p. 192.

115 Barbara Hanawalt, *The Ties That Bound: Peasant Families in Medieval England* (Oxford, 1986), p. 209.

116 Korpiola, 'Rethinking Incest', p. 104.

117 Sara McDougall, 'The Transformation of Adultery in France at the End of the Middle Ages', *Law and History Review*, XXXII (2014), pp. 511–13.

118 Ingram, *Carnal Knowledge*, p. 136.

119 Jamie Page, 'Masculinity and Prostitution in Late Medieval German Literature', *Speculum*, 94 (2019), p. 745.

120 Carol Lansing, 'Gender and Civic Authority: Sexual Control in a Medieval Italian Town', *Journal of Social History*, 31 (1997), pp. 48–9.

121 Ingram, *Carnal Knowledge*, p. 228.
122 John Arnold, 'Sexualité et déshonneur dans le Midi (xiiie–xive siècles): Les péchés de la chair et l'opinion collective', in *L'Église et la chair (xiie–xve siècle)*, ed. Michèle Fournié, Daniel le Blévec and Julien Théry (Toulouse, 2019), pp. 275–86.

2 Getting Together

1 Andreas Capellanus, *On Love*, trans. P. G. Walsh (London, 1982), p. 35.
2 Norman Tanner, ed., *Decrees of the Ecumenical Councils*, i: *Nicaea to Lateran v* (Washington, DC, 1990), pp. 257–8; James Brundage, 'Sex and the Canon Law', in *Handbook of Medieval Sexuality*, ed. Vern Bullough and James Brundage (New York, 1996), p. 38; Monique Vleeschouwers-Van Melkebeek, 'Incestuous Marriages: Formal Rules and Social Practice in the Southern Burgundian Netherlands', in *Love, Marriage and Family Ties in the Later Middle Ages*, ed. Isabel Davis, Miriam Müller and Sarah Rees Jones (Turnhout, 2010), p. 78.
3 Margaret Berger, trans., *Hildegard of Bingen: On Natural Philosophy and Medicine* (Cambridge, 1999), pp. 50, 55, 82.
4 Fiona Harris-Stoertz, 'Sex and the Medieval Adolescent', in *The Pre-modern Teenager: Youth in Society, 1150–1650*, ed. Konrad Eisenbichkler (Toronto, 2002), pp. 226–33.
5 James Craigie Robertson, ed., *Materials for the History of Thomas Becket*, 7 vols (London, 1875–85), vol. i, pp. 469–70.
6 Elisabeth van Houts, *Married Life in the Middle Ages, 900–1300* (Oxford, 2019), pp. 90–91.
7 Capellanus, *On Love*, pp. 38–41.
8 Berger, ed., *Hildegard of Bingen*, pp. 55–6.
9 Houts, *Married Life*, pp. 32–49, 52–7.
10 Ibid., pp. 88–9.
11 Kim Phillips, *Medieval Maidens: Young Women and Gender in England, 1270–1540* (Manchester, 2003), p. 36.
12 Jeremy Goldberg, ed. and trans., *Women in England, c. 1275–1525* (Manchester, 1995), p. 98.
13 Shannon McSheffrey, ed. and trans., *Love and Marriage in Late Medieval London* (Kalamazoo, MI, 1995), pp. 23–5.
14 Phillips, *Medieval Maidens*, pp. 156–7.
15 Ruth Mazo Karras, *Unmarriages: Women, Men and Sexual Unions in the Middle Ages* (Philadelphia, PA, 2012), pp. 98–9.
16 Ibid., p. 71.
17 Capellanus, *On Love*, pp. 43–5.
18 Kim Phillips, 'Beauty', in *Women and Gender in Medieval Europe: An Encyclopaedia*, ed. Margaret Schaus (London, 2006), pp. 64–6.
19 Montserrat Cabré, 'Beautiful Bodies', in *A Cultural History of the Human Body in the Medieval Age*, ed. Linda Kalof (London, 2010), pp. 125–6; Claudio Soller, 'The Beautiful Woman in Medieval Iberia', PhD thesis, University of Missouri, 2005, p. 2.
20 Cabré, 'Beautiful Bodies', pp. 125–6.
21 Capellanus, *On Love*, pp. 43–5.
22 Marilyn Yalom, *A History of the Breast* (New York, 1997), pp. 39, 52; Ann Marie Rasmussen, *Wandering Genitalia: Sexuality and the Body in German*

Culture between the Late Middle Ages and Early Modernity (London, 2009), p. 6.

23 Kim Phillips, 'The Breasts of Virgins: Sexual Reputation and Young Women's Bodies in Medieval Culture and Society', *Cultural and Social History*, xv/1 (2018), pp. 1–19.

24 Cabré, 'Beautiful Bodies', pp. 125–7.

25 Michael Solomon, ed. and trans., *The Mirror of Coitus: A Translation and Edition of the Fifteenth-century 'Speculum al Foderi'* (Madison, WI, 1990), p. 33

26 Nathaniel Dubin, ed. and trans., *The Fabliaux* (New York, 2013), pp. 918–29.

27 Jacqueline Murray, ed. and trans., *Love, Marriage, and Family in the Middle Ages: A Reader* (Peterborough, ON, 2001), p. 261.

28 Barbara Hanawalt, *The Ties That Bound: Peasant Families in Medieval England* (Oxford, 1986), pp. 194–5.

29 Guido Ruggiero, *The Boundaries of Eros* (Oxford, 1985), p. 29.

30 Hanawalt, *Ties That Bound*, p. 196.

31 Heath Dillard, *Daughters of the Reconquest: Women in Castilian Town Society, 1100–1300* (Cambridge, 1984), pp. 56–7.

32 Houts, *Married Life*, p. 91; Harris-Stoertz, 'Sex and the Medieval Adolescent', p. 233.

33 Harris-Stoertz, 'Sex and the Medieval Adolescent', pp. 236–8; Barbara Hanawalt, *The Wealth of Wives: Women, Law and Economy in Late Medieval London* (Oxford, 2007), p. 72.

34 Harris-Stoertz, 'Sex and the Medieval Adolescent', p. 234.

35 Carissa Harris, *Obscene Pedagogies: Transgressive Talk and Sexual Education in Late Medieval Britain* (Ithaca, NY, 2018), p. 24.

36 Shannon McSheffrey, *Marriage, Sex and Civic Culture in Late Medieval London* (Philadelphia, PA, 2006), pp. 67–9; Goldberg, ed., *Women in England*, p. 124.

37 Ruggiero, *Boundaries of Eros*, pp. 36–9.

38 McSheffrey, ed., *Marriage, Sex and Civic Culture*, pp. 67–9; Goldberg, ed., *Women in England*, p. 124.

39 McSheffrey, ed., *Marriage, Sex and Civic Culture*, pp. 69–70, 150–51.

40 Ibid., pp. 21–2, 31.

41 Karras, *Unmarriages*, p. 185.

42 Ibid., pp. 171, 186, 196–7.

43 Houts, *Married Life*, pp. 220, 223.

44 Conor McCarthy, ed. and trans., *Love, Sex and Marriage in the Middle Ages: A Sourcebook* (London, 2004), p. 74.

45 Karras, *Unmarriages*, p. 176.

46 Gene Brucker, *Giovanni and Lusanna: Love and Marriage in Renaissance Florence* (Berkeley, CA, 1986).

47 Frederik Pedersen, *Marriage Disputes in Medieval England* (London, 2000), pp. 78–82.

48 Martha Brożyna, ed. and trans., *Gender and Sexuality in the Middle Ages* (Jefferson, NC, 2005), p. 136.

49 Kirsi Salonen, 'Marriage Disputes in the Consistorial Court of Freising in the Late Middle Ages', in *Regional Variations in Matrimonial Law and Custom in Europe, 1150–1600*, ed. Mia Korpiola (Leiden, 2011), pp. 196–7.

50 McSheffrey, ed., *Marriage, Sex and Civic Culture*, pp. 1–2.

51 Ruggiero, *Boundaries of Eros*, pp. 27–8.
52 Goldberg, ed., *Women in England*, pp. 110–14.
53 Salonen, 'Marriage Disputes', pp. 194–5.
54 Sara Butler, '"I Will Never Consent to Be Wedded with You!" Coerced Marriage in the Courts of Medieval England', *Canadian Journal of History*, XXXIX/2 (2004), pp. 255–6.
55 Catherine Rider, 'Men, Women and Love Magic in Late Medieval English Pastoral Manuals', *Magic, Ritual and Witchcraft*, 7 (2012), pp. 202–5.
56 Domenico Mammoli, *The Record of the Trial and Condemnation of a Witch, Matteuccia di Francesco, at Todi, 20 March 1428* (Rome, 1972).
57 Richard Kieckhefer, 'Mythologies of Witchcraft in the Fifteenth Century', *Magic, Ritual and Witchcraft*, 1 (2006), p. 87.
58 Ibid., pp. 38, 42–3.
59 Caesarius of Heisterbach, *The Dialogue on Miracles*, trans. H. von Schott and C. Swinton Bland, 2 vols (London, 1929), vol. II, pp. 112–13.
60 Rider, 'Men, Women and Love Magic', p. 208.
61 Richard Kieckhefer, 'Erotic Magic in Medieval Europe', in *Sex in the Middle Ages*, ed. Joyce Salisbury (New York, 1991), pp. 40–41.
62 Diana Wolfthal, *Images of Rape: The 'Heroic' Tradition and Its Alternatives* (Cambridge, 1999), pp. 152–4.
63 Ruggiero, *Boundaries of Eros*, pp. 33–5.
64 Hildegard of Bingen, *Physica*, ed. and trans. Priscilla Throop (Rochester, VT, 1998), pp. 67–8.
65 Ibid., p. 143.
66 Mary Wack, *Lovesickness in the Middle Ages* (Philadelphia, PA, 1990), pp. xi–xii.
67 Ibid., pp. 186–91.
68 Ibid., pp. 256–7.
69 Ibid., pp. 94–6, 218–19.
70 Ibid., pp. xi–xii, 66–70, 190–91, 202–3, 262–3.
71 Ibid., pp. 112–13.
72 Ibid., pp. 220–23.
73 *The Lais of Marie de France*, trans. Glyn Burgess and Keith Busby (London, 1986), pp. 82–5.
74 John Gower, *Confessio Amantis*, ed. Russell Peck (Toronto, 1980).
75 Geoffrey Chaucer, *The Canterbury Tales*, trans. Nevill Coghill (London, 1951), pp. 26–86.

3 Sex within Marriage

1 James Brundage, 'Implied Consent to Intercourse', and John Baldwin, 'Consent and the Marital Debt: Five Discourses in Northern France around 1200', in *Consent and Coercion to Sex and Marriage in Ancient and Medieval Societies*, ed. Angeliki Laiou (Washington, DC, 1993), pp. 245–70.
2 Heath Dillard, *Daughters of the Reconquest: Women in Castilian Town Society, 1100–1300* (Cambridge, 1984), p. 58.
3 Jacqueline Murray, ed. and trans., *Love, Marriage, and Family in the Middle Ages: A Reader* (Peterborough, ON, 2001), pp. 261, 269–70; Daphna Oren-Magidor, *Infertility in Early Modern England* (London, 2017), pp. 124–5.
4 Dillard, *Daughters of the Reconquest*, p. 64.

5 Peter Biller, 'Birth-control in the West in the Thirteenth and Early Fourteenth Centuries', *Past and Present*, xciv/i (1982), p. 19.

6 Monika Otter, 'Medieval Sex Education, or: What About Canidia?', *Interfaces*, 3 (2016), pp. 71–89.

7 Joan Cadden, *Meanings of Sex Difference in the Middle Ages: Medicine, Science and Culture* (Cambridge, 1993), pp. 262–3.

8 Guido Ruggiero, *The Boundaries of Eros* (Oxford, 1985), p. 25.

9 Kathleen Coyne Kelly, *Performing Virginity and Testing Chastity in the Middle Ages* (Abingdon, 2000), pp. 27–8.

10 Esther Lastique and Helen Rodnite Lemay, 'A Medieval Physician's Guide to Virginity', in *Sex in the Middle Ages*, ed. Joyce Salisbury (New York, 1991), p. 64.

11 Ibid., pp. 59–60.

12 Kelly, *Performing Virginity*, pp. 27–8.

13 Ibid., pp. 17–18, 37.

14 Kim Phillips, 'The Breasts of Virgins: Sexual Reputation and Young Women's Bodies in Medieval Culture and Society', *Cultural and Social History*, xv/i (2018), pp. 9–12.

15 Joseph Ziegler, 'Sexuality and the Sexual Organs in Latin Physiognomy, 1200–1500', in *Sexuality and Culture in Medieval and Renaissance Europe*, ed. Philip Soergel (New York, 2005), pp. 85–6.

16 Lastique and Lemay, 'Guide to Virginity', p. 61.

17 Ibid., p. 63.

18 Helen Rodnite Lemay, 'Human Sexuality in Twelfth- through Fifteenth-century Scientific Writings', in *Sexual Practices and the Medieval Church*, ed. Vern Bullough and James Brundage (New York, 1982), pp. 193–4.

19 Monica Green, ed. and trans., *The Trotula* (Philadelphia, pa, 2001), pp. 103–4.

20 Kelly, *Performing Virginity*, p. 32.

21 Helen Rodnite Lemay, 'William of Saliceto on Human Sexuality', *Viator*, xii (1981), pp. 175–6.

22 1 Corinthians 7:4.

23 Dyan Elliott, 'Bernardino of Siena versus the Marriage Debt', in *Desire and Discipline: Sex and Sexuality in the Premodern West*, ed. Jacqueline Murray and Konrad Eisenbichler (Toronto, 1996), pp. 168–9; Baldwin, 'Consent and the Marital Debt', p. 261.

24 Elliott, 'Bernardino of Siena', pp. 168–9.

25 Ibid., pp. 199–200.

26 Thomas Tentler, *Sin and Confession on the Eve of the Reformation* (Princeton, nj, 1977), pp. 209–10.

27 Elliott, 'Bernardino of Siena', pp. 168–9; Tentler, *Sin and Confession*, p. 171.

28 Brenda Bolton, 'The Absentee Lord? Alexander iii and the Patrimony', in *Pope Alexander iii (1159–81): The Art of Survival*, ed. Peter D. Clarke and Anne J. Duggan (Abingdon, 2012), p. 177.

29 Elliott, 'Bernardino of Siena', pp. 172–3; Carole Rawcliffe, *Leprosy in Medieval England* (Woodbridge, 2006), pp. 267–70.

30 Dyan Elliott, *Fallen Bodies: Pollution, Sexuality and Demonology in the Middle Ages* (Philadelphia, pa, 1999), pp. 61–80; Tentler, *Sin and Confession*, pp. 171–2.

31 Sarah Salih, 'Unpleasures of the Flesh: Medieval Marriage, Masochism,

and the History of Heterosexuality', *Studies in the Age of Chaucer*, XXXIII (2011), pp. 125–47.

32 Tentler, *Sin and Confession*, pp. 174–5, 179.

33 Benedetto Cotrugli, *The Book of the Art of Trade*, ed. Carlo Carraro and Giovanni Favero, trans. John Phillimore (London, 2017), pp. 156–7.

34 Ibid., pp. 161–2.

35 Salih, 'Unpleasures of the Flesh', pp. 125–47.

36 Elliott, 'Bernardino of Siena', pp. 173, 183–4.

37 Ibid., p. 179.

38 Ibid., pp. 180–81.

39 Ibid., pp. 154, 171.

40 Salih, 'Unpleasures of the Flesh', pp. 125–47.

41 Dyan Elliott, *Spiritual Marriage: Sexual Abstinence in Medieval Wedlock* (Princeton, NJ, 1993), pp. 3, 9, 158, 163.

42 C. H. Talbot, ed. and trans., *The Life of Christina of Markyate*, rev. Samuel Fanous and Henrietta Leyser (Oxford, 2008), p. 3.

43 Elizabeth Spearing, ed. and trans., *Medieval Writings on Female Spirituality* (London, 2002), pp. 88–9.

44 Elliott, *Spiritual Marriage*, p. 282.

45 Ibid., pp. 247–8.

46 Ibid., pp. 225–6.

47 Ibid., pp. 228, 246.

48 Barry Windeatt, ed. and trans., *The Book of Margery Kempe*, pp. 46–7, 58–9, 69–72.

49 Ibid., pp. 219–21.

50 Ibid., p. 253.

51 Angus McLaren, *Impotence: A Cultural History* (Chicago, IL, 2007), p. 36.

52 Bronach Kane, *Impotence and Virginity in the Late Medieval Ecclesiastical Court of York* (York, 2008), p. 8.

53 Jacqueline Murray, 'On the Origins and Role of Wise Women in Causes for Annulment on the Grounds of Male Impotence', *Journal of Medieval History*, 16 (1990), pp. 238, 245.

54 Catherine Rider, 'Men, Women and Love Magic in Late Medieval English Pastoral Manuals', *Magic, Ritual and Witchcraft*, 7 (2012), p. 207.

55 Murray, 'On the Origins', p. 238.

56 McLaren, *Impotence*, pp. 36–7.

57 Murray, 'On the Origins', pp. 242–5.

58 Kane, *Impotence and Virginity*, pp. 13, 15.

59 Ibid., p. 9.

60 Ibid., pp. 5, 9–10.

61 Kirsi Salonen, 'Marriage Disputes in the Consistorial Court of Freising in the Late Middle Ages', in *Regional Variations in Matrimonial Law and Custom in Europe, 1150–1600*, ed. Mia Korpiola (Leiden, 2011), pp. 204–5.

62 Martha Brożyna, ed. and trans., *Gender and Sexuality in the Middle Ages* (Jefferson, NC, 2005), p. 135.

63 Kane, *Impotence and Virginity*, pp. 10–15, 27–8.

64 Salonen, 'Marriage Disputes', p. 204.

65 Murray, 'On the Origins', p. 238.

66 Catherine Rider, *Magic and Impotence in the Middle Ages* (Oxford, 2006), p. 230.

67 Ibid., pp. 65–6, 95–7, 106.

68 Ibid., p. 1.
69 Ibid., pp. 168–9.
70 Ibid., p. 124.
71 Ibid., p. 230.
72 Ibid., p. 99.
73 Stephen Mitchell, 'Nordic Witchcraft in Transition: Impotence, Heresy and Diabolism in Fourteenth-century Bergen', *Scandia*, LXIII/1 (1997), pp. 18–19.
74 Rider, *Magic and Impotence*, p. 231.
75 Michael Solomon, ed. and trans., *The Mirror of Coitus: A Translation and Edition of the Fifteenth-century 'Speculum al Foderi'* (Madison, WI, 1990), pp. 23, 25–6.
76 Ibid., p. 27.
77 McLaren, *Impotence*, p. 41.
78 Rider, *Magic and Impotence*, p. 79.
79 Lydia Harris, 'Evacuating the Womb: Abortion and Contraception in the High Middle Ages, *c.* 1050–1300', PhD thesis, Durham University, 2017, pp. 65–6.
80 Elliott, *Spiritual Marriage*, p. 146.
81 Ibid., pp. 146–8.
82 Thomas Head, ed., *Medieval Hagiography: An Anthology* (New York, 2000), pp. 646–51.

4 Reproduction

1 Joan Cadden, 'Western Medicine and Natural Philosophy', in *Handbook of Medieval Sexuality*, ed. Vern Bullough and James Brundage (New York, 1996), pp. 55–6.
2 Helen Rodnite Lemay, 'William of Saliceto on Human Sexuality', *Viator*, XII (1981), pp. 166–7; Danielle Jacquart and Claude Thomasset, *Sexuality and Medicine in the Middle Ages* (Oxford, 1988), p. 59.
3 Hiram Kümper, 'Learned Men and Skilful Matrons: Medical Expertise and the Forensics of Rape in the Middle Ages', in *Medicine and the Law in the Middle Ages*, ed. Wendy Turner and Sara Butler (Leiden, 2014), pp. 104–5.
4 Lemay, 'William of Saliceto', pp. 169–70.
5 Melissa Mohr, *Holy Sh*t: A Brief History of Swearing* (Oxford, 2013), p. 98.
6 Lemay, 'William of Saliceto', p. 172.
7 Ibid., p. 171.
8 Albertus Magnus, *On Animals: A Medieval Summa Zoologica*, trans. Kenneth Mitchell and Irven Resnick, 2 vols (Baltimore, MD, 1999), vol. I, pp. 844–5.
9 Helen Rodnite Lemay, ed. and trans., *Women's Secrets* (New York, 1992), p. 67.
10 Lemay, 'William of Saliceto', p. 173; Lemay, ed., *Women's Secrets*, p. 115.
11 Benedetto Cotrugli, *The Book of the Art of Trade*, ed. Carlo Carraro and Giovanni Favero, trans. John Phillimore (London, 2017), p. 163.
12 Paul Delany, 'Constantinus Africanus' *De Coitu*: A Translation', *Chaucer Review*, 4 (1969), p. 59.
13 Margaret Berger, trans., *Hildegard of Bingen: On Natural Philosophy and Medicine* (Cambridge, 1999), p. 50.

14 Lemay, ed., *Women's Secrets*, pp. 105, 114.
15 Berger, trans., *Hildegard of Bingen*, pp. 63, 123–4.
16 Albertus Magnus, *On Animals*, I, p. 796.
17 Lemay, ed., *Women's Secrets*, p. 115.
18 Joan Cadden, *Meanings of Sex Difference in the Middle Ages: Medicine, Science and Culture* (Cambridge, 1993), p. 197.
19 Monica Green, ed. and trans., *The Trotula* (Philadelphia, PA, 2001), p. 76.
20 Ibid., p. 66; Albertus Magnus, *On Animals*, I, p. 782; Lemay, 'William of Saliceto', p. 169.
21 Catherine Rider, 'Men and Infertility in Late Medieval English Medicine', *Social History of Medicine*, XXIX (2016), p. 261.
22 Albertus Magnus, *On Animals*, I, p. 843.
23 Green, ed., *Trotula*, pp. 85–6.
24 Albertus Magnus, *On Animals*, I, pp. 832–4, 844; Green, ed., *Trotula*, p. 76.
25 Green, ed., *Trotula*, pp. 76, 91–2.
26 Albertus Magnus, *On Animals*, I, pp. 828–30.
27 Cadden, 'Western Medicine', p. 60.
28 Albertus Magnus, *On Animals*, II, p. 1235.
29 Rider, 'Men and Infertility', p. 245; Green, ed., *Trotula*, p. 85.
30 Rider, 'Men and Infertility', pp. 262–6; Cadden, *Sex Difference*, p. 253.
31 Green, ed., *Trotula*, p. 87; Rider, 'Men and Infertility', pp. 254–5.
32 Albertus Magnus, *On Animals*, I, p. 844.
33 Rider, 'Men and Infertility', p. 247.
34 Lemay, 'William of Saliceto', pp. 173–4.
35 Rider, 'Men and Infertility', p. 258.
36 Lemay, 'William of Saliceto', p. 173; Green, ed., *Trotula*, p. 76.
37 Albertus Magnus, *On Animals*, I, p. 845.
38 Ibid., I, p. 795.
39 Catherine Rider, *Magic and Impotence in the Middle Ages* (Oxford, 2006), pp. 108–9, 170.
40 Helen Rodnite Lemay, 'Human Sexuality in Twelfth- through Fifteenth-century Scientific Writings', in *Sexual Practices and the Medieval Church*, ed. Vern Bullough and James Brundage (New York, 1982), p. 199.
41 Elisabeth van Houts, *Married Life in the Middle Ages* (Oxford, 2019), pp. 97–8; Fiona Harris-Stoertz, 'Pregnancy and Childbirth in Twelfth- and Thirteenth-century French and English Law', *Journal of the History of Sexuality*, 21 (2012), p. 276; Berger, ed., *Hildegard of Bingen*, p. 111.
42 Peter Murray Jones and Lea Olsan, 'Performative Rituals for Conception and Childbirth in England, 900–1500', *Bulletin of the History of Medicine*, 89 (2015), pp. 412–13; Lea Olsan, 'Charms and Prayers in Medieval Medical Theory and Practice', *Social History of Medicine*, XVI/3 (2003), p. 352.
43 Christine Walsh, *The Cult of St Katherine of Alexandria in Early Medieval Europe* (Farnham, 2007), pp. 175–6.
44 Carole Rawcliffe, 'Women, Childbirth and Religion in Later Medieval England', in *Women and Religion in Later Medieval England*, ed. Diana Wood (Oxford, 2003), pp. 104–5; Daphna Oren-Magidor, *Infertility in Early Modern England* (London, 2017), pp. 124–5.
45 William of Malmesbury, *Gesta Regum Anglorum: The History of the Kings of England*, ed. and trans. R.A.B. Mynors, Rodney Thomson and Michael Winterbottom, 2 vols (Oxford, 1998–9), vol. I, pp. 406–7.

46 Rawcliffe, 'Women, Childbirth and Religion', pp. 104–5.
47 Iris Origo, *The Merchant of Prato* (London, 1957), pp. 161–3.
48 Joseph Shatzmiller, ed., *Médecine et justice en Provence médiévale: Documents de Manosque, 1262–1348* (Aix-en-Provence, 1989), pp. 176–83.
49 Lydia Harris, 'Evacuating the Womb: Abortion and Contraception in the High Middle Ages, *c.* 1050–1300', PhD thesis, Durham University, 2017, p. 131.
50 Peter Biller, 'Confessors' Manuals and the Avoidance of Offspring', in *Handling Sin: Confession in the Middle Ages,* ed. Peter Biller and A. J. Minnis (York, 1998), p. 184.
51 Ibid., p. 169.
52 Ibid., pp. 176–7.
53 Peter Biller, 'Birth-control in the West in the Thirteenth and Early Fourteenth Centuries', *Past and Present*, XCIV/1 (1982), pp. 3–26.
54 Katharine Park, 'Managing Childbirth and Fertility in Medieval Europe', in *Reproduction: Antiquity to the Present Day*, ed. Nicholas Hopwood, Rebecca Flemming and Lauren Kassell (Cambridge, 2018), p. 166.
55 John Riddle, *Contraception and Abortion from the Ancient World to the Renaissance* (Cambridge, MA, 1992), pp. 128–9.
56 Park, 'Managing Childbirth', p. 166.
57 Biller, 'Confessors' Manuals', pp. 178–80.
58 Riddle, *Contraception and Abortion*, pp. 128–9.
59 Martha Brożyna, ed., *Gender and Sexuality in the Middle Ages: A Sourcebook* (Jefferson, NC, 2005), pp. 167–9.
60 Harris, 'Evacuating the Womb', pp. 154–7.
61 Guido Ruggiero, *The Boundaries of Eros* (Oxford, 1985), p. 42.
62 Pierre Dubuis, 'Enfants refusés dans les Alpes Occidentales (XIV–XVe siècles)', in *Enfance abandonée et société en Europe, XIV–XXe siècle* (Rome, 1991), p. 576.
63 Domenico Mammoli, *The Record of the Trial and Condemnation of a Witch, Matteucia di Francesco, at Todi, 20 March 1428* (Rome, 1972), p. 36.
64 Emmanuel Le Roy Ladurie, *Montaillou*, trans. Barbara Bray (Harmondsworth, 1980), pp. 172–4.
65 Lydia Harris, 'Old Ideas for a New Debate: Medieval and Modern Attitudes to Abortion', *Medieval Feminist Forum* (December 2017), pp. 143–5.
66 Maaike van der Lugt, 'Formed Foetuses and Healthy Children in Scholastic Theology, Medicine and Law', in *Reproduction*, ed. Hopwood, Flemming and Kassell, pp. 168–70.
67 Harris, 'Old Ideas for a New Debate', pp. 143–5.
68 Wolfgang Müller, *The Criminalization of Abortion in the West* (New York, 2012), p. 194.
69 Fiona Harris-Stoertz, 'Pregnancy and Childbirth in Twelfth- and Thirteenth-century England', *Journal of the History of Sexuality*, 21 (2012), p. 271.
70 Harris, 'Evacuating the Womb', pp. 186–7.
71 Müller, *Criminalization*, p. 202.
72 Dubuis, 'Enfants refusés', pp. 577–9.
73 Park, 'Managing Childbirth', p. 164.
74 Marija Karbić, 'Prostitutes and Urban Communities of Medieval Slavonia: Examples from Gradec', in *Same Bodies, Different Women: 'Other' Women*

in the Middle Ages and Early Modern Period, ed. Christopher Mielke and Andrea-Bianka Znorovszky (Budapest, 2019), p. 89.

75 Riddle, *Contraception and Abortion*, p. 136.

76 Müller, *Criminalization*, p. 167.

77 Jamie Page, 'Inside the Medieval Brothel', *History Today*, LXIX/6 (2019), pp. 30–39.

78 Shatzmiller, ed., *Médecine et justice*, pp. 80–85.

79 Park, 'Managing Childbirth', p. 165.

80 Jacquart and Thomasset, *Sexuality and Medicine*, p. 93.

81 Müller, *Criminalization*, p. 164.

82 Park, 'Managing Childbirth', p. 164; Müller, *Criminalization*, pp. 163–4, 166.

83 Lemay, ed., *Women's Secrets*, pp. 120–22.

84 Cotrugli, *Art of Trade*, p. 163.

85 Albertus Magnus, *On Animals*, I, pp. 793–4; Barbara Hanawalt, *The Ties That Bound: Peasant Families in Medieval England* (Oxford, 1986), p. 215.

86 Albertus Magnus, *On Animals*, I, p. 792.

87 Dyan Elliott, 'Bernardino of Siena versus the Marriage Debt', in *Desire and Discipline: Sex and Sexuality in the Premodern West*, ed. Jacqueline Murray and Konrad Eisenbichler (Toronto, 1996), p. 172.

88 Pierre Payer, *The Bridling of Desire: Views of Sex in the Later Middle Ages* (Toronto, 1993), pp. 103–4; Harris, 'Evacuating the Womb', pp. 198–200.

89 Albertus Magnus, *On Animals*, I, p. 789.

90 Harris, 'Evacuating the Womb', p. 198.

91 Jacqueline Murray, ed. and trans., *Love, Marriage, and Family in the Middle Ages: A Reader* (Peterborough, ON, 2001), pp. 304–5.

92 Thomas Tentler, *Sin and Confession on the Eve of the Reformation* (Princeton, NJ, 1977), p. 171; Elliott, 'Bernardino of Siena', pp. 199–200.

93 Payer, *Bridling of Desire*, p. 78.

94 Henrietta Leyser, *Medieval Women: A Social History of Women in England, 450–1500* (London, 1995), p. 130.

95 Payer, *Bridling of Desire*, pp. 105–8.

96 Louis Landouzy and Roger Pépin, eds, *Le régime du corps de maître Aldebrandin de Sienne* (Paris, 1911), p. 77.

97 Heath Dillard, *Daughters of the Reconquest: Women in Castilian Town Society, 1100–1300* (Cambridge, 1984), pp. 178–9.

98 Elisheva Baumgarten, *Mothers and Children: Jewish Family Life in Medieval Europe* (Princeton, NJ, 2004), pp. 145–7.

5 The Battle for Chastity

1 Hugh Thomas, *The Secular Clergy in England, 1066–1216* (Oxford, 2014), pp. 155–9.

2 Ibid., pp. 32–4.

3 Dyan Elliott, *Fallen Bodies: Pollution, Sexuality and Demonology in the Middle Ages* (Philadelphia, PA, 1999), pp. 21–3.

4 Ruth Mazo Karras, *Unmarriages: Women, Men and Sexual Unions in the Middle Ages* (Philadelphia, PA, 2012), pp. 120–21.

5 Thomas, *Secular Clergy*, p. 32.

6 Jacqueline Murray, 'Men's Bodies, Men's Minds: Seminal Emissions and Sexual Anxiety in the Middle Ages', *Annual Review of Sex Research*,

8 (1997), pp. 1–26; Pierre Payer, *Sex and the New Medieval Literature of Confession* (Toronto, 2009), pp. 139–41.

7 Michael Goodich, *The Unmentionable Vice* (Santa Barbara, CA, 1979), pp. 65–6.

8 Elisabeth van Houts, *Married Life in the Middle Ages, 900–1300* (Oxford, 2019), p. 189.

9 Thomas, *Secular Clergy*, pp. 160, 173–6.

10 J. Patrick Hornbeck, 'Theologies of Sexuality in English "Lollardy"', *Journal of Ecclesiastical History*, LX/1 (2009), pp. 32–3, 41.

11 Houts, *Married Life*, p. 184.

12 Guido Ruggiero, *The Boundaries of Eros* (Oxford, 1985), pp. 73–4.

13 Trevor Dean, 'Fornicating with Nuns in Fifteenth-century Bologna', *Journal of Medieval History*, XXXIV/2 (2008), pp. 374–6.

14 Caesarius of Heisterbach, *The Dialogue on Miracles*, trans. H. von Scott and C. Swinton Bland, 2 vols (London, 1929), vol. II, p. 283.

15 Gerald of Wales, *The Jewel of the Church*, trans. John Hagen (Leiden, 1979), pp. 189–90.

16 Decima Douie and Hugh Farmer, eds and trans, *Magna Vita Sancti Hugonis*, 2 vols (London, 1961–2), vol. I, pp. 49–52.

17 Jacqueline Murray, 'Masculinizing Religious Life: Sexual Prowess, the Battle for Chastity and Monastic Identity', in *Holiness and Masculinity in the Middle Ages*, ed. Patricia Cullum and Katharine Lewis (Cardiff, 2005), pp. 24–37; John Arnold, 'The Labour of Continence: Masculinity and Clerical Virginity', in *Medieval Virginities*, ed. Anke Bernau, Ruth Evans and Sarah Salih (Cardiff, 2003), pp. 102–18.

18 Gerald of Wales, *Jewel of the Church*, pp. 170–71.

19 Caesarius of Heisterbach, *The Dialogue on Miracles*, trans. H. von Scott and C. Swinton Bland, 2 vols (London, 1929), vol. I, pp. 501–2.

20 Jacqueline Murray, 'The Battle for Chastity: Miraculous Castration and the Quelling of Desire in the Middle Ages', *Journal of the History of Sexuality*, XXVIII/1 (2019), p. 109.

21 Emma Gurney-Salter, ed. and trans., *The Coming of the Friars to England and Germany, Being the Chronicles of Brother Thomas of Eccleston and Brother Jordan of Giano* (London, 1926), p. 9.

22 William Bliss et al., *Calendar of Entries in the Papal Registers Relating to Great Britain and Ireland*, 18 vols (London and Dublin, 1893–), vol. II, pp. 412–13; X, p. 401.

23 David Preest and Harriet Webster, trans., *The Annals of Dunstable Priory* (Woodbridge, 2018), p. 199.

24 Lydia Harris, 'Evacuating the Womb: Abortion and Contraception in the High Middle Ages, c. 1050–1300', PhD thesis, Durham University, 2017, pp. 105–9.

25 Julie Kerr, *Life in the Medieval Cloister* (London, 2009), p. 142.

26 Ibid., pp. 139–40.

27 Fiona Harris-Stoertz, 'Sex and the Medieval Adolescent', in *The Premodern Teenager: Youth in Society, 1150–1650*, ed. Konrad Eisenbichler (Toronto, 2002), pp. 228–31.

28 Kerr, *Medieval Cloister*, p. 141.

29 Gerald of Wales, *Jewel of the Church*, pp. 179, 182.

30 B. J. Parkinson, 'The Life of Robert de Bethune by William de Wycombe', BLitt thesis, Oxford University, 1951, pp. 159–60.

31 Katherine Harvey, 'Episcopal Virginity in Medieval England', *Journal of the History of Sexuality*, XXVI/2 (2017), pp. 278–9.

32 Katherine Harvey, 'Food, Drink and the Bishop in Medieval England', *Viator*, 26 (2015), pp. 170–71.

33 Ibid., pp. 169–71.

34 C. H. Talbot, Samuel Fanous and Henrietta Leyser, trans. and rev., *The Life of Christina of Markyate* (Oxford, 2008), pp. 46–8.

35 Walter Daniel, *The Life of Aelred of Rievaulx*, trans. F. M. Powicke (Kalamazoo, MI, 1994), p. 108.

36 Tom Licence, *Hermits and Recluses in English Society, 950–1200* (Oxford, 2011), p. 136.

37 Van Houts, *Married Life*, pp. 194–5.

38 Bruce Vernarde, ed., *Robert of Arbrissel: A Medieval Religious Life* (Washington, DC, 2003), pp. 103–5.

39 Peter Arnade and Walter Prevenier, *Honor, Vengeance, and Social Trouble* (Ithaca, NY, 2015), p. 96.

40 Karras, *Unmarriages*, p. 250.

41 Thomas, *Secular Clergy*, p. 185.

42 Sydney Brown, trans., *The Register of Eudes of Rouen* (New York, 1964), pp. 20–21.

43 Ibid., p. 210.

44 Ibid., p. 336.

45 Roisin Cossar, 'Clerical "Concubines" in Northern Italy during the Fourteenth Century', *Journal of Women's History*, 23 (2011), pp. 110–19.

46 Michelle Armstrong-Patrida, *Defiant Priests* (Ithaca, NY, 2017), pp. 33–5.

47 Ibid., p. 74.

48 Ibid., pp. 64–5.

49 Ibid., pp. 33–5.

50 A. Hamilton Thompson, ed., *Visitations of Religious Houses in the Diocese of Lincoln: Records of Visitations Held by William Alnwick, Bishop of Lincoln, 1436–1449* (Horncastle, 1918), pp. 69–83.

51 Dyan Elliott, *The Bride of Christ Goes to Hell: Metaphor and Embodiment in the Lives of Pious Women, 200–1500* (Philadelphia, PA, 2012), pp. 209–10.

52 Brown, *Register of Eudes*, pp. 285, 319, 470–71, 537.

53 Cossar, 'Clerical "Concubines"', pp. 117–19.

54 Penelope Johnson, *Equal in Monastic Profession: Religious Women in Medieval France* (Chicago, IL, 1991), pp. 112–28.

55 Christian Knudsen, 'Promiscuous Monks and Naughty Nuns: Poverty, Sex and Apostasy in Later Medieval England', in *Poverty and Prosperity: The Rich and the Poor in the Middle Ages and Renaissance*, ed. Anne Scott and Cindy Kosso (Turnhout, 2012), pp. 85–6.

56 Eileen Power, *Medieval English Nunneries, c. 1275–1535* (Cambridge, 1922), pp. 466–70.

57 Ibid., pp. 455–6.

58 Ibid., pp. 436, 445, 460–61.

59 On which see Dyan Elliott, *The Corrupter of Boys: Sodomy, Scandal and the Medieval Clergy* (Philadelphia, PA, 2020).

60 Brown, *Register of Eudes*, p. 691.

61 Karras, *Unmarriages*, p. 155.

62 Helmut Puff, *Sodomy in Reformation Germany and Switzerland, 1400–1600* (Chicago, IL, 2003), pp. 37–8.

6 Immoral Behaviours

1 Jeremy Goldberg, ed., *Women in England, c. 1275–1525* (Manchester, 1995), p. 118.
2 Martin Ingram, *Carnal Knowledge: Regulating Sex in England, 1470–1600* (Cambridge, 2017), p. 182.
3 Siegfried Wenzel, ed., *Fasciculus Morum: A Preacher's Handbook* (London, 1989), pp. 668–9.
4 Guido Ruggiero, *The Boundaries of Eros* (Oxford, 1985), pp. 17–22.
5 Grethe Jacobsen, 'Sexual Irregularities in Medieval Scandinavia', in *Sexual Practices and the Medieval Church*, ed. Vern Bullough and James Brundage (New York, 1982), pp. 80–83.
6 Matthew Paris, *English History*, trans. John Giles, 3 vols (London, 1852–4), vol. II, pp. 277–8; *Calendar of Patent Rolls, Henry III*, vol. IV: *1247–1258*, ed. H. C. Maxwell Lyte (London, 1908), p. 387.
7 Martha Brożyna, ed., *Gender and Sexuality in the Middle Ages* (Jefferson, NC, 2005), pp. 137–8.
8 Louise Wilkinson, *Women in Thirteenth-century Lincolnshire* (Woodbridge, 2007), pp. 125–7.
9 Ingram, *Carnal Knowledge*, pp. 94, 109.
10 Goldberg, ed., *Women in England*, p. 118.
11 Shannon McSheffrey, ed. and trans., *Love and Marriage in Late Medieval London* (Kalamazoo, MI, 1995), pp. 84–5.
12 Peter Arnade and Walter Prevenier, *Honor, Vengeance, and Social Trouble: Pardon Letters in the Burgundian Low Countries* (Ithaca, NY, 2015), pp. 136–7.
13 Shannon McSheffrey, *Marriage, Sex and Civic Culture in Late Medieval London* (Philadelphia, PA, 2006), pp. 152–3, 156, 160.
14 Goldberg, ed., *Women in England*, p. 119.
15 Ruth Mazo Karras, *Unmarriages: Women, Men and Sexual Unions in the Middle Ages* (Philadelphia, PA, 2012), p. 89.
16 Kim Phillips, *Medieval Maidens: Young Women and Gender in England, 1270–1540* (Manchester, 2003), p. 83.
17 John Arnold, 'Sexualité et déshonneur dans le Midi (XIIIe–XIVe siècles): Les péchés de la chair et l'opinion collective', in *L'Église et la chair (XIIe–XVe siècle)*, ed. Michèle Fournié, Daniel le Blévec and Julien Théry (Toulouse, 2019), pp. 266–7.
18 Ingram, *Carnal Knowledge*, pp. 178, 182.
19 Marija Karbić, 'Illicit Love in Medieval Slavonian Cities', in *Love, Marriage and Family Ties in the Later Middle Ages*, ed. Isabel Davis, Miriam Müller and Sarah Rees Jones (Leiden, 2006), p. 335.
20 Diana Wolfthal, *In and Out of the Marital Bed: Seeing Sex in Renaissance Europe* (London, 2010), p. 165.
21 Carol Lansing, 'Gender and Civic Authority: Sexual Control in a Medieval Italian Town', *Journal of Social History*, 31 (1997), p. 46.
22 Karbić, 'Illicit Love', pp. 333–4.
23 Heath Dillard, *Daughters of the Reconquest: Women in Castilian Town Society, 1100–1300* (Cambridge, 1984), pp. 203–5.
24 Conor McCarthy, ed. and trans., *Love, Sex and Marriage in the Middle Ages: A Sourcebook* (London, 2004), pp. 88–9.
25 Arnold, 'Sexualité et déshonneur', pp. 266–7, 277–81.

26 Arnade and Prevenier, *Honor, Vengeance, and Social Trouble*, p. 96.
27 Ruggiero, *Boundaries of Eros*, p. 49.
28 Arnade and Prevenier, *Honor, Vengeance, and Social Trouble*, pp. 94–5.
29 Arnold, 'Sexualité et déshonneur', pp. 272–3.
30 Steven Bednarski, *Curia: A Social History of a Court, Crime and Conflict in a Late Medieval Town* (Montpellier, 2013), p. 190.
31 Lansing, 'Gender and Civic Authority', pp. 45–6, 48.
32 Ruggiero, *Boundaries of Eros*, p. 53.
33 Dillard, *Daughters of the Reconquest*, pp. 203–5.
34 Jacobsen, 'Sexual Irregularities', pp. 77–9.
35 Sara McDougall, 'The Transformation of Adultery in France at the End of the Middle Ages', *Law and History Review*, XXXII (2014), pp. 501–3.
36 Dillard, *Daughters of the Reconquest*, pp. 203–5; Jacobsen, 'Sexual Irregularities', p. 77.
37 Walter Prevenier, 'The Notions of Honour and Adultery in the Fifteenth-century Burgundian Netherlands', in *Comparative Perspectives on History and Historians*, ed. David Nicholas, Bernard Bachrach and James Murray (Kalamazoo, MI, 2012), pp. 260–63.
38 Leah Otis-Cour, '*De jure novo*: Dealing with Adultery in the Fifteenth-century Toulousain', *Speculum*, LXXXIV (2009), pp. 356–66.
39 Karbić, 'Illicit Love', pp. 334–5.
40 Sara McDougall, 'The Opposite of the Double Standard: Gender, Marriage and Adultery Prosecution in Late Medieval France', *Journal of the History of Sexuality*, XXIII (2014), pp. 207–8.
41 Ibid., pp. 223–4.
42 Otis-Cour, 'Dealing with Adultery', pp. 378–9.
43 Ruggiero, *Boundaries of Eros*, p. 57.
44 Otis-Cour, 'Dealing with Adultery', pp. 386–7.
45 McSheffrey, *Marriage, Sex and Civic Culture*, pp. 176–7, 181.
46 Ruggiero, *Boundaries of Eros*, p. 66.
47 Otis-Cour, 'Dealing with Adultery', pp. 354–5.
48 Andrew Finch, 'Sexual Morality and Canon Law: The Evidence of the Rochester Consistory Court', *Journal of Medieval History*, XX/3 (1994), pp. 269–70.
49 Otis-Cour, 'Dealing with Adultery', pp. 375–7.
50 Goldberg, ed., *Women in England*, p. 143.
51 McSheffrey, *Marriage, Sex and Civic Culture*, pp. 166–74.
52 Samuel Scott and Robert Burns, ed. and trans., *Las Siete Partidas*, vol. V: *Underworlds: The Dead, the Criminal and the Marginalized* (Philadelphia, PA, 2001), p. 1415.
53 Otis-Cour, 'De Jure Novo', pp. 348–54.
54 Lansing, 'Gender and Civic Authority', p. 47; Ruggiero, *Boundaries of Eros*, pp. 59–60.
55 Ingram, *Carnal Knowledge*, p. 179.
56 Kathleen Coyne Kelly, *Performing Virginity and Testing Chastity in the Middle Ages* (Abingdon, 2000), p. 31.
57 Ingram, *Carnal Knowledge*, p. 179.
58 Ibid.
59 McDougall, 'Transformation of Adultery', pp. 508–9.
60 Arnold, 'Sexualité et déshonneur', pp. 265–6.
61 Scott and Burns, *Las Siete Partidas*, pp. 1411–14.

62 Bednarski, *Curia*, pp. 77–8.
63 Caroline Dunn, 'Forfeiting the Marriage Portion: Punishing Female Adultery in the Secular Courts of England and Italy', in *Regional Variations in Matrimonial Law and Custom, 1150–1600*, ed. Mia Korpiola (Leiden, 2011), pp. 161–4.
64 John Shinners and William Dohar, eds, *Pastors and the Care of Souls in Medieval England* (Notre Dame, IN, 1998), p. 145.
65 Ibid., pp. 185–6.
66 Rosemary Horrox, ed., *The Black Death* (Manchester, 1999), pp. 87–8.
67 Caesarius of Heisterbach, *The Dialogue on Miracles*, trans. H. von Scott and C. Swinton Bland, 2 vols (London, 1929), vol. 1, pp. 84–6.
68 Norman Tanner, ed., *Decrees of the Ecumenical Councils*, 1: *Nicaea to Lateran V* (Washington, DC, 1990), pp. 257–8; James Brundage, 'Sex and the Canon Law', in *Handbook of Medieval Sexuality*, ed. Vern Bullough and James Brundage (New York, 1996), p. 38; Monique Vleeschouwers-Van Melkebeek, 'Incestuous Marriages: Formal Rules and Social Practice in the Southern Burgundian Netherlands', in *Love, Marriage and Family Ties in the Later Middle Ages*, ed. Isabel Davis, Miriam Müller and Sarah Rees Jones (Leiden, 2010), p. 78.
69 Pierre Payer, 'Sex and Confession in the Thirteenth Century', in *Sex in the Middle Ages*, ed. Joyce Salisbury (New York, 1991), p. 131.
70 Elizabeth Archibald, *Incest and the Medieval Imagination* (Oxford, 2001), pp. 42, 44, 48.
71 Shinners and Dohar, eds, *Pastors*, p. 292.
72 Archibald, *Incest*, p. 43.
73 Ibid., p. 47.
74 Torstein Jørgensen, 'Illegal Sexual Behavior in Late Medieval Norway as Testified in Supplications to the Pope', *Journal of the History of Sexuality*, XVII (2008), pp. 347–8.
75 Archibald, *Incest*, p. 35.
76 Vleeschouwers-Van Melkebeek, 'Incestuous Marriages', pp. 77–95.
77 Robert of Flamborough, *Liber Poenitentialis*, ed. J. J. Francis Firth (Toronto, 1971), p. 197.
78 Mia Korpiola, 'Rethinking Incest and Heinous Sexual Crime: Changing Boundaries of Secular and Ecclesiastical Jurisdiction in Late Medieval Sweden', in *Boundaries of the Law*, ed. Anthony Musson (Farnham, 2005), pp. 107–8.
79 Scott and Burns, *Las Siete Partidas*, pp. 1421–2.
80 Korpiola, 'Rethinking Incest', pp. 102–3.
81 Jørgensen, 'Illegal Sexual Behavior', pp. 344–5.
82 Thomas Hardy, ed., *Registrum Palatinum Dunelmense: The Register of Richard de Kellawe, Lord Palatine and Bishop of Durham, 1311–1316*, 4 vols (London, 1873–8), vol. 1, p. 464.
83 Ibid., pp. 432, 461, 484.
84 Ruggiero, *Boundaries of Eros*, p. 42.
85 Jørgensen, 'Illegal Sexual Behavior', pp. 335–6, 343.
86 Wolfgang Müller, *The Criminalization of Abortion in the West* (New York, 2012), pp. 190–91.
87 Y.-B. Brissaud, 'L'infanticide à la fin du Moyen Age, ses motivations psychologiques et sa répression', *Revue historique de droit français et étranger*, 50 (1972), pp. 238, 241.

88 Joyce Salisbury, *The Beast Within: Animals in the Middle Ages*, 2nd edn (Abingdon, 2011), pp. 62–4.

89 Ibid., pp. 68–74.

90 Ibid., pp. 72, 76–8.

91 Ibid., p. 73.

92 Scott and Burns, *Las Siete Partidas*, p. 1427; Korpiola, 'Rethinking Incest', p. 109.

93 Salisbury, *Beast Within*, pp. 78–9.

94 Dyan Elliott, *The Corrupter of Boys: Sodomy, Scandal and the Medieval Clergy* (Philadelphia, PA, 2020), p. 141.

95 Salisbury, *Beast Within*, p. 79; Edward Evans, *The Criminal Prosecution and Capital Punishment of Animals* (London, 1906), p. 147.

96 Ruggiero, *Boundaries of Eros*, pp. 114–15.

7 Defying Sexual Norms: Positions and Partners

1 Alan Bray, *The Friend* (Chicago, IL, 2003), pp. 13–19.

2 Ibid., pp. 78–82.

3 Ibid., p. 85.

4 Ibid., pp. 24–35.

5 Peter Damian, *Letters 31–60*, trans. Owen Blum (Washington, DC, 1990).

6 Ibid., pp. 6–7.

7 Ibid., pp. 34–5.

8 Ruth Mazo Karras, 'The Lechery That Dare Not Speak Its Name: Sodomy and the Vices in Medieval England', in *In the Garden of Evil: The Vices and Culture in the Middle Ages*, ed. Richard Newhauser (Toronto, 2005), p. 200.

9 Conor McCarthy, ed., *Love, Sex and Marriage in the Middle Ages: A Sourcebook* (London, 2004), pp. 65–6.

10 Thomas Tentler, *Sin and Confession on the Eve of the Reformation* (Princeton, NJ, 1977), pp. 188–90.

11 Ibid., pp. 190–91.

12 Ibid., p. 201.

13 Marc Boone, 'State Power and Illicit Sexuality: The Persecution of Sodomy in Late Medieval Bruges', *Journal of Medieval History*, XXII/2 (1996), p. 138.

14 Bernd-Ulrich Hergemöller, *Sodom and Gomorrah: On the Everyday Reality and Persecution of Homosexuals in the Middle Ages* (London, 2001), pp. 146–59.

15 Thomas Laqueur, *Solitary Sex: A Cultural History of Masturbation* (New York, 2003).

16 Tentler, *Sin and Confession*, p. 143.

17 Laqueur, *Solitary Sex*, p. 158.

18 Albertus Magnus, *On Animals: A Medieval Summa Zoologica*, trans. Kenneth Mitchell and Irven Resnick, 2 vols (Baltimore, MD, 1999), vol. I, p. 776.

19 Tentler, *Sin and Confession*, pp. 91–3.

20 Michael Goodich, *The Unmentionable Vice* (Santa Barbara, CA, 1979), pp. 115, 120.

21 Guido Ruggiero, *The Boundaries of Eros* (Oxford, 1985), p. 115.

22 Helmut Puff, *Sodomy in Reformation Germany and Switzerland, 1400–1600* (Chicago, IL, 2003), pp. 23–4.

23 Michael Solomon, ed. and trans., *The Mirror of Coitus: A Translation and Edition of the Fifteenth-century 'Speculum al Foderi'* (Madison, WI, 1990), pp. 39–42.

24 Helen Rodnite Lemay, 'Human Sexuality in Twelfth- through Fifteenth-century Scientific Writings', in *Sexual Practices and the Medieval Church*, ed. Vern Bullough and James Brundage (New York, 1982), p. 195.

25 Danielle Jacquart and Claude Thomasset, *Sexuality and Medicine in the Middle Ages* (Oxford, 1988), p. 134.

26 Jacques Roussiaud, *Medieval Prostitution* (Oxford, 1988), pp. 109–10; Jacques Roussiaud, 'Prostitution, Sex and Society in French Towns in the Fifteenth Century', in *Western Sexuality: Practice and Precept in Past and Present Times*, ed. Philippe Ariès and André Béjin (Oxford, 1985), p. 81.

27 Puff, *Sodomy*, p. 29.

28 Ruggiero, *Boundaries of Eros*, p. 119.

29 Michael Rocke, *Forbidden Friendships: Homosexuality and Male Culture in Renaissance Florence* (Oxford, 1996), pp. 130–31.

30 Will Fisher, 'Wantoning with the Thighs: The Socialization of Thigh Sex in England, 1590–1730', *Journal of the History of Sexuality*, XXIV/1 (2015), pp. 261–75.

31 Kim Phillips and Barry Reay, *Sex before Sexuality: A Premodern History* (Cambridge, 2014), pp. 61–2.

32 Hergemöller, *Sodom and Gomorrah*, p. 48.

33 Ruggiero, *Boundaries of Eros*, pp. 116–17.

34 Goodich, *Unmentionable Vice*, pp. 93–123.

35 Joan Cadden, *Nothing Natural Is Shameful: Sodomy and Science in Late Medieval Europe* (Philadelphia, PA, 2013), pp. 35–105.

36 Michael Rocke, 'Sodomites in Fifteenth-century Tuscany: The Views of Bernardino of Siena', in *The Pursuit of Sodomy: Male Homosexuality in Renaissance and Enlightenment Europe*, ed. Kurt Gerard and Gert Hekma (London, 1989), pp. 9–18.

37 Ibid., p. 18.

38 Robert Mills, 'Male-male Love and Sex in the Middle Ages, 1000–1500', in *A Gay History of Britain*, ed. Matt Cook (Oxford, 2007), p. 20.

39 Helmut Puff, 'The Sodomite's Clothes: Gift-giving and Sexual Excess in Early Modern Germany and Switzerland', in *The Material Culture of Sex, Procreation and Marriage in Premodern Europe*, ed. Anne McClanan and Karen Rosoff Encarnación (London, 2002), pp. 260–61.

40 Joseph Ziegler, 'Sexuality and the Sexual Organs in Latin Physiognomy, 1200–1500', in *Sexuality and Culture in Medieval and Renaissance Europe*, ed. Philip Soergel (New York, 2005), pp. 83–107.

41 Mathew Kuefler, 'Male Friendship and the Suspicion of Sodomy in Twelfth-century France', in *The Boswell Thesis*, ed. Mathew Kuefler (Chicago, IL, 2005), pp. 182–3.

42 Ibid., pp. 191, 201–2.

43 Ibid., p. 193.

44 Rocke, 'Sodomites', pp. 22–3.

45 Boone, 'State Power', p. 153.

46 Samuel Scott and Robert Burns, ed. and trans., *Las Siete Partidas*, vol. V: *Underworlds: The Dead, the Criminal and the Marginalized* (Philadelphia, PA, 2001), p. 1427.

47 Rocke, *Forbidden Friendships*, p. 20.

48 Ruggiero, *Boundaries of Eros*, pp. 111, 135.
49 Margaret Berger, ed., *Hildegard of Bingen: On Natural Philosophy and Medicine* (Cambridge, 1999), p. 54.
50 Puff, *Sodomy*, pp. 55–6.
51 Ibid., p. 61.
52 Rocke, 'Sodomites', pp. 7–8.
53 Karras, 'Lechery', pp. 193–4.
54 Puff, *Sodomy*, p. 17.
55 Ibid., pp. 24–5.
56 Rocke, *Forbidden Friendships*, pp. 27–9.
57 Hergemöller, *Sodom and Gomorrah*, pp. 86–126.
58 Boone, 'Illicit Sexuality', p. 135; Rocke, *Forbidden Friendships*, pp. 3, 27.
59 Ibid., pp. 21–3.
60 Ibid., p. 4.
61 Ibid., pp. 46–7.
62 Ibid., p. 74.
63 Peter Arnade and Walter Prevenier, *Honor, Vengeance, and Social Trouble* (Ithaca, NY, 2015), pp. 104–5; Boone, 'Illicit Sexuality', p. 148.
64 Ruggiero, *Boundaries of Eros*, pp. 116–17; Rocke, *Forbidden Friendships*, p. 71.
65 Rocke, *Forbidden Friendships*, pp. 69–70.
66 Ibid., pp. 48–54.
67 Ibid., pp. 89–90.
68 Ruggiero, *Boundaries of Eros*, pp. 121–2.
69 Puff, *Sodomy*, p. 29.
70 Ruggiero, *Boundaries of Eros*, p. 123.
71 Rocke, *Forbidden Friendships*, pp. 88, 96–7, 100, 104–5.
72 Ibid., pp. 80–82.
73 Ibid., pp. 175–6.
74 Ibid., pp. 150–58.
75 Ibid., pp. 183, 186–7.
76 Ibid., pp. 24–5.
77 Ibid., pp. 168, 172.
78 Goodich, *Unmentionable Vice*, pp. 95–9.
79 Ibid., pp. 99–101.
80 Ibid., pp. 101–3.
81 Ibid., pp. 105–8.
82 Ibid., pp. 108–23.
83 For an influential discussion of how to recover lesbian histories from this period, see Judith Bennett, '"Lesbian-like" and the Social History of Lesbianisms', *Journal of the History of Sexuality*, IX (2000), pp. 1–24.
84 Louis Crompton, 'The Myth of Lesbian Impunity: Capital Laws from 1270 to 1791', *Journal of Homosexuality*, VI (1981), p. 13.
85 Edith Benkov, 'The Erased Lesbian: Sodomy and the Legal Tradition in Medieval Europe', in *Same Sex Love and Desire among Women in the Middle Ages*, ed. Francesca Sautman and Pamela Sheingorn (London, 2001), p. 108.
86 Carol Lansing, 'Donna con Donna? A 1295 Inquest into Female Sodomy', in *Sexuality and Culture in Medieval and Renaissance Europe*, ed. Philip Soergel (New York, 2005), p. 115.
87 Quoted in Susan Schibanoff, 'Hildegard of Bingen and Richardis of

Stade: The Discourse of Desire', in *Same Sex Love and Desire*, ed. Sautman and Sheingorn, p. 59.

88 Benkov, 'Erased Lesbian', p. 110.

89 Helen Rodnite Lemay, 'William of Saliceto on Human Sexuality', *Viator*, XII (1981), pp. 178–9.

90 Jonas Roelens, 'Visible Women: Female Sodomy in the Early Modern Southern Netherlands (1400–1550)', *Low Countries Historical Review*, 130 (2015), pp. 12–13.

91 Lansing, 'Donna con Donna?', pp. 109–22.

92 Helmut Puff, 'The Trial of Katherine Hetzeldorger (1477)', *Journal of Medieval and Early Modern Studies*, 30 (2000), pp. 41–61.

93 Roelens, 'Visible Women', p. 15.

94 Ibid., pp. 11–12.

95 Benkov, 'Erased Lesbian', pp. 112–14.

96 Judith Bennett, 'Remembering Elizabeth Etchingham and Agnes Oxenbridge', in *The Lesbian Premodern*, ed. Noreen Giffney, Michelle Sauer and Diane Watt (London, 2011), pp. 131–43.

8 Defying Sexual Norms: Religion and Race

1 Gerald of Wales, *The History and Topography of Ireland*, trans. John O'Meara (London, 1982), p. 106.

2 Gerald of Wales, *The Journey through Wales and The Description of Wales*, trans. Lewis Thorpe (London, 1978), pp. 262–5.

3 Robert Mills, 'Male-Male Love and Sex in the Middle Ages, 1000–1500', in *A Gay History of Britain*, ed. Matt Cook (Oxford, 2007), p. 23.

4 Helmut Puff, *Sodomy in Reformation Germany and Switzerland, 1400–1600* (Chicago, IL, 2003), pp. 125–6.

5 John Boswell, *Christianity, Social Tolerance and Homosexuality* (Chicago, IL, 1985), pp. 279–82.

6 Christoph Maier, 'Crusade and Rhetoric against the Muslim Colony of Lucera: Eudes of Châteauroux's *Sermones de Rebellione Sarracenorum Lucheria in Apulia*', *Journal of Medieval History*, XXI/4 (1995), pp. 372–3.

7 William Paden, ed. and trans., *The Medieval Pastourelle*, 2 vols (New York, 1987), vol. II, pp. 434–9.

8 Judith Bruskin Diner, trans., *The One Hundred New Tales* (New York, 1990), pp. 55–7.

9 Marco Polo, *The Travels*, trans. Ronald Latham (London, 1958), p. 302.

10 Ibid., pp. 88, 172–3.

11 Ibid., pp. 215–16.

12 Sir John de Mandeville, *The Book of Marvels and Travels*, trans. Anthony Bale (Oxford, 2012), pp. 13, 62–4.

13 Ibid., p. 75.

14 Ibid., pp. 98–9, 114.

15 Ibid., p. 87.

16 Valentin Groebner, 'The Carnal Knowledge of a Coloured Body: Sleeping with Arabs and Blacks in the European Imagination, 1300–1550', in *The Origins of Racism in the West*, ed. Miriam Eliav-Feldon, Benjamin Isaac and Joseph Ziegler (Cambridge, 2009), pp. 218–19, 227–8; Peter Biller, 'Black Women in Medieval Scientific Thought', *Micrologus*, XIII (2005), pp. 477–92.

17 Francesco Gabrieli and E. J. Costello, trans., *Arab Historians of the Crusades* (Abingdon, 2010), pp. 46–7.
18 Ibid., pp. 120–21.
19 David Nirenberg, *Communities of Violence: Persecution of Minorities in the Middle Ages* (Princeton, NJ, 1998), p. 157.
20 Jonathan Ray, *The Sephardic Frontier: The 'Reconquista' and the Jewish Community in Medieval Iberia* (Ithaca, NY, 2006), pp. 171–2.
21 Tim Mackintosh-Smith, trans., *The Travels of Ibn Battutah* (London, 2002), pp. 212, 232.
22 Elisheva Baumgarten, *Mothers and Children: Jewish Family Life in Medieval Europe* (Princeton, NJ, 2004), pp. 87, 254.
23 David Biale, *Eros and the Jews: From Biblical Israel to Contemporary America* (New York, 1992), p. 101.
24 Baumgarten, *Mothers and Children*, pp. 23–5.
25 Biale, *Eros and the Jews*, p. 92.
26 Avraham Grossman, *Pious and Rebellious: Jewish Women in Medieval Europe* (Waltham, MA, 2012), p. 9; Yom Tov Assis, 'Sexual Behaviour in Mediaeval Hispano-Jewish Society', in *Jewish History: Essays in Honour of Chimen Abramsky*, ed. Ada Rapoport-Albert and Steven Zipperstein (London, 1988), pp. 35–6.
27 Biale, *Eros and the Jews*, pp. 78–9.
28 Grossman, *Pious and Rebellious*, p. 129.
29 Biale, *Eros and the Jews*, pp. 90–91.
30 Ibid., p. 94.
31 Ibid., p. 78.
32 Baumgarten, *Mothers and Children*, pp. 145–7.
33 Biale, *Eros and the Jews*, p. 82.
34 Elisheva Baumgarten, *Practicing Piety in Medieval Ashkenaz: Men, Women and Everyday Religious Observance* (Philadelphia, PA, 2014), pp. 26–35.
35 Ibid., pp. 31, 33–4.
36 Ibid., p. 45.
37 Assis, 'Sexual Behaviour', pp. 28–9, 32.
38 Biale, *Eros and the Jews*, p. 73; Baumgarten, *Practicing Piety*, pp. 74–5.
39 Biale, *Eros and the Jews*, pp. 67, 70–71; Assis, 'Sexual Behaviour', pp. 30, 54.
40 Grossman, *Pious and Rebellious*, pp. 70, 80, 83.
41 Biale, *Eros and the Jews*, pp. 73–4.
42 Grossman, *Pious and Rebellious*, p. 42.
43 Baumgarten, *Practicing Piety*, p. 81.
44 Grossman, *Pious and Rebellious*, p. 57.
45 For this and the next paragraph, see François Soyer, 'Prohibiting Sexual Relations across Religious Boundaries in Fifteenth-century Portugal: Severity and Pragmatism in Legal Theory and Practice', in *Religious Minorities in Christian, Jewish and Muslim Law*, ed. Nora Berend, Youna Hameau-Masset, Capucinè Nemo-Pekelman and John Tolan (Turnhout, 2017), pp. 301–8; James Brundage, 'Intermarriage between Christians and Jews in Medieval Canon Law', *Jewish History*, III/1 (1988), pp. 25–40; Nirenberg, *Communities of Violence*, pp. 130–32.
46 Brian Catlos, *Muslims of Medieval Latin Christendom, c. 1050–1614* (Cambridge, 2014), pp. 157–8.
47 James Brundage, 'Prostitution, Miscegenation and Sexual Purity in the First Crusade', in *Crusade and Settlement*, ed. Peter Edbury (Cardiff, 1985),

pp. 57–65; Simon Barton, *Conquerors, Brides and Concubines: Interfaith Relations and Social Power in Medieval Iberia* (Philadelphia, PA, 2015), p. 57.

48 Norman Tanner, ed. and trans., *Decrees of the Ecumenical Councils*, I: *Nicaea to Lateran V* (Washington, DC, 1990), p. 266.

49 David Nirenberg, 'Conversion, Sex and Segregation: Jews and Christians in Medieval Spain', *American Historical Review*, CVII (2002), pp. 1079–80.

50 Guido Ruggiero, *The Boundaries of Eros* (Oxford, 1985), pp. 87–8.

51 Soyer, 'Prohibiting Sexual Relations', pp. 301–8; Brundage, 'Intermarriage between Christians and Jews', pp. 25–40; Nirenberg, *Communities of Violence*, pp. 130–32.

52 Nirenberg, *Communities of Violence*, p. 150.

53 Ariel Toaff, *Love, Work and Death: Jewish Life in Medieval Umbria* (Oxford, 1996), pp. 33–5.

54 David Nirenberg, 'Conversion, Sex and Segregation', pp. 1066–9, 1075, 1078.

55 Ruggiero, *Boundaries of Eros*, p. 71.

56 Nirenberg, 'Conversion, Sex and Segregation', pp. 1070, 1081–3.

57 Barton, *Conquerors, Brides and Concubines*, pp. 69–75, 147.

58 Ibid., p. 63.

59 Nirenberg, 'Conversion, Sex and Segregation', p. 1091.

60 Barton, *Conquerors, Brides and Concubines*, p. 53.

61 Nirenberg, *Communities of Violence*, pp. 143–5.

62 Ruggiero, *Boundaries of Eros*, p. 87.

63 Steven Bednarski, *Curia: A Social History of a Court, Crime and Conflict in a Late Medieval Town* (Montpellier, 2013), p. 132.

64 Soyer, 'Relations across Religious Boundaries', p. 312.

65 Barton, *Conquerors, Brides and Concubines*, p. 58; Soyer, 'Prohibiting Sexual Relations', pp. 310–11.

66 Nirenberg, *Communities of Violence*, p. 140.

67 David Nirenberg, 'Love between Muslim and Jew in Medieval Spain: A Triangular Affair', in *Jews, Muslims and Christians in and around the Crown of Aragon*, ed. Harvey Hames (Leiden, 2004), p. 140.

68 Soyer, 'Prohibiting Sexual Relations', pp. 308–9.

69 Barton, *Conquerors, Brides and Concubines*, p. 58.

70 Ibid., pp. 54–5; Nirenberg, *Communities of Violence*, pp. 158–9.

71 Barton, *Conquerors, Brides and Concubines*, pp. 102–6.

72 Nirenberg, 'Love between Muslim and Jew', p. 135.

73 Nirenberg, *Communities of Violence*, pp. 134–7.

74 Ariel Toaff, *Love, Work and Death: Jewish Life in Medieval Umbria* (Oxford, 1996), p. 11.

75 Ray, *Sephardic Frontier*, p. 172.

76 Grossman, *Pious and Rebellious*, p. 144.

77 Nirenberg, *Communities of Violence*, pp. 134–7.

78 Grossman, *Pious and Rebellious*, p. 138.

79 Assis, 'Sexual Behaviour', pp. 36–9.

80 Toaff, *Love, Work and Death*, p. 5.

81 Biale, *Eros and the Jews*, p. 76.

82 Nirenberg, *Communities of Violence*, pp. 134–7.

83 Nirenberg, 'Love between Muslim and Jew', p. 136.

84 Nirenberg, *Communities of Violence*, pp. 136–7.

85 Nirenberg, 'Love between Muslim and Jew', p. 137.

86 Ibid., p. 132.
87 Nirenberg, *Communities of Violence*, pp. 137–8.
88 John Boswell, *The Royal Treasure: Muslim Communities under the Crown of Aragon in the Fourteenth Century* (London, 1977), p. 346; Nirenberg, 'Love between Muslim and Jew', p. 136.
89 Paul Archambault, trans., *A Monk's Confession: The Memoirs of Guibert of Nogent* (Philadelphia, PA, 1996), pp. 195–8.
90 Robert Lerner, *The Heresy of the Free Spirit in the Later Middle Ages* (Berkeley, CA, 1972), pp. 30–31.
91 Norman Cohn, *Europe's Inner Demons: The Demonization of Christians in Medieval Christendom*, revd edn (London, 1993), pp. 1–4, 10–12.
92 Jeffrey Richards, *Sex, Dissidence and Damnation: Minority Groups in the Middle Ages* (Abingdon, 1991), p. 58.
93 Dyan Elliott, *Spiritual Marriage: Sexual Abstinence in Medieval Wedlock* (Princeton, NJ, 1993), p. 96.
94 Malcolm Barber, *The Cathars*, 2nd edn (London, 2013), p. 113.
95 Mark Gregory Pegg, *The Corruption of Angels: The Great Inquisition of 1245–6* (Princeton, NJ, 2001), p. 55.
96 Ibid., pp. 76–8.
97 Barber, *Cathars*, p. 106.
98 Lerner, *Free Spirit*, pp. 10–11.
99 Ibid., p. 176.
100 J. Patrick Hornbeck, 'Theologies of Sexuality in English "Lollardy"', *Journal of Ecclesiastical History*, LX/1 (2009), pp. 38–40.
101 John Arnold and Peter Biller, eds, *Heresy and Inquisition in France, 1200–1300* (Manchester, 2016), p. 41; Lerner, *Free Spirit*, pp. 149–50.
102 Richards, *Sex, Dissidence and Damnation*, p. 60.
103 Ibid., pp. 58–9, 62.
104 Lerner, *Free Spirit*, pp. 10–11.
105 Cohn, *Inner Demons*, pp. 56–7.
106 Anne Gilmour-Bryson, 'Sodomy and the Knights Templar', *Journal of the History of Sexuality*, VII/2 (1996), pp. 151–83.
107 Emmanuel Le Roy Ladurie, *Montaillou*, trans. Barbara Bray (Harmondsworth, 1980), pp. 155–9.
108 Ibid., pp. 171–2.
109 Ibid., pp. 179, 185.
110 Richards, *Sex, Dissidence and Damnation*, pp. 62–3.
111 Lerner, *Free Spirit*, pp. 20–24.
112 Dyan Elliott, *Fallen Bodies: Pollution, Sexuality and Demonology in the Middle Ages* (Philadelphia, PA, 1999), pp. 30, 52–3.
113 Joyce Salisbury, *The Beast Within: Animals in the Middle Ages*, 2nd edn (Abingdon, 2011), p. 78.
114 Jacobus de Voragine, *The Golden Legend*, trans. William Granger Ryan (Princeton, NJ, 2012), pp. 491–2.
115 Elliott, *Fallen Bodies*, p. 54.
116 Dyan Elliott, *The Bride of Christ Goes to Hell: Metaphor and Embodiment in the Lives of Pious Women, 200–1500* (Philadelphia, PA, 2012), pp. 229–31; Renate Blumenfeld-Kosinski, 'The Strange Case of Ermine de Reims (c. 1347–1396): A Medieval Woman between Demons and Saints', *Speculum*, LXXXV/2 (2010), pp. 321–56.

117 Gerald of Wales, *The Jewel of the Church*, ed. John Hagen (Leiden, 1979), pp. 177–8.
118 Walter Stephens, *Demon Lovers: Witchcraft, Sex and the Crisis of Belief* (Chicago, IL, 2002), p. 23.
119 Elliott, *Bride of Christ*, p. 227.
120 Stephens, *Demon Lovers*, pp. 106–8; Elliott, *Fallen Bodies*, p. 57.
121 Salisbury, *Beast Within*, p. 78.
122 Richard Huscroft, *Tales from the Long Twelfth Century: The Rise and Fall of the Angevin Empire* (London, 2016), pp. xix–xx.
123 Martine Ostorero, Agostino Paravicini Bagliani, Kathrin Utz Tremp and Catherine Chène, eds, *L'imaginaire du sabbat* (Lausanne, 1999), pp. 290–91.
124 Ibid., pp. 346–7.
125 Hans Peter Broedel, 'Fifteenth-century Witch Beliefs', in *The Oxford Handbook of Witchcraft in Early Modern Europe and Colonial America*, ed. Brian Levack (Oxford, 2013), pp. 32–49.
126 Stephens, *Demon Lovers*, p. 23.
127 L. S. Davidson and J. O. Ward, ed. and trans., *The Sorcery Trial of Alice Kyteler* (Asheville, NC, 2004), pp. 29, 62–3.
128 Richard Kieckhefer, 'Mythologies of Witchcraft in the Fifteenth Century', *Magic, Ritual and Witchcraft*, I (2006), pp. 82–4, 101–2.
129 Rinaldo Comba and Angelo Nicolini, eds, *'Lucea Talvolta la luna': I processi alle 'masche' di Rifreddo e Gambasca del 1495* (Cunea, 2004), pp. 89, 92.

9 Prostitution

1 Christine de Pizan, *The Treasure of the City of Ladies*, trans. Sarah Lawson (London, 2003), pp. 158–60.
2 Ruth Mazo Karras, *Common Women: Prostitution and Sexuality in Medieval England* (Oxford, 1996), p. 3.
3 Patricia Skinner and Elisabeth van Houts, eds, *Medieval Writings on Secular Women* (London, 2011), pp. 96–7.
4 Karras, *Common Women*, p. 49.
5 Maria Serena Mazzi, *A Life of Ill Repute: Public Prostitution in the Middle Ages*, trans. Joyce Myerson (Montreal, 2020), p. 17.
6 Skinner and Houts, *Writings on Secular Women*, p. 100.
7 Sharon Farmer, *Surviving Poverty in Medieval Paris: Gender, Ideology and the Daily Lives of the Poor* (Ithaca, NY, 2002), p. 68; Skinner and Houts, *Writings on Secular Women*, p. 102.
8 Ibid., pp. 98–9.
9 Michelle Sauer, *Gender in Medieval Culture* (London, 2015), p. 71.
10 Joëlle Rollo-Koster, 'From Prostitutes to Brides of Christ: The Avignonese *Repenties* in the Late Middle Ages', *Journal of Medieval History*, XXXII/1 (2002), pp. 116–22.
11 Sharon Farmer, *Surviving Poverty in Medieval Paris: Gender, Ideology and the Daily Lives of the Poor* (Ithaca, NY, 2002), pp. 129, 147.
12 Rollo-Koster, 'From Prostitutes to Brides', p. 113.
13 Michael Hammer, 'Prostitution in Urban Brothels in Late Medieval Austria', in *Same Bodies, Different Women: 'Other' Women in the Middle Ages and Early Modern Period*, ed. Christopher Mielke and Andrea-Bianka Znorovszky (Budapest, 2019), p. 78.

14 Rollo-Koster, 'From Prostitutes to Brides', pp. 113–15; Paula Clarke, 'The Business of Prostitution in Early Renaissance Venice', *Renaissance Quarterly*, LXVIII/2 (2015), p. 454.

15 Leah Otis, *Prostitution in Medieval Society: The History of an Urban Institution in Languedoc* (Chicago, IL, 1985), p. 17.

16 Ibid., p. 25.

17 Clarke, 'Business of Prostitution', pp. 421–2.

18 Otis, *Prostitution*, pp. 101–4.

19 John Brackett, 'The Florentine Onesta and the Control of Prostitution, 1403–1680', *Sixteenth Century Journal*, XXIV/2 (1993), p. 281.

20 Jeremy Goldberg, 'Pigs and XXIV/2: Streetwalking in Comparative Perspective', in *Young Medieval Women*, ed. Katharine Lewis, Noel Menuge and Kim Phillips (Stroud, 1999), pp. 181, 186.

21 Karras, *Common Women*, p. 32.

22 Ibid., pp. 35–44.

23 Ibid., pp. 14–15.

24 Jeremy Goldberg, ed., *Women in England, c. 1275–1525* (Manchester, 1995), pp. 210, 212.

25 Barbara Hanawalt, *The Wealth of Wives: Women, Law and Economy in Late Medieval London* (Oxford, 2007), p. 204.

26 Karras, *Common Women*, p. 22.

27 Ibid., pp. 45–6.

28 Bronisław Geremek, *The Margins of Society in Late Medieval Paris* (London, 1987), pp. 226–30.

29 Marija Karbić, 'Prostitutes and Urban Communities of Medieval Slavonia: Examples from Gradec', in *Same Bodies, Different Women: 'Other' Women in the Middle Ages and Early Modern Period*, ed. Christopher Mielke and Andrea-Bianka Znorovszky (Budapest, 2019), p. 84.

30 Eleanor Janega, 'Suspect Women: Prostitution, Reputation and Gossip in Fourteenth-century Prague', in *Same Bodies, Different Women*, ed. Mielke and Znorovszky, p. 51.

31 Karras, *Common Women*, p. 72.

32 Otis, *Prostitution*, p. 70.

33 Diane Wolfthal, *In and Out of the Marital Bed: Seeing Sex in Renaissance Europe* (London, 2010), p. 127; Mazzi, *Ill Repute*, p. 39.

34 Karras, *Common Women*, p. 80.

35 Eukene Lacarra Lanz, 'Legal and Clandestine Prostitution in Medieval Spain', *Bulletin of Hispanic Studies*, 79 (2002), p. 278.

36 David Nicholas, *The Domestic Life of a Medieval City: Women, Children and the Family in Fourteenth-century Ghent* (Lincoln, NE, 1985), p. 60.

37 Geremek, *Margins of Society*, p. 221; Goldberg, 'Pigs and Prostitutes', pp. 179–81.

38 Guido Ruggiero, *The Boundaries of Eros* (Oxford, 1985), p. 71.

39 Karras, *Common Women*, pp. 21–2; Rollo-Koster, 'From Prostitutes to Brides', pp. 112–13; Otis, *Prostitution*, p. 80; Clarke, 'Business of Prostitution', pp. 426–8.

40 Carole Rawcliffe, *Urban Bodies: Communal Health in Late Medieval English Towns and Cities* (Woodbridge, 2013), p. 109.

41 Shannon McSheffrey, *Marriage, Sex and Civic Culture in Late Medieval London* (Philadelphia, PA, 2006), p. 179.

42 Goldberg, ed., *Women in England*, p. 216.

43 Clarke, 'Business of Prostitution', p. 428.
44 Jamie Page, 'Masculinity and Prostitution in Late Medieval German Literature', *Speculum*, xciv/3 (2019), pp. 745–6.
45 Farmer, *Surviving Poverty*, p. 111.
46 Karras, *Common Women*, pp. 24–5; Otis, *Prostitution*, pp. 28–9.
47 Brackett, 'Florentine Onesta', p. 286.
48 Jacques Rossiaud, *Medieval Prostitution*, trans. Lydia Cochrane (Oxford, 1988), pp. 33, 36–7.
49 Clarke, 'Business of Prostitution', pp. 432–9.
50 Erik Spindler, 'Were Medieval Prostitutes Marginals? Evidence from Sluis, 1387–1440', *Revue Belge de Philologie et d'Histoire*, 87 (2009), pp. 264–8.
51 Ruth Mazo Karras, *Unmarriages: Women, Men and Sexual Unions in the Middle Ages* (Philadelphia, pa, 2012), p. 139.
52 Rossiaud, *Medieval Prostitution*, pp. 33, 36–7.
53 Karbić, 'Prostitutes and Urban Communities', pp. 91–3.
54 Karras, *Common Women*, p. 63.
55 Carol Lansing, 'Girls in Trouble in Late Medieval Bologna', in *The Premodern Teenager: Youth in Society, 1150–1650*, ed. Konrad Eisenbichler (Toronto, 2002), pp. 305–6.
56 Goldberg, ed., *Women in England*, pp. 214–16.
57 Hanawalt, *Wealth of Wives*, p. 190.
58 Mazzi, *Ill Repute*, pp. 112–14.
59 Rossiaud, *Medieval Prostitution*, p. 33.
60 Mazzi, *Ill Repute*, p. 45.
61 Simon Barton, *Conquerors, Brides and Concubines: Interfaith Relations and Social Power in Medieval Iberia* (Philadelphia, pa, 2015), p. 61.
62 Dillard, *Daughters of the Reconquest*, pp. 197–8.
63 Mazzi, *Ill Repute*, pp. 53–4.
64 Page, 'Masculinity and Prostitution', p. 771.
65 Hammer, 'Urban Brothels', pp. 75–6.
66 Ibid.
67 Rossiaud, *Medieval Prostitution*, p. 29.
68 Mazzi, *Ill Repute*, pp. 118–20.
69 Ibid., pp. 100–101.
70 Clarke, 'Business of Prostitution', pp. 432–4; Spindler, 'Were Medieval Prostitutes Marginals?', p. 251.
71 Jamie Page, 'Inside the Medieval Brothel', *History Today*, lxix/6 (June 2019), pp. 30–39.
72 Page, 'Masculinity and Prostitution', pp. 747, 754–5.
73 Mazzi, *Ill Repute*, pp. 135–6.
74 Otis, *Prostitution*, p. 83.
75 Ruggiero, *Boundaries of Eros*, p. 120.
76 Goldberg, ed., *Women in England*, p. 213.
77 Reginald Sharpe, ed., *Calendar of Coroners Rolls of the City of London, AD 1300–1378* (London, 1913), pp. 208–9.
78 Rossiaud, *Medieval Prostitution*, pp. 35, 109.
79 Albertus Magnus, *On Animals: A Medieval Summa Zoologica*, trans. Kenneth Mitchell and Irven Resnick, 2 vols (Baltimore, md, 1999), vol. i, p. 777.
80 Skinner and Houts, *Writings on Secular Women*, p. 20.

81 Mazzi, *Ill Repute*, p. 60.
82 Ibid., pp. 39–41.
83 Janega, 'Suspect Women', p. 48.
84 Hanawalt, *Wealth of Wives*, p. 202; Goldberg, ed., *Women in England*, p. 213.
85 Karras, *Common Women*, p. 96.
86 Page, 'Masculinity and Prostitution', pp. 770–71.
87 Brackett, 'Florentine Onesta', p. 281.
88 Steven Bednarski, *Curia: A Social History of a Court, Crime and Conflict in a Late Medieval Town* (Montpellier, 2013).
89 Karras, *Common Women*, pp. 66–7.
90 Ibid., p. 97.
91 Clarke, 'Business of Prostitution', pp. 456–7.
92 Karras, *Common Women*, pp. 97–9; Otis, *Prostitution*, pp. 67–8; Skinner and Houts, *Writings on Secular Women*, p. 100.
93 Mazzi, *Ill Repute*, pp. 65–6.
94 Rollo-Koster, 'From Prostitutes to Brides', p. 130.
95 Andreas Capellanus, *On Love*, ed. and trans. P. G. Walsh (London, 1982), p. 223.
96 Ruth Mazo Karras, *From Boys to Men: Formations of Masculinity in Late Medieval Europe* (Philadelphia, PA, 2003), p. 50.
97 Farmer, *Surviving Poverty*, p. 37.
98 Rossiaud, *Medieval Prostitution*, p. 34.
99 Lanz, 'Legal and Clandestine Prostitution', p. 269; François Soyer, 'Prohibiting Sexual Relations across Religious Boundaries in Fifteenth-century Portugal: Severity and Pragmatism in Legal Theory and Practice', in *Religious Minorities in Christian, Jewish and Muslim Law*, ed. Nora Berend, Youna Hameau-Mosset, Capucinè Nemo-Pekelman and John Tolan (Turnhout, 2017), pp. 311–12.
100 Rollo-Koster, 'From Prostitutes to Brides', pp. 110–12.
101 Janega, 'Suspect Women', p. 52.
102 Goldberg, 'Pigs and Prostitutes', p. 176.
103 Karras, *Common Women*, p. 114.
104 Leah Otis-Cour, '*De jure novo*: Dealing with Adultery in the Fifteenth-century Toulousain', *Speculum*, LXXXIV (2009), p. 385.
105 McSheffrey, *Marriage, Sex and Civic Culture*, pp. 166–7.
106 Rossiaud, *Medieval Prostitution*, pp. 40–41.
107 Bednarski, *Curia*, p. 129.
108 Clarke, 'Business of Prostitution', pp. 423–4.
109 James Brundage, 'Prostitution, Miscegenation and Sexual Purity in the First Crusade', in *Crusade and Settlement*, ed. Peter Edbury (Cardiff, 1985), pp. 57–65.
110 Wolfthal, *In and Out of the Marital Bed*, p. 127.
111 Anne Curry, 'Sex and the Soldier in Lancastrian Normandy, 1415–1450', *Reading Medieval Studies*, XIV (1988), pp. 17–45.
112 Karras, *From Boys to Men*, p. 128.
113 Karras, *Common Women*, p. 19.
114 Karras, *From Boys to Men*, pp. 79–80, 102; Robert Marichal, ed., *Le livre des prieurs de Sorbonne (1431–1485)* (Paris, 1987), p. 106.
115 Martha Brożyna, ed., *Gender and Sexuality in the Middle Ages* (Jefferson, NC, 2005), p. 138.
116 Page, 'Masculinity and Prostitution', pp. 761–2.

117 Clarke, 'Business of Prostitution', p. 425.
118 Michael Rocke, *Forbidden Friendships: Homosexuality and Male Culture in Renaissance Florence* (Oxford, 1996), p. 130.
119 Ruggiero, *Boundaries of Eros*, pp. 136, 195.
120 Ruth Mazo Karras and David Boyd, '"Ut cum muliere": A Male Transvestite Prostitute in Medieval London', in *Premodern Sexualities*, ed. Louise Fradenburg (London, 1996), pp. 111–12.
121 Jeremy Goldberg, 'John Rykener, Richard II, and the Governance of London', *Leeds Studies in English*, XLV (2014), pp. 49–70.

10 Sexual Violence

1 Heath Dillard, *Daughters of the Reconquest: Women in Castilian Town Society, 1100–1300* (Cambridge, 1984), pp. 173, 175.
2 Grethe Jacobsen, 'Sexual Irregularities in Medieval Scandinavia', in *Sexual Practices and the Medieval Church*, ed. Vern Bullough and James Brundage (New York, 1982), p. 84.
3 Dillard, *Daughters of the Reconquest*, pp. 175–6.
4 Katherine Ludwig Jansen, *Peace and Penance in Late Medieval Italy* (Princeton, NJ, 2018), p. 122.
5 Bernd-Ulrich Hergemöller, *Sodom and Gomorrah: On the Everyday Reality and Persecution of Homosexuals in the Middle Ages* (London, 2001), pp. 116–21.
6 Ibid., p. 126.
7 David Nicholas, *The Domestic Life of a Medieval City: Women, Children and the Family in Fourteenth-century Ghent* (Lincoln, NE, 1985), p. 64.
8 Guido Ruggiero, *The Boundaries of Eros* (Oxford, 1985), p. 85.
9 Eckehard Simon, 'Carnival Obscenities in German Towns', in *Obscenity: Social Control and Artistic Creation in the European Middle Ages*, ed. Jan Ziolkowski (Leiden, 1998), p. 201.
10 Jeremy Goldberg, ed., *Women in England, c. 1215–1525* (Manchester, 1995), p. 255.
11 Caroline Dunn, *Stolen Women in Medieval England: Rape, Abduction and Adultery, 1100–1500* (Cambridge, 2013).
12 Kathryn Gravdal, *Ravishing Maidens: Writing Rape in Medieval French Literature and Law* (Philadelphia, PA, 1991), pp. 8–9.
13 Hiram Kümper, 'Learned Men and Skilful Matrons: Medical Expertise and the Forensics of Rape in the Middle Ages', in *Medicine and the Law in the Middle Ages*, ed. Wendy Turner and Sara Butler (Leiden, 2014), p. 93.
14 Samuel Scott and Robert Burns, ed. and trans., *Las Siete Partidas*, vol. V: *Underworlds: The Dead, the Criminal and the Marginalized* (Philadelphia, PA, 2001), pp. 1425–6.
15 Corinne Saunders, 'A Matter of Consent: Middle English Romance and the Law of Raptus', in *Medieval Women and the Law*, ed. Noël Menage (Woodbridge, 2003), pp. 106, 109–10.
16 Ibid., Gravdal, *Ravishing Maidens*, p. 123.
17 Kümper, 'Forensics of Rape', p. 91.
18 Dillard, *Daughters of the Reconquest*, pp. 184–6, 188–90.
19 Louise Wilkinson, *Women in Thirteenth-century Lincolnshire* (Woodbridge, 2007), p. 150.

20 Gravdal, *Ravishing Maidens*, p. 129.
21 Barbara Hanawalt, *'Of Good and Ill Repute': Gender and Social Control in Medieval England* (Oxford, 1998), p. 136.
22 Carol Lansing, 'Accusations of Rape in Thirteenth-century Bologna', in *Violence and Justice in Bologna*, ed. Sarah Rubin Blanshei (Lanham, MD, 2018), pp. 170–71, 176–7.
23 Kümper, 'Forensics of Rape', pp. 95–9.
24 Edna Yahil, 'A Rape Trial in Saint Eloi: Sex, Seduction and Justice in the Seigneurial Courts of Medieval Paris', in *Voices from the Bench*, ed. Michael Goodich (London, 2006), pp. 258–61.
25 David Nicholas, *The Domestic Life of a Medieval City: Women, Children and the Family in Fourteenth-century Ghent* (Lincoln, NE, 1985), p. 54.
26 Kümper, 'Forensics of Rape', p. 92.
27 Diane Wolfthal, *Images of Rape: The 'Heroic' Tradition and Its Alternatives* (Cambridge, 1989), pp. 100–103, 105–6.
28 Dillard, *Daughters of the Reconquest*, pp. 181–4.
29 Yahil, 'Rape Trial', p. 262.
30 Nicholas, *Domestic Life*, p. 54.
31 Patricia Skinner and Elisabeth van Houts, eds, *Medieval Writings on Secular Women* (London, 2011), pp. 153–4.
32 Carol Lansing, 'Girls in Trouble in Late Medieval Bologna', in *The Premodern Teenager: Youth in Society, 1150–1650*, ed. Konrad Eisenbichler (Toronto, 2002), pp. 299–300.
33 Gravdal, *Ravishing Maidens*, p. 127.
34 Jacques Rossiaud, *Medieval Prostitution* (Oxford, 1988), pp. 11–13, 20, 22–3; Ruth Mazo Karras, *From Boys to Men: Formations of Masculinity in Late Medieval Europe* (Philadelphia, PA, 2003), p. 148.
35 Andreas Capellanus, *On Love*, ed. and trans. P. G. Walsh (London, 1982), p. 223.
36 Lansing, 'Accusations of Rape', p. 174.
37 Guido Ruggiero, *The Boundaries of Eros* (Oxford, 1985), pp. 99, 107–8.
38 Dillard, *Daughters of the Reconquest*, p. 179.
39 Ruth Mazo Karras, *Unmarriages: Women, Men and Sexual Unions in the Middle Ages* (Philadelphia, PA, 2012), pp. 87, 90.
40 Christine de Pizan, *The Book of the City of Ladies*, trans. Rosalind Brown-Grant (London, 1999), p. 147.
41 Christine de Pizan, *The Treasure of the City of Ladies*, trans. Sarah Lawson (London, 2003), p. 133.
42 Carrissa Harris, *Obscene Pedagogies: Transgressive Talk and Sexual Education in Late Medieval Britain* (Ithaca, NY, 2018), pp. 20, 119, 150–83.
43 Rossiaud, *Medieval Prostitution*, p. 28.
44 Nicholas, *Domestic Life*, p. 61.
45 Kümper, 'Forensics of Rape', p. 102.
46 Goldberg, ed., *Women in England*, p. 256.
47 Skinner and Houts, ed., *Writings on Secular Women*, p. 20.
48 Kümper, 'Forensics of Rape', pp. 103–5.
49 Gravdal, *Ravishing Maidens*, pp. 8–9.
50 Lansing, 'Accusations of Rape', pp. 177–8.
51 Ruggiero, *Boundaries of Eros*, p. 98.
52 Roussiaud, *Medieval Prostitution*, pp. 29–30, 180.
53 Nicholas, *Domestic Life*, pp. 65–6.

54 Shannon McSheffrey, *Marriage, Sex and Civic Culture in Late Medieval London* (Philadelphia, PA, 2006), p. 145.
55 Yahil, 'Rape Trial', pp. 251–71.
56 Lansing, 'Accusations of Rape', pp. 175–6.
57 Wilkinson, *Women*, p. 153.
58 Dillard, *Daughters of the Reconquest*, pp. 185–6.
59 Gravdal, *Ravishing Maidens*, pp. 129–30.
60 Gerald of Wales, *The Jewel of the Church*, trans. John Hagen (Leiden, 1979), pp. 82–3.
61 Bernard of Clairvaux, *The Life and Death of St Malachy the Irishman*, trans. Robert Meyer (Kalamazoo, MI, 1978), p. 55.
62 Corinne Saunders, 'Sexual Violence in Wars: The Middle Ages', in *Transcultural Wars: From the Middle Ages to the Twenty-first Century*, ed. Hana-Henning Kortüm (Berlin, 2006), pp. 153–5.
63 Karras, *From Boys to Men*, p. 77.
64 Peter Arnade and Walter Prevenier, *Honor, Vengeance, and Social Trouble* (Ithaca, NY, 2015), pp. 102–4, 118–20.
65 Hergemöller, *Sodom and Gomorrah*, pp. 122–6.
66 Alan Kissane, 'Unnatural in Body and a Villain in Soul: Rape and Sexual Violence towards Girls under the Age of Canonical Consent in Late Medieval England', in *Fourteenth-century England*, ed. Gwilym Dodd (Woodbridge, 2018), vol. X, p. 90.
67 Ibid., p. 104.
68 Ruggiero, *Boundaries of Eros*, p. 92.
69 Gravdal, *Ravishing Maidens*, pp. 128, 136–7.
70 Kissane, 'Unnatural in Body', pp. 96–7.
71 Skinner and Houts, eds, *Writings on Secular Women*, pp. 80–88.
72 Montserrat Cabré, 'Women or Healers? Household Practices and the Categories of Health Care in Late Medieval Iberia', *Bulletin of the History of Medicine*, 82 (2008), pp. 31–5.
73 Hanawalt, *Of Good and Ill Repute*, p. 136.
74 Ruggiero, *Boundaries of Eros*, pp. 119–20.
75 Kissane, 'Unnatural in Body', p. 98.
76 Barbara Hanawalt, *The Wealth of Wives: Women, Law, and Economy in Late Medieval London* (Oxford, 2007), p. 47.
77 John Shinners and William Dohar, eds, *Pastors and the Care of Souls in Medieval England* (Notre Dame, IN, 1998), pp. 271–2.
78 Ruggiero, *Boundaries of Eros*, pp. 117–18, 125–6.
79 Ibid., p. 138.
80 Karras, *From Boys to Men*, pp. 81–2; Dyan Elliott, *The Corrupter of Boys: Sodomy, Scandal and the Medieval Clergy* (Philadelphia, PA, 2020), pp. 207–9.
81 Elliott, *Corrupter of Boys*, pp. 179–84.
82 Helmut Puff, *Sodomy in Reformation Germany and Switzerland, 1400–1600* (Chicago, IL, 2003), pp. 38–40; Elliott, *Corrupter of Boys*, pp. 184–7.

11 Sex in Culture

1 Geoffrey Chaucer, *The Canterbury Tales*, trans. Neville Coghill (London, 1951), pp. 88–106.
2 Ibid., pp. 356–88, with the sex in a tree incident at p. 386.

3 Giovanni Boccaccio, *The Decameron*, trans. Guido Waldman (Oxford, 1993), pp. 158–65.
4 Derek Brewer, ed., *Medieval Comic Tales*, 2nd edn (Cambridge, 1996), pp. 132–3.
5 Nathaniel Dubin, trans., *The Fabliaux* (New York, 2013), pp. 490–97.
6 Judith Bruskin Diner, trans., *The One Hundred New Tales* (New York, 1990), pp. 122–3.
7 Dubin, trans., *The Fabliaux*, pp. 124–43.
8 Diner, *One Hundred New Tales*, pp. 83–7.
9 Eve Salisbury, ed., *The Trials and Joys of Marriage* (Kalamazoo, MI, 2002), pp. 95–8.
10 Dubin, trans., *The Fabliaux*, pp. 438–51.
11 Diner, *One Hundred New Tales*, pp. 246–8.
12 Dubin, trans., *The Fabliaux*, pp. 324–31.
13 Boccaccio, *The Decameron*, pp. 42–5.
14 Ibid., pp. 171–7.
15 R. T. Davies, ed., *Medieval English Lyrics* (London, 1963), pp. 162–3, 204–6.
16 Brewer, ed., *Medieval Comic Tales*, pp. 136–9.
17 Ibid., pp. 97–101.
18 Boccaccio, *The Decameron*, pp. 418–26.
19 Diner, *One Hundred New Tales*, pp. 186–7.
20 Boccaccio, *The Decameron*, pp. 489–94.
21 Dubin, trans., *The Fabliaux*, pp. 860–73.
22 Diner, *One Hundred New Tales*, pp. 26–31.
23 Ibid., pp. 319–21.
24 Dubin, trans., *The Fabliaux*, pp. 884–95.
25 Ann Marie Rasmussen, *Wandering Genitalia: Sexuality and the Body in German Culture between the Late Middle Ages and Early Modernity* (London, 2009).
26 Dafydd Johnston, ed., *Medieval Welsh Erotic Poetry* (Bridgend, 1998), pp. 24–7.
27 Ibid., pp. 36–9.
28 Jeremy Goldberg, 'John Skathelok's Dick: Voyeurism and Pornography in Late Medieval England', in *Medieval Obscenities*, ed. Nicola McDonald (York, 2006), pp. 117–23.
29 William Paden, trans., *The Medieval Pastourelle*, 2 vols (New York, 1987), vol. I, pp. 284–7.
30 Ibid., pp. 294–7.
31 Kathryn Gravdal, *Ravishing Maidens: Writing Rape in Medieval French Literature and Law* (Philadelphia, PA, 1991), pp. 104–5, 110–11.
32 Nicole Nolan Sidhu, *Indecent Exposure: Gender, Politics and Obscene Comedy in Middle English Literature* (Philadelphia, PA, 2016), pp. 16–17.
33 Dyan Elliott, *Fallen Bodies: Pollution, Sexuality and Demonology in the Middle Ages* (Philadelphia, PA, 1999), pp. 61–80.
34 Sidhu, *Indecent Exposure*, pp. 6, 11.
35 Glenn Olsen, 'On the Frontiers of Eroticism: The Romanesque Monastery of San Pedro de Cervatos', *Mediterranean Studies*, VIII (1999), pp. 89–104.
36 Anthony Weir and James Jerman, *Images of Lust: Sexual Carvings on Medieval Churches* (London, 1986), pp. 7–9.
37 Marian Bleeke, 'Sheelas, Sex and Significance in Romanesque Sculpture:

The Kilpeck Corbel Series', *Studies in Iconography*, XXVI (2005), pp. 1–26; Lisa Bitel, *Land of Women: Tales of Sex and Gender from Early Ireland* (Ithaca, NY, 1996), pp. 229–34; Weir and Jerman, *Images of Lust*, pp. 11–22.

38 Penney Howell Jolly, 'Pubics and Privates: Body Hair in Late Medieval Art', in *The Meanings of Nudity in Medieval Art*, ed. Sherry Lindquist (Farnham, 2012), pp. 200–201; Michael Camille, 'Dr Witkowski's Anus: French Doctors, German Homosexuals and the Obscene in Medieval Church Art', in *Medieval Obscenities*, ed. McDonald, pp. 28–9.

39 Michael Camille, *The Medieval Art of Love* (London, 1998), pp. 18–19.

40 Sarah Salih, 'Erotica', in *A Cultural History of Sexuality in the Middle Ages*, ed. Ruth Evans (London, 2011), pp. 191–7.

41 Jolley, 'Publics and Privates', pp. 187–9.

42 The key texts in this debate include Leo Steinberg, *The Sexuality of Christ in Renaissance Art and Modern Oblivion* (Chicago, IL, 1996); Caroline Walker Bynum, 'The Body of Christ in the Later Middle Ages: A Reply to Leo Steinberg', in *Fragmentation and Redemption: Essays on Gender and the Human Body in Medieval Religion* (New York, 1991), pp. 79–117; and Margaret Miles, 'The Virgin's One Bare Breast', in *The Expanding Discourse: Feminism and Art History*, ed. Norma Broude and Mary Garrard (New York, 1992), pp. 26–37.

43 Salih, 'Erotica', pp. 208–11; Thomas Kren, Jill Burke and Stephen Campbell, eds, *The Renaissance Nude* (London, 2019), p. 19.

44 Salih, 'Erotica', pp. 182–5; Sherry Lindquist, 'The Meanings of Nudity in Medieval Art: An Introduction', in *The Meanings of Nudity in Medieval Art*, ed. Lindquist (Farnham, 2012), pp. 22–3.

45 See, for example, BL Harley MS 4979, including fols 47, 60, 72v.

46 Jean Longnon, ed., *Les très riches heures du Duc de Berry* (London, 1969).

47 BNF MS fr. 22526, especially fols 107v, 111r–v, 132v, 160r, for images of nuns and phalluses (available online via Gallica, the digital repository of the Bibliothèque nationale de France); Michael Camille, *Image on the Edge: The Margins of Medieval Art* (London, 1992), pp. 151–3.

48 Malcolm Jones, 'Sex, Popular Beliefs and Culture', in *Cultural History of Sexuality*, ed. Evans, pp. 155–6.

49 Salih, 'Erotica', pp. 186–91.

50 See, for example, the illustration of 'Adultery' in BL Royal E VI, f. 61 (a fourteenth-century encyclopaedia); the depiction of Mars in bed with Vulcan's wife in BL Harley 4425, fol. 122v (a late fifteenth-century Belgian copy of *The Romance of the Rose*); and the image of a couple in bed from BL Sloane 2435, fol. 8v (a late thirteenth-century French manuscript of Aldobrandino of Siena's *Le régime du corps*), all available via the British Library's online catalogue of illuminated manuscripts.

51 See, for example, BL Sloane 56, fol. 85v (a fifteenth-century image of cleric with sores on his penis) and BL Sloane 1977, fol. 7v (a collection of diseases of the breasts and genitals, from a fourteenth-century surgical text).

52 BL Sloane 56, fol. 30.

53 Goldberg, 'John Skathelok's Dick', pp. 113–16.

54 Michael Camille, 'Obscenity under Erasure: Censorship in Medieval Illuminated Manuscripts', in *Obscenity: Social Control and Artistic Creation in the European Middle Ages*, ed. Jan Ziolkowski (Leiden, 1998), pp. 147–53.

55 Paul Saenger, 'Silent Reading: Its Impact on Late Medieval Script and Society', *Viator*, XIII (1982), pp. 412–13.

56 Kren, Burke and Campbell, eds, *Renaissance Nude*, pp. 64–9.
57 Jos Koldeweij, 'Shameless and Naked Images: Obscene Badges as Parodies of Popular Devotion', in *Art and Architecture of Late Medieval Pilgrimage in Northern Europe and the British Isles*, ed. Sarah Blick and Rita Tekippe (Leiden, 2004), pp. 502–4.
58 Ana-Maria Gruia, 'Sex on the Stove: A Fifteenth-century Tile from Banská Bystrica', *Studia Patzinaka*, 4 (2007), pp. 85–122.
59 Jones, 'Popular Beliefs', pp. 157, 160.
60 Koldeweij, 'Shameless and Naked Images', pp. 493–4, 504–5, 508.
61 Carissa Harris, *Obscene Pedagogies: Transgressive Talk and Sexual Education in Late Medieval Britain* (Ithaca, NY, 2019), p. 12.
62 Jones, 'Popular Beliefs', p. 150; H.J.E. van Beuningen, ed., *Heilig en profaan* (Zwolle, 2018).
63 Malcolm Jones, *The Secret Middle Ages* (Stroud, 2002), p. 249.
64 Koldeweij, 'Shameless and Naked Images', p. 506.
65 Jones, 'Popular Beliefs', pp. 143–4, 148–9, 151–3.
66 Roberta Gilchrist, *Medieval Life: Archaeology and the Life Course* (Woodbridge, 2012), pp. 105–6, 260–62.
67 James Knirk, 'Love and Eroticism in Medieval Norwegian Runic Inscriptions', in *Die Faszination des Verborgenen und seine Entschlüsselung – Rådi sär kunni*, ed. Jana Krüger (Berlin, 2017), pp. 217–32.
68 Jones, 'Popular Beliefs', p. 156.
69 Sidhu, *Indecent Exposure*, pp. 18–20.
70 Harris, *Obscene Pedagogies*, p. 14.
71 David Nicholas, *The Domestic Life of a Medieval City: Women, Children and the Family in Fourteenth-century Ghent* (Lincoln, NE, 1985), p. 60.
72 Geoffrey Hughes, *Swearing: A Social History of Foul Language, Oaths, and Profanity in English* (Oxford, 1991), pp. 55–62; Melissa Mohr, *Holy Sh*t: A Brief History of Swearing* (Oxford, 2013), pp. 112–28.
73 OED.
74 Paul Booth, 'An early fourteenth-century use of the F-Word in Cheshire, 1310–11', *Transactions of the Historic Society of Lancashire and Cheshire*, CLXIV (2015), pp. 99–102.
75 Jones, ' Popular Beliefs', p. 160.
76 Richard Coates, 'Fockynggrove in Bristol', *Notes and Queries*, 54 (2007), pp. 373–6.
77 Geoffrey Hughes, *An Encyclopaedia of Swearing* (New York, 2006), p. 312; Keith Briggs, 'OE and ME Cunte in Place-names', *Journal of the English Place-name Society*, XLI (2009), p. 27.
78 OED; Briggs, 'OE and ME Cunte', pp. 26–39; Hughes, *Encyclopaedia*, pp. 110–11; Jones, 'Popular Beliefs', p. 159.
79 Hughes, *Encyclopaedia*, pp. 112–13.
80 Ibid., p. 197.
81 Ibid., pp. 86–9.
82 Ibid., pp. 101–3.
83 Trevor Dean, 'Gender and Insult in an Italian City: Bologna in the Later Middle Ages', *Social History*, XXIX/2 (2004), p. 223; L. R. Poos, 'Sex, Lies and the Church Courts of Pre-Reformation England', *Journal of Interdisciplinary History*, XXV/4 (1995), p. 587.
84 Daniel Lesnick, 'Insults and Threats in Medieval Todi', *Journal of Medieval History*, XVII (1991), p. 76; Dean, 'Gender and Insult', pp. 217–18.

85 Jelle Haemers, 'Filthy and Indecent Words: Insults, Defamation and Urban Politics in the Southern Low Countries, 1300–1550', in *The Voices of the People in Late Medieval Europe*, ed. Jon Dumolyn, Jelle Haemers, Hipólito Rafael Oliva Herrer and Vincent Challet (Turnhout, 2014), p. 261.
86 Dean, 'Gender and Insult', pp. 219–20.
87 Haemers, 'Filthy Words', p. 262; Lesnick, 'Insults and Threats', p. 71.
88 Dean, 'Gender and Insult', pp. 219, 221.
89 Ibid., p. 223.
90 Poos, 'Sex, Lies and the Church Courts', pp. 586–8.
91 Robert Helmholz, ed., *Select Cases on Defamation to 1600* (London, 1985), p. 21.
92 Ibid., p. 18.
93 Poos, 'Sex, Lies and the Church Courts', p. 590.
94 Ibid., p. 602.
95 Haemers, 'Filthy Words', p. 258.
96 Ibid., pp. 252–5.
97 Martha Brożyna, ed., *Gender and Sexuality in the Middle Ages* (Jefferson, NC, 2005), p. 138.
98 Helmut Puff, *Sodomy in Reformation Germany and Switzerland, 1400–1600* (Chicago, IL, 2003), p. 18.
99 Haemers, 'Filthy Words', p. 256; Jonas Roelens, 'Gossip, Defamation and Sodomy in the Early Modern Southern Netherlands', *Renaissance Studies*, XXXII/2 (2018), pp. 236–7.
100 Dean, 'Gender and Insult', pp. 228–9.
101 Sidhu, *Indecent Exposure*, p. 24; Emma Dillon, 'Representing Obscene Sound', in *Medieval Obscenities*, ed. Nicola McDonald (York, 2006), p. 61.
102 Salih, 'Erotica', p. 184.
103 James Stevenson, ed., *Chronicon de Lanercost* (Edinburgh, 1839), p. 109.
104 Eckehard Simon, 'Carnival Obscenities in German Towns', in *Obscenity: Social Control and Artistic Creation in the European Middle Ages*, ed. Jan Ziolowski (Leiden, 1998), pp. 193–213.
105 A. C. Cawley, ed., *Everyman and Medieval Miracle Plays* (London, 1993), pp. 125–36.
106 Sidhu, *Indecent Exposure*, pp. 208–10.
107 Emma Maggie Solberg, *Virgin Whore* (Ithaca, NY, 2018).

Conclusion

1 Shanti Das, 'Restoring Virgins Is a Big Earner for British Surgeons', *Sunday Times*, 12 January 2020.
2 Anke Bernau, *Virgins: A Cultural History* (London, 2007), pp. 168–85.
3 Julia Ebner, *Going Dark: The Social Lives of Extremists* (London, 2020), pp. 51–60.
4 Wendy Macdowall et al., 'Lifetime Prevalence, Associated Factors, and Circumstances of Non-volitional Sex in Women and Men in Britain: Findings from the third National Survey of Sexual Attitudes and Lifestyles (Natsal-3)', *The Lancet*, 382 (2013), pp. 1845–55.
5 Leïla Slimani, *Sex and Lies* (London, 2020), pp. 36–7.
6 Christina Lamb, *Our Bodies, Their Battlefield: What War Does to Women* (London, 2020).

7 Paul Archambault, trans., *A Monk's Confession: The Memoirs of Guibert of Nogent* (Philadelphia, PA, 1996), pp. 36–7.

BIBLIOGRAPHY

This bibliography is intended to point readers to accessible resources for further reading; for that reason I have given references to works in English translation wherever possible.

Archambault, Paul, trans., *A Monk's Confession: The Memoirs of Guibert of Nogent* (Philadelphia, PA, 1996)

Archibald, Elizabeth, *Incest and the Medieval Imagination* (Oxford, 2001)

Armstrong-Partida, Michelle, *Defiant Priests: Domestic Unions, Violence and Clerical Masculinity in Fourteenth-century Catalunya* (Ithaca, NY, 2017)

Arnade, Peter, and Walter Prevenier, *Honor, Vengeance, and Social Trouble: Pardon Letters in the Burgundian Low Countries* (Ithaca, NY, 2015)

Arnold, John, 'The Labour of Continence: Masculinity and Clerical Virginity', in *Medieval Virginities*, ed. Anke Bernau, Ruth Evans and Sarah Salih (Cardiff, 2003), pp. 102–18

—, 'Sexualité et déshonneur dans le Midi (XIIIe–XIVe siècles): Les péchés de la chair et l'opinion collective', in *L'Église et la chair (XIIe–XVe siècle)*, ed. Michèle Fournié, Daniel le Blévec and Julien Théry (Toulouse, 2019), pp. 261–95

—, and Peter Biller, eds, *Heresy and Inquisition in France, 1200–1300* (Manchester, 2016)

Assis, Yom Tov, 'Sexual Behaviour in Mediaeval Hispano-Jewish Society', in *Jewish History: Essays in Honour of Chimen Abramsky*, ed. Ada Rapoport-Albert and Steven Zipperstein (London, 1988), pp. 25–59

Atkinson, Clarissa, '"Precious Balsam in a Fragile Glass": The Ideology of Virginity in the Later Middle Ages', *Journal of Family History*, 8 (1983), pp. 131–43

Barber, Malcolm, *The Cathars*, 2nd edn (London, 2013)

Barr, Beth Alison, 'Three's a Crowd: Wives, Husbands and Priests in the Late Medieval Confessional', in *A Companion to Pastoral Care in the Late Middle Ages (1200–1500)*, ed. Ronald Stanbury (Leiden, 2010), pp. 213–34

Barratt, Alexandra, ed., *The Knowing of Woman's Kind in Childing: A Middle English Version of Material Derived from the 'Trotula' and Other Sources* (Turnhout, 2001)

Bartlett, Robert, *Why Can the Dead Do Such Great Things? Saints and Worshippers from the Martyrs to the Reformation* (Princeton, NJ, 2013)

Barton, Simon, *Conquerors, Brides and Concubines: Interfaith Relations and Social Power in Medieval Iberia* (Philadelphia, PA, 2015)

Baumgarten, Elisheva, *Mothers and Children: Jewish Family Life in Medieval Europe* (Princeton, NJ, 2004)
—, *Practicing Piety in Medieval Ashkenaz: Men, Women, and Everyday Religious Observance* (Philadelphia, PA, 2014)
Bednarski, Steven, *Curia: A Social History of a Court, Crime and Conflict in a Late Medieval Town* (Montpellier, 2013)
—, *A Poisoned Past: The Life and Times of Margarida de Portu, a Fourteenth-century Accused Poisoner* (Toronto, 2014)
Bennett, Judith, '"Lesbian-like" and the Social History of Lesbianisms', *Journal of the History of Sexuality*, IX (2000), pp. 1–24
—, 'Remembering Elizabeth Etchingham and Agnes Oxenbridge', in *The Lesbian Premodern*, ed. Noreen Giffney, Michelle Sauer and Diane Watt (London, 2011), pp. 131–43
Berceo, Gonzalo de, *Miracles of Our Lady*, trans. Richard Mount and Annette Cash (Lexington, KY, 1997)
Berger, Margaret, ed., *Hildegard of Bingen: On Natural Philosophy and Medicine* (Cambridge, 1999)
Bernau, Anke, *Virgins: A Cultural History* (London, 2007)
Beuningen, H.J.E. van, ed., *Heilig en profaan* (Zwolle, 2018)
Biale, David, *Eros and the Jews: From Biblical Israel to Contemporary America* (New York, 1992)
Biller, Peter, 'Birth-control in the West in the Thirteenth and Early Fourteenth Centuries', *Past and Present*, XCIV/1 (1982), pp. 3–26
—, 'Black Women in Medieval Scientific Thought', *Micrologus*, XIII (2005), pp. 477–92
—, and A. J. Minnis, eds, *Handling Sin: Confession in the Middle Ages* (York, 1998)
Bitel, Lisa, *Land of Women: Tales of Sex and Gender from Early Ireland* (Ithaca, NY, 1996)
Bleeke, Marian, 'Sheela, Sex, and Significance in Romanesque Sculpture: The Kilpeck Corbel Series', *Studies in Iconography*, XXVI (2005), pp. 1–26
Bliss, William, et al., eds, *Calendar of Entries in the Papal Registers Relating to Great Britain and Ireland*, 18 vols (London and Dublin, 1893–)
Blumenfeld-Kosinski, Renate, 'The Strange Case of Ermine de Reims (c. 1347–1396): A Medieval Woman between Demons and Saints', *Speculum*, LXXXV/2 (2010), pp. 321–56
Boccaccio, Giovanni, *The Decameron*, trans. Guido Waldman (Oxford, 1993)
Boone, Marc, 'State Power and Illicit Sexuality: The Persecution of Sodomy in Late Medieval Bruges', *Journal of Medieval History*, XXII/2 (1996), pp. 135–53
Booth, Paul, '"An Early Fourteenth-century Use of the F-word in Cheshire, 1310–11', *Transactions of the Historic Society of Lincolnshire and Cheshire*, CLXIV (2015), pp. 99–102
Boswell, John, *The Royal Treasure: Muslim Communities under the Crown of Aragon in the Fourteenth Century* (London, 1977)
—, *Christianity, Social Tolerance and Homosexuality* (1980), revd edn (Chicago, IL, 2015)
Boureau, Alain, *The Lord's First Night: The Myth of the Droit de Cuissage*, trans. Lydia Cochrane (Chicago, IL, 1998)
Brackett, John, 'The Florentine Onestà and the Control of Prostitution, 1403–1680', *Sixteenth Century Journal*, XXIV/2 (1993), pp. 273–300

Bray, Alan, *The Friend* (Chicago, IL, 2003)

Brewer, Derek, ed., *Medieval Comic Tales* (1972), 2nd edn (Cambridge, 1996)

Briggs, Keith, 'OE and ME *Cunte* in Place-names', *Journal of the English Place-name Society*, XLI (2009), pp. 26–39

Brissaud, Y.-B., 'L'infanticide à la fin du moyen âge, ses motivations psychologiques et sa répression', *Revue historique de droit français et étranger*, 50 (1972), pp. 229–56

Broedel, Hans Peter, 'Fifteenth-century Witch Beliefs', in *The Oxford Handbook of Witchcraft in Early Modern Europe and Colonial America*, ed. Brian Levack (Oxford, 2013), pp. 32–49

Brown, Rachael, 'George R. R. Martin on Sex, Fantasy, and *A Dance with Dragons*', *The Atlantic* (11 July 2011)

Brown, Sydney, ed. and trans., *The Register of Eudes of Rouen* (New York, 1964)

Brożyna, Martha, ed., *Gender and Sexuality in the Middle Ages* (Jefferson, NC, 2005)

Brucker, Gene, *Giovanni and Lusanna: Love and Marriage in Renaissance Florence* (Berkeley, CA, 1986)

Brundage, James, 'Prostitution, Miscegenation and Sexual Purity in the First Crusade', in *Crusade and Settlement*, ed. Peter Edbury (Cardiff, 1985), pp. 57–65

—, 'Intermarriage between Christians and Jews in Medieval Canon Law', *Jewish History*, III/I (1988), pp. 25–40

Bruskin Diner, Judith, ed. and trans., *The One Hundred New Tales* (New York, 1990)

Bullough, Vern, and James Brundage, eds, *Sexual Practices and the Medieval Church* (New York, 1982)

—, eds, *Handbook of Medieval Sexuality* (New York, 1996)

Burge, Amy, 'Do Knights Still Rescue Damsels in Distress? Reimagining the Medieval in Mills and Boon Historical Romance', in *The Female Figure in Contemporary Historical Fiction*, ed. K. Cooper and E. Short (London, 2012), pp. 95–114

Burgess, Glyn, and Keith Busby, trans., *The Lais of Marie de France* (London, 1986)

Butler, Sara, '"I Will Never Consent to Be Wedded with You!" Coerced Marriage in the Courts of Medieval England', *Canadian Journal of History*, XXXIX/2 (2004), pp. 247–70

Bynum, Caroline Walker, *Fragmentation and Redemption: Essays on Gender and the Human Body in Medieval Religion* (New York, 1992)

Cabré, Montserrat, 'Women or Healers? Household Practice and the Categories of Health Care in Late Medieval Iberia', *Bulletin of the History of Medicine*, 82 (2008), pp. 18–51

Cadden, Joan, *Meanings of Sex Difference in the Middle Ages: Medicine, Science, and Culture* (Cambridge, 1993)

—, *Nothing Natural Is Shameful: Sodomy and Science in Late Medieval Europe* (Philadelphia, PA, 2013)

Camille, Michael, *Image on the Edge: The Margins of Medieval Art* (London, 1992)

—, *The Medieval Art of Love* (London, 1998)

Capellanus, Andreas, *On Love*, trans. P. G. Walsh (London, 1982)

Carroll, Shiloh, *Medievalism in 'A Song of Ice and Fire' and 'Game of Thrones'* (Cambridge, 2018)

Catlos, Brian, *Muslims of Medieval Latin Christendom, c. 1050–1614*
(Cambridge, 2014)

Cawley, A. C., ed., *Everyman and Medieval Miracle Plays* (London, 1993)

Chaucer, Geoffrey, *The Canterbury Tales*, trans. Nevill Coghill (London, 1977)

Clairvaux, Bernard of, *The Life of St Malachy the Irishman*, trans. Robert Meyer
(Kalamazoo, MI, 1978)

Clarke, Paula, 'The Business of Prostitution in Early Renaissance Venice',
Renaissance Quarterly, LXVIII/2 (2015), pp. 419–64

Classen, Albrecht, *The Medieval Chastity Belt: A Myth-making Process*
(Basingstoke, 2007)

Coates, Richard, 'Fockynggroue in Bristol', *Notes and Queries*, 54 (2007),
pp. 373–6

Cohn, Norman, *Europe's Inner Demons: The Demonization of Christians
in Medieval Christendom* [1975] (London, 1993)

Comba, Rinaldo, and Angelo Nicolini, eds, *'Lucea Talvolta La Luna': I processi
alle 'masche' di Rifreddo e Gambasca del 1495* (Cunea, 2004)

Cossar, Roisin, 'Clerical "Concubines" in Northern Italy during the Fourteenth
Century', *Journal of Women's History*, XXIII/1 (2011), pp. 110–31

Cotrugli, Benedetto, *The Book of the Art of Trade*, ed. Carlo Carraro
and Giovanni Favero, trans. John Phillimore (London, 2017)

Crompton, Louis, 'The Myth of Lesbian Impunity: Capital Laws from 1270
to 1791', *Journal of Homosexuality*, VI (1981), pp. 11–25

Cullum, Patricia, '"Give Me Chastity": Masculinity and Attitudes to Chastity
and Celibacy in the Middle Ages', *Gender and History*, 25 (2013), pp. 225–40

Curry, Anne, 'Sex and the Soldier in Lancastrian Normandy, 1415–1450',
Reading Medieval Studies, XIV (1988), pp. 17–45

D'Arcens, Louise, *Comic Medievalisms: Laughing at the Middle Ages*
(Woodbridge, 2014)

Damian, Peter, *Letters 31–60*, trans. Owen Blum (Washington, DC, 1990)

Daniel, Walter, *The Life of Aelred of Rievaulx*, trans. F. Maurice Powicke
(Kalamazoo, MI, 1994)

Das, Shanti, 'Restoring Virgins Is a Big Earner for British Surgeons', *Sunday
Times*, 12 January 2020

Davidson, L. S., and J. O. Ward, eds, *The Sorcery Trial of Alice Kyteler*
(Asheville, NC, 2004)

Davies, R. T., ed., *Medieval English Lyrics* (London, 1963)

Davis, Isabel, Miriam Müller and Sarah Rees Jones, eds, *Love, Marriage
and Family Ties in the Later Middle Ages* (Turnhout, 2010)

Dean, Trevor, 'Gender and Insult in an Italian City: Bologna in the Later
Middle Ages', *Social History*, XXIX/2 (2004), pp. 217–31

—, 'Fornicating with Nuns in Fifteenth-century Bologna', *Journal of Medieval
History*, XXXIV/2 (2008), pp. 374–82

Delaney, Paul, 'Constantinus Africanus' *De Coitu*: A Translation', *Chaucer
Review*, 4 (1969), pp. 55–65

Demaitre, Luke, *Medieval Medicine: The Art of Healing, from Head to Toe*
(Santa Barbara, CA, 2013)

Dillard, Heath, *Daughters of the Reconquest: Women in Castilian Town Society,
1100–1300* (Cambridge, 1984)

Diner, Judith Bruskin, ed., *The One Hundred New Tales* (New York, 1990)

Dixon, Laurinda, *Perilous Chastity: Women and Illness in Pre-Enlightenment
Art and Medicine* (Ithaca, NY, 1995)

Douie, Decima, and Hugh Farmer, eds and trans., *Magna Vita Sancti Hugonis*, 2 vols (London, 1961–2)

Dubin, Nathaniel, ed. and trans., *The Fabliaux* (New York, 2013)

Dubuis, Pierre, 'Enfants refusés dans les Alpes Occidentales (xiv–xve siècles)', in *Enfance abandonée et société en Europe, xiv–xxe siècle* (Rome, 1991), pp. 573–90

Dunn, Caroline, *Stolen Women in Medieval England: Rape, Abduction and Adultery, 1100–1500* (Cambridge, 2013)

Ebner, Julia, *Going Dark: The Social Lives of Extremists* (London, 2020)

Eisenbichler, Konrad, ed., *The Premodern Teenager: Youth in Society, 1150–1650* (Toronto, 2002)

Elliott, Andrew, *Medievalism, Politics and Mass Media: Appropriating the Middle Ages in the Twenty-first Century* (Cambridge, 2017)

Elliott, Dyan, *Spiritual Marriage: Sexual Abstinence in Medieval Wedlock* (Princeton, NJ, 1993)

—, *Fallen Bodies: Pollution, Sexuality and Demonology in the Middle Ages* (Philadelphia, PA, 1999)

—, *The Bride of Christ Goes to Hell: Metaphor and Embodiment in the Lives of Pious Women, 200–1500* (Philadelphia, PA, 2012)

—, *The Corrupter of Boys: Sodomy, Scandal and the Medieval Clergy* (Philadelphia, PA, 2020)

Evans, Edward, *The Criminal Prosecution and Capital Punishment of Animals* (London, 1906)

Evans, Ruth, ed., *A Cultural History of Sexuality in the Middle Ages* (London, 2011)

Farmer, Sharon, *Surviving Poverty in Medieval Paris: Gender, Ideology and the Daily Lives of the Poor* (Ithaca, NY, 2002)

Finch, Andrew, 'Sexual Morality and Canon Law: The Evidence of the Rochester Consistory Court', *Journal of Medieval History*, xx/3 (1994), pp. 261–75

Fisher, Will, '"Wantoning with the Thighs": The Socialization of Thigh Sex in England, 1590–1730', *Journal of the History of Sexuality*, xxiv/1 (2015), pp. 1–24

Flamborough, Robert of, *Liber Poenitentialis*, ed. J. J. Francis Firth (Toronto, 1971)

Gabrieli, Francesco, and E. J. Costello, eds, *Arab Historians of the Crusades* (Abingdon, 2010)

Gebhardt, Torben R., 'Homosexuality in Television Medievalism', in *The Middle Ages on Television: Critical Essays*, ed. Meriem Pagès and Karolyn Kinane (Jefferson, NC, 2015), pp. 197–214

Gerald of Wales, *The Journey through Wales and The Description of Wales*, trans. Lewis Thorpe (London, 1978)

—, *The Jewel of the Church*, trans. John Hagen (Leiden, 1979)

—, *The History and Topography of Ireland*, trans. John O'Meara (London, 1982)

Geremek, Bronisław, *The Margins of Society in Late Medieval Paris* [1976] (Cambridge, 1987)

Gilchrist, Roberta, *Medieval Life: Archaeology and the Life Course* (Woodbridge, 2012)

—, *Sacred Heritage: Monastic Archaeology, Identities and Beliefs* (Woodbridge, 2019)

Gillingham, John, 'Richard 1 and the Science of War in the Middle Ages', in *Anglo-Norman Warfare*, ed. Matthew Strickland (Woodbridge, 1992), pp. 194–207

Gilmour-Bryson, Anne, 'Sodomy and the Knights Templar', *Journal of the History of Sexuality*, VII (1996), pp. 151–83

Goldberg, Jeremy, 'Pigs and Prostitutes: Streetwalking in Comparative Perspective', in *Young Medieval Women*, ed. Katherine Lewis, Noel Menuge and Kim Phillips (Stroud, 1999), pp. 172–93

—, 'John Rykener, Richard II and the Governance of London', *Leeds Studies in English*, XLIV (2014), pp. 49–70

—, ed., *Women in England, c. 1275–1525* (Manchester, 1995)

Goodich, Michael, *The Unmentionable Vice* (Santa Barbara, CA, 1979)

Goulburn, Edward, and Henry Symonds, eds, *The Life, Letters and Sermons of Bishop Herbert of Losinga*, 2 vols (Oxford, 1878)

Gower, John, *Confessio Amantis*, ed. Russell Peck (Toronto, 1980)

Gravdal, Kathryn, *Ravishing Maidens: Writing Rape in Medieval French Literature and Law* (Philadelphia, PA, 1991)

Green, Monica, ed. and trans., *The Trotula* (Philadelphia, PA, 2001)

Groebner, Valentin, 'The Carnal Knowing of the Coloured Body: Sleeping with Arabs and Blacks in the European Imagination, 1300–1550', in *The Origins of Racism in the West*, ed. Miriam Eliav-Feldon, Benjamin Isaac and Joseph Ziegler (Cambridge, 2009), pp. 217–31

Grossman, Avraham, *Pious and Rebellious: Jewish Women in Medieval Europe* (Waltham, MA, 2012)

Gruia, Ana-Maria, 'Sex on the Stove: A Fifteenth-century Tile from Bamská Bystrica', *Studia Patzinaka*, 4 (2007), pp. 85–122

Gurney-Salter, Emma, ed. and trans., *The Coming of the Friars to England and Germany, Being the Chronicles of Brother Thomas of Eccleston and Brother Jordan of Giano* (London, 1926)

Haemers, Jelle, 'Filthy and Indecent Words: Insults, Defamation and Urban Politics in the Southern Low Countries, 1300–1550', in *The Voices of the People in Late Medieval Europe*, ed. Jon Dumolyn, Jelle Haemers, Hipólito Rafael Oliva Herrer and Vincent Challet (Turnhout, 2014), pp. 247–67

Hanawalt, Barbara, *The Ties That Bound: Peasant Families in Medieval England* (Oxford, 1986)

—, *'Of Good and Ill Repute': Gender and Social Control in Medieval England* (Oxford, 1998)

—, *The Wealth of Wives: Women, Law and Economy in Late Medieval London* (Oxford, 2007)

Hardy, Thomas Duffus, ed., *Registrum Palatinum Dunelmense: The Register of Richard de Kellawe, Lord Palatine and Bishop of Durham, 1311–1316*, 4 vols (London, 1873–8)

Harris, Carissa, *Obscene Pedagogies: Transgressive Talk and Sexual Education in Late Medieval Britain* (Ithaca, NY, 2016)

Harris, Lydia, 'Evacuating the Womb: Abortion and Contraception in the High Middle Ages, c. 1050–1300', PhD thesis, Durham University, 2017

—, 'Old Ideas for a New Debate: Medieval and Modern Attitudes to Abortion', *Medieval Feminist Forum* (December 2017), pp. 131–49

Harris-Stoertz, Fiona, 'Pregnancy and Childbirth in Twelfth- and Thirteenth-century French and English', *Journal of the History of Sexuality*, XXI/2 (2012), pp. 263–81

Harvey, Katherine, 'Food, Drink and the Bishop in Medieval England', *Viator*, 26 (2015), pp. 155–76

—, 'Episcopal Virginity in Medieval England', *Journal of the History of Sexuality*, XXVI/2 (2017), pp. 273–93

Haskins, Susan, *Mary Magdalene: The Essential History* (London, 1993)

Head, Thomas, ed., *Medieval Hagiography: An Anthology* (New York, 2000)

Heisterback, Caesarius of, *The Dialogue on Miracles*, trans. H. von Schott and C. Swinton Bland, 2 vols (London, 1929)

Helmholz, R. M., ed., *Select Cases on Defamation to 1600* (London, 1985)

Hergemöller, Bernd-Ulrich, *Sodom and Gomorrah: On the Everyday Reality and Persecution of Homosexuals in the Middle Ages* (London, 2001)

Hopwood, Nicholas, Rebecca Flemming and Lauren Kassell, eds, *Reproduction: Antiquity to the Present Day* (Cambridge, 2018)

Hornbeck, J. Patrick, 'Theologies of Sexuality in English "Lollardy"', *Journal of Ecclesiastical History*, LX/1 (2009), pp. 19–44

Horrox, Rosemary, ed., *The Black Death* (Manchester, 1994)

Houts, Elisabeth van, *Married Life in the Middle Ages, 900–1300* (Oxford, 2019)

Hughes, Geoffrey, *Swearing: A Social History of Foul Language, Oaths, and Profanity in English* (Oxford, 1991)

—, *An Encyclopaedia of Swearing* (New York, 2006)

Huscroft, Richard, *Tales from the Long Twelfth Century: The Rise and Fall of the Angevin Empire* (London, 2016)

Ingram, Martin, *Carnal Knowledge: Regulating Sex in England, 1470–1600* (Cambridge, 2017)

Jacquart, Danielle, and Claude Thomasset, *Sexuality and Medicine in the Middle Ages*, trans. Matthew Adamson (Oxford, 1988)

Jansen, Katherine Ludwig, *Peace and Penance in Medieval Italy* (Princeton, NJ, 2018)

Johnson, Penelope, *Equal in Monastic Profession: Religious Women in Medieval France* (Chicago, IL, 1991)

Johnston, Dafydd, ed. and trans., *Medieval Welsh Erotic Poetry* (Bridgend, 1998)

Jones, Malcolm, *The Secret Middle Ages* (Stroud, 2002)

Jørgensen, Torstein, 'Illegal Sexual Behavior in Late Medieval Norway as Testified in Supplications to the Pope', *Journal of the History of Sexuality*, XVII (2008), pp. 335–50

Kalof, Linda, ed., *A Cultural History of the Body in the Medieval Age* (London, 2010)

Kane, Bronach, *Impotence and Virginity in the Late Medieval Ecclesiastical Court of York* (York, 2008)

—, *Popular Memory and Gender in Medieval England* (Woodbridge, 2019)

Karras, Ruth Mazo, *Common Women: Prostitution and Sexuality in Medieval England* (Oxford, 1996)

—, *From Boys to Men: Formations of Masculinity in Late Medieval Europe* (Philadelphia, PA, 2003)

—, 'The Lechery That Dare Not Speak Its Name: Sodomy and the Vices in Medieval England', in *In the Garden of Evil: The Vices and Culture in the Middle Ages*, ed. Richard Newhauser (Toronto, 2005), pp. 193–205

—, *Unmarriages: Women, Men and Sexual Unions in the Middle Ages* (Philadelphia, PA, 2012)

—, *Sexuality in Medieval Europe*, 3rd edn (Abingdon, 2017)

—, and David Boyd, '"Ut cum Muliere": A Male Transvestite Prostitute in Medieval London', in *Premodern Sexualities*, ed. Louise Fradenburg (London, 1999), pp. 101–16

Kelly, Kathleen Coyne, *Performing Virginity and Testing Chastity in the Middle Ages* (Abingdon, 2000)

Kerr, Julie, *Life in the Medieval Cloister* (London, 2009)

Kieckhefer, Richard, 'Mythologies of Witchcraft in the Fifteenth Century', *Magic, Ritual and Witchcraft*, 1 (2006), pp. 79–108

Kissane, Alan, 'Unnatural in Body and a Villain in Soul: Rape and Sexual Violence towards Girls under the Age of Canonical Consent in Late Medieval England', *Fourteenth-century England* x, ed. Gwilym Dodd (Woodbridge, 2018), pp. 89–112

Knirk, James, 'Love and Eroticism in Medieval Norwegian Runic Inscriptions', in *Die Faszination des Verborgenen und seine Entschlüsselung – Rāði sār kunni*, ed. Jana Krüger (Berlin, 2017), pp. 217–32

Knudsen, Christian, 'Promiscuous Monks and Naughty Nuns: Poverty, Sex and Apostasy in Later Medieval England', in *Poverty and Prosperity: The Rich and the Poor in the Middle Ages and Renaissance*, ed. Anne Scott and Cindy Kosse (Turnhout, 2012), pp. 75–91

Koldeweij, Jos, 'Shameless and Naked Images: Obscene Badges as Parodies of Popular Devotion', in *Art and Architecture of Late Medieval Pilgrimage in Northern Europe and the British Isles*, ed. Sarah Blick and Rita Tekippe (Leiden, 2004), vol. 1, pp. 493–510

Korpiola, Mia, 'Rethinking Incest and Heinous Sexual Crime: Changing Boundaries of Secular and Ecclesiastical Jurisdiction in Late Medieval Sweden', in *Boundaries of the Law*, ed. Anthony Musson (Farnham, 2005), pp. 102–17

—, ed., *Regional Variations in Matrimonial Law and Custom in Europe, 1150–1600* (Leiden, 2011)

Kren, Thomas, Jill Burke and Stephen Campbell, eds, *The Renaissance Nude* (London, 2019)

Kuefler, Mathew, ed., *The Boswell Thesis* (Chicago, IL, 2005)

Kümper, Hiram, 'Learned Men and Skilful Matrons: Medical Expertise and the Forensics of Rape in the Middle Ages', in *Medicine and the Law in the Middle Ages*, ed. Wendy Turner and Sara Butler (Leiden, 2014), pp. 88–108

Laiou, Angelika, ed., *Consent and Coercion to Sex and Marriage in Ancient and Medieval Societies* (Washington, DC, 1993)

Lamb, Christina, *Our Bodies, Their Battlefield: What War Does to Women* (London, 2020)

Landouzy, Louis, and Roger Pépin, eds, *Le régime du corps de maître Aldebrandin de Sienne* (Paris, 1911)

Lansing, Carol, 'Gender and Civic Authority: Sexual Control in a Medieval Italian Town', *Journal of Social History*, 31 (1997), pp. 33–59

—, 'Accusations of Rape in Thirteenth-century Bologna', in *Violence and Justice in Bologna*, ed. Sarah Rubin Blanshei (Lanham, MD, 2018), pp. 167–85

Lanz, Eukene Lacarra, 'Legal and Clandestine Prostitution in Medieval Spain', *Bulletin of Hispanic Studies*, 79 (2002), pp. 342–88

Laqueur, Thomas, *Making Sex: Body and Gender from the Greeks to Freud* (London, 1990)

—, *Solitary Sex: A Cultural History of Masturbation* (New York, 2003)

Le Roy Ladurie, Emmanuel, *Montaillou*, trans. Barbara Bray (Harmondsworth, 1980)

Lemay, Helen Rodnite, 'William of Saliceto on Human Sexuality', *Viator*, XII (1981), pp. 165–81

—, ed., *Women's Secrets* (New York, 1992)

Lerner, Robert, *The Heresy of the Free Spirit in the Later Middle Ages* (Berkeley, CA, 1972)

Lesnick, Daniel, 'Insults and Threats in Medieval Todi', *Journal of Medieval History*, XVII (1991), pp. 71–89

Leyser, Henrietta, *Medieval Women: A Social History of Women in England, 450–1550* (London, 1995)

Licence, Tom, *Hermits and Recluses in English Society, 950–1200* (Oxford, 2011)

Lindquist, Sherry, ed., *The Meanings of Nudity in Medieval Art* (Farnham, 2012)

Lochrie, Karma, *Heterosyncrasies: Female Sexuality When Normal Wasn't* (Minneapolis, MN, 2005)

Longnon, Jean, ed., *Les très riches heures du Duc de Berry* (London, 1969)

McCarthy, Conor, ed., *Love, Sex and Marriage in the Middle Ages: A Sourcebook* (London, 2004)

McDonald, Nicola, ed., *Medieval Obscenities* (York, 2006)

McDougall, Sara, 'The Opposite of the Double Standard: Gender, Marriage and Adultery Prosecution in Late Medieval France', *Journal of the History of Sexuality*, XXIII (2014), pp. 206–25

—, 'The Transformation of Adultery in France at the End of the Middle Ages', *Law and History Review*, XXXII (2014), pp. 491–524

Macdowall, Wendy, et al., 'Lifetime Prevalence, Associated Factors, and Circumstances of Non-volitional Sex in Women and Men in Britain: Findings from the Third National Survey of Sexual Attitudes and Lifestyles (Natsal-3)', *The Lancet*, 382 (2013), pp. 1845–55

Mackintosh-Smith, Tim, ed. and trans., *The Travels of Ibn Battutah* (London, 2002)

McLaren, Angus, *Impotence: A Cultural History* (Chicago, IL, 2007)

McNeill, John, and Helena Garner, ed. and trans, *Medieval Handbooks of Penance* (New York, 1938)

McSheffrey, Shannon, *Marriage, Sex and Civic Culture in Late Medieval London* (Philadelphia, PA, 2006)

—, ed. and trans., *Love and Marriage in Late Medieval London* (Kalamazoo, MI, 1995)

Magnus, Albertus, *On Animals: A Medieval Summa Zoologica*, trans. Kenneth Mitchell and Irven Resnick, 2 vols (Baltimore, MD, 1999)

Maier, Christoph, 'Crusade and Rhetoric against the Muslim Colony of Lucera: Eudes of Châteauroux's *Sermones de Rebellione Sarracenorum Lucherie in Apulia*', *Journal of Medieval History*, XXI/4 (1995), pp. 343–85

Malmesbury, William of, *Gesta Regum Anglorum: The History of the Kings of England*, ed. and trans. R.A.B. Mynors, Rodney Thompson and Michael Winterbottom, 2 vols (Oxford, 1998–9)

Mammoli, Domenico, *The Record of the Trial and Condemnation of a Witch, Matteuccia di Francesco, at Todi, 20 March 1428* (Rome, 1972)

Mandeville, John, *The Book of Marvels and Travels*, trans. Anthony Bale (Oxford, 2012)

Mazzi, Maria Serena, *A Life of Ill Repute: Public Prostitution in the Middle Ages*, trans. Joyce Myerson (Montreal, 2020)

Menuge, Noël, ed., *Medieval Women and the Law* (Woodbridge, 2003)

Mielke, Christopher, and Andrea-Bianka Znorovszky, eds, *Same Bodies, Different Women: 'Other' Women in the Middle Ages and Early Modern Period* (Budapest, 2019)

Miles, Margaret, 'The Virgin's One Breast', in *The Expanding Discourse: Feminism and Art History*, ed. Norma Broude and Mary Garrard (New York, 1992), pp. 26–37

Mills, Robert, 'Male-Male Love and Sex in the Middle Ages, 1000–1500', in *A Gay History of Britain*, ed. Matt Cook (Oxford, 2007), pp. 1–43

Minnis, Alastair, *From Eden to Eternity: Creations of Paradise in the Later Middle Ages* (Philadelphia, PA, 2016)

Mitchell, Stephen, 'Nordic Witchcraft in Transition: Impotence, Heresy and Diabolism in Fourteenth-century Bergen', *Scandia*, LXIII/3 (1997), pp. 17–33

Mohr, Melissa, *Holy Sh*t: A Brief History of Swearing* (Oxford, 2013)

Müller, Wolfgang, *The Criminalization of Abortion in the West* (New York, 2012)

Murray, Jacqueline, 'On the Origins and Role of "Wise Women" in Causes for Annulment on the Grounds of Male Impotence', *Journal of Medieval History*, XVI (1990), pp. 235–49

—, 'Men's Bodies, Men's Minds: Seminal Emissions and Sexual Anxiety in the Middle Ages', *Annual Review of Sex Research*, 8 (1997), pp. 1–26

—, 'Masculinizing Religious Life: Sexual Prowess, the Battle for Chastity, and Monastic Identity', in *Holiness and Masculinity in the Middle Ages*, ed. Patricia Cullum and Katharine Lewis (Cardiff, 2005), pp. 24–37

—, 'The Battle for Chastity: Miraculous Castration and the Quelling of Desire in the Middle Ages', *Journal of the History of Sexuality*, XXVIII/1 (2019), pp. 96–116

—, ed., *Love, Marriage, and Family in the Middle Ages: A Reader* (Peterborough, ON, 2001)

—, and Konrad Eisenbichler, eds, *Desire and Discipline: Sex in the Premodern West* (Toronto, 1996)

Murray Jones, Peter, and Lea Olsan, 'Performative Rituals for Conception and Childbirth in England, 900–1500', *Bulletin of the History of Medicine*, 89 (2015), pp. 406–33

Nicholas, David, *The Domestic Life of a Medieval City: Women, Children and the Family in Fourteenth-century Ghent* (Lincoln, NE, 1985)

Nirenberg, David, *Communities of Violence: Persecution of Minorities in the Middle Ages* (Princeton, NJ, 1998)

—, 'Conversion, Sex and Segregation: Jews and Christians in Medieval Spain', *American Historical Review*, CVII (2002), pp. 1065–93

—, 'Love between Muslim and Jew in Medieval Spain: A Triangular Affair', in *Jews, Muslims and Christians in and around the Crown of Aragon*, ed. Harvey Hames (Leiden, 2004), pp. 127–55

Olsan, Lea, 'Charms and Prayers in Medieval Medical Theory and Practice', *Social History of Medicine*, XVI/3 (2003), pp. 343–66

Olsen, Glenn, 'On the Frontiers of Eroticism: The Romanesque Monastery of San Pedro de Cervantes', *Mediterranean Studies*, 8 (1999), pp. 89–104

Oren-Magidor, Daphna, *Infertility in Early Modern England* (London, 2017)

—, and Catherine Rider, 'Introduction: Infertility in Medieval and Early Modern Medicine', *Social History of Medicine*, 29 (2016), pp. 211–23

Oriel, J. D., *The Scars of Venus: A History of Venereology* (Berlin, 1994)

Origo, Iris, *The Merchant of Prato* (London, 1957)

Ostorero, Martine, Agostino Paravicini Bagliani, Kathrin Utz Tremp and Catherine Chène, eds, *L'imaginaire du sabbat* (Lausanne, 1999)

Otis, Leah, *Prostitution in Medieval Society: The History of an Urban Institution in Languedoc* (Chicago, IL, 1985)

Otis-Cour, Leah, '*De jure novo*: Dealing with Adultery in the Fifteenth-century Toulousain', *Speculum*, LXXXIV (2009), pp. 347–92

Otter, Monika, 'Medieval Sex Education, Or: What About Canidia?', *Interfaces*, 3 (2016), pp. 71–89

Paden, William, trans., *The Medieval Pastourelle*, 2 vols (New York, 1987)

Page, Jamie, 'Inside the Medieval Brothel', *History Today*, LXIX/6 (June 2019), pp. 28–39

—, 'Masculinity and Prostitution in Late Medieval German Literature', *Speculum*, XCIV (2019), pp. 739–73

Paris, Matthew, *English History*, trans. John Giles, 3 vols (London, 1852–4)

Payer, Pierre, *The Bridling of Desire: Views of Sex in the Later Middle Ages* (Toronto, 1993)

—, *Sex and the New Medieval Literature of Confession* (Toronto, 2009)

Pedersen, Frederik, *Marriage Disputes in Medieval England* (London, 2000)

Pegg, Mark, *The Corruption of Angels: The Great Inquisition of 1245–6* (Princeton, NJ, 2001)

Phillips, Kim, *Medieval Maidens: Young Women and Gender in England, 1270–1540* (Manchester, 2003)

—, 'Beauty', in *Women and Gender in Medieval Europe: An Encyclopedia*, ed. Margaret Schaus (London, 2006), pp. 64–6

—, 'Gender and Sexuality', in *The Routledge History of Medieval Christianity, 1050-1500*, ed. Robert Swanson (Abingdon, 2015), pp. 309–21

—, 'The Breasts of Virgins: Sexual Reputation and Young Women's Bodies in Medieval Culture and Society', *Cultural and Social History*, XV/1 (2018), pp. 1–19

—, and Barry Reay, *Sex before Sexuality: A Premodern History* (Cambridge, 2011)

Pizan, Christine de, *The Book of the City of Ladies*, trans. Rosalind Brown-Grant (London, 1999)

—, *The Treasure of the City of Ladies*, trans. Sarah Lawson (rev., London, 2003)

Polo, Marco, *The Travels*, trans. Ronald Latham (London, 1958)

Poos, L. R., 'Sex, Lies and the Church Courts of Pre-Reformation England', *Journal of Interdisciplinary History*, XXV/4 (1995), pp. 585–607

Power, Eileen, *Medieval English Nunneries, c. 1275–1535* (Cambridge, 1922)

Powicke, F. M., and C. R. Cheney, eds, *Councils and Synods, with Other Documents Relating to the English Church*, vol. II: A.D. *1205–1313*, 2 vols (Oxford, 1964)

Preest, David, trans., and Harriet Webster, ed., *The Annals of Dunstable* (Woodbridge, 2018)

Prevenier, Walter, 'The Notions of Honor and Adultery in the Fifteenth-century Burgundian Netherlands', in *Comparative Perspectives on History and Historians*, ed. David Nicholas, Bernard Bachrach and James Murray (Kalamazoo, MI, 2012), pp. 259–78

Proctor, Caroline, 'Between Medicine and Morals: Sex in the Regimens of Maino de Maineri', in *Medieval Sexuality: A Casebook*, ed. April Harper and Caroline Proctor (London, 2008), pp. 113–31

Puff, Helmut, 'Female Sodomy: The Trial of Katherina Hetzeldorfer (1477)', *Journal of Medieval and Early Modern Studies*, XXX (2000), pp. 41–61

—, 'The Sodomite's Clothes: Gift-giving and Sexual Excess in Early Modern Germany and Switzerland', in *The Material Culture of Sex, Procreation and Marriage in Medieval and Renaissance Europe*, ed. Anne McClanan and Karen Rosoff Encarnación (London, 2002), pp. 251–72

—, *Sodomy in Reformation Germany and Switzerland, 1400–1600* (Chicago, IL, 2003)

Rasmussen, Ann Marie, *Wandering Genitalia: Sexuality and the Body in German Culture between the Late Middle Ages and Early Modernity* (London, 2009)

Rawcliffe, Carole, *Medicine and Society in Later Medieval England* (Stroud, 1995)

—, 'Women, Childbirth and Religion in Later Medieval England', in *Women and Religion in Medieval England*, ed. Diana Wood (Oxford, 2003), pp. 91–111

—, *Leprosy in Medieval England* (Woodbridge, 2006)

—, *Urban Bodies: Communal Health in Late Medieval English Towns and Cities* (Woodbridge, 2013)

Ray, Jonathan, *The Sephardic Frontier: The 'Renconquista' and the Jewish Community in Medieval Iberia* (Ithaca, NY, 2011)

Resnick, Irven, 'Peter Damian on the Restoration of Virginity: A Problem for Medieval Theology', *Journal of Theological Studies*, XXXIX/1 (1988), pp. 125–34

Richards, Jeffrey, *Sex, Dissidence and Damnation: Minority Groups in the Middle Ages* (Abingdon, 1991)

Riddle, John, *Contraception and Abortion from the Ancient World to the Renaissance* (Cambridge, MA, 1992)

Rider, Catherine, *Magic and Impotence in the Middle Ages* (Oxford, 2006)

—, 'Men, Women and Love Magic in Late Medieval English Pastoral Manuals', *Magic, Ritual and Witchcraft*, 7 (2012), pp. 190–211

—, 'Men and Infertility in Late Medieval English Medicine', *Social History of Medicine*, XXIX (2016), pp. 245–66

Robertson, James Craigie, ed., *Materials for the History of Thomas Becket*, 7 vols (London, 1875–85)

Rocke, Michael, 'Sodomites in Fifteenth-century Tuscany: The Views of Bernardino of Siena', in *The Pursuit of Sodomy: Male Homosexuality in Renaissance and Enlightenment Europe*, ed. Kurt Gerard and Gert Hekma (London, 1989), pp. 7–31

—, *Forbidden Friendships: Homosexuality and Male Culture in Renaissance Florence* (Oxford, 1996)

Roelens, Jonas, 'Visible Women: Female Sodomy in the Late Medieval and Early Modern Southern Netherlands (1400–1550)', *Low Countries Historical Review*, 130 (2015), pp. 3–24

—, 'Gossip, Defamation and Sodomy in the Early Modern Southern Netherlands', *Renaissance Studies*, XXXII/2 (2018), pp. 236–52

Rollo-Koster, Joëlle, 'From Prostitutes to Brides of Christ: The Avignonese *Repenties* in the Late Middle Ages', *Journal of Medieval and Early Modern Studies*, XXXII (2002), pp. 109–44

Rosewell, Roger, *Medieval Wall Paintings* (Woodbridge, 2008)

Rossiaud, Jacques, 'Prostitution, Sex and Society in French Towns in the Fifteenth Century', in *Western Sexuality: Practice and Precept in Past and Present Times*, ed. Philippe Ariès and André Béjin (Oxford, 1985), pp. 76–94

—, *Medieval Prostitution*, trans. Lydia Cochrane (Oxford, 1988)

Ruggiero, Guido, *The Boundaries of Eros* (Oxford, 1985)

Saenger, Paul, 'Silent Reading: Its Impact on Late Medieval Script and Society', *Viator*, XIII (1982), pp. 367–414

Salih, Sarah, 'Unpleasures of the Flesh: Medieval Marriage, Masochism,

and the History of Heterosexuality', *Studies in the Age of Chaucer*, XXXIII
(2011), pp. 125–47

Salisbury, Eve, ed., *The Trials and Joys of Marriage* (Kalamazoo, MI, 2002)

Salisbury, John of, *Historia Pontificalis*, ed. and trans. Marjorie Chibnall
(Oxford, 1986)

Salisbury, Joyce, *The Beast Within: Animals in the Middle Ages* (2nd edn,
Abingdon, 2011)

—, ed., *Sex in the Middle Ages* (New York, 1991)

Sauer, Michelle, *Gender in Medieval Culture* (London, 2015)

Saunders, Corinne, 'Sexual Violence in Wars: The Middle Ages',
in *Transcultural Wars: From the Middle Ages to the 21st Century*,
ed. Hans-Henning Kortüm (Berlin, 2006), pp. 151–64

Sautman, Francesca, and Pamela Sheingorn, eds, *Same Sex Love and Desire
among Women in the Middle Ages* (London, 2001)

Scott, Samuel Parsons, trans., and Robert Burns, ed., *Las Siete Partidas*,
V: *Underworlds: The Dead, the Criminal and the Marginalized*
(Philadelphia, PA, 2001)

Shahar, Shulamith, *Growing Old in the Middle Ages* (London, 1997)

Sharp, Michael, 'Remaking Medieval Heroism: Nationalism and Sexuality
in *Braveheart*', *Florilegium*, XV (1998), pp. 251–66

Sharpe, Reginald, ed., *Calendar of Coroners Rolls of the City of London*, AD
1300–1378 (London, 1913)

Shatzmiller, Joseph, ed., *Médecine et justice en Provence médiévale: Documents
de Manosque, 1262–1348* (Aix-en-Provence, 1989)

Shinners, John, and William Dohar, eds, *Pastors and the Care of Souls
in Medieval England* (Notre Dame, IN, 1998)

Sidhu, Nicole Nolan, *Indecent Exposure: Gender, Politics and Obscene Comedy
in Middle English Literature* (Philadelphia, PA, 2016)

Skinner, Patricia, and Elisabeth van Houts, eds, *Medieval Writings on Secular
Women* (London, 2011)

Slimani, Leïla, *Sex and Lies* (London, 2020)

Soergel, Peter, ed., *Sexuality and Culture in Medieval and Renaissance Europe*
(New York, 2005)

Solberg, Emma Maggie, *Virgin Whore* (Ithaca, NY, 2018)

Soller, Claudio, 'The Beautiful Woman in Medieval Iberia', PhD thesis,
University of Missouri, 2005

Solomon, Michael, ed. and trans., *The Mirror of Coitus: A Translation and
Edition of the Fifteenth-century 'Speculum al foderi'* (Madison, WI, 1990)

Soyer, François, 'Prohibiting Sexual Relations across Religious Boundaries in
Fifteenth-century Portugal', in *Religious Minorities in Christian, Jewish
and Muslim Law*, ed. Nora Bernend, Youna Hameau-Masset, Capuciné
Nemo-Pekelman and John Tolan (Turnhout, 2017), pp. 301–16

Spearing, Elizabeth, ed. and trans., *Medieval Writings on Female Spirituality*
(London, 2002)

Spindler, Erik, 'Were Medieval Prostitutes Marginals? Evidence from Sluis,
1387–1440', *Revue Belge de Philologie et d'Histoire*, 87 (2009), pp. 239–72

Steinberg, Leo, *The Sexuality of Christ in Renaissance Art and Modern Oblivion*
(Chicago, IL, 1996)

Stephens, Walter, *Demon Lovers: Witchcraft, Sex, and the Crisis of Belief*
(Chicago, IL, 2002)

Stevenson, James, ed., *Chronicon de Lanercost* (Edinburgh, 1839)

Talbot, C. H., trans., *The Life of Christina of Markyate*, rev. Samuel Fanous
and Henrietta Leyser (Oxford, 2008)

Tanner, Norman, ed., *Decrees of the Ecumenical Councils*, I: *Nicaea to Lateran* V
(Washington, DC, 1990)

Tentler, Thomas, *Sin and Confession on the Eve of the Reformation*
(Princeton, NJ, 1977)

Thomas, Hugh, *The Secular Clergy in England, 1066–1216* (Oxford, 2014)

Thompson, A. Hamilton, ed., *Visitations of Religious Houses in the Diocese
of Lincoln: Records of Visitations Held by William Alnwick, Bishop of Lincoln,
1436–1449* (Horncastle, 1918)

Throop, Priscilla, ed., *Hildegard von Bingen's Physica* (Rochester, VT, 1998)

Tibbetts Schulenberg, Jane, 'The Heroics of Virginity: Brides of Christ and
Sacrificial Mutilation', in *Women in the Middle Ages and Renaissance*,
ed. Mary Beth Rose (Syracuse, NY, 1986), pp. 29–72

Toaff, Ariel, *Love, Work and Death: Jewish Life in Medieval Umbria*
(Oxford, 1996)

Vernarde, Bruce, ed., *Robert of Arbrissel: A Medieval Religious Life*
(Washington, DC, 1994)

Voragine, Jacobus de, *The Golden Legend*, trans. William Granger Ryan
(Princeton, NJ, 2012)

Wack, Mary, *Lovesickness in the Middle Ages* (Philadelphia, PA, 1990)

Walsh, Christine, *The Cult of St Katherine of Alexandria in Early Medieval
Europe* (Farnham, 2007)

Weir, Anthony, and James Jerman, *Images of Lust: Sexual Carvings on Medieval
Churches* (London, 1986)

Wenzel, Siegfried, ed., *Fasciculus Morum: A Fourteenth-century Preacher's
Handbook* (London, 1989)

Wilkinson, Louise, *Women in Thirteenth-century Lincolnshire*
(Woodbridge, 2007)

Windeatt, Barry, ed. and trans., *The Book of Margery Kempe* (London, 1985)

Wolfthal, Diane, *Images of Rape: The 'Heroic' Tradition and Its Alternatives*
(Cambridge, 1999)

——, *In and Out of the Marital Bed: Seeing Sex in Renaissance Europe*
(London, 2010)

Wood, Charles, 'The Doctor's Dilemma: Sin, Salvation and the Menstrual
Cycle in Medieval Thought', *Speculum*, LVI (1981), pp. 710–27

Yahil, Edna, 'A Rape Trial in Saint Eloi: Sex, Seduction and Justice
in the Seigneurial Courts of Medieval Paris', in *Voices from the Bench*,
ed. Michael Goodich (London, 2006), pp. 251–71

Yalom, Marilyn, *A History of the Breast* (New York, 1997)

Ziegler, Joseph, *Medicine and Religion c. 1300: The Case of Arnau de Vilanova*
(Oxford, 1998)

Ziolkowski, Jan, ed., *Obscenity: Social Control and Artistic Creation
in the European Middle Ages* (Leiden, 1998)

ACKNOWLEDGEMENTS

Writing a book is never an easy task, and this one was completed during the first half of 2020 – a period which posed considerable extra challenges for us all! I am therefore extremely grateful to everyone who helped me along the way, starting with the Department of History, Classics and Archaeology at Birkbeck, University of London, which has provided me with a congenial academic home for nearly a decade. I am also greatly indebted to numerous libraries and their staff, especially the Birkbeck Library, Senate House Library, the British Library, the Wellcome Library and the Institute of Historical Research. Thank you to everyone who has answered my questions, discussed medieval sex with me, or sent me copies of their publications; to audiences at conferences and seminars across the UK, who have provided valuable feedback on various aspects of this project; and to the Birkbeck students who have studied this subject with me. For several years now I have been involved in two projects that have helped to shape my thinking about the history of sexuality: NOTCHES (a blog about the history of sexuality) and the History of Sexuality Seminar at the Institute of Historical Research. Thank you to the contributors at the former, the speakers at the latter, and to my colleagues at both. Thank you to Reaktion Books for helping me to turn my proposal into a manuscript and my manuscript into a book, and especially to Dave Watkins and Amy Salter. Above all, I am grateful to my family for their continued support and interest, and especially to my sisters Elisabeth and Eleanor, who both read the book in draft, for their feedback and encouragement.

PHOTO
ACKNOWLEDGEMENTS

The author and publishers wish to express their thanks to the below sources of illustrative material and/or permission to reproduce it. Every effort has been made to contact copyright holders; should there be any we have been unable to reach or to whom inaccurate acknowledgements have been made, please contact the publishers, and full adjustments will be made to subsequent printings.

Bibliothèque municipal d'Agen: p. 103; Bibliothèque nationale de France: p. 213; British Library: pp. 18, 25, 93, 119, 141; Fitzwilliam Museum, Cambridge: p. 195; Getty Museum: pp. 33, 173, 215; Julian P. Guffogg/Wikimedia Commons: p. 137; Nessy-Pic/Wikimedia Commons: p. 211; Poliphilo/Wikimedia Commons: p. 13; Royal Society: p. 71; Walters Art Museum: p. 61; Wellcome Collection: p. 21.

INDEX

Page numbers for illustrations are in *italics*